THE GUINNESS
FOOTBALL
ENCYCLOPEDIA

3RD EDITION
3

**EDITED BY
GRAHAM HART**

GUINNESS PUBLISHING

Introduction

Since the last edition of the Guinness Football Encyclopedia the game has experienced the normal run of highs and lows. There has been a successful, though not brilliant, World Cup, a handful of welcome law changes and some exciting domestic league and cup performances. Manchester United won a League and Cup double in a season (1993/94) they completely dominated. Jurgen Klinsmann chose to play in England, joined Tottenham Hotspur and inspired both the team and the rest of the country. And throughout Britain crowds have been on the increase, trouble on the decrease and some wonderful ground improvements (and some completely new grounds) have been unveiled.

Sadly there has been a downside too. The last couple of years have witnessed the loss of several great names, including Sir Matt Busby and Bobby Moore. The Colombian player, Andres Escobar, was murdered on his return home from the 1994 World Cup finals, apparently because he scored an own goal. There have been serious allegations, some proved, about financial mismanagement and dishonesty. And there have been well documented incidents that, to coin a phrase, have brought the game into disrepute: Eric Cantona at Crystal Palace, English yobs in Dublin and more of the same in Bruges spring readily to mind.

All these things, the good and the bad, deserve reflection and discussion. They must not be dismissed lightly, but the game has survived much worse, and enjoyed much better. Nothing really is new... except that over the past two years there has been talk of a development that would be completely new.

I refer to the proposals to start a second division of the Premier League in England. This, in itself, is not a revolutionary idea, but two aspects of it are. First, that teams should be invited to play in it, not chosen on merit; and second, that there would be no automatic relegation/promotion with the leagues below.

Both concepts, if adopted, will crush, at a single blow, the hopes and plans of scores of teams and hundreds of thousands of fans. More importantly the game as a whole will suffer. When performance on the pitch is secondary to money in the bank, everything is lost. If smaller clubs can't dream of reaching the big time, where is the point of it all?

Sir John Hall, Newcastle's chairman and a supporter of the plan, has no answer to critics except to say that this is progress and football is now big business. No, Sir John, you are wrong. Football is a game. And if you, in Newcastle of all places, can't see that, you really must have let those millions blinker your vision. Your fans are some of the best in the world, which was proved when your team was down; the 'Toon Army' still travelled the length and breadth of Britain in the hope of better times. They deserve success, and were prepared to wait until it came... on the pitch. I trust all of them would be simply too embarrassed at having their achievement guaranteed by a no-relegation league.

Let's hope the plan is put into the bin where it belongs, and that football, while empowered and employed by big business, is not enslaved and emasculated by it. Let's hope.

To other, happier, matters. As always there are many thanks to offer. I am particularly grateful to the writing team of:

Moira Banks
Rob Cameron
Bob Ferrier
Derek Hodgson
Guy Hodgson
Simon Inglis
Ken Jones
Peter Lovering
Charles Richards
Sean MacSweeney
Kevin McCarra
Tony Morris
Ivan Ponting
Phil Shaw
Andy Ward

Matthew Impey at Colorsport, Marc Glanville and Lee Martin at Allsport, were especially helpful in providing photographs and Stephen Adamson at Guinness and Simon Duncan, formerly at Guinness, also provided valuable assistance. On the production side Susannah Wills, Gill McLeod, Chris McLeod and Cathy Willis (who laid out the pages) all played a significant part.

Very special thanks go to Charles Richards, Ivan Ponting, and my brother Nick. They all provided great editorial support and tried to cheer me up when Southend United looked doomed to relegation.

And finally a word about Moira Banks who was heavily involved in the writing and proof reading of the first two editions of the Encyclopedia. Moira, who would have worked on this edition, died very young in 1994. She was a well respected editor of countless sports titles and, while unknown by the punter, will be greatly missed in the trade. We all miss you very much; Wimbledon just won't be the same this year.

Graham Hart

Acknowledgements

The Editor and Publishers would like to thank the following for permission to use photographs:

Allsport: 2-3, 9, 14, 15, 19, 20, 33 (bottom), 34, 36 (top), 37 (top), 38, 39, 40, 45 (top), 47, 48, 50-51, 52-53, 57, 62, 63, 68 (top), 72, 72-73, 78, 80, 85, 86, 88, 89, 94, 95, 96, 104, 108, 112-113, 115, 116, 123, 124, 130, 131, 132, 137, 140, 143, 154, 157, 175, 176, 177, 178-179, 183, 189 (bottom), 190, 192, 193, 196, 197

(bottom), 207. Colorsport: Title page, introduction, 2, 5, 6-7, 8, 10-11, 17 (both), 21 (both), 23, 24, 25, 26-27, 28, 29, 30, 31, 33, (top), 35, 36 (bottom), 37 (bottom), 41, 42, 43, 44-45 (bottom), 46, 49, 50, 54, 55, 56, 58, 59, 60, 64, 65, 66 (both), 68, 71, 73 (top), 75, 76, 81, 82, 83, 87, 90-91, 92, 92, 98-99, 100-101, 102-103, 103, 105, 106, 107, 109, 110, 111, 113, 114, 117, 118, 119, 120, 121, 122, 125, 126, 126-127, 128, 129, 133, 134, 136, 138, 139, 141, 144,

145, 146-147, 148, 149, 150-151, 152-153, 156 (both), 158, 159, 160, 161, 162, 162-163, 165, 166, 167, 168-169, 172-173, 174, 174-175, 181, 182, 185, 186-187, 187, 189 (top), 191, 194, 195, 197 (top), 198-199, 199, 200, 202, 202-203, 204, 205 (both), 206, 209, 210, 211, 213, 215, 216. Illustrated London Weekly News: 93 (both). John Frost Historical Newspaper Collection: 12-13. Andy Ward: 16 (both).

England Coach Terry Venables with Paul Gascoigne before England's 3-1 defeat at the hands of World Champions Brazil in the summer of 1995. This reverse was the first for Venables since he took over the job from Graham Taylor.

Venables' reign as England boss has, to date, been free of the wild criticism that plagued his predecessors. Anything short of victory in the 1996 European Championships, however, may well bring recriminations from fans and press alike. The omens are good. Not only has 'El Tel' got some of the most talented England players for some time to choose from, but the Tournament is being held on home territory… where England last achieved a major football success.

Copyright © 1995 Guinness Publishing Ltd

The moral right of the Authors has been asserted.

First published 1991
Second edition 1993
Third edition 1995
Reprint 10 9 8 7 6 5 4

Published in Great Britain by Guinness Publishing Ltd, 338 Euston Road, London NW1 3BD

Illustrations © 1995 as credited

Editorial, design and production by Hart McLeod, Cambridge

Printed and bound in Great Britain by The Bath Press, Bath

"GUINNESS" is a registered trademark of guinness Publishing Ltd

A catalogue record for this book is available from the British Library

ISBN 0-85112-664-2

The Guinness Football Encyclopedia

ABERDEEN

Founded 1903

Joined League 1904
(Division 2)

Honours Scottish League
Championship Division 1
1955, Premier Division 1980,
1984, 1985, Scottish Cup
1947, 1970, 1982, 1983,
1984, 1986, 1990, League
Cup 1955/56, 1976/77,
1985/86, 1989/90, European
Cup Winners' Cup 1983

Ground Pittodrie Stadium

Aberdeen have done far more
than win trophies. In the
1980s they did not just come
through to take silverware,
they repeatedly trounced both
Celtic and Rangers. It was the
greatest disruption to the
status quo in the modern
history of Scottish football.

Their confidence and
pugnacity seemed to originate
in the personality of manager
Alex Ferguson. A
marvellously blended side
deployed the rigour of
defenders Willie Miller and
Alex McLeish as well as the
deft skills of Gordon Strachan,
Mark McGhee and Peter Weir
in attack.

Their finest two hours
came in the extra-time
victory over Real Madrid in
the 1983 Cup Winners' Cup
final. The 2-1 scoreline
masked the annihilation of
the celebrated opposition.

Aberdeen's prominence is
aided by remoteness (fans
cannot easily be wooed away
to watch the Old Firm) and
the fact that they are their
city's only senior club.
Shrewd administration down
the years, seen in the fact that
Pittodrie was all-seated long
before the Taylor Report, has
also been significant.

There had been celebrated
figures before, such as
goalscorer Benny Yorston
between the wars and Martin
Buchan who, as a 21-year

old, captained them to the
Scottish Cup triumph over
Celtic in 1970. Sadly,
Aberdeen found success to be
elusive in the nineties. A series
of failures or near misses in all
the major competitions led to
disquiet which came to a head
when in February 1995, they
found themselves near the
bottom of the Premier
Division. A narrow escape
from relegation followed.
Manager Willie Miller, their
most famous player with 65
Scotland caps, was dismissed,
almost exactly three years
since he took the job. His
assistant Roy Aitken, the
former Celtic and Scotland
captain, succeeded him.

AFRICA

To describe a tournament in
which 14 goals were
conceded in three successive
defeats as a basis for optimism
might seem far-fetched, but
in 1974 Zaire became the first
non-Arabic speaking African
state to appear in the World
Cup finals; to compete at

François Omam Biyik of Cameroon scoring the only goal of the opening match of the 1990 World Cup in Italy. Their shock victory against Argentina, the defending World Champions, was initially greeted with disbelief. However, Cameroon's performances later in a competition where they so nearly made the semi-finals ensured that African football would, in future, be treated much more seriously. So seriously, in fact, that the idea of an African country staging a future World Cup was first discussed.

world level was significant in itself and the confidence and self-belief of that continent's other teams were raised. Sixteen years later, Cameroon, with a style that might euphemistically be termed robust, reached the quarter-finals, and that, plus Morocco winning their first-stage group in 1986,

Aberdeen's success in the 1980s was not limited to the football field; the city was growing in prosperity as a result of the offshore oil and gas business. One highlight of the boom period was the 1983 European Cup Winners' Cup victory. The Dons beat Real Madrid 2-1 on a wet night in Gothenburg with Eric Black opening the scoring, putting the ball past the diving Augustin. Only 17,804 watched the match – it sounded as if they were all Scots.

prompted FIFA to increase Africa's contingent for 1994 to three teams.

Football in Africa, as might be expected, has colonial origins, and ironically the political, economic and cultural consequences of post-imperialism are among the many things holding up the sport's development in that part of the world. To a European the words Congo, Biafra, Uganda, Ethiopia, Zimbabwe and Mozambique represent not so much countries as disasters: famine, drought, civil war. A 1989 survey showed that, in almost every country in a broad band sweeping across central Africa from Mozambique in the south-east to the western Sahara, economic growth was negligible and the average annual income less than 500 dollars per head. The climate and attendant disease are also not to be underestimated as problems. It is against such a background that African soccer is trying to make its

own mark on the world.

Football, a school as well as a street sport, is tremendously popular throughout the continent, but it is in north Africa, particularly the Francophone states – France arguably having done more to promote world soccer than the game's mother nation – that the game's traditions are strongest. In the 1982 World Cup, Algeria, with African footballer of the year Lakhdar Belloumi in the side, beat West Germany 2-1 and might have reached the second round had not the Germans been able to contrive a mutually beneficial 1-0 result with Austria. In colonial Morocco and Tunisia, football became identified with nationalist sentiment. (Today, in central and eastern Africa, regional pride is greatly in evidence, many national teams taking on nicknames which celebrate the power of African fauna: the Green Eagles, the Lions, the

Elephants, the Scorpions.) Egypt joined FIFA in 1923 and was one of the first African states to organise a league and gain international recognition. It still is a power, having won the 1986 African Nations Cup and qualified for the 1990 World Cup finals.

Unlike Britain, France and Portugal maintained links with the football scene in their former colonies, often poaching the best players for their club – and national – teams. France's record-holding Just Fontaine was Moroccan. Benfica in the 1960s had three Angolans in their team including goalkeeper Alberto Costa Pereira, and two famous players from Mozambique who also represented Portugal – skipper Mario Coluña and Eusebio. Such signings are still a rarity in England but continue in France.

Since the 1950s, countries south of the Sahara, notably Cameroon, Zaire, Ghana and most recently Nigeria, have emerged as football powers. The Confederation of African Football (CAF) was formed in 1957 with four member nations – today there are some fifty. Almost their first act was to expel South Africa because of apartheid. FIFA suspended the South Africans in 1964 and did the same to Rhodesia in 1970. Among South African whites, football comes a poor second to rugby union. The national league was disbanded in 1978 despite the enrolment of stars such as Ian St John and Francis Lee. But the game is hugely popular among the non-white population. Formal structure, facilities and coaching are all lacking, but moves towards racial integration, in particular the formation in late 1990 of one ruling body, the SAFA, led CAF and FIFA to reconsider South Africa's position, finally reinstating them with the abolition of apartheid in 1994. CAF's influence in FIFA has grown and in 1985 Africa staged the first Junior World Cup.

As well as the African Cup of Nations there are continental club competitions based on European models, and wisely for a continent larger than South America, regional international tournaments. No East African country has won the Nations Cup since 1970; rivalry between Kenya, the region's top team, and Uganda is intense but the two sides do not experience enough competition with north African and European sides to improve – a replication in miniature of one of Africa's main problems. The average Kenyan footballer has an excellent physique for the sport but his country's approach often emphasises individual excellence at the expense of teamwork.

Idi Amin, a football enthusiast, brought Uganda financial ruin and civil war – conditions which make sport seem trivial. Tanzania lost her best players of the 1970s and 1980s to Europe, the Middle East and the USA – another disadvantage experienced by most African nations. Malawi, with their tough brand of football, and Zambia, a nation boasting home-grown coaches and staff, also exhibit keen rivalry. However, Zambian progress suffered a catastrophic setback in April 1993 when all but four of the national squad perished in an air crash en route to play in a World Cup qualifier. Subsequent resistance shown by Zambians has been both remarkable and moving.

The lowly status of a small, under-resourced country such as Gambia has been

understandable; more puzzling was Nigeria's lack of success until the 1994 World Cup. Football is widely played in this populous country but the league, established in 1972, took some years to get off the ground and the national team rarely lived up to expectations. The Biafran war was obviously a hindrance. Less apparent was the disturbing effect of emigré stars returning and trying to adapt to the national style. Ghana, on the other hand, has a proud record. As the game took hold, European administrators were phased out until, strangely enough, independence in 1957. Then a commemorative tour by Stanley Matthews so inspired the national association that European coaches were brought over to increase their players' technical skills and tactics. In 1963 the national side toured Europe, holding Real Madrid to a 3-3 draw. The following year they beat Italy. Ghana's four victories in the Cup of Nations is a record. Another success story in the making is that of the Ivory Coast, whose football has made huge advances in recent years, the highlight being victory in the 1992 Cup of Nations.

Although various styles exist in African soccer, with greater or lesser European influences, the climate to a large extent determines the basic approach. Individual dribbling skills, accurate passing and willingness to take direct, long-range shots are at a premium in slow, patient build-ups. This is as true for Cameroon as Algeria; British footballers admired the poise and fluent passing of the central Africans – players such as M'bouh, Makanaky and Omam-Biyik spring to mind.

In the United States in 1994 Africa set out her stall; Nigeria excelled as they reached the second phase of the tournament, while Cameroon and Morocco disappointed in terms of results yet displayed vast potential. Now it is equally important that, meanwhile, the main problems within African football are tackled. Political, economic and

ecological issues are, of course, beyond the power of sporting bodies, but work can be done in other areas. Professionalism needs to be established to encourage Africa's best players to stay at home. National and club sides must gain more experience abroad; CAF might try to persuade other FIFA countries to help finance tours.

The 1990 World Cup made Cameroon, with the remarkable Roger Milla, the best known African team of recent times. In 1994 Nigeria stepped up, with the likes of Daniel Amokachi – later to join Everton – taking the limelight. Other countries such as Ghana, Libya and Senegal are itching to get on the world stage. Players such as George Weah (Liberia) and Tony Yeboah (Leeds United and Ghana), already stars in European club football, are waiting in the wings to show what they can do.

AFRICAN CUP OF NATIONS

Set up in 1957 with the establishment of the Confederation of African Football, this competition has taken place every two years, almost without exception – no small achievement in a huge Third World continent. The range of winners is testimony to a healthy competitive element in African football. Ghana emerges as the most consistent nation.

AIRDRIEONIANS

Founded 1878 (as Excelsior, renamed Airdrieonians 1881)

Joined League 1894 (Division 2)

Honours Scottish League Division 2 Champions 1903, 1955, 1974, Scottish Cup Winners 1924

Ground Broomfield Park

Lanarkshire is a footballing heartland but Airdrie lose potential support to nearby Celtic and Rangers. However they are a durable club.

Their fine side of the 1920s, which won the 1924 Scottish Cup, included Bob McPhail, who became a Rangers legend, and Hughie Gallacher, one of the 'Wembley Wizards' who defeated England 5-1 in 1928.

Airdrie survived only two seasons in the Premier Division (1980-82) but returned to it in 1991. They reached the Scottish Cup Final in 1992, losing to Rangers, but a year later they were relegated. In 1995 they were losing Scottish Cup finalists again.

ALBION ROVERS

Founded 1882

Joined League 1903 (Division 2)

Honours Scottish League Division 2 Champions 1989

Ground Cliftonhill Stadium

AFRICAN CUP OF NATIONS			
Year	Winner	Runner-up	Score
1957	Egypt	Sudan	
1959	Egypt	Sudan	
1962	Ethiopia	Egypt	4-2*
1963	Ghana	Sudan	3-0
1965	Ghana	Tunisia	3-2*
1968	Congo	Ghana	1-0
1970	Sudan	Ghana	1-0
1972	Congo	Mali	3-2
1974	Zaire	Zambia	2-2* 2-0
1976	Morocco	Guinea	
1978	Ghana	Uganda	2-0
1980	Nigeria	Algeria	3-0
1982	Ghana	Libya	1-1**
1984	Cameroon	Nigeria	3-1
1986	Egypt	Cameroon	0-0**
1988	Cameroon	Nigeria	1-0
1989/90	Algeria	Nigeria	1-0
1992	Ivory Coast	Ghana	0-0**
1994	Nigeria	Zambia	2-1

* after extra time ** on penalties
In 1957, 1959 and 1976 the tournament was decided on a league basis.

Ivor Allchurch made 330 League appearances for Swansea Town, the team later to be called Swansea City, before moving off to Newcastle United and then Cardiff City. This second move saw him play for Swansea's main rivals. Home fans were appeased (a bit) when their hero returned to play a further 116 League games for the Swans. Ivor's younger brother Len also made a career detour to Sheffield United and Stockport County before returning to play for Swansea.

Overshadowed even in Lanarkshire by nearby Airdrie and Motherwell, life has always been trying for Albion Rovers. Their principal moment of national celebrity came in 1920 when they outlasted Rangers to win the second replay of a Scottish Cup semi-final. The final was lost all the same.

Jubilation of a more contemporary nature came with their Second Division Championship in 1989, although relegation followed a year later. The club can boast of service from future internationalists such as Tony Green (Scotland) and Bernie Slaven (Republic of Ireland).

ALLCHURCH, Ivor

1929 Born in Swansea

1947 Joins Swansea Town

1949 Makes first-team debut

1951 Wins first of 68 Welsh caps, v England

1958 Transferred to Newcastle United for £27,000; World Cup quarter-finalist, 0-1 v Brazil

1962 Transferred to Cardiff

1965 Returns to Swansea

1967 Retires

Grace and touch were the hallmarks of Ivor Allchurch. A wonderfully skilful inside-forward, he always seemed to have plenty of time on the ball, a sure sign of a good footballer.

He could pass brilliantly with either foot, dribbled perceptively and was a prolific scorer for a midfield player, getting more than 250 goals in an 18-year career. His tally of 160 is still a club record at Swansea.

National Service delayed Allchurch's first-team debut until he was 20 but almost immediately he stood out. Tall and blond, he drew attention like a magnet and throughout the 1950s his elegant skills were coveted by many First Division clubs. Swansea managed to resist all offers until Newcastle paid £27,000, then a considerable sum, in 1958.

His four years at St James's Park were probably his best. Ron Greenwood, the former West Ham United and England manager, said: 'You could do nothing but admire him. He was a great prompter, a creative player who could always find his centre-forward with a great through pass.'

Allchurch, whose brother Len also played for his country on 11 occasions, won 68 caps for Wales between 1951 and 1966, which stood as a record for 20 years until overtaken by Joey Jones.

ALLOA

Founded 1883

Joined League 1921 (Division 2)

Honours Scottish League Division 2 Champions 1922

Ground Recreation Park

Since League reconstruction (1974) Alloa have oscillated mostly between the First and Second Divisions, though by 1995 they were in the Third. The experience of modest success which has proved difficult to sustain is typical of the club.

Their Second Division Championship of 1922 (Alloa's first season in the League) was the most spectacular with 49 goals coming from diminutive centre-forward Willie Crilley who was soon to join Celtic. Then, and often since, the club has had to take pride in simply grooming stars for others' benefit. In more recent decades they have nurtured fledglings such as the late John White and Tommy Hutchison who went on to play for Scotland and who had considerable success south of the border.

AMATEUR CUP

The FA Amateur Cup was the major knock-out competition for amateur teams between 1893 and 1974 (when the distinction between 'amateurs' and 'professionals' was made obsolete by the Football Association). From 1949 the Final was held at Wembley. Bishop Auckland's record ten wins included three in succession in the mid-1950s.

AMATEUR FOOTBALL

Amateurs were responsible for the emergence of many of football's most important features: the early laws, national Football Associations in Britain, the FA Cup and Scottish Cup, international matches and the network of local associations. The power of amateurism dwindled after 1885, when the FA legalised professionalism, but amateur

The Amateur Cup is a fading memory but the competition, and in particular the final, were once major features of the footballing calendar. Crowds of 100,000 would watch Wembley finals with the same interest as viewed the professional equivalent. The 1954 final features the two sides that won it most often, Bishop Auckland (ten wins) and Crook Town (five – equal with Clapton). Here J Major (left) of Bishop Auckland and R Davison of Crook lead out their teams for the second replay of the final at Middlesbrough. Crook Town won 1-0 following 2-2 draws at Wembley and Newcastle.

football is still the foundation on which the game is based.

Top amateur teams competed with professionals until well into the twentieth century. The Corinthians, for instance, thrashed Cup winners Blackburn Rovers and double-winning Preston North End in their heyday in the 1880s. They also beat 1903 Cup winners Bury 10-3 and achieved good FA Cup results until the late 1930s. As late as 1974, an Isthmian League amateur team, Hendon, held Newcastle United to a 1-1 draw at St James's Park in the FA Cup. Newcastle won the replay and went on to reach the Final.

The Amateur Football Association was formed in 1907 to ensure the distinction between the increasingly popular professional game and the 'old school' of amateurism. The AFA stated: 'It is essential for the good of the game of Association football as played by amateurs that an Amateur Football Association be formed.' (The title was changed to the Amateur Football Alliance in May 1934.)

An example of amateur-professional conflict was the debate over the penalty kick, introduced in 1891. Those in the public-school tradition believed that the new law was not needed, and the

Arthur Dunn Cup, inaugurated in 1902/03 as a competition for old boys' teams from Eton and elsewhere, refused to recognise the penalty kick until reprimanded by the FA. Even in the 1920s some amateur teams were so appalled at conceding a penalty that they instructed their goalkeeper to stand aside and permit the just punishment of a goal into the empty net.

The Scottish Amateur FA was formed in 1909, but it

was a combined United Kingdom amateur team that won the first two football tournaments in the Olympic Games – in London (1908) and Stockholm (1912).

In 1914 the breach between the Football Association and the breakaway Amateur Football Association was healed. They had fallen out over the acceptance of professional clubs to local football associations.

In 1928 the four British Football Associations resigned

membership of FIFA over problems of defining 'amateurism' and 'broken time' (the payment of wages lost by amateurs while absent from work playing football). The British bodies were in favour of allowing 'broken time' payments but FIFA voted against them, with the exception of part payments in special circumstances.

When Britain returned to FIFA in 1946, 'broken time' payments were still contentious and 'shamateurism' remained an issue in Britain. 'Shamateurism' was the payment of expenses and compensation to amateurs, some of whom played in the Football League. The debate was finally ended in 1974 when the FA classified all footballers as 'players'. The problem of deciding whether or not a player was paid was therefore passed to the tax authorities. A notable exception was the Olympic Games football tournament, which, under the jurisdiction of the Olympic Committee, continued to be plagued with problems of defining who were truly amateurs.

The 1974 decision effectively ended the FA Amateur Cup and the home internationals amateur tournament introduced in 1953/54. Some famous amateur leagues have adapted to survive the new legislation. These include the Northern League (formed in 1889) and the Isthmian League (1905). The Athenian League, formed in 1912, lasted until 1984.

Many amateur players have ranked alongside professionals in their contribution to the game. G.O. Smith, who scored 12 goals in 20 full England games at the turn of the century, was an outstanding centre-forward of any era. Bernard Joy was an amateur when capped for the full England team in 1936. Jim Lewis, who achieved 49 England amateur international caps, played in Chelsea's 1954/55 Championship team, and the 1948 Great Britain Olympic team included Queen's Park's Ronnie Simpson, who later played as a professional for Newcastle United, Celtic and Scotland.

Today, amateur football is still the grass roots of the game. There are far more amateur players than professional, and most professionals start as amateurs, even if only in schoolboy football. The development of the Sunday game in the 1960s helped increase the number of teams, leading to the inauguration of the FA Sunday Cup in 1965. The number of clubs continues to grow in the 1990s.

ARBROATH

Founded 1878

Joined League 1921 (Division 2)

Honours None

Ground Gayfield Park

A club founded by rugby enthusiasts produced a football score to match. Their world record victory in senior football – 36-0 against Bon Accord (an Aberdeen club) in a Scottish Cup tie on 12 September 1885 – still stands. Perhaps they felt that was sufficient impact, for they have scarcely troubled the statisticians since.

Arbroath, though, have often possessed an air of diligent stability. Albert Henderson was manager for 17 years until 1980 during which period the club twice won promotion to the old Division 1. Earlier times saw the rapid-fire achievement of Dave Easson, who notched up 45 goals in season 1958/59.

ARDILES, Osvaldo

1952 Born in Cordoba, Argentina

1978 June – takes the eye as his country wins the World Cup on home soil; July – joins Tottenham Hotspur from Huracan of Buenos Aires for £325,000

1981 Plays prominent role in Spurs' FA Cup Final victory over Manchester City

1982 April – helps Spurs beat Leicester City in FA Cup semi-final, then misses final because of Falklands War; June – plays for Argentinian side knocked out in second phase of World Cup in Spain; starts season on loan with Paris St Germain while Falklands furore dies down

1983 January – returns to White Hart Lane

1984 Comes on as substitute to earn UEFA Cup winner's medal against Anderlecht

1988 March – joins Blackburn Rovers on loan; July – moves to Queen's Park Rangers, but makes only a handful of appearances

1989 Succeeds Lou Macari as Swindon Town manager

1990 Swindon qualify for Division 1 in play-offs, but stay down because of financial irregularities

1991 Takes over as Newcastle boss

1992 February – gets sack from Magpies; May – becomes West Bromwich Albion manager

1993 Leads Albion to promotion from Division 2 via play-offs, then quits controversially to take charge at White Hart Lane

1994 Dismissed by Tottenham after disappointing, often turbulent reign

The purchase of 'Ossie' Ardiles, and fellow countryman Ricardo Villa, represented a brave gamble by Spurs manager Keith Burkinshaw. After their dazzling displays in the World Cup, the players' talent was not in question but many critics were sceptical about their ability to adapt to the hurly-burly of the English League. Both men laid such doubts to rest, but Ardiles in particular was a revelation.

A slightly-built, nimble midfield general blessed with glorious all-round skills and deceptive strength, he was a masterful passer and intelligent reader of the game whose experience and enthusiasm proved a splendidly positive influence at White Hart Lane.

Ardiles became one of the most popular overseas footballers to come to these shores, and a testimony to his stature was his successful return to Tottenham in the wake of the Falklands conflict when Britain was at war with Argentina. As manager of Swindon Town he transformed a lacklustre side into an attractive one, and was desperately unfortunate to see his first season's work count for nothing. There followed a brief, turbulent spell at Newcastle before Ardiles slipped into the hot seat at West Bromwich. In the summer of 1993 he upset the Hawthorns regime by accepting his 'dream' job, managing Spurs, but it was to end in tears. After 16 months of lacklustre results and the trauma of the club being docked 12 league points and ejected from the FA Cup – a sentence imposed for alleged 'financial misdeeds' by the previous board and later reduced to a cash fine – Ardiles was sacked by chairman Alan Sugar in November 1994.

ARSENAL

Founded 1886

Joined League 1893 (Division 2)

Honours Division 1 Champions 1931, 1933, 1934, 1935, 1938, 1948, 1953, 1971, 1989, 1991; FA Cup Winners 1930, 1936, 1950, 1971, 1979, 1993; League Cup Winners 1987, 1993; European Cup Winners' Cup Winners 1994; European Fairs Cup Winners 1970

Ground Highbury

Arsenal are an institution throughout the soccer-playing world. Even when their fortunes dip alarmingly, as they did throughout most of the 1950s and 1960s, the 'Gunners' retain their eminence. Such is the weight of achievement, the sense of tradition and sheer splendour exuded by Highbury's marble halls, that a fall from grace seems unthinkable. It was not always the case.

After winning election to Division 2, Woolwich Arsenal, as they were then known, experienced several decades of dour consolidation and financial struggle. Indeed, during this unimpressive interlude the Gunners were relegated for the only time in their history – in 1913 when they chalked up only one home win, a record that no other club has matched.

The turning point was the arrival of Herbert Chapman in 1925. The brilliant Yorkshireman, who had just led Huddersfield Town to the first two legs of their League Championship hat-trick, predicted that he would need five years to transform Arsenal from nonentities to a power in the land, and so it proved. The darkness began to lighten with the lifting of the FA Cup in 1930, and there followed the club's most successful period, which saw five League titles and another FA Cup triumph before the Second World War ended the bonanza.

Stars of that era included deadly marksman Charlie Buchan (who missed out on the trophies but helped lay the foundations of a great team), visionary play-maker Alex James, goalscoring wingers Cliff Bastin and Joe Hulme, prolific forwards David Jack and Ted Drake, and a posse of defenders and half-backs including George Male, Eddie Hapgood, Wilf Copping, Jack Crayston, Bob John, Tom Parker and Herbie Roberts.

When peacetime soccer resumed, Arsenal were no longer the same all-dominant force, although with Tom

Whittaker at the helm they collected more silverware, thanks to the likes of wing-half and skipper Joe Mercer, schemer Jimmy Logie, and gifted brothers Les and Denis Compton. There was also Welsh international goalkeeper Jack Kelsey, who helped the Gunners take the title in 1953 and then proved their only truly top-class performer throughout a period of distressing mediocrity. Despite acquiring skilled individuals such as inside-forward George Eastham and striker Joe Baker, a succession of managers – including former England captain Billy Wright – failed to effect a revival.

The glory days were not to return until club physiotherapist Bertie Mee took command. Then, with on-the-field drive from centre-half Frank McLintock, the creative ability of George Graham and Charlie George, devoted and accomplished service from forwards such as John Radford and George Armstrong, and a seemingly iron-clad defence, Arsenal won the League and FA Cup double in 1971. Mee's side was functional rather than

Arsenal, certainly since the 1960s, have never earned the same admiration from the general footballing public of, say, Manchester United or Liverpool. Their achievements probably deserve better. Their 1971 double success, here celebrated by Charlie George (left), the scorer of the winning goal at Wembley, and Frank McLintock, the captain, was achieved in a very competitive season. George, who could be described as mercurial or cocky, gifted or arrogant, depending upon your viewpoint, probably typified Arsenal's 'image' problem. As for the Gunners' fans, who cares if nobody loves you?

exciting, and the feat received but grudging acclaim, an unfair reflection on a magnificent season's work.

The rest of the 1970s and the first half of the 1980s – though enlivened at times by the contributions of sublimely talented midfielder Liam Brady and stylish defender David O'Leary, among others – were something of an anti-climax, and it was not until the appointment of George Graham as manager in 1986 that deeds to rival past successes again proved possible. The Scot led the side to six major prizes in eight years, including the Championship in both 1989 and 1991, and a cup double, the FA Cup and League Cup, in 1993. In 1994 Graham's side won the European Cup Winners' Cup... but this was to be his last trophy. Poor domestic form, and then allegations about transfer irregularities, led to the Scot's dismissal. His immediate successor, caretaker boss Stewart Houston, took the side to a second successive Cup Winners Final – which was lost to Real Zaragoza. Houston was then replaced by Bruce Rioch.

ASIA

FIFA and a geographer would not agree on their identification of Asia. For administrative purposes the International Federation includes the countries of the Middle East in the continent. This does pose problems with regard to Israel, something of a nomad in the football world because of the boycotts by Arab countries, and at different times her teams have contested World Cup qualifiers in Asia, Europe and Oceania. In 1970 Israel competed in the finals of the competition, and held both Italy and Sweden to draws.

Politics has often interfered with sport in the East. In 1991 Iraq's national and club teams were suspended from FIFA competitions following the invasion of Kuwait and the subsequent war. Japan and China have both been expelled from FIFA in their history, although they are now well-established members. China was readmitted to FIFA in 1975, and three years later West Bromwich Albion became the first Western club to tour communist China. In 1976 Taiwan and Israel were expelled from the Asian Football Confederation, which in turn found itself threatened with a FIFA ban

for its actions. The Confederation was formed in 1954 to promote the sport and it set up much-needed coaching schemes and instigated the Asian Cup for national teams in 1956.

It was North Korea, beneficiaries of Soviet coaching, who first put Asia on the football map with their spirited performances in the 1966 World Cup in England. Their Group games were played in Middlesbrough where the crowd took to the small Asians. They drew against Chile and played intelligently against Italy to win 1-0. Their quarter-final at Goodison Park against Portugal was even more of a sensation. They led 3-0 before their opponents scored five goals (four from Eusebio). The North Koreans were fit, dedicated and played a lively, short-passing game, but, like so many nations new to the international arena, lack of tactical understanding was their undoing. Their outstanding footballer was the play-maker Pak Seung Jin who set up their attacks, and Pak Doo Ik will be remembered for his goal against Italy. South Korea had played in the 1954 World Cup but they didn't win a single point and in

1986 and 1990 they were also unimpressive. However, in 1994 they gave a stirring account of themselves, drawing with Spain and Bolivia, then impressing mightily in a 3-2 defeat by Germany.

Korea, before the Second World War and before the division created by its own civil war, had been occupied by the Japanese who appreciated their subject people's footballing skills and made them represent Japan in the 1936 Olympic Games. Japan's FA was formed in 1921 and they were admitted to FIFA eight years later, although their national league didn't start until 1965, after failure to qualify for the 1960 Olympics prompted them to bring over a prominent West German coach who trained new coaches. After the war American influence was strong, so that baseball was more popular than soccer – except in Hiroshima, where British troops were based.

However, revolution was at hand. Huge amounts of cash were pumped into launching the much-trumpeted J-League in 1993, and well-known players from all over the world were recruited. Among those enticed last was England's

Seo Jung Won of South Korea in jubilant mood having scored a last minute equaliser in the 2-2 draw with Spain during the 1994 World Cup finals. South Korea failed to qualify for the next stages of the tournament but were far from disgraced. The game in Asia generally has not made the same impact on the world stage as Africa, although the 1966 North Koreans will always be remembered. The relative economic and political security of many of the Asian football playing nations, however, coupled with the enthusiasm that exists for the game, may soon change this.

Gary Lineker, though sadly his career was ended prematurely by injury. There seemed to be no limits to the ambition of Japan's administrators and the country prepared a bid to host the World Cup in 2002. Those close to the campaign, including Sir Bobby Charlton, were confident that it would end in success. In the long term, though, the future of Japanese football will depend on fostering grass-roots enthusiasm.

In Pakistan, British traders and military personnel brought hockey as well as soccer and it was the former which proved more popular. In other Asian countries, traditional sports prevailed. However, the increasing popularity of football is evident: India's amateur game was strong in the 1950s and early 1960s and the game has a great following in Hong Kong, Malaysia and Bangladesh. Chinese students played international games in the early years of this century and the game's roots might be stronger if political events had turned out differently.

Forms of football existed in the Far East in ancient times. In Japan this was mainly as a type of ball juggling, although there is evidence from 1004 BC and AD 611 of a competitive game played on a pitch, and in 50 BC there was an international between Japan and China! A game known as tsu chu (kick-ball), played two and a half thousand years ago on the Chinese Emperor's birthday, involved kicking a ball through a hole in silk netting; there was physical punishment for the losers.

In the Middle East, however, the British Imperial influence is more apparent. Iran (Persia at the time) formed its national association in 1920 and Afghanistan in 1922; Arab countries were to follow in the course of the next three decades. Iran, coached by former Manchester United boss Frank O'Farrell, reached the 1978 World Cup finals. The following year the Ayatollah banned the sport, but today there are 300,000 registered players compared with 43,000 in 1980 and Iran is one of the strongest teams in the area. Other nations to boost the region's soccer stature by reaching the World Cup Finals have been Kuwait (1982), Iraq (1986), the United Arab Emirates (1990) and Saudi Arabia (1994). The Saudis were particularly impressive, beating Morocco and Belgium on their way to the second stage of the tournament, before bowing out to Sweden.

Since 1980 football's position in the Middle East has been stable. The number of clubs ranges from 12 in Qatar to 154 in Saudi Arabia, 40 in Iraq and 6236 in Iran.

Most of the countries in Asia and the Middle East play their international football in the Olympics, the Asian Games and the Asian Cup, which means they do not get enough experience of top-flight competition. To this are added well-publicised political and economic problems.

ASTON VILLA

Founded 1874

Joined League 1888 (founder member)

Honours Division 1 Champions 1894, 1896, 1897, 1899, 1900, 1910, 1981; Division 2 Champions 1938, 1960; Division 3 Champions 1972; FA Cup Winners 1887, 1895, 1897, 1905, 1913, 1920, 1957; League Cup Winners 1961, 1975, 1977, 1994; European Cup Winners 1982

Ground Villa Park

Although the bulk of Aston Villa's honours were won during the reign of Queen Victoria, they remain one of the leading clubs in the land, a status they have good prospects of maintaining into the next century. It does seem unlikely, however, that they will ever outstrip those early achievements. After being formed at a meeting under a street-corner gas-lamp, the

Birmingham club made rapid strides. Doubtless inspired by the fact that one of their officials, William McGregor, had founded the Football League, Villa proceeded to place considerable strain on their trophy cabinet. In the seven seasons leading to the turn of the century they won five Championships and lifted the FA Cup twice, with the coveted double being secured in 1897.

As the standard of competition grew, the rate of success slowed, but Villa continued to be Division 1 bastions. Stars included combative centre-forward Harry Hampton, who scored 242 goals for the club between 1904 and 1920, and England's Sam Hardy, who guarded Villa's net on either side of the First World War. Then, in the 1920s and 1930s, it was masterful inside-forward Billy Walker and the prolific Pongo Waring – he once notched 49 League goals in a single campaign – who held sway. It was not until 1936 that Villa slipped into

Although Aston Villa have achieved some great successes since the 1898/99 season this photograph still takes some beating. The trophies they collected were (left to right, back row) the Walsall Cup, the Sheriff of London Charity Shield, the Mayor of Birmingham Charity Cup, the Birmingham Challenge Cup, the Football League Championship (won by two points from Liverpool) and the Staffordshire Cup. And some people say that there is too much football today!

the Second Division for the first time. They soon regained their seniority, but then began a lengthy period of mediocrity. The 1950s, mostly disappointing, offered brief hope of revival with an FA Cup triumph over Manchester United – albeit a controversial one in which two-goal match-winner Peter McParland was involved in a sickening collision with the United 'keeper. But relegation followed and although new boss Joe Mercer soon achieved promotion and saw

his side become the first winners of the League Cup – which at that time attracted entries from few top clubs – there was worse to follow. England marksman Gerry Hitchens headed for Italy, and an inexorable slide began. Successive managers, including the tempestuous Tommy Docherty, failed and Villa sank to the Third Division. After much boardroom upheaval, it was left to former wing-half Vic Crowe to rebuild.

It was not until Ron Saunders arrived in 1975 that

the glory days returned. His side restored Villa's Division 1 status, won two League Cups and then lifted the League Championship for the first time in 71 years. With midfielders Dennis Mortimer and Gordon Cowans outstanding, Villa went on to win the European Cup a year later, but even that did not signal ultimate consistency, and there was another one-season sojourn in Division 2 before the decade was out. Next, with Graham Taylor having left to guide England,

the appointment of extrovert Ron Atkinson as manager seemed to herald a new era; he certainly brought a hint of the 'big time' with him, and in players such as Paul McGrath, Dean Saunders and Dalian Atkinson, in the early nineties, had the nucleus of a title-winning side. But despite lifting the League Cup in 1994, Atkinson was sacked after a poor start to the new term, and was replaced by Villa old-boy Brian Little, under whom relegation was avoided only at the last gasp.

A famous event as covered by the Sunday Pictorial in 1923. This was the day that a policeman on a white horse eventually helped clear the pitch to enable the first Wembley FA Cup final to begin. The game, in which Bolton Wanderers beat West Ham 2-0, was watched by a crowd estimated at around 200,000; officially it was 126,047. Today's all-seater Wembley houses about 80,000 for a major final.

FINAL WEEKS OF £7,000 FILM

SUNDAY·PI

SALE MORE THAN DOUBLE THAT OF ANY

No. 424.   Registered at the G.P.O. as a Newspaper.   SUNDAY, APRIL 29

WEMBLEY STADIUM STORMED BY EX

A striking aerial photograph of the scene at Wembley Stadium yesterday after the gates had been closed. ... flood the playing pitch, while thousands clustered outside are clamouring for

ATTENDANCES

The paying customer provides the life-blood of professional football, so it is not surprising that a great deal of interest is shown in the numbers of supporters who attend matches. Even beyond the professional game, a large crowd can be important in lifting a team and elevating an occasion.

The British game, although generally enjoying increasing attendances in the late 1980s and early 1990s, is still poorly supported when compared with the halcyon days immediately after the Second World War. The record for one day's English League matches was set on 27 December 1949 when 1,272,185 spectators attended the 44 matches. That day 70,000 saw Aston Villa lose at home to Wolves, while 56,000 watched Sheffield United draw with Preston North End in the Second Division.

Apart from falling interest, nearly all Football and Scottish League teams have current ground capacities well below their record attendances. Ground reconstruction and safety regulations account for this trend that produces such examples as Blackburn Rovers (capacity 31,000 – record 61,783) and Aberdeen (capacity 22,568 – record 45,061).

The record English League match attendance was set at Maine Road (Manchester City's ground) where 83,260 saw Manchester United play Arsenal in 1948, although this falls well short of Rangers'

118,567 for the 1939 New Year League match with Celtic at Ibrox Park. Glasgow's Hampden Park has been the scene of enormous crowds such as the 135,826 that saw Celtic v Leeds United in the second leg of the European Cup semi-final in 1970, and the 146,433 for the Celtic v Aberdeen Scottish Cup Final of 1937.

Cup matches have often accounted for individual club records throughout Britain. The 1923 FA Cup Final between West Ham United

and Bolton Wanderers had an official attendance of 126,047, but these were only the paying customers; gatecrashers are estimated to have put the final figure up to 200,000. A far cry from the 2000 who witnessed the first Final in 1872.

That 1923 figure compares well with the recognised world record of 199,854 who saw the 1950 World Cup Final between Brazil and Uruguay at Rio's Maracana Stadium.

Over the years there have

been small crowds too, records that have been added to by the occasional instructions to play a match 'behind closed doors' as a punishment for a club's misdemeanours. A British example was the European Cup Winners' Cup match (second leg) between West Ham United and Castilla of Spain. Each team was permitted a 70-man delegation (including players) and 16 ballboys manned the empty terraces. The official attendance figure was 262; there were 500 police outside the ground!

CONTEST – See Page 5

TORIAL

ER SUNDAY PICTURE PAPER

[24 PAGES]   Twopence,

ED CUP FINAL CROWDS

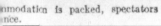
nmodation is packed, spectators
nce.

One of four daring souls who climbed a drain-pipe to secure an entrance at the back of the lofty covered stand.

AUSTRALASIA

Australia and New Zealand have failed to make an impact on the World Cup to rival that of North Korea or the African countries, but both have reached the finals and Australia ended the 1980s with some excellent results which promised well for the future.

In Australasia soccer has had to compete with rugby league, rugby union and, in Australia's southern states, Australian Rules football. Progress has been slow. The first Australian soccer club was formed in Sydney in 1880, but the Australian Football Association was not formed until 1920 and the first World Cup entry was as late as 1964. The Australians celebrated 100 years of soccer in 1980, when England won 2-1 in Sydney and Northern Ireland won two out of three, the game in Melbourne being drawn.

Australia gave Scotland a fright in a two-leg qualifying play-off for the 1986 World Cup finals: Scotland won 2-0 in Glasgow but only drew 0-0 in Australia. This was undoubtedly an improvement on some of Australia's earlier showings against British international teams such as the 17-0 defeat by England in Sydney in 1951.

The variety of ethnic origins of Australian soccer, with players and supporters having roots in Europe and elsewhere, adds a touch of volatility to the National League and regional leagues, and there have been recent bans on national flags, emblems and ethnic names such as Croatia, Juventus and North End. The names of many minor-league Australian teams are known in Britain through their appearance on football pools coupons during the British summer, but top Australian teams play during their own summer, the British winter.

The catalyst for one of the biggest booms in Australian soccer came when Jim Mackay's goal against South Korea brought a 1-0 win in a qualifying play-off for a place in the 1974 World Cup finals. In West Germany, Australia held Chile to a goalless draw; otherwise, there were predictable defeats against East Germany and the West German hosts.

In 1981 Australia staged the FIFA Youth Championship. Around the same time, the New Zealand team was working towards the 1982 World Cup finals. For a few minutes, in their first game of the finals, New Zealand threatened an upset, having pulled back from 3-0 down to 3-2, but Scotland eventually won 5-2. The Kiwis also lost to the USSR and Brazil – it wasn't an easy group – but the World Cup finals provided a boost for the New Zealand FA, which was formed in 1891.

In 1988 there was a double success for Australian soccer. The national team beat world champions Argentina 4-1 in a four-nation tournament to celebrate the Australian bicentenary. Australia lost 2-0 to Brazil in the final, watched by 28,161 people. The other success came in the 1988 Seoul Olympics. Wins against Yugoslavia and Nigeria brought a runners-up place in a group won by Brazil. Australia's quarter-final was lost 3-0 to the Soviet Union, the eventual gold medallists. In 1993 Australia again staged the finals of the World Youth Cup and took 4th place; then the senior side narrowly missed out on a place in the 1994 World Cup finals when they lost a play-off with no less than Argentina.

Australasia has always been a popular place for touring club teams. In addition, players have been recruited from the area for the British leagues, such as Tony Dorigo, who has played for Aston Villa, Chelsea and Leeds United and won international honours for England, and Craig Johnston, who played for Middlesbrough and Liverpool in the 1980s; Mark Bosnich, who served Manchester United briefly before realising his considerable potential with Aston Villa in the early 1990s, and Robbie Slater, who joined Blackburn Rovers in 1994.

AYR UNITED

Founded 1910

Joined League 1910 (Division 2)

Honours Scottish League Division 2 Champions 1912, 1913, 1928, 1937, 1959, 1966; Second Division Champions 1988

Ground Somerset Park

Ayr United achieved their highest profile under the exuberant Ally MacLeod (the first of his three spells as manager) in the late 1960s and early 1970s. They were then a frequent threat in cup competitions.

Of earlier feats the most remarkable was Jimmy Smith's tally of 66 League goals in season 1927/28.

Ayr United take pride in having produced three players from the recent international scene: Steve Nicol, Bobby Connor and Alan McInally.

BANKS, Gordon

1937 Born in Sheffield

1955 Turns professional with Chesterfield

1959 Joins Leicester City for £6000

1961 Takes home FA Cup runners-up medal as Tottenham Hotspur clinch League and Cup double

1963 Another FA Cup Final defeat, this time by Manchester United; England debut, against Brazil at Wembley

1964 At last, a club honour: League Cup Final victory over Stoke City

1966 The ultimate glory: World Cup triumph

1967 Moves to Stoke City for £52,000

1970 Performs World Cup heroics in Mexico

1972 Helps Stoke City beat Chelsea and win the League Cup; voted Footballer of the Year by the Football Writers' Association; car accident ends career

At his peak, Banks was regarded as the greatest goalkeeper in the world, yet he never played for a 'fashionable' club. After learning his trade for four seasons with Chesterfield, he moved into the top flight and it soon became apparent that Leicester had unearthed a rare gem. Brave, strong and blessed with an acute positional sense, he was not an habitually flashy custodian, but at times his natural elasticity between the posts was astonishing.

Accomplished though it was, Banks' club career was overshadowed by his international exploits. He was an ever-present member of Alf Ramsey's team which won the 1966 World Cup, conceding only three goals during the finals. But the moment for which he is

lionised came four years later in a World Cup confrontation with Brazil in Mexico. The incomparable Pele rose above the England defence to send an apparently unstoppable header arrowing towards the unguarded corner of Banks' net. The 'keeper dived but seemed to have been beaten by the bounce when he somehow managed to twist upwards and divert the ball over his crossbar. Sadly, illness forced him out of the subsequent quarter-final against West Germany, and his deputy, poor Peter Bonetti, will be forever vilified for his part in England's 3-2 defeat. Banks, who had been allowed to leave Leicester for Stoke due to the emergence of the

A young Gordon Banks conceding a goal during Leicester City's 2-0 defeat at the hands of Spurs in the 1961 FA Cup final. Up until the final Banks played in nine matches, including replays, and conceded only four goals. Although recognised as the greatest 'keeper in the world during the period between 1966 and 1972, Banks wasn't noted for any particular aspect of his play. With hindsight it was probably his all-round ability, and his knack of making the difficult look easy, that set him apart.

young Peter Shilton, went on to win 73 caps before damaging his right eye in a road accident and being forced to quit the game. Though 35 at the time, Banks, whose popularity was fuelled by a natural dignity and amiable disposition, was still in majestic form.

BARNES, John

1963 Born in Jamaica

1981 Turns professional with Watford

1982 Hits sparkling form as 'Hornets' win promotion to Division 1

1983 Makes England debut as substitute against Northern Ireland in Belfast

1984 Takes home FA Cup runners-up medal after Wembley defeat by Everton; dribbles through Brazil's defence in Rio to score one of the most breathtaking England goals of modern times

1987 Moves to Liverpool for £900,000

1988 Holds centre stage as 'Reds' lift title but becomes two-time Wembley loser as Wimbledon win FA Cup; receives Player of the Year awards from football writers and his fellow professionals

1989 Helps beat Everton to claim FA Cup winner's medal at last

1990 Wins a second Championship medal but disappoints for England in World Cup finals

1994 Improved form and fitness raise hopes of an 'Indian summer'

Breathtakingly brilliant for Liverpool, frustratingly inconsistent for England, Barnes was arguably the supreme soccer artist of the late 1980s and early 1990s.

Whether patrolling the left flank or adopting a free-roaming role, he was, at his best, well-nigh unstoppable when he ran at defences. Big, strong and blessed with magnetic ball control, Barnes boasted the intricate wiles to trick his opponents and deceptive pace which left them stranded in his wake. He was also a lethal finisher, with a particularly wicked free-kick technique which made him a 'keeper's nightmare anywhere within 30 yards of goal.

Perhaps Barnes's greatest achievement was in bringing, almost instantly, a new dimension to Liverpool after his move from Vicarage Road. For all their success, the Reds had been sometimes described detrimentally as 'machine-like', and it took the West Indian-born winger to bestow on them the panache and glitter that had traditionally been the preserve of Manchester

Apart from all the things that could be said about John Barnes' talent and achievements it might be appropriate to recall that he has been a good model for youngsters coming into the game. His dignified response to criticism and his modesty in televised interviews have been as impressive as the help he has given to people in Liverpool when they have been faced with various crises. He has made his way in the game through ability and with dignity, and even as late as 1994/95 the new England manager, Terry Venables, refused to close the door on his England career prospects.

soccer headlines in the early 1990s.

In fact, the Bees were no strangers to drama, having been closed in 1901, then re-formed, undergoing various title changes and becoming Barnet in 1919. Subsequent accomplishments included winning the FA Amateur Cup in 1946 and reaching the FA Cup third round three times in the 1970s.

After narrowly missing promotion to the Football League three times in four years, Barnet finally made it in 1991, and promptly proclaimed their endearing eccentricity by losing their first match 7-4 at home to Crewe. They were to be no whipping boys, however, as they showed with a 6-0 away victory at Lincoln two weeks later, and by qualifying for the promotion play-offs at season's end. They lost to Blackpool but had done more than enough to suggest they were capable of 'doing a Wimbledon'.

Come 1992/93 there were frequent public rows between Flashman (who had saved the club from bankruptcy) and Fry, who was sacked and reinstated on at least three occasions. With both Flashman and Fry having departed, and with Ray Clemence installed as the new manager, the future looked interesting, even after relegation to Division 3 in 1994.

United and Spurs. The mystery of his fluctuations of form remains. But even after his World Cup anti-climax in Italy, and severe injury problems in 1991 and 1992, he remains one of the most thrilling entertainers on the football fields of England.

BARNET

Founded 1888

Joined League 1991 (Division 4)

Honours None

Ground Underhill Stadium

By turns joyous, traumatic and bewildering, life for a Barnet supporter is never boring. Thanks to the antics, achievements and enthusiasm of their former chairman Stan Flashman and ex-manager Barry Fry, the club was rarely far from the

BARNSLEY

Founded 1887

Joined League 1898

Honours FA Cup winners 1912; Division 3 (N) Champions 1934, 1939, 1955

Ground Oakwell

Located in the coal-mining area of South Yorkshire, Barnsley has a very strong football tradition. The club has promised more than most small-town clubs, but top-flight League soccer has always proved elusive. The greatest honours have come in the FA Cup. Barnsley lost to Newcastle United in the 1910 FA Cup Final, but won the 1912 FA Cup Final replay against West Brom, the only goal of the two games coming in the last minute of extra time when Harry Tufnell ran from the halfway line to score

brilliantly. The 1912 Cup-winning team was nicknamed 'Battling Barnsley', partly for their long, 12-game battle to the trophy – six 0-0 draws, five odd-goal victories and a 3-1 win over Birmingham – and partly because of the team's rugged approach.

The club had a rough time through the late 1960s and 1970s, spending ten seasons in the Fourth Division and surviving financial crises, but the 1981/82 season saw Barnsley restored to what many would see as the club's rightful place, the old Second Division. In fact, Barnsley's strange League record is that they spent more seasons in Division 2 than any other club, seven more than Leicester City.

As befits many smaller town clubs, Barnsley have often transferred star players for large fees. Post-war examples include Danny Blanchflower (to Aston Villa),

Tommy Taylor (Manchester United), Mick McCarthy (Manchester City), David Hirst (Sheffield Wednesday), John Beresford (Portsmouth) and David Currie (Nottingham Forest). Barry Murphy holds the club appearance record with 514 League appearances between 1962 and 1978.

BAXTER, Jim

1939 Born in Hill o'Beath, Fifeshire, Scotland

1957 Raith Rovers pay Crossgates Primrose £200 to sign Baxter as a part-timer.

1960 Signs for Rangers (£20,000); first of 34 Scotland caps (v Northern Ireland)

1963 Scores two goals (one a penalty) to defeat England 2-1 at Wembley

1964 Suffers broken leg in Rangers' European Cup tie

with Rapid Vienna

1965 Signs for Sunderland

1967 Plays brilliantly in Scotland's 3-2 defeat of world champions England at Wembley; signs for Nottingham Forest at a new record fee for a half-back (£100,000)

1969 Leaves for Rangers on a free transfer after only 48 games for Forest

1970 Retires to become a Glasgow licensee

In five years at Rangers, Baxter helped the club win three Scottish League Championships, three Scottish Cup Finals and four League Cup Finals. In contrast, his English clubs were always worried more about relegation from the First Division than winning honours. Baxter himself never justified his big fees. Known as 'Slim Jim' in Scotland, he put on weight in England and his autobiography describes his liking for 'bets, birds and booze'. Altogether he played 347 Football and Scottish League games.

North of the border Baxter was a cult hero, as much for his style of play as for his achievements. He was an unhurried attacking wing-half whose lazy-looking left-footed skill somehow left him time to spare. He could torment opponents and was never more cocky than when teasing England at Wembley. His most outrageous taunts were during the 1967 Wembley international when he kept the ball in the air with

ENGLISH CUP-TIE.   BARNSLEY v. QUEEN'S PARK RANGERS.   FOURTH ROUND, MARCH 5TH. 1910.
Barnes (Capt. Q P R)   Mr F. Heath (Referee)   Boyle (Capt. Barnsley)   Photo by A. W. Fenby

BARNSLEY ENGLISH CUP WINNERS 1911-12.

Nothing is new under the sun; in the early part of the century clubs were 'merchandising' for extra cash. These two postcards of Barnsley's exploits show (top) a step on the path to the 1910 FA Cup final, where the team lost to Newcastle 2-0 after a 1-1 draw, and the successful side that won the Cup two years later, beating West Bromwich Albion 1-0 after extra time and a 0-0 draw.

The closest the Tykes have been to Wembley since then is the last eight; not so worthy of a commemorative postcard perhaps, but were they to make the top flight for the first time in their history, no doubt the club shop would be doing a roaring trade in 'Premiership souvenirs'.

BECKENBAUER, Franz

1945 Born in Munich, Germany

1958 Joins Bayern Munich

1963 Makes first-team debut

1965 First full cap, West Germany v Sweden

1966 World Cup finalist, 2-4 v England

1967 Wins European Cup Winners' Cup medal, 1-0 v Rangers

1970 World Cup semi-finalist, 3-4 v Italy

1971 Appointed captain of West Germany

1972 Wins European Championship, 3-0 v Soviet Union; European Footballer of the Year

1974 Wins European Cup, 4-0 (replay) v Atletico Madrid; leads West Germany to World Cup, 2-1 v Netherlands

1975 Wins European Cup, 2-0 v Leeds United

1976 Leads Bayern to a hat-trick of European Cups, 1-0 v St Etienne; European Footballer of the Year

1977 Transferred to New York Cosmos

1982 Returns to Germany to play for Hamburg

1983 Back to New York Cosmos

Some players, no matter what the record books show, demand a place in an encyclopedia because of the magic that attends their name. Jim Baxter, here in his Rangers shirt, is such a player. Only 34 caps, but a legend in Scotland, perhaps because of his skills, his leadership ability or because his performance inspired Scotland's famous 3-2 victory over England at Wembley in 1967, thus making Scotland, of course, holders of the 'World Championship'.

a juggling exhibition and then, on another occasion, calmly walked away from the ball knowing a team-mate would probably reach it first. In 1963 he walked off the Wembley pitch with the ball stuffed up his jersey after excelling in a stirring victory.

Franz Beckenbauer, 'The Kaiser' at the 1970 World Cup finals, here competing for the ball with Brazil's Rivelino. West Germany were to finish third in the tournament with Beckenbauer establishing himself as a world class performer. His unflappable style was important, but his ability to turn defence into attack, with long runs through undefended midfields, was also crucial to his game. Like Sir Bobby Charlton in England, Beckenbauer has become a spokesman for the game.

1984 Retires from playing; appointed manager of West Germany

1986 World Cup runners-up, 2-3 v Argentina

1990 Becomes the first man to have captained and managed a World Cup-winning team, 1-0 v Argentina; appointed coach of Marseille, but later demoted to technical staff

1992 Involved in USA's preparation for 1994 World Cup; joins Japanese car firm Mitsubishi as worldwide sales spokesman and adviser to the company's soccer team, Urawa Red Diamonds

1993 Returns to club management with Bayern Munich

1994 Moves upstairs as senior executive with club

Beckenbauer's influence on football over the three decades from the 1960s cannot be overstated. Credited as the inventor of the modern, attacking sweeper, and hence 'Total Football', his curriculum vitae since graduating into management could scarcely be more impressive: two World Cup Finals, one won, one lost.

An admirer of Giacinto Facchetti, the overlapping Italian left-back with Internazionale, Beckenbauer wished to practise the art of attack from defence in a more central position but had to wait until he had won half his 103 caps before the German manager, Helmut Schoen, was persuaded. The rest of the world was won over more quickly, Germany winning the European Championship in 1972 and the World Cup on home soil two years later.

A wonderfully elegant footballer with faultless distribution and a bewildering change of pace, Beckenbauer won international honours at schoolboy, youth and full level as an attacking right-half, having outstanding World Cups in 1966 and 1970 before switching to sweeper where his influence on the national side became absolute. His club Bayern was

similarly dominated by the man whose nickname, 'The Kaiser', was worn with the comfort of a favourite sweater, and they dominated German football, winning a hat-trick of European Cups in the mid 1970s.

A superb strategist, Beckenbauer's zenith was probably the European Championships of 1972 after which he became more cautious, much less ready to foray upfield. He carried this more defensive attitude into management where the Germans, for all their success, established a reputation for efficiency rather than flair. The 1990 World Cup Final against Argentina was something of an anti-climax and it was with respect rather than affection that Beckenbauer was regarded as he bowed out of international management immediately afterwards. He announced his intention to work in football promotion and administration but was lured back to management for a brief spell in France, before returning to his beloved Bayern.

BERWICK RANGERS

Founded 1881

Joined League 1951 (C Division)

Honours Scottish League Second Division Champions 1979

Ground Shielfield Park

Berwick Rangers were in no hurry. It took 70 years for them fully to enter Scottish football. Appropriately for a club on English soil, they spent their early years in the Northumberland Association.

There was nothing peripheral about their role in Scottish football one Saturday in January 1967. In the Scottish Cup's most remarkable result of modern times they beat Rangers 1-0 at Shielfield through a goal by Sammy Reid.

Feats such as Ken Bowron's 50 goals in 1963/64 do not disguise the fact that Berwick have sometimes been competing merely for survival.

BEST, George

1946 Born in Belfast

1961 Homesick youngster arrives at Old Trafford

1963 Turns professional with Manchester United

1964 Makes Northern Ireland debut, against Wales at Swansea

1965 Wins first club honour, a League Championship medal

1966 Earns the nickname 'El Beatle' by destroying Benfica in Lisbon

1967 Helps United take another League title

1968 Footballer of the Year; scores in Red Devils' European Cup Final triumph; December – European Footballer of the Year

1970 Nets six times in FA Cup tie against Northampton Town, first game after suspension following clash with referee

1971 Withdraws from international match after threats on his life

1972 Announces retirement after repeated brushes with authority

1973 Makes short-lived United comeback

1975 Joins Stockport County on loan, then Los Angeles Aztecs and Cork Celtic

1976 Moves to Fulham

1977 Wins 37th and final cap, against Holland in Belfast

1978 Switches to Fort Lauderdale Strikers

1979 Plays briefly for Hibernian

1980 Signs for San Jose Earthquakes before seeking treatment for alcoholism

1983 Appears five times for Bournemouth, then retires

Few would dispute that George Best was the most naturally gifted British footballer of the modern era. Most, however, would bemoan the fact that the Irish genius allowed the second half of his career to be wasted in a self-destructive maelstrom of personal problems.

With the perspective that time brings, it is more pertinent to dwell on the seven or eight of his eleven campaigns at Old Trafford in which Best was a purveyor of sheer delight. He was at his peak during the mid and late 1960s, in harness with fellow greats Bobby Charlton and Denis Law, when his irresistible ball skill created countless undying memories. He was quick, too, could tackle like a full-back, and there wasn't a more deadly finisher in the First Division. Sometimes he infuriated team-mates by holding the ball too long, but he more than paid for such self-indulgence with magical match-winning interludes of sublime beauty. Eventually he became a victim of the goldfish-bowl existence that was thrust upon him, and his subsequent fall from grace was profoundly distressing. But no one can take away from George the knowledge that, for a time, he entertained more royally than any other player in the world.

No one image of George Best can show all aspects of his diverse, charismatic and sometimes unhappy character. This photograph of the ageing hero, playing for Los Angeles Aztecs in the North American Soccer League, does not picture him on the big stage, scoring a brilliant goal or dumbfounding his poor marker. However, it does hint at the marvellous balance, and the great control, to say nothing of the swarthy, slightly dissolute, good looks that epitomised 'Besty'. And it was sometimes in these days, removed from the pressures of the English press and Football League marking, that he was able to turn on quite brilliant displays of control and skill and simple football mastery.

BINGHAM, Billy

1931 Born in Belfast

1950 Leaves Irish League club Glentoran for Sunderland

1951 Debut for Northern Ireland against France in Belfast

1958 June – plays a leading part in Northern Ireland's progress to the World Cup quarter-finals in Sweden; July – moves to Luton Town for £15,000

1959 Stars in Luton's progress to the FA Cup Final, where the 'Hatters' are beaten by Nottingham Forest

1960 Joins Everton for £20,000 plus two players

1963 Helps Everton win League title and then moves to Port Vale; November – wins last of 56 caps, against England at Wembley

1965 Takes over as Southport manager

1968 Becomes boss of Plymouth Argyle and Northern Ireland

1970 Assumes control of Greek national side

1973 Succeeds Harry Catterick as Everton boss

1977 January – gets the sack; April – returns to Greece to run PAOK Salonika

1978 Takes over at Mansfield Town

1980 Starts second spell as manager of Northern Ireland

1982 His team reach second round of World Cup in Spain

1986 Northern Ireland qualify for World Cup Finals in Mexico

1993 Accepts directorship of Blackpool, combining new work with international responsibilities

1994 Retires as Northern Ireland boss

Bingham has enjoyed two illustrious careers at soccer's top level, and his subsequent success as a manager should

Billy Bingham preparing his Northern Ireland squad for the 1985 World Cup qualifying match against Romania. Bingham's side won 1-0 and this helped the Northern Irish go to Mexico where they lost to Spain and Brazil before going out of the tournament. Bingham might like this picture as it shows him very much as a 'tracksuit' manager, enjoying getting down with the players on the training ground as much as giving press interviews and doing the PR round.

not obscure the peaks he scaled as one of Britain's most gifted wingers throughout the 1950s and early 1960s.

A fast, slightly built raider possessed of intricate skills and a deceptively powerful shot, he first came to prominence with a brilliant display for the Irish League against the Football League in 1950. After Sunderland snapped him up, he became one of the First Division's star attractions and a key member of the Irish side, although his talents were more unpredictable than those of team-mates Danny Blanchflower and Jimmy McIlroy, with whom he often linked so effectively.

As a manager, Bingham seemed to have reached his zenith when he took the Everton job, but he failed to bring glory to Goodison and it was not until his second stint in charge of his country that he found his most productive niche. He is a genial, shrewd character who served Northern Ireland with rare distinction.

BIRMINGHAM CITY

Founded 1875

Joined League 1892 (Division 2)

Honours Division 2 Champions 1893, 1921, 1948, 1955, 1995; League Cup Winners 1963

Ground St Andrews

For a long-established club which carries the name of England's second city, the Blues have a dreadful record. They have never won either the League Championship or the FA Cup, and even though they boast a fine new stadium and can tap vast support – in 1972/73 their average gate exceeded 36,000 – they have offered but token resistance to the superiority of neighbouring Aston Villa.

Birmingham, originally named Small Heath, made a bright start to League life, topping the inaugural Second Division table but staying down because they failed in promotion test matches. There was to be no lack of movement between divisions, however. At the end of their second season they rose to the top flight, the first of nine such ascents in 90 years; depressingly, of course, there was an equal number of journeys the other way.

It wasn't until the 1920s that City showed real mettle, with centre-forward Joe Bradford and England goalkeeper Harry Hibbs claiming most headlines. During this period the Blues remained in Division 1 for 18 years – still their longest stay – and reached their first FA Cup Final, losing to West Bromwich Albion in 1931.

But they were demoted in 1939 and after the war, with the excellent Gil Merrick replacing Hibbs, they resumed their ups and downs before enjoying another short spell of relative success. In 1955/56, newly promoted City finished sixth in the First Division and lost to Manchester City at Wembley. Building on this – thanks to a defence in which Jeff Hall, who was soon to die of polio, and Trevor Smith were outstanding – Birmingham

Birmingham City, often taunted for lack of success, made the headlines for several off-the-field developments in the early 1990s. In one, joint owner, and major investor, David Sullivan caused a few eyebrows to raise when he appointed Karren Brady to the role of Blues' chief executive. She settled quickly into the difficult world of football administration and proved her ambition for Birmingham when she attracted Barry Fry, then with Southend United, to take over in charge at St Andrews.

became the first Britons to reach a European final, that of the Fairs Cup. In fact they did so twice, losing to Barcelona in 1960 and Roma the following year.

But stability vanished, they were relegated in 1965, and even former Wolves boss Stan Cullis could not achieve a revival. His successor in the 1970s, Freddie Goodwin, did better, discovering precocious goalscorer Trevor Francis and fellow striker Bob Latchford, but when the manager left the yo-yo tendency returned, and in 1989 the Blues reached their lowest ebb, tasting life in Division 3. A club with so much potential could not remain in the depths for long, however, and in 1995 – owned by millionaire tycoon David Sullivan and managed by the ebullient Barry Fry – they won the Second Division title and the Auto Windscreens Shield.

BLACKBURN ROVERS

Founded 1875

Joined League 1888 (founder member)

Honours Leage Champions 1912, 1914, 1995; Division 2 Champions 1939; Division 3 Champions 1975; FA Cup Winners 1884, 1885, 1886, 1890, 1891, 1928

Ground Ewood Park

When Blackburn Rovers won the 1994/95 Premiership much was made of this being their first such success for more than 80 years. Little mention, however, was made of the earlier side that won the Cup in 1891, pictured here. This team's triumph was the club's fifth in eight years. They won the final by beating Notts County 3-1, with Townley (extreme right, front row) scoring one goal to add to the three he had scored in the previous year's final when Rovers beat Sheffield Wednesday 6-1.

Who said money couldn't buy success? Certainly not Blackburn Rovers, whose fortunes were transformed in the early 1990s by multi-millionaire Jack Walker. Employing one of the game's most accomplished managers, Kenny Dalglish, and buying a collection of leading players including England striker Alan Shearer for £3.6 million and the promising Chris Sutton from Norwich for £5 million, he saw Rovers rise from the old Second Division to become champions of the Premiership.

Of course, Blackburn can point to a tradition of lifting honours, but nearly all of them were won before the First World War.

Towards the end of the nineteenth century, Rovers were among the game's giants, and they are the only surviving club with a hat-trick of FA Cups to their name. With play-maker Jim Forrest prominent, they were at the forefront of the northern professionals' challenge to the southern amateurs who had dominated in pre-League days. Such glory came too early for Bob Crompton, but the great full-back and captain, the most revered figure in Blackburn's history, made up for it by playing a major role in lifting two titles before war intervened.

Despite an isolated FA Cup victory, there was a gradual decline between the wars which culminated in a first ever relegation in 1936. Rovers soon climbed back, only to sink again, and it was not until Johnny Carey became manager in 1953 that a revival began. He led a side which included such stars as wing marvel Bryan Douglas, constructive wing-half Ronnie Clayton, full-back Bill Eckersley and centre-forward Tommy Briggs back to the top flight in 1957, and then celebrated by reaching Wembley three years later.

Defeat by Wolves proved the prelude to major changes, and promising youngsters such as defenders Mike England and Keith Newton and striker Fred Pickering were introduced. Blackburn consolidated encouragingly but key players were sold and 1966 brought demotion.

Thereafter Rovers remained mostly in Division 2, although there were two stints in the Third. Notable personalities of that lacklustre era included long-serving defender Derek Fazackerly, the club's record goalscorer Simon Garner, and managers Howard Kendall and Don Mackay.

A series of failures in the promotion play-offs during the late 1980s gave rise to the notion that times were likely to remain hard for all but the giants in crowded Lancashire. But then along came Jack Walker, Rovers at last tasted play-off glory and the brave new world of the Premier League was at their feet.

BLACKPOOL

Founded 1887

Joined League 1896 (Division 2)

Honours Division 2 Champions 1930; FA Cup Winners 1953

Ground Bloomfield Road

One golden era dominates the history of Blackpool. From the late 1940s to the mid 1950s, the 'Seasiders' were one of the most entertaining sides in the land, and in Stanley Matthews they boasted arguably the finest player in the world.

Their beginnings were infinitely more modest. After three campaigns in the Second Division, Blackpool failed to gain re-election, although one year later they were back in the League to stay. There followed three decades of consolidation before they reached the top grade, inspired by 45 goals from Johnny Hampson. After suffering relegation in 1933, Blackpool rose again four years later to signal their arrival as a footballing power. With shrewd manager Joe Smith now in command, they settled quickly and topped the table as war broke out in 1939. When normality returned, Blackpool were ready to compete with the best. Between 1948 and 1953 they reached three FA Cup Finals, finished runners-up in the title race in 1956 and throughout the 1950s were rarely out of the League's leading group. The highlight was the legendary 'Matthews Final' of 1953, which ended in victory after the great winger inspired a stirring comeback. Stan Mortensen scored a hat-trick that day, with other leading lights including half-back and skipper Harry Johnston, goalkeeper George Farm, and inside-forwards Jackie Mudie and Ernie Taylor.

Ron Stuart replaced Smith in 1958 and, with the lifting of the maximum wage shifting the balance of power ever more towards the big clubs, Blackpool began a gradual decline, despite the sterling efforts of England captain and full-back Jimmy Armfield, England World Cup hero Alan Ball, goalkeeper Tony Waiters, defender Roy Gratrix and centre-forward Ray Charnley.

When the Seasiders were demoted in 1967, only Arsenal could boast longer consecutive membership of Division 1, but alas, such heady days were not to return. A brief resurgence, in which schemer Tony Green was outstanding, produced promotion before Blackpool plunged, reaching Division 4 in 1981 and returning there, after brief relief, in 1990.

Two years later they climbed, via the promotion play-offs, into the new Second Division. But with the advent of cheap overseas holidays the town is no longer so popular with travelling fans, and, beset by the usual financial difficulties under which many clubs labour, Blackpool face a mammoth task to achieve sustained resurgence.

BLANCHFLOWER, Danny

1926 Born in Belfast

1945 Makes senior debut with Irish side Glentoran

1949 Signs for Barnsley, at a cost of £6500; wins first cap for Northern Ireland in 8-2 home defeat by Scotland

1951 Moves to Aston Villa for £15,000

1954 Joins Tottenham Hotspur for £30,000

1958 Captains Northern Ireland in the World Cup finals in Sweden; becomes Footballer of the Year, an honour which is repeated three years later

1961 Skippers Spurs to League and FA Cup double

1962 Lifts the FA Cup for the second successive season

1963 Leads the side to triumph in the European Cup Winners' Cup

1964 Retires and turns to journalism

1978 Begins a short, unsuccessful spell as manager of Chelsea

1979 Ends managerial career after brief stint in charge of Northern Ireland

1993 Dies after a long and debilitating illness

Blanchflower ranks as one of the outstanding British sporting personalities since the Second World War. After richly promising years with Barnsley and Aston Villa, he blossomed as the leader and creative hub of Tottenham Hotspur's greatest side. Playing at right-half, he forged two constructive midfield partnerships; first with Tommy Harmer as the north Londoners emerged as challengers to the dominance in the late 1950s of Wolves and Manchester United; then with the subtly brilliant Scot John White, as manager Bill Nicholson moulded the team which was to become the first this century to win the League and FA Cup double, before going on to further triumphs.

The Irish play-maker dominated Spurs' approach with his vision, ball control and cultured long-distance passing, and he was equally influential when on duty for his country. During the course of a 56-cap international career – a record at that time – he was an inspirational figure in the 1958 World Cup campaign.

As eloquent off the field as he was elegant on it, Blanchflower – whose brother Jackie played for Manchester United until injuries sustained in the Munich aircrash put him out of the game – was an intellectual, far removed from the normal run of professional footballers, and his forcefully expressed opinions sometimes led him into conflict with authority. Some 14 years after he retired a brief fling with management ended badly, but his glory days at Tottenham had already assured him a place in soccer's hall of fame. Sadly, come the 1990s Blanchflower's health had deteriorated and he was increasingly less able to retain contact with the game he had graced for so long.

As proud as the Spurs cockerel on his chest, Danny Blanchflower leads out his team in 1956. Although calm and composed on the field of play, and despite a later, successful career as a journalist, Blanchflower always wore the look of a troubled man.

BLOOMER, Steve

1874 Born in Cradley Heath, Staffordshire

1891 Signs for Derby County for 7s 6d a week

1895 First of 23 England caps (scores twice against Ireland)

1906 Signs for Middlesbrough (£750)

1910 Returns to Derby County (£100)

1912 Derby County's leading League goalscorer for the 15th season, he helps the club to the Second Division Championship

1914 Plays his last game for Derby County five days after his 40th birthday

1915 Coaches in Germany, where he is interned during First World War

1938 Dies in Derby

Steve Bloomer's goalscoring achievements set the standard for British football. He scored 331 League and Cup goals for Derby County, 63 for Middlesbrough and 28 international goals for England, the latter a record until Nat Lofthouse improved upon it in 1956. But Bloomer scored in each of his first ten internationals and played only 23 England games – a phenomenal scoring ratio. He played 524 League and Cup games for Derby County and 130 for Middlesbrough, yet his only honour was a Second Division Championship medal with Derby. With County he played in eight FA Cup semi-finals (six goals), including two replays against Sheffield United, and two finals (one goal), but never in a Cup-winning team.

Having Steve Bloomer in this encyclopedia means an opportunity to show this picture of the 1902 England side that drew 2-2 with Scotland in Birmingham. The team is left to right, back row: George, Crompton, Molyneux, Wilkes, Forman, Houlker; Hogg, Bloomer, Beats, Settle, Cox. Beats from Wolves (this was his second of two caps) and Settle of Everton clearly went to the same cobbler.

Bloomer, along with Welshman Billy Meredith, was the star of the period up to the First World War. He appeared physically deficient, being pale and slender, but had underlying strength and ability. His goalscoring secret lay in sudden, surprise shots with either foot. He used hardly any backlift when shooting. He was a strong, skilful runner with the ball, but, like Jimmy Greaves half a century later, he was dedicated to one task only in the opposition penalty area – scoring goals.

BOLTON WANDERERS

Founded 1874

Joined League 1888 (founder member)

Honours Division 2 Champions 1909, 1978; Division 3 Champions 1973; FA Cup Winners 1923, 1926, 1929, 1958

Ground Burnden Park

Bolton Wanderers are a club of proud tradition whose star began to fall with the abolition of the maximum wage in 1961. Since then top players have left – understandably – for richer pickings, all but the most loyal fans have been drawn inexorably to Manchester and Liverpool. Indeed, until promotion to the Premiership and a place in the League Cup Final made 1995 a year to remember, life has frequently been a struggle for the 'Trotters'.

It wasn't always easy, either, in the 1880s, when Bolton were at the forefront of the battle to legalise professionalism. They prevailed but reaped no immediate dividend in trophies, losing one early FA Cup Final. Around the turn of the century, League consistency also became elusive and they suffered four demotions to Division 2 in 12 years.

Success came in the 1920s, when they won the FA Cup three times and twice finished third in the First Division. Stars of the day included prolific inside-forwards David Jack and Joe Smith and winger Ted Vizard. There followed a descent into mediocrity, with the Wanderers' only national headlines being of the wrong kind, when 33 supporters died following the collapse of a barrier at Burnden Park in 1946. But Bill Ridding took over as manager in 1951 and built a competitive side around England centre-forward Nat Lofthouse and a formidably physical defence, in which Malcolm Barrass and Tommy Banks were outstanding. They reached the celebrated 'Matthews Final' of 1953, which they lost to Blackpool, but, after recruiting accomplished 'keeper Eddie Hopkinson, made amends five years later against a Manchester United side ravaged at Munich.

The Wembley triumph was well deserved, yet it did not presage further glories. Harsh economic realities forced the sale of strikers Wyn Davies and Francis Lee and, despite the delightful prompting of schemer Freddie Hill, the team were in the Second Division by 1964 and the Third by 1971.

Enterprising boss Ian Greaves, ably assisted by stalwart midfielders Roy Greaves and Peter Reid, hauled them back to the top flight in 1978, but new horrors awaited. They kicked off the 1987/88 campaign in Division 4, before Phil Neal lifted them one rung up the League ladder a year later and Bruce Rioch guided them into Division 1 in 1993. Several rousing cup runs under the enterprising Rioch heralded a return to the top flight in 1995, but much depends on whether they can hang on to young stars such as Alan Stubbs and Jason McAteer.

Jason McAteer (left), John McGinlay and Andy Walker, the three scorers in Bolton's 1994 FA Cup 4th round extra-time replay victory against Arsenal at Highbury. In the early 1990s Bolton always looked happier in cup competitions than league football. Their promotion to the Premiership, achieved at the end of the 1994/95 season, was managed only via the play-offs.

BOOKS

The cliche that football literature lags far behind cricket literature is becoming dated. In the past two decades there has been a rise in the wealth of published material: reference books, statistical histories of clubs, academic contributions and fanzines. 'Football has rediscovered its history,' says John Gaustad of Sportspages, London's specialist sports bookshop. His shop sells more literature on football than on cricket, but this may not represent the national picture.

Rothmans *Football Yearbook*, first published in 1970, has become football's equivalent to cricket's *Wisden*, with an annual summary of clubs, games, teams and records. Several smaller reference books – *The Football Association Yearbook*, the *News of the World Football Annual* and the *Playfair Football Annual* – have a much longer history than Rothmans, however.

For a true feel of the sport, there are several entertaining books. Two 1960s classics, John Moynihan's *Soccer Syndrome* and Arthur Hopcraft's *The Football Man*, have recently been republished. Two from the 1970s, Eamon Dunphy's *Only A Game?* and Hunter Davies' *The Glory Game*, have also reappeared, the former still the most illuminating autobiographical comment on life as a professional footballer, the latter a journalist's insightful observations on Tottenham Hotspur's 1971/72 season. Two easy-to-read books from the 1980s are *The Book of Football Quotations* by Peter Ball and Phil Shaw, and *One Afternoon in Lisbon* by Kevin McCarra and Pat Woods, an account of Celtic's 1967 European Cup triumph based on evocative interview material, while perhaps the pick of the offerings in the early 1990s was Nick Hornby's vivid, humorous *Fever Pitch – A Fan's Life*.

Autobiographies are abundant, some more famous for their titles than their insight, a favourite being Ian Ure's *Ure's Truly*. Good biographies are very limited, but Tony Francis challenged this with *Clough*. The 1980s also saw classic biographies of Stanley Matthews (by David Miller), Jock Stein (by Ken Gallacher), Bill Meredith and Alex James (both by John Harding).

The encyclopedia tradition began with Pickford and Gibson's four-volume *Association Football and the Men Who Made It* in 1906, and the same publisher repeated the enterprise with *Association Football*, edited by A.H. Fabian and Geoffrey Green, in 1960. The 1906 set was recently republished by the Association of Football Statisticians in photocopied form. This association has a big publication list, much of it original material on the statistical history of the game.

Almost every club has its history documented. One of the best is *The Glory and the Dream: The History of Celtic FC, 1887-1987* by Tom Campbell and Pat Woods. A Derby firm, Breedon Books, has become a market leader in club statistical histories. Their 'Complete Record' series covers some 40 English and Scottish League clubs, giving team records for every game in the club's history and background text on players and club. Many individuals have also taken initiatives to publish club histories.

For sound historical background to the game, the best starting point is Tony Mason's *Association Football and English Society 1863-1915* and Nick Fishwick's *English Football and Society*. Richard Holt's *Sport and the British* is strong on football history, while Simon Inglis, a journalist with architectural experience, is the author of *The Football Grounds of Great Britain* and *The Football Grounds of Europe*, the former one of the most popular books of the 1980s. Many other books are mentioned elsewhere in this encyclopedia, but the best place to browse through new books is Sportspages, Caxton Walk, 94-96 Charing Cross Road, London. Out-of-print books are available through John Whittaker, 51 Western Hill, Durham City while general information can be obtained from the Association of Football Statisticians, 22 Bretons, Basildon, Essex.

BOURNEMOUTH

Founded 1899

Joined League 1923 (Division 3 S)

Honours Division 3 Champions 1987

Ground Dean Court

Anyone curious to find out about life in the old Third Division could hardly do better than study the history of Bournemouth. Between their election to the League in 1923 and their relegation in 1970, the 'Cherries' chalked up a record number of campaigns in the Third, a statistic which points, with reasonable accuracy, to decade upon decade of mediocrity.

Such predictability – enlivened by the occasional FA Cup run, notably that of 1957 when stirring victories over Wolves and Spurs preceded a plucky quarter-final exit against Manchester United – ended in the year of their demotion with the appointment of John Bond as manager. The extrovert newcomer changed the Dean Court club's staid image, found a hero for the fans in goal merchant Ted MacDougall, and soon won promotion.

Alas, Bournemouth were not destined for a fairytale rise. Bond departed, a seven-year sojourn in Division 4 ensued and it was not until the arrival of another enterprising boss, Harry Redknapp, in 1983 that real

hope for the future blossomed anew. Redknapp took his team into the Second Division in 1987, but then came the unexpected disappointment of a return to the Third after three years. Redknapp departed for West Ham and the Cherries were back once more in the shadows of south coast neighbours Southampton and Portsmouth.

BRADFORD CITY

Founded 1903

Joined League 1903

Honours Division 2 Champions 1908; Division 3 (N) Champions 1929; Division 3 Champions 1985; FA Cup Winners 1911

Ground Valley Parade

Despite hailing from a city with a 300,000-plus population, and losing their closest competition when neighbours Park Avenue failed to gain re-election to the League in 1970, Bradford City have continued to make little lasting impact in the modern era.

In fact, they must look back to the days before the First World War for evidence of real success. Then, just three years after climbing out of Division 2 – to which, remarkably, they had been elected in the year of their formation – the 'Bantams' finished fifth in the top flight, capping their campaign by winning the FA Cup. Sadly that victory, gained after a replay against mighty Newcastle United, still represents the peak of their achievements.

After being relegated in 1922, City spent the next 15 years to-ing and fro-ing between the Second and Third Divisions before settling at the lower level until 1961. The remainder of the decade was spent in the Fourth, and they did not succeed in escaping the lower reaches for another 24 terms. Bradford's playing fortunes finally took a turn for the better in 1985 when manager Trevor Cherry led them to the Second Division, although the promotion celebrations were

eclipsed by horror when a fire in the main stand during an end-of-season Valley Parade encounter with Lincoln City cost more than 50 lives.

City overcame the shock of the disaster to remain in Division 2 for five years but, after selling outstanding midfielder Stuart McCall and sacking Cherry's worthy successor Terry Dolan, they were demoted in 1990. More support – never overwhelming, even when nearby Leeds United are in a trough – is essential before real progress can be made.

BRECHIN CITY

Founded 1906

Joined League 1924 (Division 3)

Honours Scottish League Division 2 Champions 1983; Second Division Champions 1990; Division C Champions 1954

Ground Glebe Park

Survival will always be Brechin's most remarkable achievement. The city's population is 7000, giving them the smallest catchment area of any senior club in Britain.

No player has ever won international honours while with them (although Davie Duncan did play for the club towards the end of his career in the late 1950s) but they have manoeuvred well in the transfer market and, remarkably, won the Second Division in 1990. Local astuteness has been recognised in the career of chairman David Will. He has been President of the SFA and is a vice-president of FIFA.

BREMNER, Billy

1942 Born in Stirling, Scotland

1959 December – turns professional with Leeds United

1960 January – makes League debut at Chelsea

1965 May – wins first Scottish cap against Spain at Hampden Park

1968 Plays crucial role in League Cup and European Fairs Cup triumphs

1969 Skippers Leeds to League Championship

1970 Footballer of the Year

1972 Lifts the FA Cup at last, as Leeds beat Arsenal

1974 Wins second League Championship medal

1975 September – plays

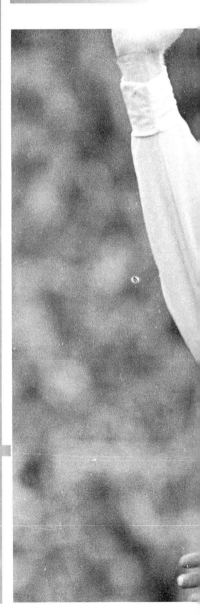

Billy Bremner had many disappointments in his playing career but also some great highlights. He had the knack of scoring goals on important occasions too. Here he's got another, and is congratulated by fellow Don Revie 'wonders', Mick Jones and Jack Charlton.

54th and last game for Scotland, against Denmark in Copenhagen

1976 September – moves to Hull City for £35,000

1978 Becomes manager of Doncaster Rovers and plays for his new club

1985 Succeeds Eddie Gray as Leeds boss

1987 United reach FA Cup semi-finals but miss out on promotion to Division 1

1988 Sacked by Leeds

1989 Takes over at Doncaster for the second time

1992 Departs Belle Vue

Bremner was the dynamic little fireball at the heart of Don Revie's successful sides of the 1960s and 1970s. Together with Johnny Giles,

whose subtle guile was the perfect counterpart to Bremner's all-action style, he formed one of the most memorable midfield partnerships modern football has seen.

The pale-faced, red-haired Scot hurled himself into every game as if his life depended on it and, especially early in his career, he was often in trouble with referees. He was sometimes criticised for being over-physical, yet there was far more to his contribution than mere combativeness. Bremner was an astute reader of the game, a skilful passer and, often in important matches, a fine finisher. But above all there was the boundless energy, which made him a vital member of both attack and defence for the Leeds and Scotland teams he captained with such passion.

BRENTFORD

Founded 1889

Joined League 1920 (Division 3)

Honours Division 2 Champions 1935; Division 3 (S) Champions 1933; Division 3 Champions 1992; Division 4 Champions 1963

Ground Griffin Park

There was a time when Brentford were the rising stars of English football. After joining the Football League as founder members of Division 3, the 'Bees' showed indifferent form in the 1920s but took flight with an exhilarating surge in the subsequent decade. After topping the Third and then the Second Division with only one season between their triumphs, they enjoyed

three campaigns in Division 1's top six and, for good measure, reached the FA Cup quarter-final in 1938. Griffin Park luminaries in those heady days included manager Harry Curtis, goalscorer John Holliday and winger Idris Hopkins.

After the war, however, Brentford's fortunes took a turn for the worse from which they have never fully recovered. Two more runs to the last eight of the FA Cup did nothing to obscure disappointing League displays and they were relegated in 1947, slumping to the Third Division – despite a brief interlude with Tommy Lawton in the managerial chair, and the doughty efforts of long-serving defender Kenny Coote – in 1954.

Since then the Bees, who came close to merger with Queen's Park Rangers during a financial crisis in the 1960s, have endured three spells in the Fourth Division, but from 1978 onwards they stabilised in the Third. In 1989 their fourth appearance in an FA Cup quarter-final brought renewed hope, which soared higher as the Third Division title was claimed in 1992. Ups and downs followed, but if manager David Webb can build on this advance, there should be enough support in West London to ensure a secure future.

BRIGHTON AND HOVE ALBION

Founded 1900

Joined League 1920 (Division 3)

Honours Division 3 (S) Champions 1958; Division 4 Champions 1965

Ground Goldstone Ground

For a club as old as a century in which the world has witnessed staggering upheaval, Brighton and Hove Albion can point to a remarkably tranquil history – but they have had their moments. In 1910, as Southern League champions, they beat Aston Villa to win the Charity Shield, but perhaps their most exciting hour came in 1983 when the 'Seagulls', already relegated from

Gary Stevens equalising for Brighton in the 1983 FA Cup Final against Bailey in the Manchester United goal. The match, which Brighton came close to winning, ended 2-2. For Brighton, a Football League team for nearly 75 years, this represents the highlight of their history. For Manchester United, just another final; they won the replay 4-0.

Division 1 in that same season, were within an ace of winning the FA Cup. With the end of extra time looming and the scores level, midfielder Gordon Smith muffed a fabulous chance and mighty Manchester United breathed again. Predictably, Jimmy Melia's men were eclipsed in the replay and quickly returned to their familiar place in the football world, far removed from such unaccustomed limelight.

The 'Shrimps', as they were first nicknamed, had entered the League as founder members of Division 3 and remained there for the next 38 years. When they finally climbed out as champions in 1958, they must have wondered if it had been worth the effort, going down 9-0 at Middlesbrough – their record defeat – in the opening Division 2 encounter. Brighton stabilised and hung on for four campaigns before entering a slump which saw them plummet to the Fourth Division. Recovery was swift, however, and the next decade and a half was divided between Third and Second Divisions before manager Alan Mullery, the former England wing-half, led them into the top flight. While never looking secure in Division 1, the south coast club competed pluckily both on the pitch and in the transfer market, with £900,000 being garnered from defender Mark Lawrenson's sale to Liverpool, and £500,000 being invested in Manchester United striker Andy Ritchie.

Sojourns in both Second and Third Divisions followed, and with the big London clubs an all too convenient alternative for supporters, another century of unspectacular, if worthy, activity may be in prospect.

BRISTOL CITY

Founded 1894

Joined League 1901 (Division 2)

Honours Division 2 Champions 1906; Division 3 (S) Champions 1923, 1927, 1955

Ground Ashton Gate

Bristol City are a club with vast unrealised potential. Blessed with a splendidly appointed stadium and a wide, fairly affluent, largely untapped area from which to draw support, the 'Robins' should by now have established themselves as a major long-term power in English soccer. Indeed, there have been periods in their history when City seemed to have arrived, but consistent success has always eluded them. Their most prosperous playing era coincided with their first decade of League competition, in which they won the Second Division title, were runners-up in the top flight, and lost the 1909 FA Cup Final to Manchester United. Their leading light in those halcyon days was Billy Wedlock, a dominant centre-half who won 26 England caps and around whom City built their side.

Somehow, though, the impetus slipped away and for more than half a century the West Countrymen made regular journeys between the Second and Third Divisions. In the 1950s and early 1960s even the prolific goal-scoring of England international John Atyeo, who found the net 350 times in more than 600 City appearances, was not enough to propel the Robins back among the elite.

It wasn't until 1976 that a First Division place was reclaimed by manager Alan Dicks' workmanlike team but, sadly, that hard-won status was lost after only four seasons. Then began an alarming nosedive which saw the Robins plumb the Fourth Division depths and teeter on the very brink of oblivion during a financial crisis in 1982. There followed a steady rebuilding process and City, ensconced in the new First Division, seemed equipped once more for greater things, an impression heightened by their FA Cup defeat of Liverpool in January 1994.

However, manager Russell Osman was sacked later in the year and his replacement, Joe Jordan – in his second term at Ashton Gate – could not avoid relegation.

John Atyeo, a local lad, made over 600 appearances for Bristol City between 1951 and 1965. Despite playing most of his football in the lower divisions, he still managed to win six England caps. He scored 350 goals in 647 games for the Bristol club. He died in 1993, still remembered as one of City's best players.

BRISTOL ROVERS

Founded 1883

Joined League 1920 (Division 3)

Honours Division 3 (S) Champions 1953; Division 3 Champions 1990

Ground Twerton Park, Bath

Bristol Rovers, a club of indomitable spirit, are used to taking setbacks in their stride. The ill-advised sale of their Eastville ground to a greyhound racing company in 1940, a bribes scandal that resulted in two players being suspended for life in 1963, a fire that destroyed their main stand in 1980, another blaze which severely damaged their temporary Bath home a decade later, and a cash crisis which never ends – somehow the 'Pirates' have risen gloriously, if at times precariously, above the lot.

Having joined the League as founder members of Division 3, Rovers settled into something of a rut, but the appointment of Bert Tann as

manager in 1950 changed all that. A dedicated believer in the long-ball game, he produced a side which reached the FA Cup quarter-final against Newcastle in 1951 – bowing to the 'Magpies' only after a replay – and lifted the Division 3 (S) title in 1953. Star of the side was free-scoring Geoff Bradford, who remains the club's sole England international, and when he was partnered later in the 1950s by the richly gifted Alfie Biggs, the club had a strike force to be envied.

Since then, homely Rovers – less grand than neighbours City, yet always endowed with more larger-than-life characters – have split their time between the middle Divisions, never really threatening to join the elite but always avoiding the drop to the basement. From winger Harold Jarman in the 1960s to Nigel Martyn, who became Britain's first £1 million goalkeeper when he joined Crystal Palace in 1989, there have been plenty of heroes.

Under enterprising manager Gerry Francis, Rovers – currently tenants of non-League Bath City – stepped up their bid to find a new ground. When Francis left in 1991, the future clouded and they were relegated to the new Division Two in 1993, but one thing is certain – the Pirates will fight on.

BURNLEY

Founded 1882

Joined League 1888 (founder member)

Honours Division 1 Champions 1921, 1960; Division 2 Champions 1898, 1973; Division 3 Champions 1982; Division 4 Champions 1992; FA Cup Winners 1914

Ground Turf Moor

The plight of Burnley in May 1987 was enough to make any genuine lover of English soccer weep. The 'Clarets', their history studded with heady triumphs, were bottom of the Fourth Division and

had to win the last match of the season to stand a chance of retaining League status. Burnley survived – just – but their fans were left to rue a sad decline.

Not that the Lancashire cotton-town club were accustomed to undiluted success. Their earliest years saw several journeys between divisions before they won their first trophy, the FA Cup. But just as they threatened to become a real power, the First World War intervened and it was the early 1920s before the title landed at Turf Moor. The honour was due largely to a majestic half-back line of George Halley, Tommy Boyle and William Watson, with 'keeper Jerry Dawson also outstanding. A slump soon ensued, however, culminating in demotion as the decade closed.

Revival came after the Second World War when new manager Cliff Britton assembled a competitive side in which two future Burnley bosses, defender Alan Brown

Burnley line up for the 1959/60 season before going on to win the League Championship and reach the sixth round of the FA Cup. The squad was (back row, left to right) Talbut, Cummings, Miller, Blacklaw, Seith, Scott, White; Harris Connelly, McIlroy, Pointer, Adamson, Robson, Pilkington, Fenton.

and forward Harry Potts, took the eye. In 1947 they won promotion and reached Wembley, where they lost to Charlton Athletic.

Expectations ran high, but it was not until Potts assumed control in the late 1950s that the Clarets reached their peak. Backed vociferously by controversial chairman Bob Lord, Potts led the club to the Championship in 1960 and an FA Cup Final defeat in 1962. The stars were midfield creators Jimmy Adamson and Jimmy McIlroy, winger John Connelly and centre-forward Ray Pointer.

Talented youngsters replaced the old guard, but Burnley had always had to sell to survive, and against a background of departures – winger Leighton James and midfielder Ralph Coates were two of many released reluctantly in the 1970s – the slide began. At first it was slow, with relegation in 1971 being followed by promotion after two terms, but by 1980 Turf Moor was hosting Division 3 matches and by 1985 Burnley, unthinkably, were in the basement.

Yet the ground is well-equipped and gates for important games have shown that there is still plenty of potential support. As they demonstrated by winning the Fourth Division title in 1992, and going on to reach the new First Division via the play-offs in 1994, there is still hope for the Clarets, though relegation a year later was a bitter blow.

BURY

Founded 1885

Joined League 1894 (Division 2)

Honours Division 2 Champions 1895; Division 3 Champions 1961; FA Cup Winners 1900, 1903

Ground Gigg Lane

Which club won two FA Cup Finals, only three years apart, by an aggregate of ten goals to nil? Might it be Liverpool? Or Manchester United perhaps? No, it was their unfashionable neighbours, gallant little Bury, who beat Southampton 4-0 in 1900 and three years later set the record for the biggest victory margin in the Final with the 6-0 annihilation of Derby County.

That, of course, was in the days when the 'Shakers' enjoyed far greater standing in the game than today. Until 1929 most of their football had been played in the First Division, and they did not taste Third Division fare until 1957. Since then, they have divided their time between the lower flights, having constant difficulty in competing for support with the north-west giants, as well as the other League clubs which proliferate throughout Lancashire.

In consequence, talented young players – 1960s midfielder Colin Bell, who went on to win 48 England

caps, was a prime example – have had to be sold so that small-town Bury can survive. But there are few grounds with more character than Gigg Lane, and the Shakers appear endearingly ready to carry their unequal struggle into the next century.

BUSBY, Sir Matt

1909 Born in Lanarkshire mining village of Orbiston, Scotland

1928 Signs for Manchester City

1933 Wins sole Scottish cap, against Wales at Cardiff

1934 Helps City beat Portsmouth to win FA Cup

1936 Joins Liverpool for £8000

1945 Takes over as Manchester United manager

1948 FA Cup victory over Blackpool, first trophy of Busby era

1952 United take League title

1953 Birth of the 'Busby Babes' as youth is given its head

1956 First of two successive Championships; September – pioneers British clubs' continental challenge as United enter European Cup

1957 FA Cup Final defeat by Aston Villa costs United the double

1958 Busby narrowly survives Munich air disaster, which claims the lives of eight players

1963 His rebuilt team lift the FA Cup, beating Leicester City

1965 United win first of two League titles in three years

1968 Receives knighthood in wake of European Cup triumph against Benfica

1969 Relinquishes team control to Wilf McGuinness; continues as general manager

1970 Resumes charge of side as McGuinness is sacked

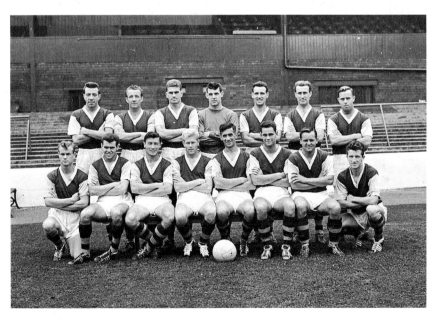

Sir Matt Busby, with the European Cup, in 1968, the year of his knighthood and Manchester United's famous victory. In 1993, when Manchester United won the Premier League title, Sir Matt was still involved with the club. The manager, Alex Ferguson, remarked at the last home match of the season: 'This is Sir Matt's club – he built it.'

1971 Frank O'Farrell is new United boss; Busby takes seat on board and later becomes club president

1980s Remains quiet but authoritative voice in background at United

1994 Dies in Manchester, aged 84, and is mourned by football folk the world over.

Matt Busby is the man who made Manchester United. Admittedly, the 'Red Devils' already had six decades of history behind them when he arrived at Old Trafford; but the United the world knows today, that magical institution whose appeal somehow transcends its periodic traumas, is essentially the creation of the visionary Scot.

After the Second World War, Busby, a benevolent figure with a core of steel, took on a club with no money and a bombed-out ground. Before long he had breathed life into the place, built the first of his three magnificent sides and was soon lifting soccer's most glittering prizes. The flair and charisma Busby had shown in his own career as a constructive wing-half was evident in each team. His creed was to entertain and, crucially, he had the priceless ability to communicate it to his players.

But despite all the triumphs on the field, his most awesome achievement was fighting back from the brink of death after Munich to bring further glories to Old Trafford.

On retirement Busby was criticised for letting his stars grow old together. But this could not detract from his monumental career.

CAMBRIDGE UNITED

Founded 1919

Joined League 1970
(Division 4)

Honours Division 3
Champions 1991; Division
4 Champions 1977

Ground Abbey Stadium

Relative newcomers to the
League, Cambridge United
have achieved their successes
on limited budgets in a town
not noted for its fervent
support of soccer.

United joined Division 4
in 1970, beating both
Bradford Park Avenue
(applying for re-election) and
neighbours Cambridge City
in the voting for League
status. The side that took
them to the Division 4
Championship in 1976/77
held together and went on to
win promotion to the Second
Division in the following
season. Stars of that era
included Alan Biley and
George Reilly, both of whom
went on to bigger clubs, and
skipper Steve Spriggs who
made a club record 417
League appearances.

Following the League's
longest ever run of games
without a win (31),
Cambridge finished bottom
of Division 2 in 1983/84.
Their return to Division 3 in
1990 was via a play-off final
against Chesterfield and they
repeated their two-
promotions-in-two-seasons
feat in 1991 by winning the
Division 3 Championship.
However, despite reaching
the Division 2 play-offs in
1992, United attracted much
criticism for their long-ball
game, and after a poor start
to the following season they
parted company with
controversial boss John Beck.
Another three managers and
two relegations later, and the
immediate future does not
look too promising for the
'U's. Tommy Taylor's first full
season in charge will be in
Division 3.

CALEDONIAN THISTLE

Founded 1994

Joined League 1994

Ground Telford Street Park,
Inverness

Caledonian Thistle FC is the
result of the amalgamation of
Inverness Thistle and
Inverness Caledonian,
designed to bring Scottish
League football to the
Highland capital. It was not an
easy marriage, but the new
club, with Ross County, joined
the Scottish League in 1994
when the number of member
clubs was increased.

Both clubs had long and
honourable histories, Thistle
dating from 1895, Caledonian
from 1896. The latter's name
derived from the Caledonian
Canal close by its ground, and
'Caley' proved to be one of
the Highland League's most
successful clubs. From 1896 to
1988, fifteen league
championships were won. In
cup competitions, the club
had a formidable reputation,
winning the North of Scotland
Cup no fewer than 14 times.
In the Scottish Cup proper
over the years, Caley beat Ayr
United at Somerset Park, and
such other league clubs as
Clyde and Stenhousemuir.

The Thistle club, a year
older, was one of six Inverness
clubs in the 1880s and
amalgamation is nothing new
to them – they absorbed the
'Citadel' and 'Union' clubs in
those early days. One match
against the former in 1895
made history throughout the
North as the 'two-minute
match' – Citadel walked off
the field disputing a Thistle
goal scored in just two
minutes of play!

Another remarkable
encounter was the match that
almost never was. Thistle
were drawn to play Falkirk in
the Scottish Cup at Inverness.
Such was the severity of the
winter that the tie was
postponed a record 29 times.

With the amalgamation of
these clubs, Inverness should
soon be a force on the Scottish
football scene. There is a
precedent; back in the
twenties, their joint XI played
Tottenham Hotspur, then FA
Cup holders. The Highlanders
won, 6-3.

CANTONA, Eric

1966 Born at Caillols, near
Marseilles

1983 Signs for Auxerre, his
first professional club

1985 Moves to another
French club, Martigues, but
doesn't make a senior
appearance

1986 Returns to Auxerre

1987 Fined for punching his
own goalkeeper; wins first
full cap for France

1988 Transferred to
Marseille, banned from
French team for a year after
insulting the national coach

1989 Suspended indefinitely
by club after angry reaction
to being substituted; loaned
to Bordeaux, then
Montpellier, with whom he
pockets French Cup
winner's medal

1990 Back to Marseille after
dressing-room brawl at
Montpellier

1991 Helps to win the
French Championship, then
joins Nimes; calls disciplinary
tribunal members 'idiots',
then announces retirement

1992 February – loaned to
Leeds United, who then pip
Manchester United for the
League title; July – move to
Elland Road made
'permanent'; November –
switches to Old Trafford in a
shock £1.2 million deal

1993 Plays inspirational part
in Red Devils' first
Championship triumph for
26 years

1994 Performs sublimely,
though his record is
blemished by periodic
petulance, as United win the
League and FA Cup double;
PFA Player of the Year;
captains disappointing
French side

1995 Loses control after
being sent off against Crystal
Palace at Selhurst Park; kicks
abusive supporter and is
suspended until the
following September

Adore him or loathe him, few
could reasonably deny that
Eric Cantona was the most
gifted and influential
footballer operating in the

British leagues during the
mid 1990s.

Not only did the tall,
tempestuous Frenchman
illuminate match after match
with his innovative talent; he
also achieved the seemingly
impossible – he ended
Manchester United's
apparently interminable wait
for the Championship.

Of course, he didn't do it
single-handed, but Cantona
was the catalyst for the Old
Trafford revolution. He it was
who supplied the final frisson
of flair and imagination that
transformed a collection of
outstanding but disparate
individuals into a superb
team.

When he was signed by
Alex Ferguson – the
negligible fee of £1.2 million
being explained by his
turbulent past – there were
many who doubted his
worth, despite his telling part
in Leeds' 1992 title triumph.
His critics dismissed him as
an unwarranted luxury
whose flicks and tricks were
an attractive but impractical
adornment, yet Cantona
made a mockery of the
doubters.

Sometimes he seemed to
saunter disdainfully while
lesser beings around him
strained every sinew but, out
of nothing, no matter how
tight the marking, he would
find space where there had
been none. Then the
swaggering Frenchman
would reveal the perfection
of his touch, the subtlety of
his passing, the explosiveness
of his finish; and he had the
strength to withstand the
fearsome physical challenges
which, inevitably, came his
way.

However, there was a
price to pay for the
spectacular goals, the sublime
set-ups, the ever-present
promise of brilliance. There
were moments, too many of
them, when Cantona's bad
temper got the better of him.
Sendings-off and suspensions
were almost de rigeur and
controversy was never far
away. The situation came to a
head in January 1995 when
he was sent off at Selhurst
Park and reacted with an
astonishing Kung-Fu attack
on a Palace fan who had
been taunting him. Cantona

Eric Cantona in celebratory mood, having scored in a Manchester derby victory as United closed in on the 1993/94 title. His affinity with the fans was slightly at odds with his aloofness in other aspects of his demeanour.

CARDIFF CITY

Founded 1899

Joined League 1920 (Division 2)

Honours Division 3 (S) Champions 1947; FA Cup Winners 1927; Division 3 Champions 1993

Ground Ninian Park

Cardiff City's first decade of League life was enough to make the opposition tremble. By the end of their opening campaign they had gained promotion to the top flight; three years later, in 1924, they missed the League Championship only on goal average; the next term ended with a single-goal Wembley defeat; and in 1927 they became the first (and still the only) Welsh club to win the FA Cup.

Unfortunately for the 'Bluebirds' the success of that golden era, when half-back Fred Keenor was their driving force, was not to continue. By 1931 they had slithered ignominiously to the Third Division and were not to reappear in the First until 1952. This time they lasted for five years, with goalscorers Trevor Ford and Gerry Hitchens

was banned for the remainder of that season and the first six weeks of the next, and his future in English football was called into question. Despite everything, though, it would be a rare Manchester United fan who didn't bless the day that he pulled on that famous red shirt.

making key contributions. Since then, apart from two campaigns in the early 1960s, they have not joined the elite.

As that decade progressed, the exertions of manager Jimmy Scoular and striker John Toshack did much to ensure Cardiff's security, and sometimes prosperity, in the Second Division. But by the late 1980s the team – who have had to labour hard to survive in a rugby fastness – had grown accustomed to floundering in the lower reaches, and a financial crisis in 1991 nearly brought about their downfall.

For many years the Welsh Cup, which they have won 21 times, offered the greatest chance of glory through entry to the European Cup Winners' Cup. Indeed, fans with modest memories still talk of 1968, when they lost in the semi-finals to Hamburg, and 1971, when they beat Real Madrid in a quarter-final first leg only to bow out by one goal. But from 1996 the Welsh Cup will no longer offer entry to Europe and Cardiff, relegated to Division 3 in 1995, are left to strive for more prosaic goals.

CARLISLE UNITED

Founded 1903

Joined League 1928 (Division 3 N)

Honours Division 3 Champions 1965, 1995

Ground Brunton Park

After three matches of 1974/75, Carlisle United sat

'Which team is in the record books as the only side to take the FA Cup out of England?' Answer: the Cardiff City side from Wales, 1926/27. They lost the 1924 FA Cup Final 1-0 to Sheffield United, before beating Arsenal by the same scoreline in 1927. Although successive Cardiff teams have won the Welsh Cup on numerous occasions, they have rarely threatened to repeat the feat of the 1926/27 side: (back row, left to right) Latham (trainer), Nelson, Farquharson, Watson, McLachlan; Sloan, Irving, Keenor, Hardy, Davies; Curtis, Ferguson (scorer of the all-important goal in the Final win over Arsenal).

The Guinness Football Encyclopedia 33

proudly at the head of Division 1. It was a supremely satisfying experience for the unfashionable Cumbrians, but not a lasting one. After being relegated at the end of their sole campaign at the top level, they slipped all the way to the Fourth Division.

United's moment of glory was all the more sweet in view of their lacklustre past. Thirty years of frugal Third Division existence were followed by two sojourns in the newly created Fourth before they began their climb to that lofty pinnacle of the mid 1970s.

Achievements in knockout competition have been few, though Carlisle did reach the FA Cup quarter-finals during their season among the elite and the League Cup semi-finals five years earlier.

Outstanding performers in the Cumbrians' blue shirts have been schemer Ivor Broadis in two spells after the Second World War; 1950s centre-forward Alan Ashman, who as manager led them into the First Division; inside-forward Stan Bowles in the early 1970s; and striker Peter Beardsley nearly a decade later. Notable bosses have included Bill Shankly (1949-51) and Bob Stokoe (three stints between 1968 and 1986).

The problem facing Carlisle in the 1990s was typical of many clubs – how to survive financially. Their solution came in a slightly less typical fashion... a 'white knight' in the shape of Michael Knighton, the man who once tried to buy Manchester United. His undoubted enthusiasm for the game, and a little cash, inspired Carlisle to a runaway championship of Division 3 in 1995.

CARTER, Raich

1913 Born in Sunderland

1930 Rejected by Leicester City as 'too small'

1931 Turns professional with hometown club

1934 Full England debut

against Scotland at Wembley

1936 Becomes youngest title-winning skipper as he inspires Sunderland to League Championship

1937 Stars in FA Cup Final victory over Preston North End

1943 Recalled to England side after lengthy absence and regains regular place for wartime internationals

1945 Joins Derby County in £8,000 deal

1946 Helps Rams lift the FA Cup, then plays first-class cricket for Derbyshire

1947 Wins 13th and last England cap

1948 Transferred to Hull City for £6,000, becomes player-manager

1949 Leads Tigers to Third Division (North) title

1951 Resigns as Hull boss having failed to reach top flight

1952 Retires as League footballer, having scored 216 goals in 451 outings

1953 Helps Cork Athletic win Irish Cup, becomes manager of Leeds

1956 Guides Elland Road club to promotion to First Division

1958 Surprisingly sacked as Leeds boss

1960 Appointed manager of Mansfield Town

1963 Leads Mansfield out of Fourth Division, takes over at Middlesbrough

1966 Sacked with 'Boro on brink of relegation to Third Division

1994 Dies on Humberside

By common consent, Raich Carter was the finest English inside-forward of his generation. But for the Second World War, which sliced his playing career in two, he would have accumulated many more than his 13 full caps, though that relatively meagre total had something to do with a distinctly abrasive side to his character.

Carter was a magnificent maker and taker of goals. During his peak years and beyond, when his black hair had turned prematurely to a distinguished silver, he cut an imperious figure, radiating self-confidence as he strutted around the pitch, invariably dictating the course of a game.

Some called him arrogant, but there was no denying the Carter class. He shot thunderously with either foot,

his ball-control and distribution was impeccable and his body-swerve was positively breathtaking.

Crucially, too, he possessed the intelligence to put these natural gifts to maximum use.

After his retirement as a player, Carter was the enterprising manager of four clubs, notably Leeds United in the mid 1950s, but probably he ruffled too many feathers to reach the very top as a boss.

CELTIC

Founded 1887 (first match: 1888)

Joined League 1890 (Division 1, founder club)

Honours Scottish League Championship Division 1, 1893, 1894, 1896, 1898, 1905, 1906, 1907, 1908, 1909, 1910, 1914, 1915, 1916, 1917, 1919, 1922, 1926, 1936, 1938, 1954, 1966, 1967, 1968, 1969, 1970, 1971, 1972, 1973, 1974; Premier Division, 1977, 1979, 1981, 1982, 1986, 1988; Scottish Cup, 1892, 1899, 1900, 1904, 1907, 1908, 1911, 1912, 1914, 1923, 1925, 1927, 1931, 1933, 1937, 1951, 1954, 1965, 1967, 1969, 1971, 1972, 1974, 1975, 1977, 1980, 1985, 1988, 1989, 1995; League Cup, 1956/66, 1966/67, 1967/68, 1968/69, 1969/70, 1974/75, 1982/83; European Cup, 1967

Ground Celtic Park

Celtic are a club of distinctive origins. They were formed to support soup kitchens operating among the impoverished Irish Catholic immigrants of Glasgow's East End. Celtic, however, were also intended to reinforce that community's self-respect by providing a focal point of pride and achievement.

They and their fans have drawn sustenance from the questionable notion that they are romantic rebels. Despite the considerable resources they have always enjoyed, the club likes to cast itself as underdogs to arch-rivals Rangers with the latter as representatives of a Protestant Establishment in Scotland. The reality has never been quite so simple.

In the early years Celtic were guided by aspiring middle-class businessmen who sought success single-mindedly. They utterly ignored the rules of amateurism (under which Scottish football supposedly operated before 1893) and were even able to take defender Dan Doyle from openly professional Everton. In Scotland Celtic plundered the ranks of the other clubs, tempting away their best players.

The effect was to rouse the domestic game. Attendances boomed and Rangers, especially, grew in strength by way of response. Before long Celtic moved on to a new policy of producing home-grown sides. The development

was nurtured by Willie Maley, who served the club first as player and then as manager from its foundation until 1939. The best of his teams won six League Championships in succession from 1905 to 1910.

Perhaps, though, the most cherished memories in Celtic's history are associated with Cup competition. Victories in the All British Empire Exhibition Cup of 1938 and the Coronation Cup of 1953 are bedded in the club's folklore. Celtic have always had men capable of the explosive moment which decides a Cup tie.

The individualistic Patsy Gallacher equalised in the 1925 Scottish Cup Final by somersaulting out of a goalmouth melee and over the line with the ball wedged between his feet. Celtic's great centre-forward of the 1920s and 1930s, Jimmy McGrory, scored the winner that day. Probably the club's greatest-ever player, he hit a British record 550 goals in first-class football, mostly for Celtic, including eight in one match against Dunfermline in 1928.

Despite an extraordinary 7-1 victory over Rangers in the 1957 League Cup Final, Celtic were a club in decline over the years following the Second World War. That changed with the appointment of Jock Stein, a former captain, as manager in 1965. With very few excursions into the transfer market he built a team which possessed the athleticism, skill and tactical know-how to match the Continent's best.

They produced overwhelming attacking football to become the first British club to win the European Cup in 1967, beating Inter Milan 2-1. The aerial power of centre-half Billy McNeill, the play-making of Bobby Murdoch and the trickery of winger Jimmy Johnstone were especially significant in that period. From 1966 to 1974 Celtic won nine successive Championships, equalling the world record of the time.

Towards the end of that run a new generation of talent appeared but men like Kenny Dalglish, David Hay

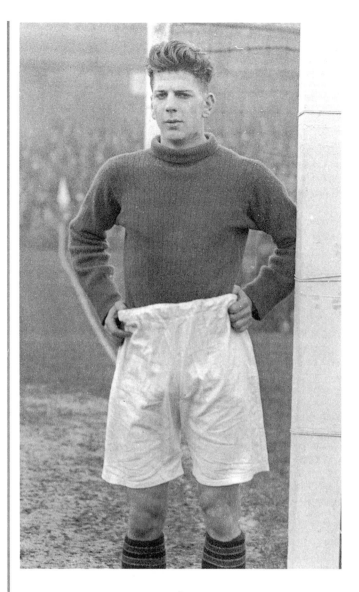

and Lou Macari were sold to English clubs. World-class full-back Danny McGrain, who stayed, was an exception. The trend continued with Charlie Nicholas's move to Arsenal in 1983. The club continued to discover gifted players, such as Paul McStay, but were surprised by the boom in Rangers' ambitions and fortunes. They sought to match it when in 1994, Fergus McCann, a Scots-Canadian businessman, headed a takeover bid which ousted the existing board of directors. He sacked manager Liam Brady and, in a controversial move, persuaded Tommy Burns and Billy Stark, former Celtic players, to leave their management of the Kilmarnock club and move to Celtic Park. McCann announced a share issue, with plans for the rebuilding of Celtic's ageing stadium to give a 60,000-seat successor, and

allowed Burns to spend £1.5 million on buying Pierre Van Hooijdonk from Breda in Holland. The Celtic fans responded to this with a staggering total of £13.5 million in the share issue, the highest such sum achieved in Britain to that date.

CENTRAL AMERICA

Central American countries are often underrated by European observers. Costa Rica's progress to the last 16 of the 1990 World Cup finals at the expense of Scotland and Sweden was no surprise to those who knew that Costa Rica had dominated the region's international football competition. Mexico's record of ten appearances in the World Cup finals is better than that of many European countries, including England, Scotland and Spain. Mexico has also hosted the tournament on two occasions (1970 and 1986).

Cuba (1938), Haiti (1974), Honduras (1982) and El Salvador (1970 and 1982) have also reached the final stages of the World Cup. The last two made world news in 1969 with the so-called 'Soccer War' game. It took three games to decide that El Salvador rather than Honduras would meet Haiti in a play-off for a place in the 1970 World Cup finals. Shortly after the final game, played in neutral Mexico, a four-day war broke out, but diplomatic relations between the two countries were already strained over land problems.

The association responsible for soccer in North and Central America is the Confederacion Norte-Centro-Americana y del Caribe de Futbol (CONCACAF), founded in 1972.

CHAPMAN, Herbert

1875 Born at Kiveton Park, Sheffield

1897-1901 While working as a mining engineer, plays as an amateur for Stalybridge, Rochdale, Grimsby, Swindon, Sheppey United and Worksop

1901 Signs professional for Northampton

1903 Moves to Notts County (£300)

1905 Transfers to Tottenham Hotspur

1907 Becomes player-manager of Northampton Town

1909 Helps Northampton to the Southern League Championship

1912 Takes over as secretary-manager of Leeds City

1917-18 Leeds City win the Football League (Midland Section) in successive seasons

1919 Temporarily suspended by an FA Commission enquiring into pre-war illegal payments at Leeds; Chapman denies involvement

1921 Takes over as Huddersfield Town manager and helps the club to win the FA Cup (1922) and the first two of three consecutive First Division Championships

1925 Becomes manager of Arsenal, where he manages another Cup-winning team (1930) and two Championship teams (1930/31 and 1932/33)

1934 Dies while still in office at Arsenal, with the club half-way through a run of three consecutive League Championships

Herbert Chapman raised the status of football club management. At both Huddersfield and Arsenal he built teams which won three consecutive Championships, and his Arsenal team of the 1930s dominated English soccer in the manner of Liverpool in the 1980s. Despite his early death in 1934, Chapman won a considerable haul of major managerial honours: four League Championships and two more for the taking when interrupted by migration (at Huddersfield) and death (at Arsenal), two FA Cup wins and two other FA Cup Finals.

After a modest playing career, Chapman displayed

A legend in British football, Herbert Chapman's reputation is founded on the Huddersfield and Arsenal teams that each won the Championship three times in a row. His style was a blend of solid authority and innovative thinking. Although not a 'tracksuit manager', he seriously thought about team tactics and individual skills.

managerial showmanship, persuasion, discipline and innovation. He arrested spectator interest with gimmicky signings such as 5ft 2in Fanny Walden (later an international) at Northampton and Charles Buchan (£2000 plus £100 for each goal) at Arsenal. He successfully persuaded the London Passenger Transport Board to change the name of the Gillespie Road tube station to 'Arsenal'. A regular churchgoer, he commanded authority, and the inter-war period became the 'Chapman era'. His innovations included experiments with a white ball, rubber-studded boots, all-weather pitches and floodlights, but his biggest impact was on tactics. He was one of the instigators of the 'stopper centre-half' system to deal with the new offside law. At Arsenal he paid big fees to attract players like Alex James (£9000), David Jack (£11,000) and Wilf Copping (£6000), but he also signed players such as Eddie Hapgood and Cliff Bastin for bargain fees.

CHARITY SHIELD

The FA Charity Shield competition was introduced in 1908, when League Champions Manchester United played Southern League Champions Queen's Park Rangers at Stamford Bridge. This format, Football League Champions against Southern League Champions, was used for the next four years, but the FA refused to sanction the game in 1913 (and again in 1923) because they considered the FA Cup Final so unsporting.

Celebrating with trademark headstand and flip at the 1986 World Cup finals, Hugo Sanchez is one of the few stars of Central American football to make a success of a career in Europe.

Holding the Charity Shield are Eric Cantona and Tony Dorigo (right) of Leeds United, after their thrilling 4-3 victory over Liverpool in 1992. Leeds had won the 1991/92 League Championship, finishing ahead of Manchester United; Liverpool had beaten Sunderland 2-0 in the FA Cup Final. Soon after this match, Eric Cantona signed for Manchester United and played a large part in their 1992/93 Premier League Championship success.

In the 1920s it was common for a team chosen from the game's Amateurs to play a team of Professionals, and the games were evenly balanced. In 1920 Spurs (Second Division Champions) lost to West Bromwich (First Division Champions), and in 1927 Cup winners Cardiff City beat crack amateurs Corinthians 2-1. In 1928 the Shield settled into the more familiar contest between FA Cup winners and League Champions. In post-war years this has been interrupted on six occasions: when Spurs (1961), Arsenal (1971), Liverpool (1986) and Manchester United (1994) won the 'double'; in 1950,

when two representative teams were chosen from summer touring parties; and in 1972 when Manchester City (fourth in Division 1) and Aston Villa (Division 3 champions) took up an invitation. Although the FA Cup winners beat the League Champions in both 1921 and 1922, the League Champions have won far more of the games.

Since 1959 the game has been played as a curtain-raiser at the start of the season. In the 1967 game Tottenham Hotspur goalkeeper Pat Jennings scored a goal against Manchester United at Old Trafford with a clearance from his own penalty area. The contest was switched to Wembley in 1974 in a match (decided by penalties) in which Keegan (Liverpool) and Bremner (Leeds) were sent off for fighting.

The neutral setting of Wembley has helped to attract large crowds and raise extra money for charity. For some years the FA employed a system of sharing the trophy (six months each) in the event of a draw, but in 1993 it was decided on penalties. Liverpool have contested the Shield 17 times since 1964 and have a record 13 wins (including shares of the trophy), followed by Manchester United (12).

CHARITY SHIELD AT WEMBLEY

Year	Winners	Runners-up	Score
1974	Liverpool	Leeds United	1-1**
1975	Derby County	West Ham United	2-0
1976	Liverpool	Southampton	1-0
1977	Liverpool	Manchester United	2-0
1978	Nottingham Forest	Ipswich Town	5-0
1979	Liverpool	Arsenal	3-1
1980	Liverpool	West Ham United	1-0
1981	Aston Villa	Tottenham Hotspur	2-2*
1982	Liverpool	Tottenham Hotspur	1-0
1983	Manchester United	Liverpool	2-0
1984	Everton	Liverpool	1-0
1985	Everton	Manchester United	2-0
1986	Everton	Liverpool	1-1*
1987	Everton	Coventry City	1-0
1988	Liverpool	Wimbledon	2-1
1989	Liverpool	Arsenal	1-0
1990	Liverpool	Manchester United	1-1*
1991	Arsenal	Tottenham Hotspur	0-0*
1992	Leeds United	Liverpool	4-3
1993	Manchester United	Arsenal	1-1**
1994	Manchester United	Blackburn Rovers	2-0

*trophy shared ** won on penalties

A big man with an imposing presence, John Charles of Juventus lines up with team-mates Terry Medwin (on his left) of Spurs and Colin Webster of Manchester United before a Wales match in the 1958 World Cup finals held in Sweden. Oddly, it seems as if John Charles is wearing brand-new boots for this game – presumably not fearful of blisters. Wales, during their only appearance in the finals, did well, drawing three matches, beating the Hungarians and only losing 1-0 to Brazil (eventual winners).

CHARLES, John

1931 Born in Swansea

1947 Joins Leeds United as a 15-year-old

1949 Makes first-team debut

1950 At the age of 18 years 71 days he becomes the youngest player to win a Welsh cap

1956 Helps Leeds win promotion to the First Division

1957 Top scorer in First Division with 38 goals;

transferred to Juventus for £65,000

1962 Returns to Leeds; joins Roma for £70,000

1963 Transferred to Cardiff City

1966 Ends League career

John Charles was supremely gifted, almost unfairly so. At 6ft 2in and nearly 14 stone he was a magnificent physical specimen, and unlike many men of his size his talent was also enormous. His touch was sensitive, his control precise, his finishing decisive; but most of all he was a master in the air.

Originally on Swansea Town's ground staff, Charles was signed by Leeds United as an amateur when he was 15. By the age of 17 he was in the first team at centre-half and within a year he had won the first of 38 Welsh caps. In the 1952/53 season Leeds experimented with him at centre-forward where he scored 27 goals in 30 matches. The following season he was the League's top marksman with 42 goals, which is still a club record. In 1956 Charles helped Leeds to the Second Division Championship.

The following year Juventus broke the British transfer record with £65,000 to lure Charles to Turin, where he enjoyed the five best seasons of his career. Playing alongside Boniperti (Italy) and Sivori (Argentina), he helped Juventus to three Italian League championships in the next four years in addition to two Italian Cups. In all he scored 93 goals in 155 League games for Juventus, a staggering record in the ultra-defensive Italian League.

In 1962 he returned briefly to Leeds before going back to Italy with Roma. The old dash was gone, however, and he finished his League career with Cardiff alongside his brother Mel, also a Welsh international.

Throughout his career Charles was never sent off or even cautioned. He had a lovely temperament, so much so that the Italians christened him 'Il Buon Gigante' (the gentle giant). A giant he truly was, the greatest Welsh player of all time.

CHARLTON ATHLETIC

Founded 1905

Joined League 1921 (Division 3 S)

Honours Division 3 (S) Champions 1929, 1935; FA Cup Winners 1947

Ground The Valley

Charlton Athletic may now be typecast as gutsy little survivors against all odds, but there was a time when they held their own among England's top clubs and were second only to Arsenal in the London pecking order. That was in the 1930s when the 'Valiants', having spent an inauspicious first decade in the League, suddenly assumed new stature.

Under the shrewd management of Jimmy Seed they rose from the Third to the First Division in successive seasons, and missed the Championship by only four points in 1936/37, their first campaign in the top flight. Thus established, even the Second World War did not shatter their momentum and they reached the FA Cup Finals of 1946 and 1947, losing first to Derby County and beating Burnley in the second. Throughout this era, and into the 1950s, the most notable playing personality was red-head Sam Bartram, often described as the finest 'keeper never to play for England.

In 1957, Seed having departed, Charlton were relegated, and it was to be 31 years before they climbed back. In between came a 15-year stay in the Second Division, which saw distinguished service from the likes of South African strikers Eddie Firmani (who also did a stint in the boss's chair) and Stuart Leary, followed by two short spells in Division Three.

The 1980s brought fundamental change. With the big clubs taking an ever higher percentage of fans, Charlton struggled to make ends meet, and in 1985 they left the Valley, that vast concrete amphitheatre, to become tenants of Crystal Palace. The admirable Lennie Lawrence, manager from 1983 to 1991, contrived success on a shoestring and

Chairman Roger Alwen opens up the gates to the 'new' Valley ground in 1992. The Valley had stood undeveloped since 1985 when Charlton Athletic were forced to leave their home due to financial pressures. For several years they had been playing their 'home' matches at Selhurst Park in a ground-sharing scheme with south London neighbours Crystal Palace. Charlton celebrated their return with a 1-0 victory over Portsmouth.

took his side into the First Division, where he pulled off a series of eleventh-hour escapes before the Valiants finally dropped in 1990. In 1992 they returned to the Valley, but the need for economy remained urgent.

CHARLTON, Bobby

1937 Born in Ashington, Northumberland, a member of the Milburn footballing clan.

1954 Signs for Manchester United

1956 Scores twice on debut, against Charlton Athletic

1957 Wins first club honour, a League Championship medal

1958 February – survives Munich air crash; April – scores against Scotland as he wins first of record 106 England caps; May – picks up second successive FA Cup runners-up medal

1963 Helps United beat Leicester City to become Wembley winners at last

1965 Shows brilliant form as 'Red Devils' take first of two League Championships in three years

1966 Plays major role in England's World Cup victory; English and European Footballer of the Year

1968 Skippers United to European Cup glory, scoring twice in final against Benfica.

1973 April – bows out of Old Trafford after scoring 247 goals in 754 games; samples management with Preston North End

1974 Comes out of retirement to boost his side on the pitch

1975 Leaves Deepdale after disagreement with board over transfer policy

1983 Short spell as caretaker boss of Wigan, of which he was a director

1984 Joins Manchester United board, combining the work with his soccer schools for youngsters

1994 Becomes Sir Bobby

Bobby Charlton possessed a sublime talent, and those who witnessed him at his peak were privileged indeed. One of sport's most graceful movers, he was blessed with a pulverising shot, a thrilling body-swerve and an ability to pass the ball over long distances with devastating accuracy. As one of Manchester United's 'Busby Babes', he was an inside-forward who played with a carefree exuberance which was to vanish forever when he took on extra responsibility in the wake of the Munich disaster. Then, for a time, he became a left-winger and there are those who reckon that was his most effective position.

But most shrewd judges agree that Charlton realised his full potential only as a deep-lying schemer, a more demanding role in which he achieved his most spectacular successes with club and country. There were many majestic international performances as a record 49 England goals would suggest, yet it was his breathtaking combination with fellow Old Trafford greats George Best and Denis Law which will linger longest in the memory.

A self-effacing man, he was an idol without the proverbial feet of clay and was loved the world over. He remains the British game's finest international ambassador.

In typical action pose, Bobby Charlton has his less favoured right leg raised as he prepares to take a corner. He was a sweet striker of a dead ball who scored 49 goals in 106 appearances for England. Bobby was a member of the England team that won the World Cup in 1966 – the year in which he was voted European Player of the Year. He was a marvellous ambassador for the sport – a true legend in his own lifetime. Bobby was also a fighter, a great team player and a man who hated losing. Today, as pundit or administrator, he is highly respected.

CHARLTON, Jack

1935 Born in Ashington, Northumberland

1956 Turns professional with Leeds United, his only club as a player

1957 Plays for Football League

1960 Charlton's efforts can't keep Leeds in top flight

1964 In dominant form as United top Division 2

1965 Disappointment of FA Cup Final defeat by Liverpool is offset by winning first of 35 England caps, against Scotland at Wembley

1966 Plays crucial part in England's World Cup triumph

1967 Footballer of the Year

1968 Helps Leeds win League Cup and European Fairs Cup

1969 Adds League Championship medal to his collection

1971 A second European Fairs Cup triumph

1972 Finally pockets an FA Cup winner's medal, two days short of 37th birthday

1973 Retires as player to become Middlesbrough manager

1974 Manager of the Year as 'Boro' win Division 2 title

1977 Takes over at Sheffield Wednesday

1980 Leads 'Owls' up to Division 2; later narrowly misses promotion to top flight

1984 Moves on to Newcastle United

1985 Shocks 'Magpies' by resigning on eve of new season following criticism over sale of Chris Waddle

1986 Appointed Republic of Ireland boss

1988 Charlton's side reach the European Championship Finals ...

1990 ... then top that as World Cup quarter-finalists in Italy

1994 Guides the Republic to the second phase of World Cup Finals in USA

Jack Charlton was never gifted with the silken skills that epitomised his younger brother, Bobby. What he lacked in the skills department, he more than made up for in determination and that 'never-say-die' spirit. Jack had the nickname of 'Giraffe'. He played for Leeds United for 20 years, and like his brother was a member of England's 1966 World Cup winning team. He has probably received most adulation from fans of the Republic of Ireland. His achievements as manager of the national side, with a small pool of players, are well chronicled. The key to his success is hard to discover: perhaps it is his honest approach that wins the trust of his team.

Bobby Charlton was elected Footballer of the Year in 1966. He was succeeded 12 months later by his brother Jack. It was yet another outstanding achievement by two members of a remarkable family. And it was in the then relatively unfamiliar role of speech-making that the two brothers underlined the contrast in temperament which is almost a denial of their kinship.

Bobby spoke well, but Jack's speech was more memorable. Bobby was warm and sincere: Jack was no less sincere, but he was different. Unlike his brother he has never paid much account to tact. Two years older, he remains independent and stubborn.

Tall and bonily hard, Jack Charlton made no pretence at being a graceful footballer, but no defender won the ball more consistently in the air or sent it further from the danger area. And there was plenty of skill concealed in this apparent clumsiness. He could cope with tight situations and his passing was often surprisingly accomplished. The turning point in Charlton's career came in 1963 when Leeds were in peril of being relegated to the Third Division. 'If you get your attitude right, there is no reason why you shouldn't play for England,' said Don Revie, the Leeds manager. Two years later Leeds were emerging as a major force and Charlton made his international debut.

When Jack and Bobby collapsed in each other's arms on the turf after England won the World Cup in 1966, the romance appeared to be complete. But all that Jack Charlton made of his playing career would be overshadowed by the remarkable success he achieved as a manager with the Republic of Ireland. After experiencing success with Middlesbrough and Sheffield Wednesday, then finding life more difficult with Newcastle, it looked as though Charlton had abandoned the game until his interest was sparked by an offer from Dublin. Within two years he had revitalised the Irish cause, before taking them, and himself, forward to greater glory than they had ever known. Increasingly feisty with advancing years, Charlton became one of the most formidable characters in international sport.

CHELSEA

Founded 1905

Joined League 1905 (Division 2)

Honours Division 1 Champions 1955; Division 2 Champions 1984, 1989; FA Cup Winners 1970; League Cup Winners 1965; European Cup Winners' Cup 1971

Ground Stamford Bridge

For many years Chelsea were not taken entirely seriously; they were regarded with amused affection rather than awe or envy. There was no lack of ambition when they were formed by Gus Mears, specifically to play at the Stamford Bridge athletics stadium which he had recently acquired, but they soon gained a reputation for unpredictability. The glamour and, perhaps, some of the attitudes of the nearby West End of London became associated with the club. The team frequently boasted a galaxy of stars, but they combined effectively too rarely for any sustained success to be achieved.

A new era dawned when Ted Drake became manager in 1952. He replaced Chelsea's familiar symbol, the Pensioner, and built a hard-working journeyman side which won the League, albeit with a modest points total. He then placed his faith in 'Drake's Ducklings', the young players emerging from the club's prolific youth scheme, but too many of them failed to maintain their early progress and, when the goalscoring genius of Jimmy Greaves was lost to Italy, relegation soon followed.

Tommy Docherty succeeded Drake in 1961 and the energetic team he fashioned from a new generation of home-produced talent won promotion at the first attempt. Chelsea became established as serious contenders for honours, but these stormy years yielded only one major trophy despite a number of near-misses and an exciting period ended in bitterness and recriminations. The thoughtful, measured approach of Dave Sexton, who took over in 1967, was rewarded by two Cup triumphs, but the club then became infected by complacency and by the time the signs of decline had been recognised, it was almost irreversible. Relegation coincided with a financial crisis which threatened Chelsea's very existence and they remained in the grip of a seemingly terminal malaise until the advent of a new owner, Ken Bates, in 1982. After a drop into the Third Division had been narrowly avoided, manager John Neal was given the means to recruit a side which restored the Blues' pride and reclaimed their place among English football's leading teams. Despite a brief return to Division 2 in 1988/89, the foundations of the club appeared to be sound, with the future of their traditional home now secure. The playing side received a stylish uplift when Glenn Hoddle became manager in 1993 and

Chelsea stars Glenn Hoddle with Dennis Wise in 1994. The next year was Hoddle's last as a player for Chelsea and one in which he was able to watch Wise develop as a gifted midfielder... with more guile and skill than some people had thought possible from him. Wise is one of a handful of strong contenders for England places in the 1996 European Championships.

By the end of the 1994/95 season Hoddle had achieved a good rapport with the supporters, but his position, like that of other Premiership managers, was under the spotlight.

the Blues performed creditably in losing the 1994 FA Cup final. There was deserved consolation for that Wembley defeat: because Manchester United, their conquerors, had also won the Premiership, Chelsea gained entry to the European Cup Winners Cup, managing to reach the semi-finals.

CHESTER CITY

Founded 1884

Joined League 1931 (Division 3)

Honours None

Ground Deva Stadium

Chester have been 'small fry' throughout their Football League history, and with so much of their potential support being lost to the Merseyside giants, there is scant hope of impending long-term advancement. Having sold their long-time home, Sealand Road, to developers in 1990, they embarked on a new era as guests of non-League Macclesfield before moving into their own purpose-built Deva Stadium. But despite such enterprise, their main claim to fame – offering Welsh centre-forwards Ron Davies and Ian Rush their professional baptisms – seems unlikely to be superseded in the immediate future. After spending nearly three decades in Division 3 (N), the 'Cestrians' became founder members of Division 4 in

1958 and made several re-election applications before winning promotion in 1975. There followed seven years in the higher grade and four back in the basement before they rose again as runners-up in 1986; then came another drop in 1993, another ascent a year later, and yet another relegation in 1995. Chester's most illustrious achievement was reaching the League Cup semi-final in 1975, when they lost 5-4 on aggregate to Aston Villa.

CHESTERFIELD

Founded 1866

Joined League 1899 (Division 2)

Honours Division 3 (N) Champions 1931, 1936; Division 4 Champions 1970, 1985

Ground Recreation Ground, Saltergate

Chesterfield, one of the oldest clubs in the Football League, have remained homely and small throughout their history, unable to emerge from the shadows of big-time competition at nearby Derby and Sheffield. Their first stint in the League ended with failure to secure re-election to the Second Division in 1909 and they had to wait until the Third (N) was formed in 1921 to gain re-entry.

This time they were in to stay and enjoyed some modest success, even tasting the excitement of a Second Division promotion battle in 1947. Eventually they finished fourth and failed to consolidate their standing, slipping back into the lower reaches. Since then the 'Spireites' – whose tradition for discovering fine goalkeepers has produced England internationals Sam Hardy and Gordon Banks, among others – have divided their time between the two bottom flights, with occasional silverware to reward their few loyal fans.

CHESTER REPORTS

In 1966, and again in 1982, Sir Norman Chester (1907-1986) was invited to chair

committees investigating the state of British football. The eventual reports, published in 1968 and 1983, contained important recommendations, many of which were at first ignored but then eventually accepted by football's ruling bodies.

Sir Norman – he was knighted in 1976 – was a passionate football enthusiast from an unprivileged Manchester background. Son of a factory worker, he left school at 14, then took an external degree and embarked on a high-flying academic career. He became an expert on local government and public administration and was warden of Nuffield College, Oxford, when asked by Minister of Sport Dennis Howell to chair the 1966 enquiry. Two years later, after countless interviews, the 135-page report was published with 36 recommendations. They included: the establishment of a Football Levy Board to match that of horse racing; a restructuring of the Football League into five divisions (two regional) of 100 clubs; the replacement of the retention-and-transfer system by fixed-term contracts with an option clause for both player and club; a new category of player to cover so-called 'amateurs' who receive limited payments; an overhaul of disciplinary committees; a fresh look at taxation; and a Director of Referees who could appoint top referees on a substantial retainer.

Chester's second study was commissioned by the Football League in 1982, when the grass-roots game was thriving but Football League clubs had a combined debt of around £37 million. Then a member of the Football Trust, Chester chaired a five-man committee which also included Jack Dunnett (Football League president), John Smith (Liverpool chairman), Cliff Lloyd (ex-PFA chairman) and Tony Boyce (Torquay United director). The final report, published in March 1983, again recommended a reduction of Division 1 clubs and regional lower divisions.

The committee proposed a 20-club Division 1 (by the end of 1983/84) and four lower leagues, each of 12 clubs with a system of mini-series and play-offs. Other recommendations were to allow natural wastage of clubs to reduce the size of the Football League, to permit home clubs to keep all receipts from League games, to allow the top non-League club automatic promotion, and to distribute a greater proportion of television money to the home club.

CLOUGH, Brian

1935 Born in Middlesbrough

1952 Turns professional with Boro

1959 October – first full England cap v Wales

1961 Signs for Sunderland

1962 Boxing Day – serious knee injury v Bury

1964 Plays for last time – injury forces him out

1965 Becomes manager of Hartlepool United, with Peter Taylor assistant

1967 With Taylor, joins Derby County as manager

1972 Wins League Championship

1973 Clough and Taylor join Brighton

1974 Joins Leeds United – Taylor stays at Brighton; Clough quits Leeds after 44 days

1975 January – becomes manager of Nottingham Forest

1978 Wins League Championship

1979 Wins European Cup, 1-0 v Malmo ...

1980 ... and repeats the performance, 1-0 v Hamburg

1990 Wins Littlewoods (League) Cup Final, 1-0 v Oldham Athletic – Forest's fourth such victory in five finals under Clough; Peter Taylor dies

1993 Announces retirement from football

Brian Clough at his last home match in charge of Nottingham Forest. He retired following this 1992/93 season, in which Forest were relegated from the Premier League. It was a sad day for Clough, one of the great managers of the modern game and certainly one who brought Forest success beyond their dreams. Interestingly Clough is flanked by policemen in this photograph. Clough, perhaps more than any other manager of his time, spoke out against hooliganism and in support of the police. He did not, however, simply produce platitudes but tried hard to address the causes of the problems. On one famous occasion, however, he perhaps overstepped the mark when he 'clipped the ears' of two fans who had invaded the City Ground pitch to celebrate a cup victory over Queen's Park Rangers. As a result, he was fined £5,000 by the FA, eventually making up with the fans by giving each a kiss on the cheek, his trademark greeting. He has remained just as outspoken in retirement and caused a stir with the publication of his autobiography in 1994.

Clough played mostly in the Second Division, appearing in only three First Division matches for Sunderland. The injury that eventually ended his playing days was suffered after a hopeless chase for the ball on a slushy Roker Park. He scored 251 League goals in only 274 appearances and won several representative honours including two full England caps, playing centre-forward.

Clough is best known as a successful – and controversial – manager. His League Championship with Derby was a major surprise to the football world, as was his and Peter Taylor's sudden departure from the club. Clough's Brighton sojourn was short-lived. He then joined Leeds United, at the time England's representatives in the European Cup. Poor results and disagreements with the players, among other reasons, saw Clough leave after only 44 days.

Nottingham Forest enjoyed considerable success under Clough, with consistent League performances matched by regular Cup success. Clough's style was built on bringing the best out of players who had sometimes not performed well for other managers. Outspoken and thriving on publicity, he was generally popular with the fans, although not always with administrators and directors. Reckoned by many to be the best manager England never had, he was once offered the part-time managership of Wales. Out of football, but also in the public eye, he was outspoken about politics and a champion of family life.

CLYDE

Founded 1878

Joined League 1891 (Division 1)

Honours Scottish League Division 2 Champions 1905, 1952, 1957, 1962, 1973; Second Division Champions 1978, 1982; Scottish Cup Winners 1939, 1955, 1958; Scottish League Division 2 Champions 1993

Ground Broadwood Stadium, Cumbernauld.

The Glasgow club's history is particularly distinguished by its three Scottish Cup victories, with the triumphs of 1955 and 1958 particularly renowned.

The first match of the Final against Celtic in 1955 was also the first Scottish Cup Final to be televised live. Clyde's stars of the era included internationals Tommy Ring and Harry Haddock. The club also performed notably in the late 1960s.

Sharing Partick Thistle's ground since 1986 drained Clyde's vitality, and they were relegated to the Second Division in 1991. With a new manager in the experienced Alex Smith, formerly of Aberdeen, and having moved to the purpose-built Broadwood Stadium in Cumbernauld, Clyde's fortunes seemed to be on the mend although good performances and reasonable support have not yet been translated into results.

CLYDEBANK

Founded 1965

Joined League 1966 (Division 2)

Honours Scottish League Second Division Champions 1976

Ground Kilbowie Park

Clydebank emerged from the failed attempt to move East Stirling to the town. They are a sprightly club both on and off the field. Clydebank possess an innovative streak and were pioneers in establishing a social club to generate revenue.

They employ a coach, not a manager. All important decisions are taken by the Steedman family (Jack has been president of the Scottish Football League) and a happy knack of finding gifted youngsters has

usually kept the club buoyant in the First Division and, after transfer, solvent. Clydebank were Scottish Cup semi-finalists in 1990. The late Davie Cooper, an outstandingly talented internationalist with Rangers and Motherwell, was their most famous discovery. Cooper returned to the club as a player-coach but tragically died following a brain haemorrhage on 22 March 1995.

COLCHESTER UNITED

Founded 1937

Joined League 1950 Division 3 (S), 1992 new Division 3

Honours None

Ground Layer Road

One result shines like a beacon from the modest, but enterprising history of Colchester United. In 1971 they were pitted against Don Revie's Leeds, then in their imperious pomp, for a place in the FA Cup quarter-finals and shocked the soccer world with a 3-2 victory, thanks largely to two goals from former England centre-forward Ray Crawford. Though they perished in the next round, it was the prelude to success of sorts for the Essex club, who that August won the Watney Cup

The highlight to date for Coventry City supporters was the memorable 1987 FA Cup Final victory over Tottenham Hotspur. One of the Coventry goalscorers in the 3-2 win, David Bennett, is flanked by George Curtis (left) and John Sillett, a popular partnership who both coached and managed the team at various times. Since first gaining promotion to the First Division in 1967, Coventry City have had an uninterrupted run in the top flight. The club place great importance on a good relationship with their fans and the game at large.

(a short-lived competition for high-scoring teams).

Before that, United's most notable achievement had been reaching the fifth round of the FA Cup in 1948 while not yet members of the League, a stirring run which helped their successful election campaign when Division 3 South was expanded two years later. Since then there have been four temporary promotions from the basement, a narrow and unlucky failure to reach Division 2 in 1957 and a place in the League Cup fifth round in 1974/75. However, in 1990 Colchester suffered the crushing experience of relegation to the Vauxhall Conference, but they refused to buckle and bounced back into the League in 1992.

COVENTRY CITY

Founded 1883

Joined League 1919 (Division 2)

Honours Division 2 Champions 1967; Division 3 (S) Champions 1936; Division 3 Champions 1964; FA Cup Winners 1987

Ground Highfield Road

Until the 1960s Coventry City hardly caught the eye. Then came a revolution which placed them among the most talked about soccer phenomena of the decade and paved the way for a lengthy tenure in Division 1. Indeed, as the 1990s dawned, the Midlanders' top-flight longevity was exceeded by that of just three rivals, Arsenal, Everton and Liverpool.

After graduating from the Southern League, Coventry had made a faltering start in the senior competition, six seasons of Second Division travail ending with relegation in 1925. Under the guidance of Harry Storer and boosted by the marksmanship of Clarrie Bourton, they gained promotion in 1936 and retained their regained status until the early 1950s.

A drab period – enlivened by one victorious term in the newly created Fourth Division, and England caps for goalkeeper Reg Matthews – was ended emphatically by the arrival in 1961 of dynamic chairman Derrick Robbins and innovative manager Jimmy Hill. Together they transformed not only City's playing fortunes but also the club's entire approach to the business of selling football to the public. Given a new sky-blue strip with a nickname to match, Coventry came up with bright schemes – Sky Blue special trains, Sky Blue Radio, etc – which were often dismissed as gimmicks at the time but were later copied by their competitors. The razzamatazz was matched by rapid progress on the field, with players such as 'keeper Bill Glazier, winger Ronnie Rees and, most influential of all, iron-man centre-half George Curtis – destined to become team boss and then managing director in the 1980s – being moulded into a side which, in 1967, claimed a place among the elite.

Since then, Coventry have waged more relegation battles than they would care to recall and though they have finished as high as sixth, have more frequently been in the bottom half. Highfield Road has, however, seen some talented performers – notably midfielder Willie Carr and winger Tommy Hutchison in the 1970s and forwards Cyrille Regis and David Speedie in the 1980s – and in 1987 extrovert manager John Sillett led the Sky Blues to their finest hour, FA Cup triumph over Tottenham. In 1990 former England star Terry Butcher took on the task of consolidating still further the club's top-flight tradition, initially in the role of player-manager, but he clashed with the board and in 1992 Bobby Gould slipped back into the hot seat he had vacated in 1984. He resigned after 16 months, however, and it was left to the enterprising Phil Neal to guide the Sky Blues through the mid 1990s. Surprisingly to many, Neal did not succeed and in 1995 Ron Atkinson was appointed, with his assistant, Gordon Strachan, nominated as his long-term successor.

COWDENBEATH

Founded 1881

Joined League 1905 (Division 2)

Honours Scottish League Division 2 Champions 1914, 1915, 1939

Ground Central Park

Cowdenbeath's last success in a national trophy went unrecognised. They swashbuckled their way to the Division 2 title in 1939 with 120 goals, but in the reorganisation which followed the Second World War they were left in the lower division.

The early 1930s had been good for the club and, as they held their own in Division 1, men like Jim Paterson and Alex Venters won Scotland caps. In general though spells in the top flight have been short, but promotion from Division 2 in 1992 gave birth to new hope. Alas, that was followed by a slump back to the basement.

Current Scotland defender Craig Levein received his first taste of senior football with Cowdenbeath before being sold to Hearts in 1983.

CREWE ALEXANDRA

Founded 1877

Joined League 1892 (Division 2)

Honours None

Ground Gresty Road

Crewe Alexandra may be a humble club – having spent all but a handful of their Football League seasons in the lowest available division – but no one can deny that they are born survivors. Since being formed by a group of railway workers in a pub, the 'Alex' have somehow managed to avoid the financial and footballing disasters which have befallen several of their contemporaries, and are now soldiering on into their second century.

One early and uncharacteristic highlight was an appearance in an FA Cup semi-final against Preston in 1888. Thus encouraged, Crewe became original members of Division 2, only to be outclassed and drop ignominiously out of the competition. Resurfacing in Division 3 (N) in 1921, they henceforth usually managed to avoid the re-election zone but were naturals for Division 4 when it was created in 1958. Thereafter they reached the Third Division three times, returning most recently to the new Second Division in 1994.

CRUYFF, Johan

1947 Born in Amsterdam, Holland

1965 Senior debut for Ajax

1966 Debut for Holland v Hungary

1971 Voted European Footballer of the Year as Ajax win the European Cup ...

1972 ... which they do again; top scorer in the competition (5 goals) and in the Dutch League (25 goals)

1973 Another European Cup victory; European Footballer of the Year again; joins ex-Ajax boss Rinus Michels at Barcelona for £922,300

1974 Captains his country in the World Cup Final and picks up another European Footballer of the Year award

1978 Announces retirement to concentrate on business

1979 Comes out of retirement to sign for Los Angeles Aztecs; receives NASL's Most Valuable Player award

1982 Returns to Ajax as player and then coach

1987 Guides his old team to Cup Winners' Cup victory

1989 Having taken his coaching skills to Barcelona, does the same for them.

1991 Suffers mild heart attack; resumes duties after operation

1992 Barcelona win European Cup

1994 Catalans take Spanish League title for fourth successive season

A natural and consistent goalscorer like Cruyff, blessed Johan Cruyff on the ball playing for Holland. He was an exceptionally gifted player, blessed with breath-taking ball control and superb balance. Cruyff was the first Dutch player to be voted European Footballer of the Year. His association with Ajax Amsterdam, his first team, is well rooted. He was born near the ground and his mother worked there as a cleaner. His soccer talents were spotted at the age of 10 and he worked his way up through the youth system.

His later career with Barcelona has been cemented by the presence of his son in the Spanish side.

with breathtaking ball control, deadly acceleration and superb balance, would have flourished in any era. As it is, he was fortunate that his peak coincided with that of Dutch football, both at club and national team level, thus providing him with an international arena in which to display and perfect his talent. The success of Cruyff, and that of Ajax, Holland and indeed Feyenoord, are, however, inextricably linked and the debt is a reciprocal one. He was surrounded by gifted players such as Neeskens, Krol and Rep, whose football intelligence was the key to the 'total football' practised in 1970s Holland – a

tactical system so suited to Cruyff's versatility. His awareness of colleagues' positions, his vision and ability to hit accurate passes (much in evidence later in his career when he dropped deeper and wider) could unsettle even the best defences; to this must be added his prowess in front of goal (33 goals in 48 internationals, 215 League goals in Holland).

At times the questionable temperament of the tall, lean Dutchman threatened to undermine his ability, but he was able to command respect as a captain. His travels took him to North America, Spain and back to Holland where he played for old rivals Feyenoord before proving his talent spectacularly in management.

CRYSTAL PALACE

Founded 1905

Joined League 1920 (Division 3)

Honours Division 1 Champions 1994; Division 2 Champions 1979; Division 3 (S) Champions 1921

Ground Selhurst Park

After a largely unremarkable history, Crystal Palace experienced a highly eventful

Substitute Ian Wright slides in to score his second goal for Crystal Palace in the 1990 FA Cup Final, to put his side 3-2 up. However, the score at the end of extra time was 3-3. Manchester United went on to win the replay 1-0 despite Wright's pre-match prediction that he was both going to score and be on the Cup-winner's side. This was Crystal Palace's only FA Cup Final appearance to date. Ian Wright was transferred to Arsenal in 1991 and has since been picked to play for England on a number of occasions.

first half of the 1990s. The surge which took them to the FA Cup Final in 1990 – they lost to Manchester United after a replay – was followed by third place in the top division in the subsequent campaign. Relegation followed, together with the resignation of long-serving boss Steve Coppell in 1993. Under new manager Alan Smith came promotion back to the top flight, then instant demotion. It was Smith's turn to go, replaced by new supremo, Coppell!

Palace made an auspicious start to their League life, topping the newly created Third Division in their first term. But they soon returned to the lowest level, there to remain until they won promotion from the Fourth Division in 1961 under the guidance of former Tottenham boss Arthur Rowe. The 1960s proved prosperous for the 'Eagles', as first Dick Graham and then Bert Head carried on Rowe's good work. In 1969 they tasted top-flight soccer for the first time, before plunging back to Division 3 with Malcolm Allison in the mid 1970s. Terry Venables effected a revival, taking the club back to the First Division, but most of the 1980s were spent in the Second before Coppell extricated them in 1989.

Star names have been few down the years, but players of note have included 1930s goal-poacher Peter Simpson, skilful centre-forward Johnny Byrne, who won an England cap as a Division 3 player in 1961, England left-back Kenny Sansom in the 1970s, and striker Ian Wright, who joined Arsenal in 1991. It was the sale of Wright and his striking partner Mark Bright, however, that appeared to signal the limits of the club's ambitions. But come 1995, Smith having been sacked, there seemed to be challenging times ahead for this less fashionable London outfit. Good cup performances, were counter-balanced by poor league form, and exciting, highly-prized young players were watched by relatively meagre crowds. The return of Steve Coppell as 'Director of Football' may bring interesting results.

CULLIS, Stan

1915 Born in Ellesmere Port, Cheshire

1934 Makes debut for Wolverhampton Wanderers

1938 Wins first of 12 England caps v Scotland

1939 Losing FA Cup finalist, 1-4 v Portsmouth

1947 Appointed Wolves assistant manager

1948 Elevated to secretary-manager

1949 Leads Wolves to FA Cup win, 3-1 v Leicester City

1954 Wins Championship, Wolves' first ...

1958 ... again

1959 ... and again

1960 Second FA Cup victory, 3-0 v Blackburn Rovers

1964 Leaves Wolves

1965 Appointed manager of Birmingham City

1970 Leaves Birmingham

Although he was relatively short – 5ft 10in – Stan Cullis was one of the finest centre-halves England has produced. An aggressive though stylish player with an ability to deliver piercing through-balls, he won 12 caps and would have collected many more but for the Second World War.

The manager of Wolverhampton Wanderers, Stan Cullis, holds the League Championship trophy after the 1953/54 season. Billy Wright is second from the left. Cullis gave so much to Wolves both as a player and as a manager. Under his autocratic leadership, the club went on to win the League title again in 1958 and in 1959. They also won the FA Cup twice, in 1949 and 1960. Their style of play under Cullis was described as 'kick and rush', but it was obviously effective.

It was as manager of Wolverhampton Wanderers, however, that he left his most indelible mark. A sergeant-major of a man, he was an autocrat whose confidence was absolute and whose criticism, it was suggested, could strip paint from 20 paces. He believed in the most direct route to goal, insisting that the ball should be hoisted into the opposition penalty area as swiftly as possible and kept there. Individual expression was frowned upon. 'Our forwards,' he said, 'are not encouraged to parade their ability in an ostentatious fashion.'

The tactics were condemned as 'kick and rush', although no one could argue with their effectiveness. Wolves had their most prosperous times under Cullis, winning the First Division Championship three times in the 1950s, a record matched only by Matt Busby and Manchester United.

Cullis, like Busby, had the foresight to look beyond Britain's boundaries and it was he who brought Moscow Dynamo and Honved, two of Europe's best sides, to Molineux for famous floodlit matches in 1954. After beating both, he claimed Wolves were the 'champions of the world'. It was a remark that threw down the gauntlet to the Continent, anticipating shrewdly the creation of the European Cup.

CUP COMPETITIONS

Cliches abound at the mere mention of knock-out cup football. A 'one-off' with 'eleven men against eleven men' ensures that the 'magic of the cup' is what, after all, 'football is all about'. It probably is this natural sense of familiarity with cup football that makes it so popular. So popular, indeed, that numerous tournaments have been proposed and competed for over the years in a bid to kindle that so-called 'magic'.

In addition to thousands of local competitions that exist up and down Britain, the professional game has not been slow in trying to introduce new, largely sponsored, tournaments to win a bit of interest and a bit of cash. In recent years the main intention seems to have been to include teams who are otherwise disenfranchised by, for example, playing in the wrong division, being

banned from Europe or generally not being good enough for the senior competitions.

The Watney Mann Invitation Cup (1970-73) was one of the first and is noted for its early use of penalties to decide finals. The Texaco Cup, followed by the Anglo-Scottish Cup, were apparently well-intentioned attempts to bring English and Scottish teams into competition – but they faded away with poor gates and almost no national reporting.

The late eighties saw a handful of tournaments

trying to bring the top English clubs, banned from Europe, into meaningful competition, and to give lesser clubs a contrived opportunity for a place at Wembley. But examples like the Screensport Super Cup for would-be European representatives (dead after one season) and the Autoglass Trophy (for Third and Fourth Division teams) never really captured the imagination. By 1995 doubts were sounded too about the future of the Anglo-Italian Cup when a tiny Wembley crowd witnessed Notts County's Final success.

The modern plethora of tournaments in addition to the big three of League, FA Cup and League Cup is viewed by some as being to the detriment of football. However, who would deny clubs from the lower divisions their moments of glory? Here, Brian Gayle celebrates Birmingham City winning the Leyland Daf Final in 1991. Gayle scored the winning goal in his side's 3-2 win over Tranmere Rovers. In 1995 Wembley was full once more for Birmingham's 1-0 sudden death victory over Carlisle.

D

DALGLISH, Kenny

1951 Born in Glasgow

1970 Makes debut for Celtic

1972 Plays leading role as Celtic win League and Cup double

1977 Joins Liverpool for a record £440,000, having helped the Scottish club lift a further seven major domestic trophies

1978 Scores only goal of European Cup Final against FC Bruges

1979 Footballer of the Year after performing brilliantly as Liverpool lift the first of five League Championships in six seasons

1981 Pockets the first of four consecutive League Cup winner's medals

1983 Footballer of the Year and players' Player of the Year

1984 Takes home his third European Cup winner's medal after 'Reds' beat Roma

1985 Succeeds Joe Fagan as Liverpool boss, continues as player

1986 Leads club to League and FA Cup double and is named Manager of the Year; November – completes international career with 102nd cap, v Luxembourg at Hampden Park

1989 Liverpool win FA Cup in aftermath of Hillsborough disaster

1990 Third League title and Manager of the Year award in five campaigns in charge at Anfield; final senior appearance as player

1991 February – stuns football world, and Liverpool in particular, by announcing 'retirement' with three months of season to go; October – takes over as Blackburn boss, with benefactor Jack Walker's

millions to spend

1992 Rovers reach the new Premier League via the promotion play-offs

1994 Blackburn mount a thrilling Premiership title challenge, eventually finishing as runners-up to Manchester United.

1995 Dalglish leads Blackburn to the Premiership title, with victory secured, at Anfield, on the last day of the season.

Throughout more than a century of British soccer, no man has assembled a catalogue of achievements to rival that of Kenny Dalglish. There may have been finer players – although not many – but none of them could point to a managerial record which remotely approaches the lustre of the single-minded Glaswegian's. The combination of two such honour-strewn careers puts Dalglish in a class of his own.

As a footballer he had shining natural talent, his game both aesthetically pleasing and exhilarating. After prodigious deeds with Celtic he headed for Anfield to fill the gap left by Kevin Keegan, and succeeded beyond even the Kop's wildest dreams. The goals flowed, and they were often spectacular, but they represented only the most superficial aspect of his value.

A favourite with the Liverpool Kop, Kenny Dalglish is seen here playing against Manchester United in the 1983 Milk (League) Cup Final, which Liverpool won 2-1 after extra time. Dalglish had the ability as a player to make goalscoring look quite simple. His darting runs, close skills and an ability to shield the ball were Dalglish's hallmarks as a player. In his first season as manager of Liverpool they achieved the League and FA Cup double. In 1991 he resigned, only to make his managerial comeback the next season with Blackburn Rovers.

His magnetic control, superb distribution and almost uncanny anticipation made him an all-rounder par excellence, though admittedly he did not always reproduce club form for his country .

As a manager Dalglish is very much his own man. After inheriting an excellent Liverpool side, he proceeded to improve it with inspired excursions into the transfer market, and deserves monumental credit for enhancing the Anfield tradition. A private, sometimes uncommunicative individual, he has the shrewdness, steel and flair to continue his phenomenal success into the next century. If he does, though, it will not be with the 'Reds', whom he left abruptly citing stress as his reason. Six months later he was back in the game as manager of Blackburn spending heavily and quickly establishing Rovers as one of the major powers in the domestic game.

DARLINGTON

Founded 1883

Joined League 1921 (Division 3 N)

Honours Division 3 (N) Champions 1925; Division 4 Champions 1991

Ground Feethams

It hardly seemed like a shot in the arm at the time, but Darlington's demotion from the Football League in 1989 might have been just what the 'Quakers' needed. As champions of the Vauxhall Conference, they returned from the wilderness at the first attempt and then lifted the Fourth Division crown in 1991. Though they rather ruined the effect by going straight back down in 1992, it was nice to win something, even if it wasn't a senior competition, after a history of struggle in the shadow of their more illustrious north-eastern neighbours. Apart

from two Second Division seasons in the 1920s, Darlington have spent all their time in the lower reaches, grappling with the economic difficulties which face all small clubs.

Highlights have been few, two of the brightest being in the FA Cup. In 1911, while still amateurs, they reached the last 16, and repeated the feat in 1958 thanks to a 4-1 thrashing of Chelsea in a replay at Feethams. During the 1980s the club's most positive spell came during the managerial era of the late Cyril Knowles, who inspired their promotion in 1985.

DEAN, Dixie

1907 Born in Birkenhead

1924 Makes debut for Tranmere Rovers

1925 Moves to Everton for £3000

1926 Fractures skull in motorcycle accident; makes rapid recovery

1927 Scores twice for England on international debut v Wales

1928 Breaks League scoring record with 60 goals in season as Everton win title

1932 Helps Everton to another Championship

1936 Passes Steve Bloomer's League record of 352 goals

1938 Joins Notts County

1939 Ends English career, having scored 379 goals in 437 games, and signs for Sligo Rovers

1940 Retires to keep a pub in Chester

1980 Dies at Goodison Park

William Ralph Dean – how he hated the nickname Dixie, preferring the more ordinary Bill – was a goalscorer supreme whose memory will be revered, especially on Merseyside, as long as football is played.

He began his career as a teenage prodigy with

Tranmere Rovers, but such was his talent that an early departure from Prenton Park was inevitable.

He duly crossed the river to Goodison and rapidly established a well-nigh peerless reputation.

Tall and immensely powerful, Dean was majestic in the air and became Everton's main attraction during one of their most successful periods. Dean's golden season was 1927/28, when he notched his record-breaking 60 goals, sealing the achievement – which is unlikely to be emulated – with a hat-trick in the final game against Arsenal.

The Everton star was also a lethal performer for England, scoring 18 times in a mere 16 games, and it's a mystery that he was not selected more often.

On retirement he kept a pub in Chester, and later became a popular after-dinner speaker.

William Ralph Dean – Dixie – was a prolific goalscorer: 349 goals for Everton from 1925 to 1937. He once scored 60 in a season – the all-time League record which looks likely to stand for ever and a day. His goalscoring continued on the international scene – netting 18 times in 16 games for England. He was also a good friend to football – ever willing to give advice to youngsters and to shake hands with people who wanted to meet the great Dixie Dean. And 'great' he was, with his achievements forming a yardstick for goalscorers to this day.

It was somehow fitting that he should die at the home of his beloved Everton, shortly after watching a derby clash with Liverpool.

DERBY COUNTY

Founded 1884

Joined League 1888 (founder member)

Honours Division 1 Champions 1972, 1975; Division 2 Champions 1912, 1915, 1969, 1987; Division 3 (N) Champions 1957; FA Cup Winners 1946

Ground Baseball Ground

From the early days, Derby County's history has been dramatic. Although the club were founder members of the Football League, early achievements were in the FA Cup, with eight semi-finals in 13 seasons (1895-1909). They reached three finals during this period but all were lost, including the record 6-0 defeat by Bury in 1903.

George Jobey, manager from 1925 to 1941, assembled internationals such as Sammy Crooks, Jack Barker, Tom Cooper, Jack Bowers, Hughie Gallacher and 'Dally' Duncan, but second place (twice) was the best League position in the inter-war years. The momentum was broken by the Second World War and FA suspensions after the discovery of illegal payments.

On a wave of euphoria Derby County won the first post-war FA Cup Final, beating Charlton 4-1 after extra-time. The stars were inside-forwards Raich Carter and Peter Doherty, while centre-forward Jack Stamps scored two goals in the Final. Derby were one of the country's top teams in the late 1940s, paying record transfer fees for Billy Steel and Johnny Morris, but a slump in the early 1950s saw them drop from Division 1 to Division 3 (N) in three seasons.

Derby returned to the First Division in 1969 under the management of Brian Clough and Peter Taylor with new signings including Roy McFarland, Dave Mackay, John McGovern, John O'Hare, Alan Hinton and Willie Carlin. Three more important signings – Colin

Archie Gemmill hitting a long cross-field pass during the 1974/75 season when Derby County became League Champions under the managership of Dave Mackay. With players like Gemmill, Colin Todd, Alan Hinton and Francis Lee, the Derby County sides of the 1970s were attractive to watch. Gemmill is now manager at Rotherham, passing on his experience and expertise to a crop of young players.

Todd, Terry Hennessey and Archie Gemmill – finally brought the League Championship. Three years later, under new manager Dave Mackay, there was a second Championship success. Colin Boulton, Ron Webster, David Nish, Peter Daniel and Henry Newton all made important contributions, and goals came from Bruce Rioch, Roger Davies, Francis Lee and, inevitably, Kevin Hector, who made a record 581 appearances (201 goals) for the club.

The club's low point came in the centenary season (1984), when relegation to Division 3 coincided with a winding-up petition from the Inland Revenue and seven High Court appearances. A rescue package, involving the Maxwell family headed by publisher Robert Maxwell, preceded success in the late 1980s, when manager Arthur Cox achieved two promotions and signed internationals such as Englishmen Peter Shilton and Mark Wright and Welshman Dean Saunders. However, 1991 found them ten points adrift at the foot of Division 1, the stars departed and Cox faced the challenge of reviving the club all over again. With the Maxwells no longer involved, new owner Lionel Pickering having cash to spend, and a move to a new purpose-built stadium in the offing, the indications were that he could bring success back to Derby County. But neither Cox nor his successor, Roy McFarland, was to find the task as easy as many pundits and fans had predicted.

McFarland was, in fact, axed at the end of the 1994/95 season when a home defeat by Southend denied chances of a play-off. Derby were left to watch how the big money at Blackburn had been spent very differently to that at the Baseball Ground.

DERBY MATCHES

Such was the importance of one particular horse-race – the Derby Stakes at Epsom – that the name 'derby' came to be applied to any sporting contest of equal note. A derby game is often one of the most important of the year, and games between teams from the same city (local derbies) are the most hotly contested of all. There is always extra tension, because rival supporters are likely to meet in the days surrounding the match.

The Glasgow games between Celtic and Rangers are legendary. The two teams have met in 24 major finals (11 Scottish League Cup and 13 Scottish Cup) including the 1909 Scottish Cup Final, when the trophy was withheld after two drawn games and crowd trouble. A 1905 League game was also abandoned, and more recently there was a riot on the pitch after the 1980 Scottish Cup Final. Extra tension emanates from the religious backcloth to these games, Celtic being associated with the Catholic faith and Rangers having been reluctant to sign Catholic players until the late 1980s.

Everton-Liverpool league games have been frequent since 1962, when Liverpool returned to Division 1. In the late 1980s Liverpool passed Everton in number of wins, and big Cup games have definitely favoured the Reds, who won all three post-war FA Cup semi-finals (but lost in 1906). The most controversial was in 1977, when Bryan Hamilton appeared to have scored an Everton winner in the last minute of the drawn first match, only to see it disallowed. Surprisingly, the first Everton-Liverpool League Cup meeting was as late as 1984, when a goalless Milk Cup Final ended with the crowd chanting 'Merseyside, Merseyside ...' Liverpool won the replay 1-0. In the late 1980s they met in two FA Cup Finals; Liverpool won 3-1 in 1986 and 3-2 in 1989, and Ian Rush scored twice in each final.

Results in Manchester derbies (City v United) are tipped slightly in favour of United. There have been almost as many away wins as home wins. The Manchester clubs haven't emulated the

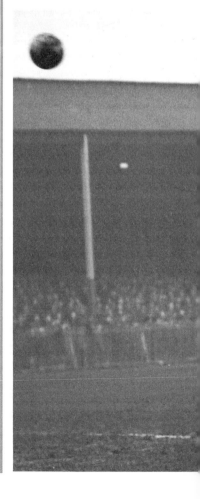

Merseyside Wembley achievements, but they have met in the semi-final of both the FA Cup and the League Cup. City beat United in the 1926 FA Cup semi-final, and won a thrilling League Cup semi-final in 1970, a late goal by Mike Summerbee taking the final aggregate score to 4-3. United won the only Charity Shield meeting, in 1956. Perhaps the most dramatic game was the last but one of the 1973/74 season, when the only goal was scored by City's Denis Law, ironically an ex-United player. Although the crowd invaded the pitch and the game was abandoned, the 1-0 result stood and United were relegated to Division 2. Big goalscorers in Manchester derby games include Joe Hayes and Francis Lee (10 each for City), Bobby Charlton (9 for United), Colin Bell (8 for City), Brian Kidd (5 for United and 3 for City) and Eric Cantona (6 for United in only four starts).

Another evenly balanced fixture is the north London derby between Arsenal and Tottenham Hotspur. The last League game of 1970/71, at White Hart Lane, ranks highly, a late goal by Arsenal's Ray Kennedy ensuring that the League Championship and FA Cup double was achieved. The two sides met twice in three seasons in the FA Cup semi-finals (1991 and 1993) with one victory apiece.

The north-east has had its fair share of exciting derby matches, none more staggering than Sunderland's 9-1 win at Newcastle United in 1908 in which Sunderland scored eight second-half goals in less than 30 minutes. The 1989/90 season ended with Sunderland (sixth) winning a vital promotion play-off game 2-0 at Newcastle (third) after the first leg was drawn.

Aston Villa have slightly the better record in games against Birmingham City, and Sheffield United have the edge on Sheffield Wednesday, despite the latter having won their FA Cup semi-final at Wembley in 1993. Derby matches between Bristol Rovers and Bristol City achieved new significance in 1989/90 when the clubs finished first and second in Division 3, but by that time Rovers had moved to Bath.

In 1987/88 the Football League included four Welsh clubs and all four were in Division 4, although Wrexham were some distance from the others. For Bradford City and Bradford Park Avenue the record is now complete, Park Avenue showing one more League win than City. And for Nottingham Forest and Notts County, rivalry was resurrected when County were promoted to Division 1 in 1991. Neil Warnock's club went straight back down, but Forest joined them for a further season in 1993/94.

The first 38 Wembley FA Cup Finals failed to produce an all-London local derby, but the next 16 finals compensated with four such occasions. Tottenham Hotspur were involved as Cup-winners in 1967 (against Chelsea) and 1982 (against Queen's Park Rangers), and West Ham United beat Fulham (1975) and Arsenal (1980).

The concept of a local derby could be applied to the international arena. A Scotland fan's description of England as the 'auld enemy' highlights a fierce rivalry of neighbours which spills over into political history. A more obvious example of political rivalry was that of Germany when the Berlin Wall divided East from West, and the game between East Germany and West Germany in the 1974 World Cup finals was a unique occasion. Vital World Cup qualifying games between Holland and Belgium have added something extra to games between these bordering countries. In other areas of the world, rivalry has at times been so belligerent that countries have been deliberately kept apart in World Cup draws.

There are so many club rivalries outside the British Isles that it is impossible to begin to compile a comprehensive list. In the Italian League four pairs of old rivals now share grounds – AC Milan and Inter (Milan), Juventus and Torino (Turin), Roma and Lazio (Rome), and Genoa and Sampdoria (Genoa). In other countries, inter-city rivalry has a national profile to compare with that of Rangers and Celtic. Examples that spring to mind are Barcelona and Real Madrid in Spain, and Feyenoord and Ajax in Holland.

DISASTERS

The biggest soccer disaster in the world may have been the crush in the Lenin Stadium in Luzhniki Park, Moscow, on 20 October 1982, at the end of a UEFA Cup second-round first-leg match between Spartak Moscow and Haarlem of Holland. Some post-glasnost accounts estimate that 340 people were killed, although the official Soviet figure put the number at 69. The exact number may be impossible to determine. When spectators streamed towards the exits in one part of the ground they found all but one door closed, and the situation was aggravated by a last-minute Spartak goal and the icy conditions.

Excluding the Moscow crush, the biggest soccer disaster was that at Lima, Peru, on 24 May 1964, a few minutes before the end of a Peru-Argentina Olympic qualifying tie. The referee disallowed a Peruvian goal, a riot broke out, police stepped

Derby matches between Sheffield Wednesday and Sheffield United often seem to involve matters of relegation and promotion; between them, the two clubs have enjoyed more than their fair share of ups and downs. In February 1955 United went to Hillsborough and won 2-1, Jack Cross (right of photo, attended by Wednesday's centre-forward Don Watson) scoring one of the goals. The season saw Wednesday relegated from the First Division, conceding 100 goals in the process.

in with tear-gas and 301 were killed and 500 injured in a rush for the exits.

Britain's worst football disaster occurred at the Hillsborough Stadium, Sheffield, on 15 April 1989, when 95 people were killed and 170 injured. The tragedy happened at the start of the FA Cup semi-final between Liverpool and Nottingham Forest, when a gate was opened to admit Liverpool supporters into the overcrowded Leppings Lane enclosure and spectators at the front of the stand were crushed or suffocated. South Yorkshire police were heavily criticised in the resultant enquiry, but the decisions to stage the game at Hillsborough and to allocate the smaller Leppings Lane end to Liverpool supporters were also considered culpable (see Taylor Report).

Sixty-six people were killed and over 140 injured at Ibrox Park, Glasgow, on 2 January 1971. The occasion was a Rangers-Celtic Scottish League derby, and at the end of the match, as the huge crowd poured off the terraces at the Rangers end, a fatal crush developed on Stairway 13. Eventually, the Safety of Sports Grounds Act (1975) was introduced as a result of the enquiry into the 1971 Ibrox disaster.

Similarly tragic, but with no criminal overtones, was the Burnden Park disaster of March 1946, when 33 lives were lost at an FA Cup tie between Bolton Wanderers and Stoke City. Barriers collapsed under pressure from a huge crowd and the victims were crushed.

On the last day of the 1984/85 season, a stand burned down in five minutes at Bradford City's Valley Parade ground. Fifty-five people were killed and 210 injured, either by the fire or the crush to get out. The fire started after 40 minutes of the game between Bradford City and Lincoln City, when a crowd of 12,000 were present to celebrate Bradford winning the Division 3 Championship. An enquiry by Mr Justice Popplewell investigated the Bradford City fire and a riot at Birmingham City's ground

This is the memorial at Liverpool's Anfield ground after the 1989 Hillsborough disaster when many supporters tragically died through being crushed against protective fencing. The FA Cup semi-final against Nottingham Forest was abandoned after 6 minutes; Liverpool won the replayed game 3-1, and then beat Everton 3-2 in the final. The Kop terrace was a mass of scarves and banners, and the Liverpool pitch was covered with floral tributes as thousands of fans paid their respects. One response to the Hillsborough disaster was the removal of perimeter fencing from around League grounds.

the same day (11 May 1985). Popplewell recommended numerous safety measures and membership cards for supporters. He found that the Bradford fire was caused by the accidental lighting of debris below the floorboards of the stand.

On 29 May 1985, less than three weeks after the Bradford fire, 38 people died and 454 were injured in a crush inside the Heysel Stadium in Brussels, Belgium. Forty minutes before the start of the European Cup Final between Juventus and Liverpool, fans of the English side broke down a flimsy fence that was holding them in their overcrowded section of the ground. They overpowered the Belgian police and charged at spectators in a supposedly neutral area. A wall collapsed and people were suffocated or crushed. All but seven of the dead were Italian. FIFA reacted by banning English clubs from European competition indefinitely. The ban was lifted in 1990 for all English clubs except Liverpool. In 1989, 14 Liverpool fans were given prison sentences in a Belgian court for their part in the Heysel Stadium disaster.

On 14 May 1949 a plane carrying the Torino club back from a game in Lisbon crashed into a hillside at

Superga, near Turin. Among the 28 dead were 17 players – including eight internationals – and the Italian club's manager, trainer and coach. Torino's youth team completed the season, and opponents sportingly fielded youth teams too. Torino's youths won all four games to complete four successive Italian League Championships.

In February 1958 the aircraft bringing the Manchester United party home from a European Cup tie against Red Star (Belgrade) crashed on take-off at Munich airport. Eight players – Geoff Bent, Roger Byrne, Eddie Colman, Duncan Edwards, Mark Jones, David Pegg, Tommy Taylor and Bill Whelan – died as a result of the crash. Eight journalists, including ex-England goalkeeper Frank Swift, and seven others were also killed. The 20 survivors included seriously injured manager Matt Busby and

two players, Jackie Blanchflower and John Berry, who never played again. Two books deal specifically with the Munich disaster: The Day a Team Died written by Frank Taylor, a journalist who survived the crash, and The Team that Wouldn't Die by John Roberts.

At least five other major air disasters have involved football teams: in 1961 eight players from Green Cross (Chile) were killed on Las Lastimas mountain; in 1969 19 players and officials of The Strongest (Bolivia) were killed in the Andes; in 1979 Pakhtator Tashkent (Soviet Union) lost 17 in an internal flight; on 9 December 1987 Alianza Lima (Peru) lost all 34 players, officials, wives and supporters on board; and on 28 April 1993, 30 people, including all but four of the Zambian nation squad, were killed when their plane crashed into the sea on the way to play in a World Cup match.

Seventy-four people were killed in a disaster at the River Plate Stadium, Buenos Aires, Argentina, on 23 June 1968. The crowd stampeded for the exits after lighted newspaper torches were thrown by spectators.

Seventy-one spectators died in Katmandu in 1988, when a hailstorm caused crowd panic during a game between teams from Nepal and Bangladesh.

The scenes of the two worst British disasters, Hillsborough and Ibrox Park, figured in other tragic incidents earlier this century. At Hillsborough, on 4 February 1914, a Cup replay between Sheffield Wednesday and Wolves was halted for 20 minutes after a retaining wall collapsed and 75 people were injured. The Wolves goalkeeper was unable to resume after fainting in the dressing room at the sight of the injured. And at Ibrox Park, on 5 April 1902, 26 were killed and 587

later compensated for injuries when part of the West Stand collapsed during a Scotland–England international.

DI STEFANO, Alfredo

1926 Born in Buenos Aires

1944 Makes debut for River Plate

1947 Joins Milionarios in Colombia

1953 Transferred to Real Madrid

1956 Wins European Cup 4-3 v Reims ...

1957 ... and again, 2-0 v Fiorentina; awarded first of 31 Spanish caps; European Footballer of the Year

1958 Completes European hat-trick, 3-2 v AC Milan

1959 Fourth European Cup, 2-0 v Reims; European Footballer of the Year

1960 Scores hat-trick as Real win fifth European Cup, 7-3 v Eintracht Frankfurt

1964 Free transfer to Español

1968 Becomes technical manager of Boca Juniors

1969 Promoted to manager

1970 Returns to Spain as manager of Valencia

1971 Valencia win Spanish Championship

1982 Appointed boss of Real Madrid

1983 Leaves Bernabeu

1990 Back again for a short spell as manager of Real

When Sir Matt Busby was asked which player he would most like to have signed for Manchester United, his reply was instant: Alfredo Di Stefano. Given that his career coincided with Pele's, it underlines Di Stefano's stature. He is arguably the best post-war player and possibly the greatest of all time.

Di Stefano, a deep-lying centre-forward, played with an intensity that Busby described as 'win at all times'. Stocky and strong, his

phenomenal stamina, cultivated by running in the streets of his native Buenos Aires, enabled him to play flat-out for 90 minutes – a quality that was beyond even the genius of Pele. He had the body and the brain to allow the game to flow through him.

Strategy rather than individual virtuosity preoccupied him. Di Stefano rarely sought to beat someone – although it was well within his powers – but he held the ball, waiting, watching for the right moment to release it. Consequently his greatest partnerships were with Puskas and Gento, both brilliant runners off the ball, rather than with fellow tacticians such as Didi and Kopa, who both had spells at Real in Di Stefano's time.

The fact that the man brandishing the field marshal's baton was also one of Real's most potent weapons was a wonderful bonus. In 59 European club matches he scored 49 goals, including one in each of the first four European Cup Finals and a hat-trick in the fifth, against Eintracht Frankfurt at Hampden in 1960. In 11 seasons in the Spanish League he found the net 219 times, while he also scored on 26 occasions at international level for Argentina and Spain.

When, at the age of 38, Di Stefano was given a free transfer, only one player could fill the gap. Real offered Santos £350,000 for Pele (at the time the British record was the £115,000 Busby paid for Denis Law) but it was declined. So, almost inevitably, did Real. Di Stefano's relationship with Real continued into the 1980s and 1990s as he had two spells of management with the club with which his name will always be linked.

DOCHERTY, Tommy

1928 Born in Glasgow

1948 Signs for Celtic

1949 Transfers to Preston North End (£4000)

1958 Joins Arsenal for £28,000

1961 Joins Chelsea (as player-coach, later manager)

1967 Goes to Rotherham United as manager

1968 Brief spell as manager of Queen's Park Rangers; appointed Aston Villa manager

1970 Becomes FC Porto manager

1971 Hull City assistant manager; manages Scotland (only three defeats in 12 games)

1972 Takes over at Manchester United

1977 Manages FA Cup-winning team; sacked at Manchester United; takes over at Derby County

1979 Queen's Park Rangers manager again

1980 Sydney Olympic (Australia) manager

1981 Returns to become Preston North End manager

1982 South Melbourne (Australia) manager

1984 Wolves manager

1987 Altrincham manager

As a player Tommy Docherty won an FA Cup runners-up medal with Preston North End in 1954 and 25 Scotland caps (eight as captain). He managed FA Cup Final teams at Chelsea (1967) and Manchester United (1976 and 1977) after taking each club into the First Division. On the other hand, there were problems – relegation at Rotherham, the sack at Aston Villa during a relegation season, and further relegation at Manchester United.

Docherty represented a new wave of management: controversial, outspoken, quotable, impulsive and occasionally wayward. He was always 'news', whether he was sending home eight Chelsea players for disciplinary reasons, trading players by the handful and being probed by the police at Derby County, being sacked

A controversial and outspoken character with a sharp wit, Tommy Docherty has experienced the highs and the lows as a player and as a manager. Here he is as Altrincham manager. No matter what his critics said – and they said quite a lot – nobody could doubt Docherty's devotion to the game of football. His experience helped a lot of players, but he may be remembered for off-the-field performances as much as those on the park.

twice by Queen's Park Rangers, being cleared of perjury offences, or simply entertaining with comments like 'I've had more clubs than Jack Nicklaus.'

DONCASTER ROVERS

Founded 1879

Joined League 1901 (Division 2)

Honours Division 3 (N) Champions 1935, 1947, 1950; Division 4 Champions 1966, 1969

Ground Belle Vue

Despite languishing in the League's lower reaches throughout most of their history, Doncaster Rovers can point to one enterprising period. In the 1950s, under the guidance of former Northern Ireland forward Peter Doherty, Rovers won promotion to Division 2 and remained there for eight campaigns.

During that glorious decade they reached the fifth round of the FA Cup four times and unearthed two top-class players. Harry Gregg was sold to Manchester United for £23,500, then a world record for a goalkeeper. Inside-forward Alick Jeffrey was not so fortunate; he seemed a certainty for stardom when injury wrecked his career.

Doncaster's earlier League experiences were more prosaic. Twice in their first four years they failed to win re-election, rejoining as members of Division 3(N) in 1923. Occasional promotions followed but success was never sustained until the Doherty days. Subsequently the club moved regularly between Divisions 3 and 4, employing such managers as Lawrie McMenemy, Dave Mackay and Billy Bremner without ever looking likely to acquire the stature of their Yorkshire rivals in Leeds and Sheffield.

DUMBARTON

Founded 1872

Joined League 1890 (Division 1, founder member)

Honours Scottish League Division 1 Champions 1891 (shared with Rangers), 1892; Division 2 Champions 1911, 1972; Second Division Champions 1992; Scottish Cup Winners 1883

Ground Boghead Park

For a spell in its early history Scottish football was dominated by Dumbarton clubs. Vale of Leven and Renton no longer exist at senior level, but Dumbarton survive as a reminder of that era.

Although soon eclipsed by the big-city clubs, Dumbarton have proved durable. When their existence was threatened in the early 1950s, local support swelled. Recent internationalists Graeme Sharp and Murdo MacLeod began their careers at Boghead. Their Division 2 title triumph in 1992 was a welcome if short-lived echo of earlier triumphs.

DUNDEE

Founded 1893

Joined League 1893 (Division 1)

Honours Scottish League Division 1 Champions 1962; First Division Champions 1979, 1992; Division 2 Champions 1947; Scottish Cup Winners 1910; Scottish League Cup Winners 1951/52, 1952/53, 1973/74

Ground Dens Park

Dundee, encouraged by their First Division Championship triumph of 1992, are out to remove the impression of a club burdened by memories of a more exalted history. The recollection of great achievements rendered recent years of mediocrity especially unpalatable, and the fact that neighbours Dundee United have prospered has hardly helped.

Dundee won the Scottish Cup in 1910 after a final which stretched to three matches, but were at their greatest in the years following the Second World War. Their devious signing of Billy Street from Derby, for £17,500, was quickly rewarded when he helped them win the 1951/52 League Cup and retain it the following season.

Their finest ever side, including names like Alan Gilzean, Ian Ure and Alex Hamilton, took them to the Championship in 1962. Dundee then went on to reach the semi-finals of the European Cup but soon lost players such as Gilzean and, a little later, Charlie Cooke to richer clubs.

Victory in the League Cup in 1973/74 did little to reverse a generally depressing trend. Indeed, since then the club has not always retained top-flight status, and promotion to the Premier Division in 1992 was followed by relegation in 1994.

Dundee United's four Scottish Cup Final appearances (all losing) and one League title in the 1980s, with Aberdeen doing well at the same time, seemed part of the shift of power away from the big Glasgow clubs. Paul Sturrock was one of The Terrors' top players at that time, winning 20 Scottish caps during the decade. He is now manager at St Johnstone, having previously had a spell in charge at Tannadice.

The rise of Dundee United demonstrates the extraordinary effect one individual can have in football. Under Jim McLean they progressed from being the second club in the city to being, at times, in the forefront of European football.

Some of the Continent's wealthiest clubs fell to them as they reached the European Cup semi-finals in 1984 and the UEFA Cup Final in 1987. McLean may have been a difficult and demanding manager, but his nurturing of young talent was unsurpassed. He resigned and became chairman in 1993.

Year after year knowledgeable footballers with sound technique emerged at Tannadice. Perhaps the finest examples were Richard Gough, David Narey and Maurice Malpas, all members of the side which won the League in 1983. The club has not always won the trophies it deserved and 1991 saw their sixth defeat in a Scottish Cup Final, yet in the first year of the reign of Yugoslav manager Ivan Golac, destined to depart after relegation in 1995, they enjoyed a storming victory over Rangers in the 1994 final.

Dunfermline vied with Kilmarnock for the position of Scotland's most successful provincial club in the 1960s. Their Scottish Cup Final victories over Celtic and Hearts, the first achieved under the management of Jock Stein, may be the substance of their achievements, but there were other glittering displays as well.

There was an aptitude for Europe especially. Everton were beaten in the 1962/63 Fairs Cup and Dunfermline saw off West Brom en route to the Cup Winners' Cup semi-finals in 1968/69. In the early part of the decade Charlie Dickson was a regular scorer of vital goals. Much of the flair flowed from winger Alex Edwards who was in the side soon after his 16th birthday.

Dunfermline's slump in the 1970s and 1980s took them as low as the Second Division. Since then they have regained their place among the elite, only to lose it again as bottom club in 1992.

EAST FIFE

Founded 1903

Joined League 1921
(Division 2)

Honours Scottish League
Division 2 Champions 1948;
Scottish Cup Winners 1938;
League Cup Winners
1947/48, 1949/50, 1953/54

Ground Bayview Park

East Fife are the only Division
2 team ever to win the Scottish
Cup. Their hastily assembled
side (two of whom had been
acquired on loan) triumphed
over Kilmarnock in 1938.

Their Cup achievements
after the Second World War
were also extraordinary, with
three triumphs in the League
Cup. The half-back line of
Philp, Findlay and Aitken was
daunting. Centre-forward
Henry Morris scored three for
Scotland on his 1949 debut
against Northern Ireland but
was never capped again.

EAST STIRLINGSHIRE

Founded 1881

Joined League 1900
(Division 2)

Honours Scottish League
Division 2 Champions 1932

Ground Firs Park

East Stirlingshire were the
subject of Scottish football's
most celebrated court case. In
1964, amid furious protests,
the Steedman family moved
the club to Clydebank and
amalgamated it with the
Junior club there to form E.S.
Clydebank.

The new club competed in
Division 2 throughout the
1964/65 season before the
Court of Session ruled that a
share transfer of the
Steedmans was invalid. East
Stirlingshire recovered their
autonomy and returned to
Falkirk. Sadly, the townspeople
have otherwise failed to take
much interest in them.

EDWARDS, Duncan

1936 Born in Dudley,
Worcestershire

1948 As an 11-year-old,
becomes regular member of
Dudley Boys, average age
15

1952 Joins Manchester
United as an amateur

1953 April – makes his
Division 1 debut as a 16-
year-old; October – turns
professional with United on
his 17th birthday

1955 At 18 years 183 days,
he is the fourth youngest
player to win a full England
cap – impressive debut in a
7-2 victory over Scotland at
Wembley

1956 Wins first of two
successive League
Championship medals

1958 Dies in a German
hospital two weeks after
sustaining multiple injuries
in the Munich air crash.

Bobby Charlton once said: 'If
I had to play for my life and
could take one man with me,
it would be Duncan
Edwards.' It was an eloquent
way of summing up the
worth of the multi-talented
young Midlander to
Manchester United and
England during his tragically
short career.

Edwards was a soccer
colossus, the sort of player
who surfaces once in a
lifetime. He had everything:
exemplary ball control and
passing skills, a titan's tackle,
awesome aerial and shooting

Duncan Edwards, in his
Manchester United shirt,
was already a regular
England international when
this picture was taken
during the 1956/57 season.
Edwards certainly shows the
classic build for a footballer.
Those who saw him play
talk of strength, skill, vision,
speed, stamina ...indeed,
there seemed to be no
shortcomings to his game.
What a shame that such a
talented player was lost to
football at such a young
age.

power, an ability to read the
game that was mature
beyond his years, and a level
head to ensure that all these
gifts were not squandered.

Throughout the mid
1950s Edwards was the
principal symbol of all that
was best about the 'Busby
Babes', as well as
representing his country's
brightest hope. There are
those who reckon that had
he not perished at Munich,
he would have been England
captain for a decade and that
Bobby Moore would never
have lifted the World Cup.
Certainly, as a 21-year-old
with 18 caps to his credit, he
appeared to have boundless
potential. Edwards played
most of his club games at left-
half but he was outstanding
in practically any position,
being a particularly lethal
emergency centre-forward,
and invested every aspect of
his play with a spirit that was
seemingly unquenchable.
Even when disaster struck at
Munich he did not give in

easily, fighting a two-week
battle for life in the face of
insurmountable odds. His
death left the football world
aching for what might have
been.

ENGLAND

In the beginning, English
football was a rough, unruly
folk game played in the
streets, rival villages defending
their territory. Vestiges of
these origins remain today in
rituals such as the annual
Shrove Tuesday game at
Ashbourne, Derbyshire. In
1863 the formation of the
Football Association and
formalisation of the first set of
standardised laws led to
football as an institution,
although disputes between
the London-based Football
Association and the Sheffield
Association lingered (see
Laws).

Writing in 1900 in The
Real Football, journalist
James Catton described the

diffusion of the game to the working class, a spread helped by the half-day Saturday holiday: 'Time was when football was the innocent diversion of the upper and middle classes who had no other thought than to pay for their own boots and clothes, take their own railway tickets, discharge their own hotel bills and entertain the teams which visited them. But the game was taken up by the mechanics, the artisans, the clerks, and thousands of others who depended upon weekly wages.'

Scottish stone-masons, encouraged by football clubs to work in England in the 1870s, complained that the stone was harder than in the north. Their hands swelled, they needed to rest, and their clubs took to supporting them financially. Other clubs then argued that they were 'professional'. In January 1884 Preston chairman William Sudell admitted that his players were paid. Preston were expelled from the FA Cup competition, and the debate stepped up. Threatened with the withdrawal of 'professional'

clubs into a new association, the FA agreed in July 1885 that 'it is expedient to legalise professionalism under stringent conditions'. Three years later the world's first professional league, the Football League, was formed, and professional clubs grew from various origins – churches (like Liverpool), chapels (like Aston Villa), schools (like Tottenham Hotspur), railway workers (like Manchester United) and cricket clubs (like Derby County).

A network of other leagues developed. By the early 1900s there were half a million or more players in leagues affiliated to the Football Association in England and Wales. Football became an easy game to arrange. It fitted in with factory life and needed little outlay on equipment; it offered players an outlet for their masculinity and physical prowess; and it emphasised teamwork and the competitive pursuit of victory. These values were particularly sought after in the post-war years. Such was the interest after the First World War that

the Football League was extended to include Division 3 (South) in 1920 and Division 3 (North) in 1921. Similarly, there was a boom in the late 1940s when English football peaked in its popularity. In 1947/48 Newcastle United averaged 56,299 spectators for home League games and 33,912 away ... and they were in the Second Division. The following season (1948/49) saw an aggregate attendance of 41,271,414 for Football League games – an all-time record.

Football's appeal was especially strong in the industrial regions of Lancashire, South Yorkshire, the Midlands and the North-East. In the 1930s Arsenal broke through the dominance of northern and Midlands clubs, and the economic decline of the north in the 1950s changed the geographical map of football. Southern towns like Luton, Oxford and Peterborough grew in both industry and football prestige, whereas Preston, Blackburn, Bolton and Huddersfield lost their First Division places.

Martin Peters (left edge of photograph) scores for England in the 1966 World Cup final at Wembley. This goal made the score 2-1 and looked, until the last moments of normal time, to have given England victory against their West German opponents. This goal would have been well remembered had it not been for Weber's dramatic equaliser and two goals – one of which was extremely controversial – by England's hat-trick hero Geoff Hurst in extra time. Importantly this victory lifted the game in England, bringing back crowds and drawing extra interest from many sections of society.

Lancastrian interest became concentrated on the big four – Liverpool, Everton, Manchester United and Manchester City.

Smaller clubs in the north were affected by a number of other problems. The restructuring of Division 3 (N) and Division 3 (S) into national Divisions 3 and 4 increased travel expenditure; the removal of the maximum wage in 1961 increased the gap between wages of top and bottom clubs; and the legal ruling in 1963 that clubs could not restrain the trading of players made it more difficult to hold on to good players.

The amateur game continued to develop dramatically, aided by the Football Association's recognition of Sunday football leagues in 1960.

The moment when it looked as if 1966 might be possible all over again. Gary Lineker steers the ball into the West German net for the equalising goal in the drawn (1-1) World Cup semi-final. Throughout the tournament England had been improving and scoring goals late into the match. As Lineker scored (with Illgner, in goal, and Kohler, watching) England fans could have been forgiven for optimism. Sadly a penalty shoot-out defeat followed.

Religious groups had opposed Sunday games, and only in 1955 had the FA permitted clubs or players under their jurisdiction to take part in Sunday football. In 1973/74 a coal-mining strike and the imposition of a shorter working week restricted floodlit games, so the professional game was forced to confront the Sunday football issue. Four FA Cup ties were played on Sunday 6 January 1974. Two weeks later came the first Sunday Football League games.

In 1966 English football received a tremendous fillip from the World Cup win. Playing interest increased, and the steady post-war decline in Football League attendances was reversed during the two seasons after 1966.

English football, however, underwent rapid change in the 1970s. Substitution rules affected players and managers, sponsorship interested directors, and television and hooliganism made their impact on supporters. English clubs broke through European barriers and at times took an

almost permanent hold on two major club trophies. The last four Inter-Cities Fairs Cup Finals (1968-1971) and three of the first five UEFA Cup Finals (1972-76) were won by English clubs. Then, seven out of eight European Cups between 1977 and 1984 went to England – four for Liverpool, two for Nottingham Forest and one for Aston Villa.

The European run literally ended in disaster. After the 1985 Heysel Stadium riot, English clubs were banned from Europe for an indefinite period, which turned out to be five years. The ban was not surprising. Hooliganism had become tagged as the 'English disease' after previous riots by Spurs fans in Holland (1974), Leeds United fans in Paris (1975), West Ham fans in Spain (1980) and England fans in Luxembourg (1977) and Italy (1980), just to mention a few.

Despite the adverse publicity following disasters at Valley Parade, Heysel and Hillsborough, aggregate Football League attendances rose for the last four seasons of the 1980s. But at the end

of the decade they were still less than half the record 1948/49 figure (and there had been an increase of 10 per cent in the number of games). English football will probably never regain the popularity it had in the late 1940s, but the nation is always willing to react to World Cup success like that achieved by Bobby Robson's team at Italia '90. Many professional clubs may be ailing economically – though Manchester United and other leading lights in the newly-formed FA Carling Premiership are doing very nicely, thank you – but the semi-professional game is healthy, and in the first half of the 1990s more people were playing soccer in England than ever before.

The really big issue in the game, by the mid-1990s, was money. Bigger transfer fees, sponsorship deals and television payouts all seemed to increase the gap between rich and poor. The national Lottery also hit many clubs and their 'scratch card' earnings. The game in England seemed poised for change – but when has that not been the case?

Since the days of Alf Ramsey the performance of England's national team manager has been closely scrutinised by the press. Rarely praised, but often pilloried, the manager's job is very hard. Manager Graham Taylor did not make life easy for himself, however. Apart from making several controversial team selections, he caused embarrassment and amusement by his behaviour during England's defeat against Holland in 1993, a match that killed off England's hopes of World Cup qualification. Taylor's comments and criticisms, many of which were aimed at the UEFA official standing next to him, were captured by a television documentary. Taylor gave way to Terry Venables in 1994 and he enjoyed a successful 'honeymoon' with the team and the press. The 1996 European Championships will be Venables' big test.

ENGLAND, NATIONAL TEAM

The history of the England national team begins with the first ever international, the goalless Scotland-England game in Glasgow on 30 November 1872. Scotland dominated early fixtures but the appearance of Wales (1880) and Ireland (1882) sparked some easier games and the birth of the home international championship. Between 1890 and 1896 England had an invincible period of 20 unbeaten games, assisted by Scotland's rejection of international-class Scots playing professionally in England.

The 1908 tour of Austria, Hungary and Bohemia – four wins and 28 goals – was the first continental excursion, but foreign fixtures were not regular until the 1920s. Predictable wins against nations like Belgium and France were often achieved with understrength teams,

but a 4-3 defeat in Spain in 1929 was the first warning sign of things to come. The most famous inter-war internationals included the brutal 'Battle of Highbury' in 1934 when England, with seven Arsenal players, beat world champions Italy 3-2, and the 6-3 win in Germany in 1938 when the English team gave the Nazi salute. A surprise defeat in Switzerland a week later was blamed on the garlic!

During the 1940s England boasted a superb team. The wartime half-back line of Britton, Cullis and Mercer linked with forwards like Matthews, Carter and Lawton to produce some scintillating wins against Scotland, including scorelines of 4-0, 8-0, 6-2, 6-2 and 6-1. Only one of the first 18 post-war internationals was lost, and the 4-0 win against Italy in Turin in 1948 was one of England's best results.

England, priding themselves on an unbeaten home record against

continental opposition, were hit hard when the Republic of Ireland beat them 2-0 in 1949 and Hungary won 6-3 at Wembley in 1953. The return match in Hungary six months later, a 7-1 defeat, reinforced the view that changes were needed. When they came, England went 16 games unbeaten (1955-57) before being unsettled by the loss of three players in the Munich air crash.

Early in 1963, Ipswich Town manager Alf (later Sir Alf) Ramsey took over from Walter Winterbottom as England manager. England lost the first two games under Ramsey but only four of the next 42, winning the 1966 World Cup in England. The win was achieved after games against Uruguay (0-0), Mexico (2-0), France (2-0), Argentina (1-0), Portugal (2-1) and West Germany (4-2 after extra time). The winning team in the final was: Banks, Cohen, Wilson, Stiles, Charlton (Jack), Moore, Ball, Hunt, Charlton (Bobby),

Hurst and Peters. Two years later England achieved their best ever European Championship placing (third) but in the 1970 World Cup West Germany turned a 2-0 quarter-final deficit into a 3-2 victory to stop England's attempt to retain the trophy.

The 11-year Ramsey era was the most successful in England's history; his teams notched 69 wins in 113 internationals with only 17 defeats. It ended with failure to qualify for the 1974 World Cup finals after a frustrating 1-1 draw with Poland. Since Ramsey, England have been managed by Joe Mercer, Don Revie, Ron Greenwood, Bobby Robson, Graham Taylor and Terry Venables. In the 1980s Greenwood and Robson consistently steered England into the World Cup finals, but only in 1990 did they make an impact, when their run ended in the semi-final with a penalty shoot-out against West Germany. Less success was to be had in the European Championship finals, with England losing all three games in 1988 and four years later performing dismally in Sweden. That proved a depressingly reliable sign of the times as, under Taylor, England failed to qualify for the 1994 World Cup Finals. Enter Terry Venables, who got off to a mildly promising start, but clearly he faced a long and difficult task.

EQUIPMENT

The knickerbocker-type shorts worn in football's early years soon developed into the baggier knee-length variety, commonly called 'knickers', which lasted until the mid 1950s. Briefer shorts, worn by mainland European and South American players, were brought to British attention through the World Cup and European club competitions. In recent years some players have taken to wearing tights or clinging cycle-shorts under their team strip.

Shirts have had a multitude of styles, ranging from early tie-at-the-neck, long-sleeved shirts to V-

collared short-sleeve versions. In the late 1970s sponsors recognised that they could use shirt fronts to advertise company names, and other design trimmings developed. Experiments with numbered shirts took place occasionally in the 1930s, most notably for the 1933 FA Cup Final when the shirts were numbered from 1 to 22 rather than two sets of 1 to 11. A new departure from convention was announced in 1993 when the Premier League introduced squad numbers. Thus a glance at Arsenal's line-up for that year's FA Cup Final reveals that midfielders Paul Davis and John Jensen wore numbers 14 and 17 respectively, while substitute David O'Leary sported number 22! Numbering was not compulsory in England until 1939. In Scotland Celtic strongly resisted shirt numbering and resorted to numbering shorts instead. In the very early days of

There has been much criticism, and amusement, concerning the new kits that clubs now wear. The criticism comes because of the pressure it puts on fans to continually pay for replica strips. The amusement arises because some of the styles are quite unlike anything seen at British grounds before. The new Hull City kit (modelled here by Steve Moran), matching the Tigers of their nickname, was a justifiable target for visiting fans.

football, players were identified by the colours of their caps and stockings. In the early 1970s Don Revie's Leeds United team pioneered numbered tie-ups which they gave to the crowd as souvenirs at the end of the game.

Goalkeepers have often been to the fore as fashion pacesetters. When restrictions on shirt colours were lifted in the late 1970s – Football League rules had previously limited goalkeepers to royal green, royal blue, scarlet and white – other designs appeared. Goalkeepers have also experimented more practically with different forms of padding, gloves and caps. Superstition was fuelled by Cardiff City's FA Cup-winning goal in 1927, Arsenal goalkeeper Lewis blaming his slippy new jersey after Ferguson's shot had squeezed the ball between his arms and body.

Shinpads were invented by Sam Widdowson (Nottingham Forest and England), who patented them in 1874; the early versions were worn outside the socks. Charlie Bambridge, a famous England winger in the 1880s, once fooled the Scots when wearing only one shinpad. Aware of Bambridge's publicised shin injury, the Scots hacked at the protected leg only to discover after the game that Bambridge had craftily worn the shinpad on his sound leg. Around 1890 began the custom of putting shinpads inside socks. In the 1960s and 1970s it was common for players such as George Best to play without shinpads, but modern players sensibly use them as standard safety equipment. Other kit accessories include headbands, worn by players such as one-time England international Steve Foster.

The original boots were made of strong, unsupple leather. They had hard toe-caps and ankle protection, and studs were knocked in with nails. Players dreaded breaking in a new pair. The invention of the screw-in stud and use of rubber moulded soles revolutionised the options available to footballers. Certain players – Alan Ball (Everton) and Peter Taylor (Spurs) come to mind – wore white boots for a time in the 1970s.

The Laws of football state that the ball must be spherical with an outer casing of leather or other approved materials. At the start of the game the ball must not weigh more than 16 oz or less than 14 oz. The laced-up leather-case balls used by early footballers often collected water and mud, so they probably weighed more than 16 oz during a game; reliable plastic coatings are now generally used. Valve balls replaced laced balls in the 1950s, and white balls became the norm around 1970, with the patterned ball arriving in the late 1970s. When England played West Germany in the 1966 World Cup Final the ball was the traditional brown.

Goal equipment evolved rapidly. Crossbars became compulsory in 1882 (they had been used in some areas as early as 1875), and goal-nets were invented and patented by JA Brodie of Liverpool in 1890. Attention to the detail of equipment is important. In November 1989 Portsmouth officials were embarrassed when a Danish referee discovered that one Fratton Park crossbar was an inch too low when he made his check before a youth international.

EUROPE

Once the British, codified form of football was introduced to mainland Europe it didn't take long to become popular, associations being formed in Belgium, Holland, Denmark, Switzerland and Italy before the turn of the century. The seeds were already there: primitive free-for-all types of the game already existed – and Ancient Greece, too, had had its form, episkyros. The other great empire of the ancient world, that of Rome, had a version called harpastum and there is evidence to suggest that this was introduced to occupied Britain, so possibly making the city of the 1990 World Cup Final the originator of the sport.

Although early British teams did tour Europe, the development of the game on the continent prospered in spite of, rather than because of, the established game and its officiating bodies in the United Kingdom; their tendency to remain aloof from the game overseas continued well into the twentieth century (attitudes towards the inauguration of first FIFA and then the World Cup being examples). It was largely through the efforts of British individuals (business representatives working in Vienna, the son of an expatriate mill-owner in tsarist Russia, etc.) and the infectious nature of casual recreational matches, as played by British sailors in the Balkans, for example, that football took root in Europe. Early this century, Scottish coaches introduced a short-passing style to central European sides; and the British influence in Italy is evidenced by the English spelling of two of that country's top teams' names (Genoa and AC Milan).

But much is owed to Switzerland (home of FIFA and UEFA) and France, founders of so many tournaments and awards, for the organisation and development of international competitive soccer within Europe and, indeed, worldwide. Ironically Swiss football has made little impact internationally, and for a long time the French did not have a great deal of success in the competitions they initiated. But they were European Championship winners in 1984, propelled by Michel Platini's nine goals, and had looked an increasingly useful outside bet in the World Cup two years earlier. By the time they met an impressive West German side in an enthralling semi-final, the team had gelled; with the experienced Tresor forming the nucleus of a springboard defence, Rocheteau providing the fire-power up front, and Platini, Genghini, Giresse and Tigana harmonising in midfield, France played some of the most beautiful football of that or any World Cup. However, it was not to be, and the national team has struggled to find its form since then.

Their victorious opponents on that day, Germany – or West Germany as they were then – are the most successful footballing nation in Europe. Some might say in the world, and they would have an impressive case: three World Cup victories and three times runners-up (a record) and two European Championships (a record). They suffer the occasional inexplicable defeat at the hands of inferior opposition, but seem to have the knack of winning important matches, and at their best appear supremely confident with an air of almost arrogant invincibility.

The German game is a combination of the direct, pragmatic approach favoured in Britain and the patient, skilful build-up typical of continental Europe. Most of their successes are identified with the names Beckenbauer and Schoen. Current coach Berti Vogts now has the pick of East Germany's footballers to help him. A limited number of East German teams have been admitted to the Bundesliga, whose club sides have always been prominent in European competitions, Bayern Munich's three consecutive European Cup victories in the mid 1970s standing out. In truth the GDR's teams achieved little, and most of the German squad will always be from the West; in Matthaus they have a player as fearsome to goalkeepers as Gerd Muller was in the 1970s. Germany's first game as a unified nation in 48 years took place on 19 December 1990 in Stuttgart against Switzerland, with East German Andreas Thom (who played in the Bundesliga) replacing Sammer, the only East German to start the game, and scoring in the 4-0 victory.

It is not only the German game which has been affected by the political changes in post-1989 Eastern Europe. If professional status is adopted by footballers in former

Ronald Koeman scores the only goal of the game in the 1992 European Cup Final. Although Koeman is a Dutchman, he was playing for Barcelona of Spain, who beat Sampdoria of Italy 1-0. When top European footballers turn out for their country, they stand a good chance of playing against their club team-mates. So easily and frequently do these players switch from one foreign club to another that, in many cases, the opposition hold no surprises for them.

communist states, their national teams might grow in strength; but 'devolution' within the Soviet Union and Yugoslavia has meant the emergence of 'new' nationalities, while Albania, something of a football desert

owing to political insularity, has become more involved in the international scene. East European teams have always been tough opposition but, Olympic football apart, have won few major honours, Czechoslovakia's 1976 European Championship title being a notable exception. The Soviet Union won the first tournament in 1960, but the strongest nations did not compete. Despite the occasional success of its club sides, the USSR, somewhat mysteriously, often showed lack of self-belief in crucial games, and individual talents such as Chivadze and Blokhin were not able to carry them.

For twenty or more years Poland sporadically promised great things with their capacity for exciting football, typified by first Lato and, more recently, Boniek. Tomaszewski in goal and Zmuda in defence were also outstanding. Unfortunately

the national team has proved unable to mount a sustained assault in a major tournament.

Hungary's golden age, May 1950 to February 1956, was blemished by only one defeat out of 48 internationals; sadly that defeat, in 1954, was Hungary's second in a World Cup Final. The Soviet invasion of their homeland in 1956 broke up the legendary team which included Puskas, Kocsis and Czibor – players whose equivalents have never surfaced in modern-day Hungary. That team's emphatic double defeat of England in 1953/54 exhibited skills and tactical subtlety which revolutionised the British attitude to the game.

Yugoslavia in the 1960s, and Romania in the 1970s, began to shake off the reputation of being dull but worthy opponents, and continued to impress with individual displays of skill

(from the likes of Jankovic, Jovanovic and, more recently, Stojkovic of Yugoslavia). The success of their club sides Red Star Belgrade (Yugoslavia) and Steaua Bucharest (Romania) in the 1980s was brought to an abrupt halt by political upheaval.

The Italians are often credited with being the tightest defenders in the world and the best practitioners of the sweeper system; their Milanese club sides of the 1960s were expert at defending slim leads in two-leg European ties. Italy has consistently produced world-class players and performances to match; of European national teams only Germany has a better record. Their rigorous defence and patient build-up are complemented by imaginative and incisive work around the penalty area. Of the modern team (who produced some of the 1990 World Cup's best soccer and reached the final of the 1994 tournament), the libero Baresi, although so different in appearance to Scirea, could be mistaken for his eminent predecessor in his style, distribution and reading of the game; and striker Roberto Baggio is proving every bit as exciting as those great names Rossi, Riva and Rivera.

Italy's northern neighbours, Austria, whose domestic league loses so many players to wealthier foreign clubs, have a poor record which does not reflect the quality of football displayed at times by their exciting, combative teams.

The Scandinavian countries have had football leagues for almost as long as any nation in Europe but until recently were handicapped in the international arena by their semi-professionalism. Since turning professional in 1978, Denmark have earned worldwide respect with their skilful and mobile brand of football, culminating in their glorious 1992 European Championship triumph. Best players, however, have always moved abroad – Jesper Olsen, Morten Olsen, Simonsen, Molby, Laudrup and Schmeichel, for example. Sweden, too, have proved their worth through club successes in Europe and by qualifying for several World Cups. Norway, and Finland especially, remain the weaker countries but have had their moments; no opponents can afford to be dismissive of them.

Spanish clubs, Real Madrid and Barcelona in particular, had great success in the early years of the three main European competitions and the national team won the 1964 European Championship, their only title. Then, as now, the domestic game relied heavily on imported players, which might explain the disparity between club and national achievements. As the Spanish challenge faded, Portugal, in the shape of Benfica and Sporting Lisbon, carried the Iberian flag. Then, in the 1966 World Cup, Eusebio, the 'Black Panther', showed just why he was being compared to Pele. But Portuguese soccer has never recovered from the decline which so rapidly followed that time. Currently the Spanish League, which still sends successful representatives into European competitions, is characterised by massive transfer fees, managerial dramas and the impossibly high expectations of the press and public.

Major European clubs have featured numbers of non-national players for many years, but the phenomenon is more recent in Britain. Recent seasons, however, have seen increasing numbers of European players in the British game. Many of them have taken advantage of more lax political controls at home to move from former eastern bloc countries to seek better rewards for their skills. Andrei Kanchelskis is one who moved from Russia to achieve great success at Manchester United. The problem, as United among others have found, is that UEFA rules restrict the numbers of non-nationals eligible for European club competitions, making it harder for sides to reproduce domestic form on the international stage.

The rise of Dutch soccer, some fifteen years after the introduction of professionalism, was breathtaking. From apparently nowhere, a new soccer power and a new approach – total football – emerged to dominate the club soccer of the early 1970s, Ajax and Feyenoord taking the spoils. The national team, inspired by Johan Cruyff, were runners-up in the 1974 and 1978 World Cups – consolation for rather poor showings in the European Championships of that decade.

The story of Belgian football seems an imitation in miniature of the Dutch success. Anderlecht, with goalscorer van der Elst, won the Cup Winners' Cup in 1976 and 1978, as the national side, organised around the midfield skills of van Moer, grew in stature and lost only by the odd goal to West Germany in the 1980 European Championship Final. Whereas Belgian football has more or less stayed on an even keel, with the emergence of new talents such as Ceulemans and Scifo, Dutch soccer seemed to lose its way in the early 1980s. But a new team was emerging including players of the calibre of Gullit and van Basten, and it swept to victory in the 1988 European Championship – only to disappoint in subsequent tournaments, partly as a consequence of low morale engendered by managerial disputes.

It is commonly said that there are no real minnows left in football, particularly in Europe, and the Faroe Islands' defeat of Austria in September 1990 underlined the danger of complacency on the part of the major teams. Even so, sides such as Luxembourg, Turkey, Greece, Cyprus, Iceland and Malta can hope for little more than the occasional thwarting of a bigger team's ambitions; it is to Holland, Italy, France, Spain and England that we look for a long-term challenge to the German hegemony.

Denmark were late entries to the 1992 European Championships, only gaining qualification when political upheavals prevented Yugoslavia from taking their allotted place. Denmark proved more than worthy substitutes by winning the final 2-0 against Germany. Brian Laudrup, who later went on to play for Glasgow Rangers, holds the cup aloft.

EUROPEAN CHAMPIONSHIPS

Like the World Cup, the European Nations Cup, as it was originally known, took some time to become fully established, with only 17 nations competing for the inaugural trophy and many of the strongest countries declining to participate. The winners that first year were the Soviet Union, who defeated Yugoslavia 2-1 in the final in Paris.

The Soviets reached the final again four years later but lost out this time to the hosts, Spain. This second tournament attracted a much healthier entry (though West Germany and Scotland still declined) with all rounds again played on a knock-out basis; matches were over two legs before switching to a single venue for a mini-tournament comprising both semi-finals and the final.

By 1968, with a new title of the European Football Championships, there were enough entries to warrant groups rather than a knock-out system in the early round. The Home Internationals over two seasons were used to decide which of the British countries would go forward to the last eight; despite a famous Scottish victory at Wembley, England won through. Home advantage again proved decisive in the finals as Italy triumphed in Rome.

West Germany's exhilarating football saw them win the 1972 tournament comfortably, with Franz Beckenbauer

imperious in defence, Gunther Netzer pulling the strings in midfield and Gerd Muller deadly up front. They reached the final again in 1976 only to lose out on penalties to an underrated Czechoslovakia, who had eliminated England at the group stage, defeated the Soviet Union in a quarter-final heavy with political tension, and then confounded Johan Cruyff and company with a semi-final win over Holland.

The Germans put matters right in 1980 as a last-minute winner from Horst Hrubesch, his second of the final, gave them victory over Belgium, but the final tournament, now featuring eight teams in a group format with the hosts qualifying automatically, was a disaster, producing stiflingly dull football played out in near-empty Italian stadia. The contrast with the 1984 Championship could not have been greater: a vibrant French side won it, but just as importantly, France proved ideal hosts. Their stadia were full, and in Michel Platini, their captain, they found a true hero as he scored in every game, including two hat-tricks.

Four years later in West Germany, the Dutch eventually justified their status as favourites, after a rather rocky opening. Ruud Gullit and Marco van Basten were the stars, and they scored the goals which

EUROPEAN CHAMPIONSHIPS			
Year	Winner	Runners-up	Score
1960	USSR	Yugoslavia	2-1*
1964	Spain	USSR	2-1
1968	Italy	Yugoslavia	1-1 2-0*
1972	West Germany	USSR	3-0
1976	Czechoslovakia	West Germany	2-2**
1980	West Germany	Belgium	2-1
1984	France	Spain	2-0
1988	Holland	USSR	2-0
1992	Denmark	Germany	2-0

* after extra time ** after extra time and penalties

Date	Fixture	Venue	Kick-off	Date	Fixture	Venue Kick-off	
Sat 8 Jun	Group A	Wembley	3.00pm	Sun 16 Jun	Group D	Hillsborough	7.30pm
Sun 9 Jun	Group B	Elland Road	2.30pm	Tue 18 Jun	Group B	St James' Park	4.30pm
Sun 9 Jun	Group C	Old Trafford	5.00pm	Tue 18 Jun	Group B	Elland Road	4.30pm
Sun 9 Jun	Group D	Hillsborough	7.30pm	Tue 18 Jun	Group A	Wembley	7.30pm
				Tue 18 Jun	Group A	Villa Park	7.30pm
Mon 10 Jun	Group A	Villa Park	4.30pm				
Mon 10 Jun	Group B	St James' Park	7.30pm	Wed 19 Jun	Group D	City Ground	4.30pm
				Wed 19 Jun	Group D	Hillsborough	4.30pm
Tue 11 Jun	Group C	Anfield	4.30pm	Wed 19 Jun	Group C	Anfield	7.30pm
Tue 11 Jun	Group D	City Ground	7.30pm	Wed 19 Jun	Group C	Old Trafford	7.30pm
Thu 13 Jun	Group B	St James' Park	4.30pm	Sat 22 Jun	Quarter-final	Wembley	3.00pm
Thu 13 Jun	Group A	Villa Park	7.30pm	Sat 22 Jun	Quarter-final	Anfield	6.30pm
Fri 14 Jun	Group D	City Ground	4.30pm	Sun 23 Jun	Quarter-final	Old Trafford	3.00pm
Fri 14 Jun	Group C	Anfield	7.30pm	Sun 23 Jun	Quarter-final	Villa Park	6.30pm
Sat 15 Jun	Group A	City Ground	3.00pm	Wed 26 Jun	Semi-final	Old Trafford	3.00pm
Sat 15 Jun	Group B	Elland Road	6.00 pm	Wed 26 Jun	Semi-final	Wembley	7.30pm
Sun 16 Jun	Group C	Old Trafford	3.00pm	Sun 30 Jun	Final	Wembley	7.00pm

defeated the USSR in the final, the Soviets finishing runners-up for a record third time. But it was the 1992 finals in Sweden which produced the most amazing story of all: when Yugoslavia were forced to withdraw just weeks before the finals, Denmark were drafted in to make up the numbers. Yet, roared on by thousands of their supporters who had made the short trip over, they upset Germany in the final, winning 2-0.

For 1996, UEFA decreed that the final tournament, to be held in England over three weeks in June, should be expanded from eight to 16 teams, and that sudden-death overtime would be used in the knockout stage.

Terry Venables, the new England manager for the 1996 European Championships, seen here with his first captain, David Platt, shortly after Venables' appointment. With home advantage and a strong squad of players from which to choose, hopes are high for success in the tournament. Both Venables and Platt have experience of managing/playing in Europe which may be a crucial factor.

EUROPEAN CUP

Europe's foremost club competition was first contested in 1955 in response to extravagant claims that Wolves were the world's best club after their defeat of star-studded Hungarian team Honved the preceding year. The first competition was by invitation but thereafter the league champions of each country were entitled to compete. It was an almost immediate success. The talented Real Madrid in their all-white strip lifted the first five trophies, but they had to wait until 1966 to win with an all-Spanish team. Italian domination in the early 1960s, felt by many to be a negative influence, was interrupted by the first British successes. In the next decade the emergence of Dutch football and Bayern Munich's heyday eventually made way for a remarkable run by English clubs which was terminated by the ban (lifted by 1991) resulting from the 1985 Heysel disaster. In the early 1990s, the straight knock-out system was replaced by the Champions League stage, although the final continued as a single match at a neutral venue.

A glorious moment for Celtic and Scotland fans as Steve Chalmers puts the ball past Inter Milan's goalkeeper Sarti for an 85th minute winner in the 1967 European Cup Final. Celtic won, deservedly, 2-1 against a negative Italian side that had tried to hang on to an early lead achieved through a penalty. That day (and night) in Lisbon will go down in Scottish folklore. Rumour has it that the team and supporters enjoyed a quiet drink afterwards too – and a handful of Scots never made the long journey back.

EUROPEAN CUP			
Year	Winners	Runners-up	Score
1956	Real Madrid	Reims	4-3
1957	Real Madrid	Fiorentina	2-0
1958	Real Madrid	AC Milan	3-2*
1959	Real Madrid	Reims	2-0
1960	Real Madrid	Eintracht Frankfurt	7-3
1961	Benfica	Barcelona	3-2
1962	Benfica	Real Madrid	5-3
1963	AC Milan	Benfica	2-1
1964	Internazionale	Real Madrid	3-1
1965	Internazionale	Benfica	1-0
1966	Real Madrid	Partizan Belgrade	2-1
1967	Celtic	Internazionale	2-1
1968	Manchester United	Benfica	4-1*
1969	AC Milan	Ajax	4-1
1970	Feyenoord	Celtic	2-1*
1971	Ajax	Panathinaikos	2-0
1972	Ajax	Internazionale	2-0
1973	Ajax	Juventus	1-0
1974	Bayern Munich	Atletico Madrid	1-1*
			4-0
1975	Bayern Munich	Leeds United	2-0
1976	Bayern Munich	St Etienne	1-0
1977	Liverpool	Borussia Mönchengladbach	3-1
1978	Liverpool	FC Brugge	1-0
1979	Nottingham Forest	Malmo	1-0
1980	Nottingham Forest	Hamburg	1-0
1981	Liverpool	Real Madrid	1-0
1982	Aston Villa	Bayern Munich	1-0
1983	Hamburg	Juventus	1-0
1984	Liverpool	Roma	1-1**
1985	Juventus	Liverpool	1-0
1986	Steaua Bucharest	Barcelona	0-0**
1987	Porto	Bayern Munich	2-1
1988	PSV Eindhoven	Benfica	0-0**
1989	AC Milan	Steaua Bucharest	4-0
1990	AC Milan	Benfica	1-0
1991	Red Star Belgrade	Marseille	0-0**
1992	Barcelona	Sampdoria	1-0*
1993	Marseille	AC Milan	1-0
1994	AC Milan	Barcelona	4-0
1995	Ajax	AC Milan	1-0

*after extra time **after extra time and penalties

EUROPEAN CUP WINNERS' CUP

Since its inception in 1960/61, this trophy has inspired many European countries to establish domestic cup competitions so that their winners will be entitled to compete. For football clubs it generates revenue as well as offering a chance of televised international success for teams which may not have done well in league competitions.

The score at the end of extra time in the 1971 final of the European Cup Winners' Cup between Chelsea and Real Madrid was 1-1. Chelsea won the replay 2-1, mirroring their FA Cup success that won them a place in the competition. Skipper Ron Harris, with a Real shirt around his shoulders, is carried by team-mates as he holds on to the Cup.

EUROPEAN CUP WINNERS' CUP

Year	Winners	Runners up	Score
1961	Fiorentina	Rangers	2-0 2-1
1962	Atletico Madrid	Fiorentina	1-1 3-0
1963	Tottenham Hotspur	Atletico Madrid	5-1
1964	Sporting Lisbon	MTK Budapest	3-3* 1-0
1965	West Ham United	Munich 1860	2-0
1966	Borussia Dortmund	Liverpool	2-1*
1967	Bayern Munich	Rangers	1-0*
1968	AC Milan	Hamburg	2-0
1969	Slovan Bratislava	Barcelona	3-2
1970	Manchester City	Gornik Zabrze	2-1
1971	Chelsea	Real Madrid	1-1* 2-1
1972	Rangers	Moscow Dynamo	3-2
1973	AC Milan	Leeds United	1-0
1974	Magdeburg	AC Milan	2-0
1975	Dynamo Kiev	Ferencvaros	3-0
1976	Anderlecht	West Ham United	4-2
1977	Hamburg	Anderlecht	2-0
1978	Anderlecht	Austria/WAC	4-0
1979	Barcelona	Fortuna Dusseldorf	4-3*
1980	Valencia	Arsenal	0-0**
1981	Dynamo Tbilisi	Carl Zeiss Jena	2-1
1982	Barcelona	Standard Liege	2-1
1983	Aberdeen	Real Madrid	2-1*
1984	Juventus	Porto	2-1
1985	Everton	Rapid Vienna	3-1
1986	Dynamo Kiev	Atletico Madrid	3-0
1987	Ajax	Lokomotiv Leipzig	1-0
1988	Mechelen	Ajax	1-0
1989	Barcelona	Sampdoria	2-0
1990	Sampdoria	Anderlecht	2-0*
1991	Manchester United	Barcelona	2-1
1992	Werder Bremen	Monaco	2-0
1993	Parma	Royal Antwerp	3-1
1994	Arsenal	Parma	1-0
1995	Real Zaragoza	Arsenal	2-1*

* after extra time **after extra time and penalties

EUROPEAN FOOTBALLER OF THE YEAR

Year	Winner	Club
1956	Stanley Matthews	Blackpool
1957	Alfredo di Stefano	Real Madrid
1958	Raymond Kopa	Real Madrid
1959	Alfredo di Stefano	Real Madrid
1960	Luis Suarez	Barcelona
1961	Omar Sivori	Juventus
1962	Josef Masopust	Dukla Prague
1963	Lev Yashin	Dynamo Moscow
1964	Denis Law	Manchester United
1965	Eusebio	Benfica
1966	Bobby Charlton	Manchester United
1967	Florian Albert	Ferencvaros
1968	George Best	Manchester United
1969	Gianni Rivera	AC Milan
1970	Gerd Muller	Bayern Munich
1971	Johan Cruyff	Ajax
1972	Franz Beckenbauer	Bayern Munich
1973	Johan Cruyff	Barcelona
1974	Johan Cruyff	Barcelona
1975	Oleg Blokhin	Dynamo Kiev
1976	Franz Beckenbauer	Bayern Munich
1977	Allan Simonsen	Borussia Mönchengladbach
1978	Kevin Keegan	Hamburg
1979	Kevin Keegan	Hamburg
1980	Karl-Heinz Rummenigge	Bayern Munich
1981	Karl-Heinz Rummenigge	Bayern Munich
1982	Paolo Rossi	Juventus
1983	Michel Platini	Juventus
1984	Michel Platini	Juventus
1985	Michel Platini	Juventus
1986	Igor Belanov	Dynamo Kiev
1987	Ruud Gullit	AC Milan
1988	Marco van Basten	AC Milan
1989	Marco van Basten	AC Milan
1990	Lothar Matthäus	Internazionale
1991	Jean-Pierre Papin	Marseille
1992	Marco van Basten	AC Milan
1993	Roberto Baggio	Juventus
1994	Hristo Stoichkov	Barcelona

The rounds are decided over home and away legs but the fact that the final is settled in one match makes it popular for television audiences. Anderlecht's thrilling performances helped to revive the popularity of the competition in the mid 1970s. No distinct pattern of domination emerges, but Barcelona enjoyed three victories in one decade. Arsenal and Rangers have appeared in three finals and West Ham in two, winning one apiece. In 1991 Manchester United celebrated the return of English clubs to Europe by winning the trophy, then Arsenal triumphed in 1994.

EUROPEAN FOOTBALLER OF THE YEAR

The Ballon d'Or is awarded on the basis of a poll among journalists. A footballer's chances of success depend upon outstanding performances in the televised European competitions, in particular the European Cup.

Three home nations were represented by the Manchester United triumvirate of the 1960s. Kevin Keegan remains the only British player to have picked up two awards and like Michel Platini (unique in winning it three years running) he won it while playing for a foreign club. When Roberto Baggio was honoured in 1993, it was the 10th time in 12 years that the prize had gone to a player from the Italian League.

EUROPEAN SUPER CUP

Contested by the winners of the European Cup and the Cup Winners' Cup; interest in the latter tournament was

EUROPEAN SUPER CUP

Year	Winners	Runners-up	Aggregate (two leg)
1973	Ajax	Rangers	6-3
1974	Ajax	AC Milan	6-1
1975	Dynamo Kiev	Bayern Munich	3-0
1976	Anderlecht	Bayern Munich	5-3
1977	Liverpool	Hamburg	7-1
1978	Anderlecht	Liverpool	4-3
1979	Nottingham Forest	Barcelona	2-1
1980	Valencia	Nottingham Forest	2-2*
1981	No competition		
1982	Aston Villa	Barcelona	3-1
1983	Aberdeen	Hamburg	2-0
1984	Juventus	Liverpool	2-0**
1985	No competition		
1986	Steaua Bucharest	Dynamo Kiev	1-0**
1987	FC Porto	Ajax	2-0
1988	Mechelen	PSV Eindhoven	3-1
1989	AC Milan	Barcelona	2-1
1990	AC Milan	Sampdoria	3-1
1991	Manchester United	Red Star Belgrade	1-0**
1992	Barcelona	Werder Bremen	3-2
1993	Parma	AC Milan	2-1
1994	AC Milan	Arsenal	2-0

*won on away goals **played as one match

Twenty-four years before such displays merited front-page copy, Eusebio cried at the end of a World Cup semi-final. England, by the simple tactic of standing off the lithe striker, had negated to a certain extent the powerful acceleration and dribbling skills which had been used to such great effect against the committed tackling of earlier rounds. The World Cup medal which would so justly have crowned a memorable career was never to be his.

Strangely enough, this popular and most sportsmanlike athlete began his European career amidst some controversy. Sporting Lisbon, the founders of Laurenco Marques, his first club, felt they, among

Jean-Pierre Papin of Marseille and France was the deserving winner of the 1991 European Footballer of the Year title, although he failed to score on this occasion – the European Cup Final against Red Star Belgrade. This game must rate as probably the dullest final ever. The score after extra time was 0-0. At no time did Red Star attempt to play attacking football. They were content to wait for the penalty shoot-out.

rekindled by this competition's inauguration. The UEFA ban on English clubs prevented Everton from playing in 1985. In 1993/94 AC Milan replaced Marseille after the French club was banned from European competition following bribery allegations. Twice clubs have not been able to agree on dates and the fixture has lapsed – an indication of the trophy's status.

EUSEBIO, Ferreira Da Silva

1943 Born in Mozambique

1958 Taken on by local

team Sporting Club of Laurenco Marques

1961 Transferred to Benfica for £7500; international debut for Portugal v Luxembourg

1962 In his first full season scores 2 goals in European Cup Final victory v Real Madrid

1965 European Footballer of the Year

1966 Top scorer in the World Cup for Portugal with 9 goals

1968 Winner of the Golden Boot award with 43 goals...

1973 ... and again with 40 goals

Ferreira Da Silva Eusebio, nearing the end of his career in top-class football, turns out for Portugal against Northern Ireland in a World Cup qualifying game in 1973. Eusebio won 77 international caps and, for Benfica in the European Cup, scored a total of 46 goals. He was a vital ingredient in the success of Portuguese football at both club and international level in the 1960s.

European teams, had first claim on the young talent, but Benfica had been tipped off. The dispute between the two Portuguese clubs took some months to settle, during which time Eusebio was obliged to lie low in an Algarve fishing village.

At Benfica, and for Portugal, his goalscoring instincts found their perfect foil in the aerial strength of Torres. A knee injury in the 1970s effectively finished Eusebio's first-class career, although he resurfaced in Mexico and the United States and in 1976 helped Toronto Metros-Croatia win the Soccer Bowl. The end of the decade saw him playing in the Portuguese Second Division.

As a player he will be best remembered for having one of the most ferocious right-foot shots ever seen, but perhaps the most abiding memories for the British public are the emotion shown at Wembley in 1966 and, at the same venue two years later, his astounded congratulations to Alex Stepney after the Manchester United 'keeper had saved a Eusebio 'special' to ensure European Cup victory for the English club.

EVERTON

Founded 1878

Joined League 1888 (founder member)

Honours Division 1 Champions 1891, 1915, 1928, 1932, 1939, 1963, 1970, 1985, 1987; Division 2 Champions 1931; FA Cup Winners 1906, 1933, 1966, 1984, 1995; European Cup Winners' Cup Winners 1985

Ground Goodison Park

When Will Cuff, the man who founded Everton, retired in 1946 he passed on a guiding principle; that only the classical and stylish players should be signed. With a few exceptions Everton have been true to this code, and the same pride in the club's style can still be sensed at Goodison. As they say in the theatre, Everton are a class act.

Founded as a church team, St Domingo's, in 1878 they began in Stanley Park and are still there. They voted to become non-denominational in 1879 in a hotel hard by Ye Ancient Everton Toffee House; six years later the club was recruiting professionals, and became a founder member of the Football League.

Another three years and Everton were champions, a prelude to a row with their landlord, which led to a move to the other side of the park. Anfield Road was vacant for the birth of another club whose name escapes most Evertonians.

By 1902 they were wearing the famous royal blue and were second in the League. They won the FA Cup at the third attempt in 1905. The First World War halted what might have been a glorious era, the next landmark coming in 1925 when William Ralph Dean (aged 19), a centre-forward, was signed from Tranmere Rovers for £3000. Despite being dropped, 'Dixie' scored 32 goals in 38 matches, and 21 the following season after having his jaw and skull fractured in a motor cycle accident; in 1927/28 history was made as Dean's 60 League goals swept Everton to their third Championship.

An increasingly ragged defence brought Everton relegation, for the first time, in 1930, but so swift was the reconstruction that the Second and First Division Championships were won in successive seasons by the 'School of Science' side. These were great years at Goodison, Joe Mercer joining Cliff Britton to give the club England's midfield. In 1935 Everton paid Burnley £6500 for Tommy Lawton, then aged 17, thus ensuring the greatest succession in football history, Dixie Dean going to meet the new boy at Lime Street Station. With the majestic Tommy Jones emerging at centre-half, Everton won a fourth Championship in 1939, a season when Everton players won 32 caps.

Everton struggled after the war and a second relegation

followed in 1951. A scrambled return in 1954 was followed four years later by John Carey's appointment as manager under John Moores' chairmanship. But it took Harry Catterick's arrival in 1961 to slake the 'Toffeemen's' thirst for glory. He built two fine sides; the first – starring Alex Young at centre-forward and Brian Labone at centre-half – won the League in 1963 and the FA Cup in 1966; the second, still with Labone but now featuring a brilliant midfield trio of Alan Ball, Howard Kendall and Colin Harvey, took the title again in 1970. Catterick left, and neither Billy Bingham nor Gordon Lee could give Everton the consistency to win top honours.

In 1981 Everton turned to Kendall, who transferred 13 players and signed 11 in his first season. In his second he signed Peter Reid, followed later by Trevor Steven and Andy Gray. From 18th in the League in January 1984, Everton went on to lose a League Cup Final replay to Liverpool but won the FA Cup. More recruiting followed and 1984/85 was a resplendent and dramatic season: the Championship was won in style, as was the European Cup Winners' Cup, but in the FA Cup Final three days later, on a humid Saturday, Everton were limp. The following season was heart-breaking – second to Liverpool in both League and Cup – but Kendall regained the title in 1987 before shaking the club by resigning to manage in Spain for two years.

Colin Harvey took the manager's chair and, despite another Cup final, was unsuccessful. Howard Kendall fared no better and under Mike Walker league form slumped. 1994/95 saw Everton's worst start to a season and Joe Royle assumed control. Premiership safety was confirmed and, when Manchester United were defeated at Wembley to crown an exciting FA Cup run, a remarkable turn-around was completed. With Royle at the helm the future looks bright for Evertonians.

EXETER CITY

Founded 1904

Joined League 1920 (Division 3)

Honours Division 4 Champions 1990

Ground St James's Park

One of the League's habitual strugglers, Exeter City can always blame their historical lack of distinction on the accident of their geography. Devon was already regarded as a rugby stronghold when the club was founded; young local talent has proved hard to find and harder to develop, and this outpost of soccer civilisation, devoid of glamour and financial resources, has seemed an uninviting lure to established players. In the circumstances, mere survival has often been the club's most meaningful target, with the occasional attainment of a decent mediocrity the highest of its realistic aspirations.

Goalkeeper Dick Pym, who later found fame with Bolton Wanderers, and subsequent Arsenal wing-ace Cliff Bastin were local products who starred in early League sides, but the first flirtations with success, in the early 1930s, were achieved with teams shrewdly developed from 'cast-offs' by wily manager Billy McDevitt. In 1931 City took Sunderland to a replay in the sixth round of the FA Cup (and attracted a still-record home gate of 20,984), and in 1933 an honourable second place in Division 3 (S) was achieved. Yet only three years later the club was bottom of the table and extinction was only narrowly averted.

Another excursion to the sixth round of the Cup (and defeat at Tottenham) in 1981 was the highlight of the post-war era until, after 70 years in the League, the first honour was won. Under dynamic manager Terry Cooper, City took the 1990 Division 4 title by a ten-point margin at the end of a campaign in which the team was undefeated at St James's Park. Injuries then dampened the fire that had been lit, and Exeter returned to the lowest division in 1994, finishing bottom in 1995.

FALKIRK

Founded 1876

Joined League 1902 (Division 2)

Honours Scottish League First Division Champions 1991, 1994; Division 2 Champions 1936, 1970, 1975; Scottish Cup Winners 1913, 1957

Ground Brockville Park

Falkirk's greatest moment had an unlikely setting. With relegation threatening in season 1956/57, Englishman Reggie Smith was appointed as manager. He not only kept them up but led Falkirk to victory in the Scottish Cup, a tournament they had also won in 1913.

Cultured talents such as internationalists Alex Parker and John White came to prominence with the club in the 1950s but were soon to find more affluent employers.

Falkirk's ambitions have never quite been killed off. The club which took Syd Puddefoot away from West Ham for a mammoth £6000 in 1922 had players such as former QPR striker Simon Stainrod on their books in the early 1990s. In 1995 they excelled themselves, finishing fifth in the Premier Division.

FERGUSON, Alex

1941 Born Govan, Glasgow

1958 Signs for Queen's Park

1960 Moves to St Johnstone

1964 Joins Dunfermline, for whom he scores heavily

1967 Rangers pay £65,000 for his signature

1969 Switches to Falkirk as player-coach in £20,000 deal

1973 Joins Ayr United

1974 July – becomes player-boss of East Stirling; October – takes similar position with St Mirren

1975 Retires as player

1977 Saints lift Scottish First Division Championship

1978 Dismissed following behind-the-scenes strife at Love Street; June – takes over at Aberdeen

1979 Dons lose two League Cup Finals, to Rangers in March, then to Dundee United in December (the competition having been rescheduled)

1980 Guides Aberdeen to Scottish League crown

1982 Dons win first of Scottish Cup hat-trick . . .

1983 . . . then beat Real Madrid to lift European Cup Winners' Cup

1984 Aberdeen take League title . . .

1985 . . . then retain it

1985 Ferguson becomes caretaker boss of Scotland following death of Jock Stein, his ten-month tenure including the 1986 World Cup Finals

1986 Aberdeen win both major Scottish knockout competitions; November – Ferguson succeeds Ron Atkinson as manager of Manchester United

1988 Red Devils finish runners-up in First Division

1989 Fans call for Fergie's head as expensive team struggles woefully

1990 United beat Crystal Palace in Wembley replay to take the FA Cup, their first trophy under Ferguson

1991 Red Devils overturn Barcelona to lift the European Cup Winners' Cup

1992 League Cup offers scant consolation for narrow miss in title race

1993 The Championship returns to Old Trafford at last . . .

1994 . . . and again, with the FA Cup thrown in for good measure; defeat in the League Cup Final prevents unique domestic treble; December – awarded CBE, to set alongside OBE received in 1984

As the only manager to win all three domestic trophies north and south of the border, Alex Ferguson stands alone as the most comprehensively successful boss of the current era.

He has done it the hard way, too. It was felt in Scotland that no one could break the vice-like stranglehold of Rangers and Celtic, but Ferguson's Aberdeen swept aside the 'Old Firm' to take an avalanche of honours to Pittodrie.

Then, at Old Trafford, many pundits predicted that the irascible Glaswegian would perish in the face of the fans' near-hysterical demands to land the long-awaited League Championship. Come 1989, it seemed that the prophets of doom might be proved correct, but Fergie is a born winner and he survived to lead Manchester United to the richest sequence of triumphs in their history.

Yet despite enjoying European success with both his major clubs, Ferguson was still lacking his crowning glory in the mid-1990s. Above all else, he yearned to emulate Sir Matt Busby by lifting the European Cup. In pursuit of that quest, he appeared ready to reshape an already-great team. It was a mammoth task, but in view of his staggering record to date, who could say that he would not achieve it?

FIFA

The inaugural meeting of FIFA (Federation Internationale de Football Association) took place in Paris on 21 May 1904; present were representatives of the French, Swiss, Belgian, Spanish, Dutch and Swedish associations. England had shown little response to two years of French overtures and initiative, but such was the country's status that on joining in 1906, the FA's treasurer D.B. Woolfall was elected president, replacing the original incumbent Robert Guerin.

The organisation, whose headquarters are in Zurich, aims to monitor and lay down guidelines for international competitions and proceedings and to promulgate new laws of the game and administrative rulings as need be. Bodies such as UEFA are answerable to it. It is during World Cups that FIFA receives more attention than at any other time, and some of its decisions are controversial: in 1982 penalty shoot-outs were introduced, and in 1986 referees were instructed not to add on stoppage time so as not to inconvenience television; in 1990 the 'professional' foul merited a dismissal but problems of interpretation arose – and persisted when the edict was carried into domestic leagues. Referees were also instructed to penalise players for untidy dress, although some officials clearly ignored the ruling. Some ideas introduced in the 1994 competition caused initial concern, but in the long term the outlawing of the unfair tackle from behind, and the use of stretchers for the speedy removal of injured players both seem likely to benefit the game.

There have been several expulsions and withdrawals from FIFA, the most noted of the latter being all four home countries in 1928 over the issue of broken-time payments.

Jules Rimet, one of the most famous past presidents (from 1921 to 1954), called soccer the jousting of modern times and saw FIFA as its protector. Sir Stanley Rous, equally popular, was president from 1961 to 1974 and strove in vain to keep football and politics apart. Membership increased in his time as he encouraged development of the game in Asia and Africa – a policy pursued by the present chief Joao Havelange. Membership in the mid-1990s was approaching 200 nations.

FINNEY, Tom

1922 Born in Preston

1940 Signs for Preston North End as a part-timer

1941 North End win

Probably the most complete all-round footballer in Britain in the 1950s, Tom Finney proudly displays the Football Writers' Association Footballer of the Year trophy for 1954. He was nearly always photographed in a white shirt, playing either for Preston or for England. Tom also won the FWA trophy in 1957.

wartime League North and Cup

1951 Wins Second Division Championship medal

1953 Preston miss the League Championship on goal average

1954 Losing FA Cup finalist against West Bromwich Albion; voted Footballer of the Year

1957 Footballer of the Year again

1958 Scores 26 goals in 34 League games at centre-forward; Preston are Championship runners-up again

1960 Retires to concentrate on his plumbing business

Despite the disruption of the Second World War, Tom Finney played 76 internationals for England and scored 30 goals. His versatility was such that he started 40 internationals on the right wing, 33 at outside-left and three at centre-forward. On two occasions – against Wales in 1949 and Scotland in 1951 – Finney played brilliantly at inside-forward to compensate for a team-mate's injury. He played 433 League games and scored 187 goals. All were for Preston North End, his only Football League club. Yet his single European appearance was for Distillery in 1963, when George Eastham enticed him from retirement to help the Irish club draw

3-3 with Benfica in the European Cup.

Nicknamed the 'Preston Plumber', Tom Finney was probably the most complete all-round footballer of his era. More direct than Stanley Matthews, he tackled like a defender and his heading ability was that of the centre-forward he became later in his career. He was two-footed to such an extent that he could adapt to either wing. He was admired by fellow professionals and gained worldwide respect for his modest personality, remaining loyal to his home-town club in spite of other offers. For 14 post-war years his name was synonymous with Preston North End. When he retired the club soon lost First

Division status. Later awarded the OBE and honoured by the PFA's merit award, Finney is also the subject of a noted biography, Paul Agnew's *Finney – A Football Legend*.

FOOTBALL ASSOCIATION

The Football Association was formed on 26 October 1863 when representatives of 11 clubs met at the Freemason's Tavern, London. As the game's first ever association, it formed a model for associations worldwide, and it is still the ruling body of English football. Its enormous range of responsibilities include England international matches, various FA challenge competitions, nationwide coaching and the overseeing of games at all levels. Its work is controlled by the FA Council, which includes representatives from the Football League and local county football associations.

The FA's earliest administrators, who were largely from a public-school background, first unified the various and conflicting local rules of the game then introduced the FA Challenge Cup competition in 1871 to develop and popularise association football. It certainly did that. However, competition brought conflict between amateurs and professionals which has since dogged relationships between the FA and the Football League. In 1885 professionalism was legalised, but all clubs, professional or amateur, were still ultimately responsible to the Football Association.

Besides the FA Cup, the

early 1870s also saw the first England-Scotland international, soon after Charles Alcock became FA Secretary. A Sunderland man who was educated at Harrow, Alcock held the secretary's post from 1870 to 1895, the last eight years as a full-time official on £200 per annum. Alcock was succeeded by Sir Frederick Wall (1895-1934), who handed over to Sir Stanley Rous (1934-1961).

The Football Association became a limited company in 1903, a move stimulated by the previous year's Ibrox disaster. The First World War brought difficult decisions for the FA – to maintain league football in 1914-15 and then curtail it the following season – but popularity increased in 1923 when the FA was linked with the new Wembley Stadium.

Under Rous's influence the FA reacted better to world developments, rejoining FIFA in 1946 and sending a team to the 1950 World Cup. Youth was given its chance, too, with the launch of the FA County Youth Challenge Cup (1944), the England Youth team (1947), FA Youth Cup (1952) and England under-23 team (1954). The immediate post-war period

also brought closer links with the English Schools' FA and the appointment of Walter Winterbottom as Director of Coaching. Later FA initiatives included the FA Sunday Cup (1964), the FA Challenge Trophy (1969) and the FA Challenge Vase (1974).

Football's problems of the 1970s, 1980s and 1990s required responses from the FA. More time has been spent on disciplinary matters, monitoring drug tests and seeking measures to combat hooliganism. There have been protracted negotiations for sponsorship money and television deals, while ongoing concerns include ticket allocation for big games, liaison with UEFA and FIFA and arranging and administrating representative games. In 1989 Ted Croker retired after 15 important years as FA Secretary. His successor, Graham Kelly, was appointed chief executive after 10 years as Football League Secretary. It seemed like another step towards minimising the inherent conflict between the Football Association and the Football League. However, this schism came to a head in 1992 with the formation of the FA Premier League.

Graham Kelly took over as Chief Executive of the FA in 1989, after 10 years at the Football League. Prior to the 1992/93 season, the FA ran the FA Cup and various other challenge competitions; the Football League was responsible for all four divisions of the League and the League Cup. In 1992 a breakaway group of 22 clubs from the then First Division resigned from the Football League and formed the new Premier League under the control of The Football Association and the guidance of Graham Kelly.

FA CUP

It seems hard to avoid using cliches when writing about the Football Association Challenge Cup, to give the FA Cup its proper title. However, phrases like 'the magic of the Cup' and 'the road to Wembley' are both singularly appropriate and universally understood to apply to this and no other competition.

The FA Cup, which is often claimed to be the oldest knock-out competition in the world despite the fact that the idea was based on a similar tournament held at Harrow School, was conceived in 1871 under the guidance of FA Secretary Charles Alcock. The first Final was played in the following year. That competition was completed in just 13 matches with such highlights as Maidenhead's 2-0 victory over Great Marlow

Lawrie Sanchez scores the only goal of the 1988 FA Cup Final to put Wimbledon's name on the trophy for the first time. Before the game only the supporters of Wimbledon fancied their team's chances in this 'David v Goliath' match. Their opponents were the hotly fancied Liverpool. But the underdogs won. As the saying goes, 'the Cup is a one-off'.

in the first round and Wanderers' 1-0 Final win over the Royal Engineers, in front of 2000 spectators at Kennington Oval, stealing what few headlines there were.

The wholly amateur tournament thrived with increasing numbers of entrants and continued southern success until the 1883 victory of Blackburn Olympic. Those early years of the Cup contained frequent oddities. In the first tournament, teams involved in drawn matches were both allowed to progress to the next round; in the following year the Final was a challenge match, with teams playing in the rounds for a chance to challenge the holders.

Blackburn Olympic's victory (their neighbours Blackburn Rovers had been runners-up the preceding year) marked the start of a period of northern, and professional, domination. Although professionalism was to remain, the northern grip on the Cup was eventually broken by Southern League Tottenham Hotspur in 1901, who played their drawn Final in front of a crowd of 114,815 at Crystal Palace before their replay success against Sheffield United at Burnden Park, Bolton. The trophy that the Spurs won was not the familiar pot that is handed to today's winning captain. They won the second cup, which was later presented to Lord Kinnaird

Blackburn Olympic were winners of the FA Cup in 1883. They beat Old Etonians 2-1 in the Final, making them the first team to break the 'public school' image of the Cup winners. The match was played not at Wembley Stadium but at Kennington Oval. The Blackburn Olympic Cup-final team contained an iron moulder, a plumber, a picture framer and two weavers.

(nine Final appearances) when he retired as FA President. The very first cup had been stolen in 1895 from a shop in Birmingham. The third trophy was first won by Bradford City in 1911 (their only Cup success) and the present trophy, an exact replica of its predecessor, was first won by Liverpool in 1992.

Following that 1901 upset the north reasserted their almost total control of the Cup, a run that continued well beyond the famous 1923 Final – the first to be played at Wembley and noted for its 126,000 paying spectators and the single police horse that gently guided the overflowing crowd off the

FA CUP

Year	Winners	Runners-up	Score	Year	Winners	Runners-up	Score
1872	Wanderers	Royal Engineers	1-0	1934	Manchester City	Portsmouth	2-1
1873	Wanderers	Oxford University	2-0	1935	Sheffield Wednesday	West Bromwich A	4-2
1874	Oxford University	Royal Engineers	2-0	1936	Arsenal	Sheffield United	1-0
1875	Royal Engineers	Old Etonians	1-1* 2-1	1937	Sunderland	Preston North End	3-1
1876	Wanderers	Old Etonians	1-1* 3-0	1938	Preston North End	Huddersfield Town	1-0*
1877	Wanderers	Oxford University	2-0*	1939	Portsmouth	Wolverhampton W	4-1
1878	Wanderers	Royal Engineers	3-1	1946	Derby County	Charlton Athletic	4-1*
1879	Old Etonians	Clapham Rovers	1-0	1947	Charlton Athletic	Burnley	1-0*
1880	Clapham Rovers	Oxford University	1-0	1948	Manchester United	Blackpool	4-2
1881	Old Carthusians	Old Etonians	3-0	1949	Wolverhampton W	Leicester City	3-1
1882	Old Etonians	Blackburn Rovers	1-0	1950	Arsenal	Liverpool	2-0
1883	Blackburn Olympic	Old Etonians	2-1*	1951	Newcastle United	Blackpool	2-0
1884	Blackburn Rovers	Queen's Park	2-1	1952	Newcastle United	Arsenal	1-0
1885	Blackburn Rovers	Queen's Park	2-0	1953	Blackpool	Bolton Wanderers	4-3
1886	Blackburn Rovers	West Bromwich A	0-0 2-0	1954	West Bromwich A	Preston North End	3-2
1887	Aston Villa	West Bromwich A	2-0	1955	Newcastle United	Manchester City	3-1
1888	West Bromwich A	Preston North End	2-1	1956	Manchester City	Birmingham City	3-1
1889	Preston North End	Wolverhampton W	3-0	1957	Aston Villa	Manchester United	2-1
1890	Blackburn Rovers	Sheffield Wednesday	6-1	1958	Bolton Wanderers	Manchester United	2-0
1891	Blackburn Rovers	Notts County	3-1	1959	Nottingham Forest	Luton Town	2-1
1892	West Bromwich A	Aston Villa	3-0	1960	Wolverhampton W	Blackburn Rovers	3-0
1893	Wolverhampton W	Everton	1-0	1961	Tottenham Hotspur	Leicester City	2-0
1894	Notts County	Bolton Wanderers	4-1	1962	Tottenham Hotspur	Burnley	3-1
1895	Aston Villa	West Bromwich A	1-0	1963	Manchester United	Leicester City	3-1
1896	Sheffield Wednesday	Wolverhampton W	2-1	1964	West Ham United	Preston North End	3-2
1897	Aston Villa	Everton	3-2	1965	Liverpool	Leeds United	2-1*
1898	Nottingham Forest	Derby County	3-1	1966	Everton	Sheffield Wednesday	3-2
1899	Sheffield United	Derby County	4-1	1967	Tottenham Hotspur	Chelsea	2-1
1900	Bury	Southampton	4-0	1968	West Bromwich A	Everton	1-0*
1901	Tottenham Hotspur	Sheffield United	2-2 3-1	1969	Manchester City	Leicester City	1-0
1902	Sheffield United	Southampton	1-1 2-1	1970	Chelsea	Leeds United	2-2* 2-1
1903	Bury	Derby County	6-0	1971	Arsenal	Liverpool	2-1*
1904	Manchester City	Bolton Wanderers	1-0	1972	Leeds United	Arsenal	1-0
1905	Aston Villa	Newcastle United	2-0	1973	Sunderland	Leeds United	1-0
1906	Everton	Newcastle United	1-0	1974	Liverpool	Newcastle United	3-0
1907	Sheffield Wednesday	Everton	2-1	1975	West Ham United	Fulham	2-0
1908	Wolverhampton W	Newcastle United	3-1	1976	Southampton	Manchester United	1-0
1909	Manchester United	Bristol City	1-0	1977	Manchester United	Liverpool	2-1
1910	Newcastle United	Barnsley	1-1 2-0	1978	Ipswich Town	Arsenal	1-0
1911	Bradford City	Newcastle United	1-0 0-0	1979	Arsenal	Manchester United	3-2
1912	Barnsley	West Bromwich A	0-0 1-0*	1980	West Ham United	Arsenal	1-0
1913	Aston Villa	Sunderland	1-0	1981	Tottenham Hotspur	Manchester City	1-1* 3-2
1914	Burnley	Liverpool	1-0	1982	Tottenham Hotspur	Queen's Park Rangers	1-1* 1-0
1915	Sheffield United	Chelsea	3-0	1983	Manchester United	Brighton & Hove Albion	2-2* 4-0
1920	Aston Villa	Huddersfield Town	1-0*	1984	Everton	Watford	2-0
1921	Tottenham Hotspur	Wolverhampton W	1-0	1985	Manchester United	Everton	1-0*
1922	Huddersfield Town	Preston North End	1-0	1986	Liverpool	Everton	3-1
1923	Bolton Wanderers	West Ham United	2-0	1987	Coventry City	Tottenham Hotspur	3-2*
1924	Newcastle United	Aston Villa	2-0	1988	Wimbledon	Liverpool	1-0
1925	Sheffield United	Cardiff City	1-0	1989	Liverpool	Everton	3-2*
1926	Bolton Wanderers	Manchester City	1-0	1990	Manchester United	Crystal Palace	3-3* 1-0
1927	Cardiff City	Arsenal	1-0	1991	Tottenham Hotspur	Nottingham Forest	2-1*
1928	Blackburn Rovers	Huddersfield Town	3-1	1992	Liverpool	Sunderland	2-0
1929	Bolton Wanderers	Portsmouth	2-0	1993	Arsenal	Sheffield Wednesday	1-1* 2-1*
1930	Arsenal	Huddersfield Town	2-0	1994	Manchester United	Chelsea	4-0
1931	West Bromwich A	Birmingham City	2-1	1995	Everton	Manchester United	1-0
1932	Newcastle United	Arsenal	2-1				
1933	Everton	Manchester City	3-0				

* after extra time

playing surface. Wembley has staged every Final since that year with the exception of the 1970 Leeds United v Chelsea replay, played at Old Trafford. Wembley finals are now part of the English national tradition, matches that attract a vast television audience both domestically and around the world. These Finals have included a number of memorable and emotional occasions, perhaps the most famous being the 1953 match in which Sir Stanley Matthews finally won his Cup winner's medal for Blackpool against Bolton Wanderers; the 1958 defeat of Manchester United's Munich survivors, this time by Bolton; and the 1973 shock defeat of Leeds United by Second Division Sunderland Of course, the Final is not the only match of importance. Every game contains its own significance for the 500-600 entrants who begin battling it out in the late summer, some nine months before the tournament's eventual climax. It's the chance for non-League and smaller League sides to battle against the 'big boys' that appeals, and most seasons throw up a few shocks, a few moments of unexpected glory. The present rules exempt Second and Third Division sides until the first round proper, normally played in November, and First Division and Premiership teams until the magical third round, played in January.

As the record books show, the Cup is often the opportunity for a team not doing well in the League to grab some glory, and also a chance to qualify for a European competition. Aston Villa, who last won the Cup in 1957, have triumphed seven times, once fewer than the most frequent victors Tottenham Hotspur and Manchester United. Teams such as Newcastle United (six wins and four League Championships) figure prominently, in contrast to Liverpool (five wins and 18 League successes). Perhaps it's the nature of the competition – a simple knock-out with no seeding – that suits the style of some clubs better than others. Whatever it is, there is something about the Cup that marks it out as special for both fans and players. Even many modern professional players, financially hardened and media-spoiled, consider their careers incomplete without a Cup winner's medal.

For many years there was increasing talk about lavish sponsorship for the tournament, although voices within the FA were loath to see their famous trophy linked to any other name save their own. However, in 1994/95 the inevitable happened and the competition was dubbed 'The FA Cup sponsored by Littlewoods Pools'. Down the decades there have been grumbles and accusations about ticket allocations for the Final, the Football Association's big day; as the capacity of Wembley falls, due to safety restrictions and the change to an all-seater stadium, so it appears that genuine fans lose out to the wealthier and more influential members of society. The Football Association has to be careful. Although the Cup may now seem inviolate, the ghosts of the Wanderers and the Royal Engineers will tell you that nothing remains the same.

FOOTBALL LEAGUE

The Football League was, until the inception of the FA Premier League in 1992, by far the most important of the 1500 or more leagues affiliated to the Football Association. The oldest in the world, it was formed by 12 northern and Midland clubs in 1888, three years after professionalism had been sanctioned reluctantly by the largely amateur and southern-dominated Football Association. The League's founder, William McGregor, a Scottish draper and Aston Villa committee man, was frustrated by the impromptu nature of Cup and friendly fixtures. He realised that pre-arranged home and away fixtures would boost gate receipts and thereby finance the fledgling professional game.

Although continually criticised for putting commerce before sport, the League has been an enduring success. It expanded to two divisions of 28 clubs in 1892 (after the absorption of the rival Alliance League), reaching 44 clubs by 1919. In 1920 it took over the Southern League's best clubs to form a Third Division, followed shortly by the best of the rest from the north and Midlands, bringing the total

Founder of the Football League, William McGregor. He was particularly popular in his native Midlands, where he died on 20 December 1911 at the age of 65. His involvement with football was total; at his funeral his daughter said he has 'the spirit of a schoolboy and the heart of a true, full-grown man'.

to 88 clubs by 1923.

By that time League players exclusively formed the English national team, while the last non-League club to have won the FA Cup was Tottenham Hotspur in 1901.

Four extra clubs joined in 1950, and in 1958 the Third Divisions North and South were replaced by nationally-based Third and Fourth Divisions. However, the formation of the breakaway FA Premier League resulted in drastic changes. The new Football League set-up comprised three divisions, the First and Second having 24 clubs each, with the Third made up of 22.

The League itself is an essentially democratic body whose main function is to organise the weekly fixtures and the Football League Cup (currently sponsored by Coca-Cola), to oversee the financial and transfer arrangements of member clubs, and to distribute income accrued from outside sources such as sponsors, television companies and the football pools. The League's current sponsors are Endsleigh Insurance. League headquarters are in Lytham St Anne's, with a commercial office in London and a chief executive based in Nottingham.

For many years one of the most contentious issues concerning the League was its reluctance to elect new clubs in place of those which frequently finished at the foot of the Fourth Division. This so-called 'closed-shop' agreement ended in 1987, Scarborough becoming the first non-League club ever to win automatic promotion to the League as winners of the Vauxhall Conference (at the expense of Lincoln City). The Conference has thus become a de facto extra division. Controversially, though, a clause demanding that the non-League champions' ground facilities reached a certain standard proved a major obstacle to advancement. Thus Conference toppers Kidderminster Harriers (1994) and Macclesfield (1995) failed to join the elite.

There have been other important rule changes in recent decades. The award of two points per win, agreed in 1888 and copied throughout the world, was modified to three points per win in 1981 in a marginally successful attempt to encourage attacking play.

To add interest at the end of the season, a controversial but profitable system of play-offs was introduced in 1987, involving clubs on the fringes of automatic promotion and relegation.

Whereas before 1973 only two clubs were promoted and two relegated between the First and Second Divisions, the format has since been altered several times, with as many as four clubs being relegated from the top division in 1995.

The pressure on League clubs to finance the implementation of the Taylor Report has put in question the entire framework of English football. As in 1888, money continues to be the dominant issue.

FOOTBALL LEAGUE CHAMPIONSHIP

The League itself consisted, until 1992, of four divisions, but the 'Championship' always referred to Division 1, often called the hardest League in the world on account of the quality of teams and the number of matches to be played. That title has of course switched to the new FA Carling Premiership.

During the history of the Football League Championship as we know it, Liverpool were far and away the most successful club. They won it 18 times, eight more than nearest rivals Arsenal. Interestingly, it appeared to be a title that, if won once, could be won again. Of the 23 clubs to lift the Championship, only five were once-only winners.

FOOTBALL LEAGUE CUP

This was first competed for in 1960/61, although the idea of a competition solely between teams within the Football League had been suggested as early as 1892. Initially it was not well supported, with many top clubs refusing to enter. The persistence of League officials Alan Hardaker and Joe Richards kept the tournament going until the mid 1960s. It was in 1967 that the final was first held at Wembley and in the same year that success in the final first brought automatic qualification for the UEFA Cup (for First Division sides). Both moves, pushed through by Hardaker, were successful in encouraging greater interest and, very quickly, an entry from every League club.

With major sides competing, and Wembley full-houses and television exposure adding to the interest, the tournament became established. Several of the early Wembley finals were memorable affairs, particularly the successes of Third Division sides Swindon and Queen's Park Rangers over First Division opponents. Today the future of the tournament seems assured, although the name changes regularly with the sponsors. From 1982-86 it was the Milk Cup, then the Littlewoods Cup, and by 1992/93 Coca-Cola was it. Time will tell if the soft drink company retains the sponsorship of what sniffy Liverpudlians (when they declined to enter) once called the 'Mickey Mouse Cup'.

Bryan Robson displays the FA Premiership Trophy following Manchester United's title success in 1993/94. This is the new trophy replacing the old Football League Championship trophy (see the photograph of Stan Cullis, page 46). This was the second successive year for Manchester United but they were edged into runners-up spot by Blackburn Rovers in 1994/95, thus failing to emulate Huddersfield Town (1924-26), Arsenal (1932-34) and Liverpool (1982-84) by winning three in a row.

LEAGUE CHAMPIONSHIP

Year	Winners	Runners-up
1888/89	Preston North End	Aston Villa
1889/90	Preston North End	Everton
1890/91	Everton	Preston North End
1891/92	Sunderland	Preston North End
1892/93	Sunderland	Preston North End
1893/94	Aston Villa	Sunderland
1894/95	Sunderland	Everton
1896/97	Aston Villa	Sheffield United
1897/98	Sheffield United	Sunderland
1898/99	Aston Villa	Liverpool
1899/1900	Aston Villa	Sheffield United
1900/01	Liverpool	Sunderland
1901/02	Sunderland	Everton
1902/03	The Wednesday	Aston Villa
1903/04	The Wednesday	Manchester City
1904/05	Newcastle United	Everton
1905/06	Liverpool	Preston North End
1906/07	Newcastle United	Bristol City
1907/08	Manchester United	Aston Villa
1908/09	Newcastle United	Bristol City
1909/10	Aston Villa	Liverpool
1910/11	Manchester United	Aston Villa
1911/12	Blackburn Rovers	Everton
1912/13	Sunderland	Aston Villa
1913/14	Blackburn Rovers	Aston Villa
1914/15	Everton	Oldham Athletic
1915-19	*No competition*	
1919/20	West Bromwich Albion	Burnley
1920/21	Burnley	Manchester City
1921/22	Liverpool	Tottenham Hotspur
1922/23	Liverpool	Sunderland
1923/24	Huddersfield Town	Cardiff City
1924/25	Huddersfield Town	West Bromwich Albion
1925/26	Huddersfield Town	Arsenal
1926/27	Newcastle United	Huddersfield Town
1927/28	Everton	Huddersfield Town
1928/29	Sheffield Wednesday	Leicester City
1929/30	Sheffield Wednesday	Derby County
1930/31	Arsenal	Aston Villa
1931/32	Everton	Arsenal
1932/33	Arsenal	Aston Villa
1933/34	Arsenal	Huddersfield Town
1934/35	Arsenal	Sunderland
1935/36	Sunderland	Derby County
1936/37	Manchester City	Charlton Athletic
1937/38	Arsenal	Wolverhampton W
1938/39	Everton	Wolverhampton W
1939-46	*No competition*	
1946/47	Liverpool	Manchester United
1947/48	Arsenal	Manchester United
1948/49	Portsmouth	Manchester United
1949/50	Portsmouth	Wolverhampton W
1950/51	Tottenham Hotspur	Manchester United
1951/52	Manchester United	Tottenham Hotspur
1952/53	Arsenal	Preston North End
1953/54	Wolverhampton W	West Bromwich Albion
1954/55	Chelsea	Wolverhampton W
1955/56	Manchester United	Blackpool
1956/57	Manchester United	Tottenham Hotspur
1957/58	Wolverhampton W	Preston North End
1958/59	Wolverhampton W	Manchester United
1959/60	Burnley	Wolverhampton W
1960/61	Tottenham Hotspur	Sheffield Wednesday
1961/62	Ipswich Town	Burnley
1962/63	Everton	Tottenham Hotspur
1963/64	Liverpool	Manchester United
1964/65	Manchester United	Leeds United
1965/66	Liverpool	Leeds United
1966/67	Manchester United	Nottingham Forest
1967/68	Manchester City	Manchester United
1968/69	Leeds United	Liverpool
1969/70	Everton	Leeds United
1970/71	Arsenal	Leeds United
1971/72	Derby County	Leeds United
1972/73	Liverpool	Arsenal
1973/74	Leeds United	Liverpool
1974/75	Derby County	Liverpool
1975/76	Liverpool	Queens Park Rangers
1976/77	Liverpool	Manchester City
1977/78	Nottingham Forest	Liverpool
1978/79	Liverpool	Nottingham Forest
1979/80	Liverpool	Manchester United
1980/81	Aston Villa	Ipswich Town
1981/82	Liverpool	Ipswich Town
1982/83	Liverpool	Watford
1983/84	Liverpool	Southampton
1984/85	Everton	Liverpool
1985/86	Liverpool	Everton
1986/87	Everton	Liverpool
1987/88	Liverpool	Manchester United
1988/89	Arsenal	Liverpool
1989/90	Liverpool	Aston Villa
1990/91	Arsenal	Liverpool
1991/92	Leeds United	Manchester United
1992/93	Manchester United	Aston Villa
1993/94	Manchester United	Blackburn Rovers
1994/95	Blackburn Rovers	Manchester United

FOOTBALL LEAGUE CUP

(Played with two-leg finals until 1966)

Year	Winners	Runners-up	Score
1961	Aston Villa	Rotherham United	0-2, 3-0*
1962	Norwich City	Rochdale	3-0, 1-0
1963	Birmingham City	Aston Villa	3-1, 0-0
1964	Leicester City	Stoke City	1-1, 3-2
1965	Chelsea	Leicester City	3-2, 0-0
1966	West Bromwich A	West Ham United	1-2, 4-1
1967	Queen's Park Rangers	West Bromwich A	3-2
1968	Leeds United	Arsenal	1-0
1969	Swindon Town	Arsenal	3-1*
1970	Manchester City	West Bromwich A	2-1*
1971	Tottenham Hotspur	Aston Villa	2-0
1972	Stoke City	Chelsea	2-1
1973	Tottenham Hotspur	Norwich City	1-0
1974	Wolverhampton W	Manchester City	2-1
1975	Aston Villa	Norwich City	1-0
1976	Manchester City	Newcastle United	2-1
1977	Aston Villa	Everton	0-0, 1-1*, 3-2*
1978	Nottingham Forest	Liverpool	0-0, 1-0
1979	Nottingham Forest	Southampton	3-2
1980	Wolverhampton W	Nottingham Forest	1-0
1981	Liverpool	West Ham United	1-1*, 2-1
1982	Liverpool	Tottenham Hotspur	3-1*
1983	Liverpool	Manchester United	2-1*
1984	Liverpool	Everton	0-0*, 1-0
1985	Norwich City	Sunderland	1-0
1986	Oxford United	Queen's Park Rangers	3-0
1987	Arsenal	Liverpool	2-1
1988	Luton Town	Arsenal	3-2
1989	Nottingham Forest	Luton Town	3-1
1990	Nottingham Forest	Oldham Athletic	1-0
1991	Sheffield Wednesday	Manchester United	1-0
1992	Manchester United	Nottingham Forest	1-0
1993	Arsenal	Sheffield Wednesday	2-1
1994	Aston Villa	Manchester United	3-1
1995	Liverpool	Bolton Wanderers	2-1

*After extra time

Formed in 1979, the Football Trust was initially funded entirely by Littlewoods, Vernons and Zetters from their spot-the-ball competitions. In 1990 the Trust was granted an additional budget from funds created by the reduction in football-pools tax announced in the Chancellor's budget.

The Trust has worked extensively to support and fund community initiatives in the professional and semi-professional game. It has also contributed to the improvement of stadium facilities and anti-hooliganism measures such as closed-circuit television. Among its work at grass-roots level is support for the Disabled Sports Foundation and the Sports Turf Research Institute. It has also funded research projects and in April 1987 helped establish the Sir Norman Chester Centre for Football Research at Leicester University.

In 1990 the Football Trust combined with the Football Grounds Improvement Trust to form 'The Football Trust 90', an important organisation with a budget of £30 million per annum to allocate to ground-safety projects, in particular the conversions to all-seater stadia. The Trust members are chosen to represent all the interested parties: the football associations and leagues of England and Scotland, local authorities, the Professional Footballers' Association, the police and the pools companies.

Nigel Jemson and Des Walker of Nottingham Forest with the Littlewoods Cup, otherwise known as the League Cup, in 1990. This was the second year running that Forest had lifted the League Cup trophy. At present this trophy is sponsored by Coca-Cola and not surprisingly known as the Coca-Cola Cup.

FOOTBALL WRITERS' ASSOCIATION

Year	Winner	Club
1948	Stanley Matthews	Blackpool
1949	Johnny Carey	Manchester United
1950	Joe Mercer	Arsenal
1951	Harry Johnston	Blackpool
1952	Billy Wright	Wolverhampton W
1953	Nat Lofthouse	Bolton Wanderers
1954	Tom Finney	Preston North End
1955	Don Revie	Manchester City
1956	Bert Trautmann	Manchester City
1957	Tom Finney	Preston North End
1958	Danny Blanchflower	Tottenham Hotspur
1959	Syd Owen	Luton Town
1960	Bill Slater	Wolverhampton W
1961	Danny Blanchflower	Tottenham Hotspur
1962	Jimmy Adamson	Burnley
1963	Stanley Matthews	Stoke City
1964	Bobby Moore	West Ham United
1965	Bobby Collins	Leeds United
1966	Bobby Charlton	Manchester United
1967	Jackie Charlton	Leeds United
1968	George Best	Manchester United
1969	Tony Book	Manchester City
	Dave Mackay	Derby County
1970	Billy Bremner	Leeds United
1971	Frank McLintock	Arsenal
1972	Gordon Banks	Stoke City
1973	Pat Jennings	Tottenham Hotspur
1974	Ian Callaghan	Liverpool
1975	Alan Mullery	Fulham
1976	Kevin Keegan	Liverpool
1977	Emlyn Hughes	Liverpool
1978	Kenny Burns	Nottingham Forest
1979	Kenny Dalglish	Liverpool
1980	Terry McDermott	Liverpool
1981	Frans Thijssen	Ipswich Town
1982	Steve Perryman	Tottenham Hotspur
1983	Kenny Dalglish	Liverpool
1984	Ian Rush	Liverpool
1985	Neville Southall	Everton
1986	Gary Lineker	Everton
1987	Clive Allen	Tottenham Hotspur
1988	John Barnes	Liverpool
1989	Steve Nicol	Liverpool
1990	John Barnes	Liverpool
1991	Gordon Strachan	Leeds United
1992	Gary Lineker	Tottenham Hotspur
1993	Chris Waddle	Sheffield Wednesday
1994	Alan Shearer	Blackburn Rovers
1995	Jurgen Klinsmann	Tottenham Hotspur

PROFESSIONAL FOOTBALLERS' ASSOCIATION

Year	Winner	Club
1974	Norman Hunter	Leeds United
1975	Colin Todd	Derby County
1976	Pat Jennings	Tottenham Hotspur
1977	Andy Gray	Aston Villa
1978	Peter Shilton	Nottingham Forest
1979	Liam Brady	Arsenal
1980	Terry McDermott	Liverpool
1981	John Wark	Ipswich Town
1982	Kevin Keegan	Southampton
1983	Kenny Dalglish	Liverpool
1984	Ian Rush	Liverpool
1985	Peter Reid	Everton
1986	Gary Lineker	Everton
1987	Clive Allen	Tottenham Hotspur
1988	John Barnes	Liverpool
1989	Mark Hughes	Manchester United
1990	David Platt	Aston Villa
1991	Mark Hughes	Manchester United
1992	Gary Pallister	Manchester United
1993	Paul McGrath	Aston Villa
1994	Eric Cantona	Manchester United
1995	Alan Shearer	Blackburn Rovers

SCOTTISH FOOTBALL WRITERS' ASSOCIATION

Year	Winner	Club
1965	Billy McNeill	Celtic
1966	John Greig	Rangers
1967	Ronnie Simpson	Celtic
1968	Gordon Wallace	Raith Rovers
1969	Bobby Murdoch	Celtic
1970	Pat Stanton	Hibernian
1971	Martin Buchan	Aberdeen
1972	Dave Smith	Rangers
1973	George Connelly	Celtic
1974	Scotland's World Cup Squad	
1975	Sandy Jardine	Rangers
1976	John Greig	Rangers
1977	Danny McGrain	Celtic
1978	Derek Johnstone	Rangers
1979	Andy Ritchie	Morton
1980	Gordon Strachan	Aberdeen
1981	Alan Rough	Partick Thistle
1982	Paul Sturrock	Dundee United
1983	Charlie Nicholas	Celtic
1984	Willie Miller	Aberdeen
1985	Hamish McAlpine	Dundee United
1986	Sandy Jardine	Hearts
1987	Brian McClair	Celtic
1988	Paul McStay	Celtic
1989	Richard Gough	Rangers
1990	Alex McLeish	Aberdeen
1991	Maurice Malpas	Dundee United
1992	Ally McCoist	Rangers
1993	Andy Goram	Rangers
1994	Mark Hateley	Rangers
1995	Brian Laudrup	Rangers

FOOTBALLER OF THE YEAR

It seems natural for there to be a trophy acknowledging the top player for a season – although perhaps not so understandable that there are two! In 1948 the Football Writers' Association began the FWA Footballer of the Year trophy for their choice of the season's top player from the Football League. This seemed fine, until 1974 when the Professional Footballers' Association set up their own awards for what they called the 'Players' Player of the Year'. The PFA also present a young player's award and give special merit awards.

The two accolades sit uneasily together, although nobody minds picking up an award and in some years the same player picks up both. In 1983 Ian Rush (Liverpool) won the PFA Young Player award and in 1984 he picked up both senior awards.

Scotland has similar awards, again with trophies being presented by two bodies, the Scottish FWA and PFA. These are for players in the Scottish League and, unlike the English awards, have been won almost exclusively by players born in Scotland.

FORFAR ATHLETIC

Founded 1885

Joined League 1921 (Division 2)

Honours Scottish League Second Division Champions

SCOTTISH PROFESSIONAL FOOTBALLERS' ASSOCIATION

Year	Winner	Club
1978	Derek Johnstone	Rangers
1979	Paul Hegarty	Dundee United
1980	Davie Provan	Celtic
1981	Sandy Clark	Airdrieonians
1982	Mark McGhee	Aberdeen
1983	Charlie Nicholas	Celtic
1984	Willie Miller	Aberdeen
1985	Jim Duff	Morton
1986	Richard Gough	Dundee
1987	Brian McClair	Celtic
1988	Paul McStay	Celtic
1989	Theo Snelders	Aberdeen
1990	Jim Bett	Aberdeen
1991	Paul Elliott	Celtic
1992	Ally McCoist	Rangers
1993	Andy Goram	Rangers
1994	Mark Hateley	Rangers
1995	Brian Laudrup	Rangers

1984; Third Division Champions 1995; Division C Champions 1949

Ground Station Park

Forfar have found their greatest fame in alarming mighty Rangers. With seven minutes to go of the 1977/78 League Cup semi-final they led the Glasgow side 2-1 before losing in extra-time, while in 1982 Rangers required two matches to dispose of them in the semi-final of the Scottish Cup.

Forfar also narrowly failed to beat the Ibrox men in a 1985 League Cup tie finally decided by a penalty shoot-out. Those stirring matches occurred in the finest period of the club's history. In 1984 Forfar won the Second Division with a record 63 points. More recently times have been harder, though the Third Division title triumph of 1995 boded well for the future.

Alan Shearer, having just scored for Blackburn Rovers during a 2-1 victory against Chelsea in March 1995, won the FWA Player of the Year award in 1994 and was the PFA choice in 1995. Shearer is known for his goalscoring ability but is also seen by many in the game to be a perfect model for young fans; he is well disciplined on the pitch and has a spotless reputation off it.

FULHAM

Founded 1879

Joined League 1907 (Division 2)

Honours Division 2 Champions 1949; Division 3 (S) Champions 1932

Ground Craven Cottage

Fulham have always been a homely club who have placed heavy accent on entertainment; their very name has been a byword for eccentricity. In the cut-throat business that soccer has become, such an admirable trait has sometimes seemed out of place, and even the most loyal Craven Cottage fan might, at times, have been willing to forgo the endearing foibles – often exemplified by the antics of long-time chairman, the late Tommy Trinder – in favour of a little more success and financial stability.

It all started when two clergymen formed the club on behalf of their churchgoers and, after twice winning the Southern League, Fulham were elected to the senior competition. At first they held their own in Division 2, but a gradual decline culminated in relegation in 1928. Four years later, bolstered by 43-goal Frank Newton, they bounced back and then consolidated.

After the war they managed three terms in the top flight, and perversely, demotion in 1952 heralded a buoyant period. Though the

Jimmy Hill played for Fulham from 1951 to 1960. He made a total of 276 appearances for them as an inside-forward and scored 41 goals. Jimmy was Chairman of the Professional Footballers' Association from 1958 to 1961, manager of Coventry City for the next six years, and has been the guiding light and saviour behind the scenes at Fulham FC since 1987. He can also be seen on television pontificating about football. His face must be a cartoonist's dream.

rest of the decade was spent in the Second Division, Fulham served up some of the capital's most attractive football and deserved promotion when it arrived in 1959. Life proved difficult in the First Division, though, and the 'Cottagers' spent the 1960s fighting rearguard actions, until a sudden slide dumped them in Division 3 in 1969.

During those two eventful decades, Fulham's most influential player was gifted schemer Johnny Haynes, with other major contributions coming from centre-forward Bedford Jezzard (who also served as manager), defenders Jim Langley and England World Cup star George Cohen, wingers Graham Leggat and the extrovert 'Tosh' Chamberlain, goalkeeper Tony Macedo, wing-halves Bobby Robson and Alan Mullery and inside-forward Jimmy Hill.

Since then Fulham have generally divided their time between the middle divisions. The 1970s were enlivened by the 1975 FA Cup Final (lost to West Ham), the presence for three years of Bobby Moore, and cameo stints from George Best and Rodney Marsh.

The early 1980s, with former Cottager Malcolm Macdonald in charge, saw many bright displays, but the promise faded and in 1987 the club came perilously close to a merger with Queen's Park Rangers. That was averted by a group headed by the aforementioned Hill, but Fulham's long-term future remained uncertain, a situation underlined by relegation to the League's basement in 1994.

GALLACHER, Hughie

1903 Born in Bellshill, Scotland

1920 Joins his first professional club, Queen of the South

1921 Signs for Airdrieonians

1924 International debut against Northern Ireland

1925 Moves to Newcastle United for £6500

1927 Captains the 'Magpies' to the League Championship

1930 Joins Chelsea for £10,000

1935 Makes a £3000 switch to Derby County

1936 Moves on to Notts County for £2000

1937 His price still dropping, he joins Grimsby Town for £1000

1938 Gateshead sign him for £500

1957 Commits suicide on a railway line

Many shrewd pundits have described Hughie Gallacher as the most complete centre-forward British soccer has known. Standing a mere 5ft 5in, Gallacher was a muscular bundle of skill, strength and energy who thrived at every level of the game, but whose private life was a sad and sorry mess.

After playing as a schoolboy alongside Alex James, he made such an impact in the Scottish League that there were protest demonstrations when his transfer to Newcastle was announced. Gallacher was an instant success on Tyneside, becoming a skipper who led by both example and scathing criticism of those less talented than himself.

He was equally effective on the international scene – netting 22 times in 20 outings for Scotland – and was one of

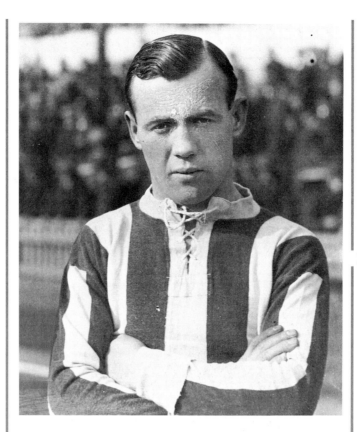

the famous 'Wembley Wizards', who thrashed England 5-1 in 1928. Gallacher went on to give five years' sterling service to Chelsea before dropping down the scale with smaller clubs, although he never stopped scoring and ended with a record of 387 strikes in 541 League games.

A temperamental, arrogant individual who was addicted to high living, he was involved in frequent controversy and would have been a gossip-writer's dream today. He ended up a lonely man who took his own life by stepping in front of a train the day before he was to appear in court accused of ill-treating his child.

GAMBLING

People have always placed bets on the outcome of football matches either privately, through bookmakers or on football pools. Odds are also quoted for football competitions such as the FA Cup and Football League. Bookmakers have also taken bets on possible goalscorers, but there is sometimes a dispute over this. One example is Arsenal's equaliser in the 1971 FA Cup

Final, thought to be scored by George Graham until close scrutiny over several days revealed that Graham had not touched Eddie Kelly's pass.

In the early 1920s a Birmingham bookmaker launched the first football coupon. The idea was developed by John Moores, Colin Askham and Bill Hughes, who formed the Littlewoods Pools organisation in 1923. John Moores bought out his colleagues during a period of early difficulties and by 1929 Littlewoods were hiring 50 girls to check coupons. A rival organisation, Vernon's Pools, was formed in the same year, and the biggest prizes became associated with forecasting drawn games.

In 1949 pools companies included Australian matches for the first time. The winter prize money grew, passing £100,000 in 1950 and £300,000 nine years later. In 1959 Football League fixtures were confirmed as the League's copyright, and the pools companies agreed to pay for reproducing them. Around the same time clubs became aware that they could raise money by small-scale commercial ventures such as lotteries and bingo tickets.

In January 1963 the pools companies inaugurated the

Hughie Gallacher captained Newcastle United to the League Championship in 1926/27. He was short for a centre-forward, yet there can be no doubting his skill and goalscoring prowess – 387 goals in 541 English and Scottish League games and 22 goals for Scotland in only 20 appearances. This photograph fails to provide a hint as to the real Hughie Gallacher, or to the tragedy that was to lie in wait for him.

'pools panel', a group of experts who could agree the results of postponed matches, enabling the pools to continue through bad weather. Changes to the rules occurred over the years and the winnings continued to rise. In April 1987 a 60-year-old woman won a then record £1,032,088 for a £1.20 stake, and 1992 saw the first £2 million jackpot.

The continuing success of football pools in Britain was put in doubt in 1995 with the launch of the National Lottery. Some weekly individual prizes from the Lottery reached more than £10m, far outweighing the big pools payouts.

Gambling, of course, can encourage attempts to fix matches. Almost every country has had a major bribery investigation associated with gambling. Sometimes the suspects are officials who have allegedly bribed opponents to ensure bonuses or trophies, but more regularly they are players attempting to win money on bets placed.

One of the most dramatic investigations in recent years was in Hungary in 1983, when 260 players and 14 referees were among those suspended and 75 people were convicted of conspiring to fix matches in lower leagues.

There have been many scandals in South America, notably concerning Colombia during the 1994 World Cup, and in Italy in the late 1970s Paolo Rossi – destined to become a national hero for his performances in the 1982 World Cup – was suspended for a year over betting offences. The top European club competitions have not been immune from corruption, with Champions Cup holders Marseille being banned for a year following bribery allegations in 1993/94. Dynamo Tbilisi were also suspended from that season's competition for allegedly bribing match officials to secure passage in the preliminary-round tie with Linfield.

The British game has not been free of scandal. In 1905 Manchester City's Billy Meredith, the most famous footballer of his age, was suspended for offering £10 to an Aston Villa player in an attempt to influence the result of a match. Ten years later a Football League game between Manchester United and Liverpool was the subject of a lengthy enquiry. Nine players were suspended from football for allegedly fixing the game, profiting from bets and defrauding bookmakers. One accused player later failed to win a libel action against the FA. Manchester United won the game 2-0.

But the most infamous instance of proven bribery in British football was unmasked in 1964, when it was revealed that three Sheffield Wednesday players – England internationals Peter Swan and Tony Kay, and the promising David 'Bronco' Layne – had bet on their own team to lose at Ipswich in December 1962. The East Anglians won 2-0 and the sorry trio were alleged to have won £100 each. As a result each man spent four months in prison and was banned from football for life, a sentence which was lifted only when it was much too late to rebuild their careers. Seven other lesser-known players with smaller clubs were jailed for terms varying between six months and four years as the ripples spread wider, and the sports-loving public reeled with shock and indignation.

The FA tightened regulations on football-club personnel betting on matches (a ban which had operated from 1892 had been lifted in 1957) and, apart from the occasional story – such as an unproved allegation in 1972 that Leeds United manager Don Revie attempted to induce Wolves players to 'take a dive' in a match crucial to the outcome of the Championship – little more was heard of bribery in British soccer until the Grobbelaar bombshell burst in November 1994.

GARRINCHA

1933 Born in Pau Grande, Brazil

1952 Joins Botafogo of Rio

1955 Gains first of 59 Brazilian caps

1958 Helps Brazil to World Cup win, 5-2 v Sweden

1962 Sent off in World Cup semi-final against Chile – hit by a bottle as he leaves the field; after a personal plea from the Brazilian president, Garrincha is allowed to play in the Final. Brazil win 3-1 v Czechoslovakia

1964 Botafogo are Brazilian champions

1965 Another championship, this time shared with Santos; car

Garrincha lining up for World Cup duty during the finals in Sweden in 1958. It was during the 1962 tournament in Chile that Garrincha really shone and, looking at film of those matches, it is hard to believe that he was partially crippled by polio as a child and displayed distinctly bowed legs as a player.

crash puts World Cup place in jeopardy

1966 Plays in World Cup in England but is not fully fit (Brazil go out in first round); transferred to Corinthians of Sao Paulo

1967 Retires

1983 Dies of alcoholic poisoning

Garrincha's life began badly and ended tragically, but in between his skills blazed with a brightness few have matched. An outstanding player in one World Cup, the dominant force in another and a goalscorer in a third, he was an innocent, flawed genius, brilliant on the football field but hopelessly equipped to cope with life off it.

Born into poverty and half crippled by polio as a small child, Garrincha (his real name was Manoel Francisco dos Santos but he was known by his nickname, meaning 'Little Bird', from an early age) learned to run on his disfigured right leg and, miraculously, at his peak was capable of explosive speed. Indeed, his twisted limb may even have been to his advantage, aiding his body-swerve. He was only 5ft 7in but could leap spectacularly, adding strong heading to his ability to shoot powerfully from outside the penalty area.

In 1958 Garrincha missed Brazil's first two World Cup matches in Sweden, but after a 0-0 draw with England his Botafogo team-mates pleaded with manager Vicente Feola for the right-winger's inclusion. Garrincha's introduction, coupled with that of the 17-year-old Pele, turned a good side into a glorious one, the only team to win outside its own continent. Four years later his contribution was even more important. Injury forced Pele out of the tournament so Garrincha, by necessity, became the focal point of Brazilian attacks. He responded magnificently, tore England to pieces in the quarter-finals and did the same to Chile in the semis, and, in addition to providing the cutting edge for several

goals, scored four himself.

Age and a car crash had taken their toll by 1966 and his one worthwhile contribution in England proved to be a devastating free-kick against Bulgaria at Goodison. For Garrincha and Brazil the rest of the tournament was an anti-climax, as indeed was the rest of his life. He died a burnt-out alcoholic, in 1983.

GASCOIGNE, Paul

1967 Born in Gateshead

1985 Makes League debut for Newcastle United

1988 Transferred to Tottenham Hotspur for £2 million

1989 Scores first goal for England in his third international appearance, coming on as a substitute against Albania and cheerfully ignoring manager Bobby Robson's tactical instructions

1990 England's star performer in the World Cup finals, his tears after the semi-final defeat against West Germany prompt 'Gazzamania' back in England. Voted BBC Sports Personality of the Year

1991 Badly injured playing for Tottenham in the FA Cup Final having agreed to a multi-million pound move to Lazio of Rome

1992 Transfer to Lazio is confirmed at £5.5 million. Returns to action with Lazio and England after a sixteen-month absence

1994 Breaks leg in training, throwing his future in doubt.

1995 Sets up a £4.3 million move to Glasgow Rangers

A truly inspirational player, a showman and a show-stealer who seems incapable of being upstaged by anyone or anything, Paul Gascoigne picked up the threads of his injury-hit career – and resumed his effortless domination of the headlines. A broken leg put the *Gazza* story on 'hold' once more in 1994.

Back in the summer of 1988, the ebullient, chubby young Geordie midfielder was at 21 already the hottest property in English football. Out of contract and unimpressed by the new deal offered him by Newcastle, he determined to move on; the silver tongue of Spurs manager Terry Venables prevailed in the face of stiff competition and so Spurs it was who for three years enjoyed the Gazza magic.

While his long-range shooting, curled free-kicks and trickery led to initial comparisons at Tottenham with Glenn Hoddle, Gascoigne's real strength always lay in his tireless running with the ball. His quick feet, body strength and sidestep, along with a complete technical mastery of the moving ball, made him well-nigh impossible to dispossess. What was more, he retained exceptional vision when dribbling at speed. As he drew panicking defenders to him, the right boot would flick out a short pass or the ball would be switched inside to release a colleague. Never one to stand back and admire, Gascoigne would then instinctively run into space to seek a return pass.

For Spurs he hit a rich vein of form, but for two years England manager Bobby Robson preferred to keep him at arm's length, using him grudgingly as substitute or confining him to the B team until he was finally let loose on Czechoslovakia in April 1990. He had a hand in three England goals and scored a thrilling fourth himself to ensure his place in the World Cup finals.

In Italy came the tears for which he is remembered, which was a pity as they came to be used against him. Those who later derided them chose to forget just how much the fearlessness of his performances, against the mighty Dutch and West Germans especially, had done to lift English spirits.

Italia '90 was the prelude to a veritable rollercoaster of a season with Tottenham in 1990-91 which seemed almost to tell the story of his

'Gazza' is an excitable and inspirational footballer, arguably England's star performer in the 1990 World Cup Finals. He is capable of scoring stunning goals, but sometimes acts like a spoilt child. His reckless tackle in the 1991 FA Cup Final when playing for Spurs left him with severely damaged knee ligaments and put his £8.5 million transfer to Lazio in Italy in jeopardy. The England side desperately needs Gascoigne's flair and influence.

entire career. Crowds flocked to see him and Lineker, but before long his overbearing superstar presence on the pitch and the relentless 'Gazzamania' off it began to grate on many outside White Hart Lane. A crucial League encounter with Liverpool culminated in him receiving a celebrated elbow in the face from Steve McMahon, as well as showing up his occasional ineffectiveness against determined man-marking, and a new low was reached on New Year's Day with his sending off against Manchester United. But just a few days later began Tottenham's FA Cup campaign which saw Gascoigne, by now the subject of frenzied transfer speculation as Spurs' financial crisis deepened, dragging his team almost single-handedly through to a Wembley semi-final against Arsenal, where he delivered what proved a sweet parting gift to Tottenham, a thumping free-kick after just five minutes that fairly screamed into the old enemy's net and set up a 3-1 victory.

For even as he revelled in his greatest club triumph, changes were afoot. Lazio had bid £8.5 million for him, Spurs' bankers demanded it be accepted, and Paul himself grew ever more enamoured of the prospect of Serie A and financial security. But the rollercoaster had one final dip to deliver on Cup Final day as Gascoigne lunged into a grotesque 'tackle' and

Giant killing traditionally refers to a Cup-tie victory by a club of lower status. The most extreme form of English giant killing, non-League clubs beating First Division clubs in the FA Cup, has occurred several times since the First World War: Sheffield Wednesday 0 Darlington 2 (first round replay in 1919/20), Corinthians 1 Blackburn Rovers 0 (first round in 1923/24), Colchester United 1 Huddersfield Town 0 (third round in 1947/48), Yeovil Town 2 Sunderland 1 (fourth round in 1948/49), Hereford United 2 Newcastle United 1 (third round replay in 1971/72), Burnley 0 Wimbledon 1 (third round in 1974/75), Birmingham City 1 Altrincham 2 (third round in 1985/86) and Sutton United 2 Coventry City 1 (third round in 1988/89).

Most of these non-League teams lost heavily in the next round – Sutton went down 8-0 to Norwich City and Yeovil lost by the same score to Manchester United in front of 81,565 spectators – but others continued to surprise. Colchester United beat Second Division Bradford Park Avenue to reach the fifth round, and Wimbledon drew 0-0 at First Division Leeds United in the fourth, helped by Dickie Guy's penalty save. They were defeated by a deflected goal in the replay.

But mention of Wimbledon illustrates the transient nature of some giant killing. Wimbledon were in the Southern League and Burnley sixth in Division 1 when they met in 1974/75. Ten years later, when they were paired together again, Burnley were a poor Division 3 team and Wimbledon in the Second Division. There was no surprise about Wimbledon's 3-1 win.

In Scotland there is a long history of surprise results, from Celtic's 4-2 defeat by non-League Arthurlie in 1896/97 through to Inverness Caledonian's win against Airdrie (on penalty-kicks after a replay) in 1989/90. Non-

wrecked his knee ligaments in the process. He left Wembley on a stretcher, his very career, let alone the move to Italy, in jeopardy.

He did not play again for over a year, and by the time he took his first tentative steps in a Lazio shirt it was not only medically that he needed rehabilitation, his reputation badly damaged by the Cup Final madness. But fittingly it was international football which provided Gazza with a timely opportunity to re-endear himself to the football public. His long absence had coincided with, or more likely resulted in, a series of depressing, lifeless displays from the national side. Come Gazza's return, England were literally transformed, his second game back illuminated by two goals after typically neat footwork and generally full of the joyful exuberance he had always radiated in an England shirt. Sadly, another serious injury cut short his reliability, and the football world waited to see if Gascoigne could survive this latest setback.

Every year the bigger clubs must wonder if it's their turn to become the headlines for the wrong reason – beaten in the FA Cup by a team from a lower division or, worst of all, from outside the Football League. In 1991/92 it was the turn of mighty Arsenal to lose 2-1 at Wrexham in the 3rd round of the FA Cup. Steve Watkin, in red on his hands and knees, beats Arsenal's goalkeeper, David Seaman. Giant killing provides the 'magic' of cup competitions and brings in much-needed revenue for the smaller clubs.

League Armadale beat three Scottish League clubs – Clyde, Hibernian and Ayr United – to reach the quarter-final of the 1919/20 Scottish Cup competition. Elgin City also beat three League clubs – Albion Rovers, Forfar Athletic and Arbroath – in 1967/68. Other major Scottish Cup upsets include Fraserburgh 1 Dundee 0 (first round in 1956/57) and Berwick Rangers 1 Rangers 0 (first round in 1966/67). The latter was especially dramatic. As Keevins and McCarra write in 100 Cups, 'There are Celtic supporters with a perverted sense of history who can tell you where they were standing when they heard Rangers had lost 1-0, and such was the barely credible result that even BBC television's afternoon sports programme refused to accept it as being true in the first place.'

Jock Wallace, manager of Berwick Rangers in 1967, later took over at Rangers. In 1980/81, however, Wallace was manager of First Division Leicester City when they drew at home to Fourth Division Exeter City and lost the replay. Exeter beat another First Division club, Newcastle United, in the fifth round before losing to Spurs in the sixth.

English League Cup winners include two Third Division clubs. In 1966/67 Queen's Park Rangers beat two First Division teams and two Second Division teams to win the trophy; in 1968/69 Swindon Town overcame three First Division teams – Coventry, Burnley and Arsenal – and Second Division leaders Derby County. Several Third Division clubs have reached the FA Cup semi-finals: Millwall (1936/37), Port Vale (1953/54), York City (1954/55), Norwich City (1958/59), Crystal Palace (1975/76) and Plymouth Argyle (1983/84).

In 1984/85, non-League Telford United beat four League teams – Preston, Lincoln, Bradford City and Darlington – before losing to First Division Everton in the fifth round. The preceding season Telford had beaten Rochdale, Northampton and Stockport to reach the fourth round. In 1979/80, the season Leicester City won the Second Division Championship, they were beaten 1-0 by non-League Harlow Town in a third-round replay. In 1963/64 non-League Bedford Town won 3-1 in a third-round game at Newcastle United, then a strong Second Division club.

On several occasions the football public has been stunned by defeat of the top team in the land. Walsall, a mid-table Third Division (S) team, beat Arsenal, the team of the decade, in a third-round FA Cup tie in 1933. Leeds United were also First Division leaders when they lost 3-2 at Fourth Division Colchester United in the fifth round of the 1970/71 FA Cup competition – perhaps one of the most popular giant-killing feats of all time.

Giant killing in the World Cup could apply to countries with relatively small populations overcoming large nations, or surprise victories for countries lacking a footballing tradition over established soccer nations. Examples in the World Cup finals include: Romania 1 Cuba 2 (1938), England 0 United States 1 (1950), Northern Ireland 2 Czechoslovakia 1 (1958), Italy 0 North Korea 1 (1966), Tunisia 3 Mexico 1 (1978), Spain 0 Northern Ireland 1 (1982) and Argentina 0 Cameroon 1 (1990). In their first ever European Championship qualifier, the Faroe Islands beat Austria 1-0 in 1990.

GILLINGHAM

Founded 1893

Joined League 1920 (Division 3, founder member)

Honours Division 4 Champions 1964

Ground Priestfield

Gillingham have failed dismally to make the most of geographical advantage. Until Maidstone United achieved League status, the 'Gills' existed in splendid isolation from other clubs yet have been perennially unable to attract the huge potential audience which exists in the Medway towns.

Their history has been modest indeed. As founder members of Division 3, Gillingham faced a constant struggle for survival and after successfully applying for re-election four times they were finally dropped in 1938. The club was liquidated, then re-formed, and entered the Southern League before being given a second chance in the senior competition in 1950.

They sank to the newly created Fourth Division in 1958, winning their sole honour six seasons later and spending all but three of the next 25 years in the Third Division. In 1979 the Gills were within a point of rising to Division 2, but subsequently have slumped back to the basement.

GREAVES, Jimmy

1940 Born in East Ham, London

1957 Scores on League debut for Chelsea

1959 First England cap in Peru

1961 Hat-trick in 9-3 defeat of Scotland at Wembley; joins AC Milan, having scored 124 goals in 157 League games for Chelsea, including four in his last match; signs for Tottenham for record fee of £99,999 after four unhappy months in Italy

1963 Scores twice in Spurs' 5-1 win in European Cup Winners' Cup Final v

Atletico Madrid; four goals for England v Northern Ireland

1965 Badly affected by an attack of hepatitis

1966 Unable to regain place in England's World Cup-winning line-up after missing quarter-final through injury

1967 Last appearance for England (44 goals in 57 games)

1970 After 321 League matches for Spurs (220 goals), moves to West Ham in part-exchange for Martin Peters

1971 Retires and disappears from public view

1980 Begins a new career in television, having struggled against alcoholism for several years

The bare statistics of Greaves's career are sufficient to demonstrate that he was the most remarkable goalscorer of his generation, but they cannot convey his unique talent. His detractors pointed

to his lack of work-rate and dependence upon others to create openings for him, but failed to appreciate that his deadly finishing could transform a match.

Although he had the born predator's ability to anticipate a half-chance, Greaves's greatest gift was perhaps his pace, which he never fully recovered after his illness. However, it was the economy of effort and coolness with which his goals were taken which set him apart from his rivals. He was always willing to take his time and felt no need to attempt the spectacular when it was more effective to wrong-foot the keeper and push the ball home. His pair of clinical far-post volleys against Atletico in 1963 were typical.

Always a popular figure, his courageous fight-back in the face of a challenge sterner than any he faced on the pitch has won him a new generation of fans and even greater admiration than he earned through his playing exploits.

GREENWOOD, Ron

1921 Born in Burnley

1945 Joins Bradford Park Avenue from his first club, Chelsea

1949 Moves to Brentford, wins England 'B' cap

1952 Starts a second stint at Stamford Bridge

1955 Turns out enough

Jimmy Greaves (in an England shirt) scoring against the 'old enemy' Scotland, at Wembley in 1961. Greaves netted a hat-trick as the final score was 9-3 to England. A regular name on the scoresheet – over 350 goals in his League career – Greaves was unfortunate not to feature in manager Alf Ramsey's team selection for the 1966 World Cup Final. It's good to see that his natural humour has given him a special place in the affections of the nation as a television personality.

A thoughtful and quiet person – perhaps those qualities alone should have automatically disqualified Ron Greenwood from the job of England manager, as successor to Alf Ramsey. He held it, with moderate success, for five years. During his reign he had only a few players of the highest quality to call on.

take on such an onerous task.

Greenwood had qualified as a coach while still an intelligent, skilful centre-half, and he went on to preach the gospel of constructive football – which produced some notable triumphs – at West Ham. When the England call came, there was little chance of securing a place in the 1978 World Cup finals, and Greenwood set his sights on subsequent tournaments. No one could reasonably accuse him of being a dismal failure, but neither could he be deemed an outstanding success.

GRIMSBY TOWN

Founded 1878

Joined League 1892 (Division 2)

Honours Division 2 Champions 1901, 1934; Division 3 (N) Champions 1926, 1956; Division 3 Champions 1980; Division 4 Champions 1972

Ground Blundell Park, Cleethorpes

Grimsby Town, who carry the name of the famous east coast fishing port but play their home games at nearby Cleethorpes, have known better days than recent modest League placings might suggest. Indeed, during their prime in the 1930s, the 'Mariners' finished fifth in Division 1 and reached two FA Cup semi-finals. Those were the days of heroes such as English international Jackie Bestall, a gifted, ball-playing inside-forward, and free-scoring marksman Pat Glover, capped seven times by Wales.

Sadly for Grimsby, the Second World War devastated

the careers of their best players and the club never recovered. They were relegated in 1948, since when they have yo-yoed between the three lower divisions. Their list of managers includes such notables as Bill Shankly, who failed to lift them out of the Third Division in the early 1950s, and Lawrie McMenemy, who converted a poor side into Fourth Division champions and the League's highest scorers in 1972. Eight years later George Kerr led Grimsby up to the second flight, although recent terms have been spent reclaiming that position following a slump to the Fourth.

Such regular movement between divisions mirrors the club's early history, most of which was spent in the old Second but also involved stints in the First and Third Divisions. Grimsby's low point came in 1910 when they failed to gain re-election, although they bounced back one season later.

GULLIT, Ruud

1962 Born in Amsterdam

1979 Joins Haarlem from minor league football

1981 September – international debut v Switzerland

1982 Moves to Feyenoord

1984 Wins league and cup medals with Feyenoord

1985 Joins PSV Eindhoven

1987 June – transferred to AC Milan for a record £6 million; European Footballer of the Year and World Footballer of the Year

1988 Highs and lows – captains club to championship title and country to European supremacy; in friendly game during summer sustains injury to right knee which is to dog him for next two years

1989 Knee injury seriously aggravated in European Cup semi-final v Real Madrid – key-hole surgery allows him to play in Final;

times to win Championship medal with 'Pensioners' then joins Fulham to end playing days

1957 Enters management with non-League Eastbourne United; coaches England youth side

1958 Becomes assistant boss of Arsenal and England under-23 team coach

1961 Takes over at West Ham United

1964 'Hammers' lift first trophy of Greenwood era, beating Preston North End in FA Cup Final...

1965 ... and the second, overcoming TSV Munich 1860 to take the European Cup Winners' Cup

1974 John Lyall takes over West Ham's team affairs; Greenwood becomes general manager

1977 Leaves Upton Park to replace Don Revie as England boss

1980 England reach European Championship finals, but fail to impress

1982 Greenwood's team qualifies for World Cup finals in Spain, where they are eliminated in second phase; manager steps down in favour of Bobby Robson

Greenwood was the deep-thinking tactician who managed England through what was – despite the presence of fine players such as Bryan Robson, Kevin Keegan, Trevor Brooking and Glenn Hoddle – a rather pedestrian era. He succeeded Revie in the face of strong public opinion that the job should have gone to Brian Clough – hardly the ideal circumstances in which to

despite not being really match-fit, scores twice v Steaua Bucharest to secure victory; further operations and lay-off necessary

1990 Recovers in time to win a second European Cup medal v Benfica, to play in World Cup, and to help AC Milan to victory in the European Super Cup and World Club Championship

1992 Still battling for fitness; plays leading part in footballers campaign against racism.

1993 Moves to Sampdoria and displays fabulous form

1994 Returns to AC Milan; walks out on Dutch World Cup squad following row with manager Dick Advocaat; rejoins 'Samp'

1995 Completes sensational move to Chelsea

Rudi Dil Gullit played as a sweeper until eventually both club and country used him as an attacking midfield player; his versatility, his intelligent approach to the game and his awareness of colleagues and opponents are typically Dutch. He is an expert finder of space, often running away from the penalty area and picking up the ball to launch an attack from an unexpected angle.

Off the field Gullit, of Surinamese origin, is confident and articulate – Dutch footballers pride themselves on expressing opinions fearlessly, and in this he is no exception. Holland's troubles since 1988, due in no small part to his injury, have been compounded by managerial squabbles, and

Gullit's views have been made plain – at times, it would seem, regardless of team morale.

The fortunes of AC Milan were bound up with those of Holland for some years, since top striker van Basten and midfielder Rijkaard turned out alongside the Dutch captain in both strips.

Gullit, winner of a half-century of international caps, has been a natural goalscorer but has often been happy to act as a provider, especially when van Basten was on song.

Ruud Gullit's name will be associated with the Dutch team of the 1980s and early 1990s, just as Cruyff's is with the 1970s side. His dreadlocks flapping as he runs, Gullit is equally at home as a goal-scorer and as goal-provider. Off the field, Gullit plays a prominent part in the footballers' campaign against racism.

HAMILTON ACADEMICAL

Founded 1875

Joined League 1897 (Division 2)

Honours Scottish League First Division Champions 1986, 1988; Division 2 Champions 1904

Ground Douglas Park

The derivation of the name from a local school gives Hamilton Academical a whimsical air but, as with all clubs of their size, survival has been a matter of grit. The club was at its most stable from 1906 to 1947, retaining Division 1 status throughout. In 1935, with high-scoring David Wilson as spearhead, they even repeated their feat of 1911 by reaching the Scottish Cup Final.

There was further success in the 1980s, when Hamilton twice won promotion to the Premier Division and in 1988 they beat Rangers at Ibrox in the Scottish Cup. Then in 1992 they won a trophy, albeit a minor one, the B & Q Cup, and pending construction of a new stadium in Hamilton, shared Partick Thistle's Firhill Park ground in Glasgow.

HARTLEPOOL UNITED

Founded 1908

Joined League 1921 (Division 3 N)

Honours None

Ground Victoria Ground

There is no getting away from the fact that Hartlepool United are a humble club. In 1991/92, their 11th place in Division 3 was the highest finish in their Football League history. Before this the best they had managed was 22nd in 1968/69, which was not enough to prevent an immediate return to the bottom flight.

Indeed their campaign was, at the time, the only one Hartlepool had spent outside the basement. Their story is one of frequent applications for re-election and constant struggle for survival in an economically depressed area.

There was brief hope of a brave new era when Brian Clough created new impetus before departing for Derby County in 1967. His successor, Angus McLean, capitalised by winning promotion the following year but could not sustain success. The 1980s saw a sequence of seven managers in six years and United's die-hard fans, while cautiously optimistic about prospects under new boss Keith Houchen in 1995, could be excused for not holding their breath.

HAYNES, Johnny

1934 Born in Edmonton, north London

1952 Turns professional with Fulham

1954 Full England debut against Northern Ireland

1959 Inspires Fulham to promotion to the First Division

1960 Takes over as England captain

1961 Becomes Britain's first £100-a-week footballer after Fulham reject bid from AC Milan

1962 Seriously damages knee in Blackpool road accident; never plays for England again

1964 Tottenham offer £90,000 for Haynes after death of their own midfield general, John White

1968 Returns to Second Division with Fulham ...

1969 ... who slide straight down to the Third

1970 Free transfer from Fulham; joins South African club Durban City

Haynes was one of the most skilful English inside-forwards of the post-war era, yet his enormous talent never won him a club honour. The dearth of medals is easily explained – he played out his entire Football League career with unfashionable Fulham, even though top clubs at home and abroad attempted to lure him away.

He first caught the public imagination with a sparkling display for England Schoolboys in a televised Wembley encounter with the Scots in 1950. But then the young Arsenal fan who was born in the Tottenham Hotspur heartland surprised everyone by opting for Craven Cottage and the Second Division. Haynes soon built a reputation as a schemer sublime; his speciality was silky, long-distance passes which sliced open defences, and his full international breakthrough was not long in coming. He won 56 caps, many of them as captain, and might have had more but for the car crash which at one time threatened his career.

Yet, despite his obvious gifts, Haynes was not beloved of the entire football world. He was a perfectionist who sometimes struck melodramatic poses when admonishing team-mates of inferior ability, and was a particular target for northern fans. Haynes, who will always be remembered as the man who broke the £100-a-week wage barrier, left English soccer after loyal service to

Peter Swan and Jimmy Armfield carry their captain, Johnny Haynes, shoulder high after England's 9-3 drubbing of Scotland in 1961. It seems incredible now, but the announcement in the same year that Haynes was to become the first £100 per week footballer brought howls of protest from outraged sections of society. That he was paid so much was evidence of his worth to his club, Fulham, and the need to pay high wages to prevent players like Haynes emigrating to Italy. Johnny Haynes was a gentleman footballer, and arguably the most skilful English inside-forward ever.

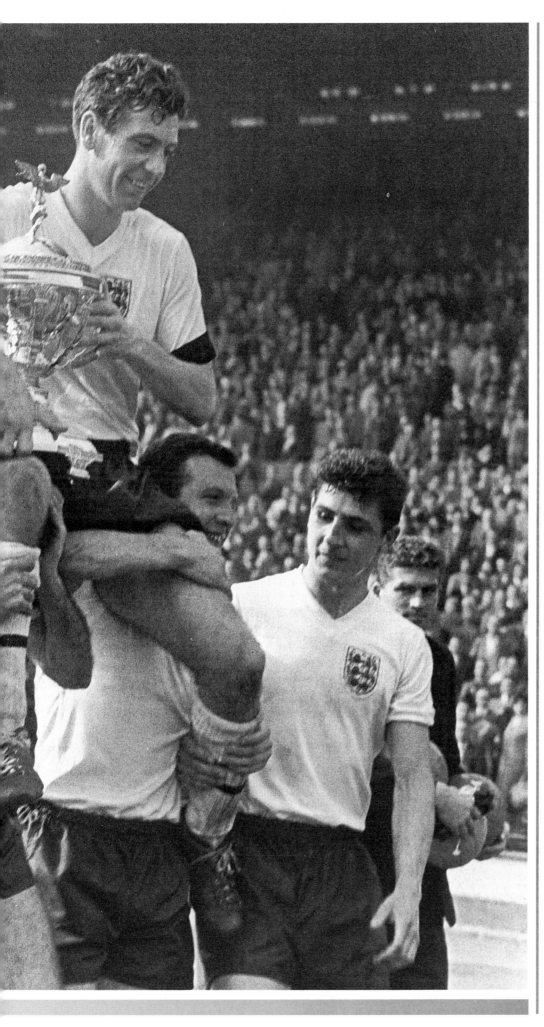

homely Fulham but with one tantalising question left unanswered: to what heights might he have risen with a leading club?

HEART OF MIDLOTHIAN

Founded 1874

Joined League 1890 (Division 1, founder club)

Honours Scottish League Championship, Division 1, 1895, 1897, 1958, 1960; First Division 1980; Scottish Cup 1891, 1896, 1901, 1906, 1956; League Cup 1954/55, 1958/59, 1959/60, 1962/63

Ground Tynecastle Park

Hearts are one of the few clubs perennially expected to mount a challenge to the Old Firm; their prestige was established from the early years with League Championships and Scottish Cups racked up before the turn of the century.

One of the great stars was Bobby Walker, a silky inside-forward who had won a club record of 29 caps, in an era when fewer internationals were played, by 1913. His namesake Tommy Walker, a great midfielder in the trophyless 1930s, was to find success as a manager two decades later.

He presided over the glorious side of the 1950s. Its 'Terrible Trio' of Alfie Conn, Willie Bauld and Jimmy Wardhaugh are renowned but they were also flanked by menacing wingers in Alex Young and Jimmy Crawford. Although Conn played less often, all five were fielded as Hearts won the League with a record 132 goals in 1958.

A 2-0 defeat at home to Kilmarnock cost Hearts the title in 1965 and their fortunes waned. Later, relegation was to bring the threat of extinction. They have recovered since the early 1980s and contributed men like Dave McPherson and John Robertson to the Scotland squad but the trophy-winning days have not yet returned. They famously missed out on the double in 1986, when Celtic, beating St Mirren in the last match of the season by 5-0, took the championship

Sandy Jardine playing for Hearts. Jardine was born in Edinburgh and rejoined his 'home' club after a successful spell as a Rangers player during the 1970s when he was considered to be the new John Greig. He was twice Scottish Player of the Year and played in over 1000 senior matches for the club and country. Jardine, as sweeper, was at the back of the Hearts line-up during the 1985/86 season, when they promised so much and achieved so little.

from them on goal difference, then they lost the Scottish Cup Final 3-0 to Aberdeen.

HEREFORD UNITED

Founded 1924

Joined League 1972 (Division 4)

Honours Division 3 Champions 1976

Ground Edgar Street

Hereford United are a club of unashamedly bucolic character, but whose opponents are – and always have been – ill-advised to dismiss them as country bumpkins. Just ask Newcastle, who became the first Division 1 side to be dumped from the FA Cup by non-League opposition for some 20 years when Hereford shocked them on an Edgar Street mudheap in 1972.

Not that they were to lack League status for long. That summer, no doubt helped immeasurably by their knock-out exploits – in the previous 24 years they had reached the FA Cup first round proper an unprecedented 23 times – United were elected to the Fourth Division, at the expense of Barrow, after a second ballot. Their first term among the big boys started slowly, but by spring they had secured promotion, and in 1976 – thanks in no small measure to ace marksman Dixie McNeil – reached the Second Division.

A one-season sojourn was all Hereford could manage, however, and since then they

have slipped back to the bottom level, though they remain a spirited, ambitious outfit who, with little competition for support, have the capacity to rise again. Influential bosses have included John Charles (in Southern League days), Colin Addison (twice) and John Sillett (also twice), while Kevin Sheedy is their most famous ex-player of the last two decades.

HIBERNIAN

Founded 1875

Joined League 1893 (Division 2)

Honours Scottish League Championship, Division 1 1903, 1948, 1951, 1952; First Division 1981; Division 2 1894, 1895, 1933; Scottish Cup 1887, 1902;

League Cup 1972/73, 1991/92

Ground Easter Road

For Hibs, as for Tottenham Hotspur, the move to Public Limited Company status has been a disaster. In 1990 their debts were approaching £6 million and they only narrowly defeated a takeover bid by Edinburgh rivals Hearts.

Hibs' plight is made all the more poignant by their illustrious history. Founded by Edinburgh's Irish immigrant community, Hibs soon had an impact on the national scene but their most vibrant era came in the early 1950s.

The 'Famous Five' forward line of Gordon Smith, Peter Johnstone, Lawrie Reilly, Eddie Turnbull and Willie Ormond contained all of football's arts and gave Hibs

unequalled attacking resources.

In 1955/56 Hibs represented Scotland in the first European Cup and reached the semi-final stage. The decline which followed was halted only in the early seventies by the cultured side which included internationalists like John Brownlie, Pat Stanton and Alex Cropley. It delighted purists but did not win the trophies it might have. However, after recent traumatic times, the 1991/92 League Cup triumph did much to restore morale at Easter Road.

HISTORY OF FOOTBALL

Although many distant corners of the world can supply evidence of a form of proto-football, it is with

The popular appeal of soccer has not been lost on advertisers over the decades. This ad, run in newspapers in the 1920s, extols the virtues of Phosferine with the help of Liverpool and England player Tom Bromilow. He only won five caps, but was a media celebrity all the same.

England that the origins, development and standardisation of the game are most strongly identified. The sport commonly assumed to be soccer's ancestor is Shrove Tuesday football, various forms of which existed throughout England; these skirmishes, with their attendant fatalities, often involved whole villages and had local rules. Some are still extant, notably in Ashbourne in Derbyshire which boasts the oldest recorded version, played annually from the thirteenth century, having been introduced by Roman soldiers a thousand years earlier. What links these games, and contemporary contests in Brittany and Italy, to modern soccer is not the use of the foot to propel the ball – indeed, the participants were

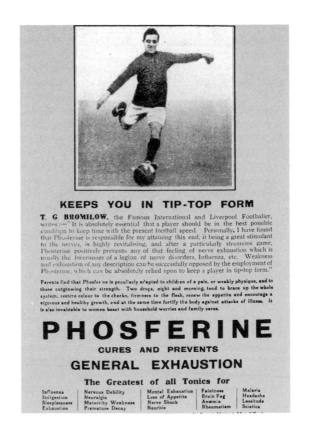

as likely to pick up the ball – but the involvement of two teams struggling to gain territory and move the ball to a specified goal (which in medieval times might have been a single identifiable landmark or an area hundreds of yards wide). The ball games of the Far East demonstrated more skilful

use of the feet but were really akin to juggling. The game in England was an outlet for aggression.

Approval was not universal, especially as, in smaller-scale versions, it ceased to confine itself to the day before Lent. A proclamation by King Edward II in 1314 forbade, on pain of

imprisonment, the playing of football in city streets. There were similar edicts from successive monarchs, notably Richard II (1389), who worried that his subjects were neglecting their archery practice on its account. Similar prohibitions testify to the game's early popularity in Scotland. (Periodically throughout this century the English judiciary have acted against people for playing football in the street – the arena in which so many great skills have been honed; the motor car now seems to have succeeded where magistrates

This illustration epitomises the amateur game: Queen's Park from Glasgow's third goal in a match against Corinthian Casuals from London as reported in the Illustrated Sporting and Dramatic News in December 1898. It was played at the Queen's Club, West Kensington, and this gentlemanly combat resulted in a win for the raiders from north of the border. Perhaps the goalkeeper could have made a better effort – although nothing too unsporting.

failed.) In 1583 one commentator described football as characterised by 'murder, homicide and great effusion of blood'. In 1581, however, Richard Mulcaster, a prominent headmaster, could write: 'Football strengtheneth and brawneth the whole body ... It is good to drive down the stone and gravel from the bladder and the kidneys.' (There is no evidence that the modern game has inherited any of these mysterious medical qualities.) Royal disapproval vanished in the seventeenth century when James I and Charles II were happy to spectate. As much as anything else, the diversity of reaction is evidence of the variety of games sharing the title 'football'.

Despite its popular origins, it is to the public schools that we owe the protracted birth of the modern game. A desire to form a common code for inter-school and inter-university matches led to the establishing of the Cambridge Rules in 1848 and these were gradually adopted by gentlemen's clubs in London and the Home Counties, with Sheffield, the first football club, eventually coming into line. Parallel to this, the predominantly working-class

game elsewhere in the north sought standardisation. It was the gradual rapprochement between the two types which formed the bedrock of association football. Equally crucial was the formation of the Rugby Union in 1871; disputes about the legitimacy of handling in open play were near an end now that two distinct games existed.

The last three decades of the nineteenth century saw the development of rules still in use today, the formation of the Football Association, the Football League, a Challenge Cup and similar institutions in the other home countries, and the participation of familiar names: Aston Villa, Blackburn Rovers, Notts County, Sheffield Wednesday. Meanwhile British engineers, entrepreneurs and servicemen were introducing the codified game abroad, laying the foundations for international competition. The prestige of the game was enhanced by its inclusion in the 1908 Olympics, its viability confirmed by the growing stature of the World Cup.

In this century, modifications to the game itself have been minimal; the simplicity of the rules and the potential of free-flowing play have been football's strong points, admitting, as they do,

a plethora of styles. The context of the sport, however, the nature of its institutions and the status of its practitioners have all been transformed by a common agent – money. This has been particularly evident in the last decade in Britain and throughout the world, with takeover bids and high-profile sponsorship, the spiralling of transfer fees, and an increase in football-related corruption all bringing the game into the headlines and transforming the image of football.

There seems little resemblance between the tumbling Shrovetide mauls of the Middle Ages and the game played by knicker-bockered Corinthians at the turn of the century; and little similarity between either of those and a game played under floodlights by sportsmen whose club crests are dwarfed by sponsors' insignia, who are supervised by a card-brandishing official and watched by a fenced-in public standing beneath executive boxes and television gantries. The evolution is remarkable, but they are, in essence, the same creature, animated by the same spirit. Pessimists and traditionalists need to be reminded that more people play and watch football

worldwide than ever before, that Saturday morning pick-up games still flourish, and that in the professional game, apprentices still clean boots.

Few players have provoked such extremes of opinion as Glenn Hoddle. His supporters claim he was the most gifted Englishman of his generation and contend that his frequent omission from the national side was little short of sacrilege. Detractors moan about inconsistency and poor work-rate, an argument which apparently found some favour with successive England managers Ron Greenwood and Bobby Robson.

Certainly, none could doubt the natural ability of the tall, elegant play-maker, who was

It is worth remembering that scenes like the one pictured were not uncommon during the history of the game; all-seater stadia and strictly controlled attendances are very modern phenomena. These huge crowds, and attendant injuries, occurred during the 1931 FA Cup semi-final between Everton and West Bromwich Albion played at Manchester United's Old Trafford. The two clubs finished first and second respectively in the Second Division at the end of the 1930/31 season and were both promoted. Everton went on to win the Football League in the following season. West Brom were the 1-0 victors in the semi-final, however, and they went on to beat Birmingham City in the final.

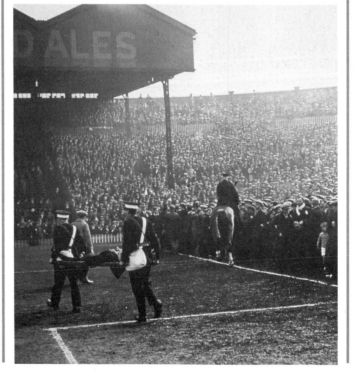

The tall, slim Hoddle celebrates scoring England's second goal in a 2-1 win over Scotland at Wembley, April 1986. Glenn was a Tottenham Hotspur and England regular in the 1980s, winning 53 caps before a knee injury sidelined him for a year. In 1988 he helped Monaco take the French Championship. As player-manager at Swindon and Chelsea he continued to dictate play from his new position as sweeper.

in 1883/84 and continued until 1983/84, interrupted only by two wars and the refusal of England and Wales to play in Belfast in 1980/81, when the programme was not completed. Poor attendances and the increasing importance of competitions like the World Cup and the European Championships led to the tournament's demise, England and Scotland being the first to pull out. The tournament ended on a bizarre note. In 1983/84 all four countries won, drew and lost a game, so Northern Ireland won on goal difference (3-2) from Wales (3-3), England (2-2) and Scotland (3-4).

In 1968/69 the tournament was moved to the end of the season in an unsuccessful attempt to revive it. As the tournament placings usually relied solely on number of points – until goal difference was taken into account in the last few years – as many as 20 championships were shared. England had more outright wins (34) than Scotland (24) and Wales (7). Ireland won a clear title in 1913/14, and Northern Ireland won two of the last four. England gained more points than any other country (378), followed by Scotland (339), Wales (202) and Ireland/Northern Ireland (142).

Given the consistency of the home international tournament – each country played three games a season – it is a good way of

blessed with breathtaking vision and had a devastating knack of changing the angle of attack with sweeping long-distance passes. His touch on the ball, with both feet, was superb, he possessed a powerful shot which was particularly effective at free-kicks, and he was one of the most delicate chippers of a ball the game has seen.

However, those who expected to see him carrying out the average midfielder's share of defensive duties were invariably disappointed; but of course, there was nothing average about Hoddle. By the

end of his Spurs days his overall involvement in matches had improved significantly, but sadly it was too late. By then, with so much of his prime gone, the football world was left to rue the fact that an exceptional talent had never been utilised to the full. As a manager he espoused the same attractive passing style he had employed throughout his career, and in the early 1990s, Swindon were serving up some of the most entertaining football in the land. Hoddle carried on the good work at Stamford Bridge, as player-boss leading

Chelsea to the FA Cup Final. They lost, but as Manchester United won the double, the Blues qualified for the European Cup Winners' Cup, surprising many by reaching the semi-finals.

HOME INTERNATIONALS

The British home international tournament was a four-way competition involving England, Scotland, Wales and Ireland (Northern Ireland after 1921). It began

Mark Hateley of England chases Scotland's Graeme Souness during the Rous Cup match at Wembley in 1986. England went on to record a 2-1 win. Although the home international tournament is no longer a regular feature of the football season, it is remembered for the passion it engendered – among the fans if not always on the park.

comparing different generations of internationals. Players with most home international tournament appearances are as follows: Pat Jennings (Northern Ireland) and Billy Meredith (Wales) 48, Billy Wright (England) 38, Danny Blanchflower (Northern Ireland) and Ivor Allchurch (Wales) 37, Jimmy McIlroy (Northern Ireland) 36, Bob Crompton (England) and Billy Bingham (Northern

Ireland) 34, Bobby Charlton (England) and Fred Keenor (Wales) 32.

Top goalscorers in the championship were Steve Bloomer (England) 28, Hughie Gallacher (Scotland) 21, Jimmy Greaves (England) 19 and Bobby Charlton (England) 16.

In 1985 the Rous Cup, named after legendary English administrator Sir Stanley Rous, was launched as a direct contest between Scotland and England, Scotland winning the first competition 1-0 at Hampden Park. England won the trophy at Wembley the following year. Then came three years of the Rous Cup as a triangular tournament involving a guest nation from South America. Brazil won in 1987, England in 1988 and 1989 when Colombia and Chile were the respective South American visitors. When Scotland pulled out of the 1990 Rous Cup, the future of home internationals

passed to the hands of those who make the draws for the World Cup and European Championships.

HOOLIGANISM

Hooliganism is not a recent phenomenon. Consider these four examples, taken from different decades of early soccer.

In 1885 Preston North End players were trapped on the field by 2000 'howling roughs' after beating Aston Villa 5-1. They were attacked with stones, sticks, umbrellas and spittle. One player (Ross) was laid out by a missile.

An 1899 semi-final replay between Sheffield United and Liverpool was abandoned at half-time. Repeated invasions of the Fallowfield pitch meant the first half took 90 minutes to complete.

The 1909 Scottish Cup Final between Rangers and Celtic was drawn, as was the replay. Spectators were

incensed when extra-time was not played in the replay. They invaded the pitch, destroyed goalposts and goalnets, set pay boxes on fire and fought with policemen. About 130 spectators received medical treatment on the ground.

At the end of the 1913 Ireland-Scotland international in Dublin, players fought for the match ball as a souvenir and a spectator was injured in the melee. An angry mob kept the Scottish team prisoners in their dressing room for about an hour as windows were smashed and property damaged.

From the late 1960s, however, hooliganism has grown to epidemic proportions throughout Europe. Examples of major British outbursts include the following.

In April 1971 about 20 Leeds United supporters invaded the Elland Road pitch shortly after a disputed goal had given West Bromwich a 2-0 lead in an important Division 1 game. A linesman was knocked out when hit by a missile. Leeds United were fined £750 and ordered to play four home matches on another ground.

In March 1974 spectators invaded the Newcastle pitch and halted a sixth-round FA Cup game with Nottingham Forest. The referee took the players off the pitch. Thirty-nine people were arrested, 23 taken to hospital and 103 others treated on the ground. Nottingham Forest, winning 3-1 at the time, eventually lost 4-3. The FA ordered a replay. Newcastle won 1-0 after a 0-0 draw.

In June 1977 Scotland beat England 2-1 at Wembley. After the game, hundreds of Scottish fans invaded the pitch and caused damage estimated at £150,000. As a consequence, fences were erected at Wembley.

A Division 2 game between Oldham Athletic and Sheffield Wednesday (September 1980) was stopped for 30 minutes when Sheffield Wednesday supporters greeted the sending-off of Terry Curran by invading the pitch. An FA disciplinary committee banned Wednesday supporters from four away games and closed terraces for four home games.

Huddersfield Town's side of 1922 at the end of a season in which they won the Charity Shield (left inset), the FA Cup (centre) and the West Riding Cup. Huddersfield beat Preston North End 1-0 in the last FA Cup Final not to be played at Wembley. This was the only time Huddersfield have won the FA Cup, despite having appeared in the final six times. The manager in 1922 was Herbert Chapman (front row, far left).

Disturbances at a sixth-round FA Cup tie at Luton on 13 March 1985 – Luton Town beat Millwall 1-0 – led to 33 arrests and £25,000 worth of damage. Having watched televised scenes, then Prime Minister Margaret Thatcher became personally involved in the problem, setting up a special task force. A £7500 fine for Millwall was later rescinded on appeal. Luton Town introduced a membership scheme which effectively banned away supporters from the start of the 1986/87 season.

All sorts of remedies have been tried: fences, segregation of fans, police escorts for fans, all-seater stadia, more sophisticated policing, closed-circuit cameras and more careful monitoring of player behaviour. The methods have succeeded in restraining hooliganism within grounds, but violence outside them has increased, often with the involvement of highly organised 'firms'.

The real causes of hooliganism are very complex. The most detailed research has been undertaken at Leicester University and its Sir Norman Chester Centre for Football Research. Eric Dunning, Patrick Murphy and John Williams have written on hooliganism in Hooligans Abroad, The Roots of Football Hooliganism and Football on Trial. Autobiographical accounts include Colin Ward's Steaming In and Jay Allan's Bloody Casuals.

HUDDERSFIELD TOWN

Founded 1908

Joined League 1910 (Division 2)

Honours Division 1 Champions 1924, 1925, 1926; Division 2 Champions 1970; Division 4 Champions 1980; FA Cup Winners 1922

Ground McAlpine Stadium

Huddersfield Town are haunted by a ghost that is unlikely to be laid; it is the spectre of the phenomenal triumphs enjoyed by the club in the 1920s, when three successive League Championships were added to an FA Cup victory. Those far-off glories – all but the final title achieved under the managership of Herbert Chapman – were astonishing in that they were attained within less than two decades of entering the Football League, and after weathering a severe cash crisis which almost saw them amalgamated with Leeds United.

They remained a major power until the late 1930s, when a decline set in. It was no surprise when they struggled after the war, and the 1950s saw the start of regular movement between the divisions. By the late 1970s they had plumbed the depths of the Fourth Division, rising again to the Second in 1983 only to slide down a grade five years later.

Notable managers have included Bill Shankly before his 1959 switch to Liverpool and, most successful in the modern era, Ian Greaves, who took Huddersfield back to the top flight, briefly, in 1970. One remarkable tradition has been a succession of fine full-backs, including Sam Wadsworth and Roy Goodall in the 1920s, Ron Staniforth and Ray Wilson in the 1950s, and Bob McNab and Derek Parkin in the 1960s, though the greatest player in their history was inside-forward Denis Law, sold for a record £55,000 in 1960.

Today Huddersfield may have turned a corner with a play-off success in 1995 seeing them achieve Division 1 status. Their new ground, and good support were not enough, however, to retain the interest of manager Neil Warnock who left for Plymouth Argyle.

HULL CITY

Founded 1904

Joined League 1905 (Division 2)

Honours Division 3 (N) Champions 1933, 1949; Division 3 Champions 1966

Ground Boothferry Park

It is surprising that Hull City, an ambitious club with plenty of potential support in the Humberside area despite strong competition from the oval-ball code, have never enjoyed a spell in the First Division. In fact, they made their most spirited attempt to gain top-flight status just five years after entering the Football League, failing only on goal average. Since then most of their time has been spent alternating between the old Second and Third Divisions, with one brief stint in the Fourth.

Two of the 'Tigers' most potent sides were those of the late 1940s and early 1950s, which featured Raich Carter (as player-manager) and Don Revie, and Cliff Britton's attacking combination of the mid and late 1960s, which contained the prolific Chris Chilton and Ken Wagstaff, both of whom notched more than 200 goals for City.

Other personalities of note have included stalwart goalkeeper Billy Bly, who served for two decades until 1959, and Terry Neill who, in his first managerial job, offered hope of a First Division breakthrough in the early 1970s. The club's best FA Cup run ended in a semi-final replay defeat by eventual winners Arsenal in 1930.

IPSWICH TOWN

Founded 1878

Joined League 1938
(Division 3 S)

Honours Division 1
Champions 1962; Division
2 Champions 1961, 1968,
1992; Division 3 (S)
Champions 1954, 1957; FA
Cup Winners 1978; UEFA
Cup Winners 1981

Ground Portman Road

Ipswich offer an inspiring example of a club whose stirring deeds have belied their small-town stature, thanks largely to two men, Sir Alf Ramsey and Bobby Robson, who both left Portman Road to manage England. Their eras brought unprecedented glory to East Anglia, which then had little reason to expect much from Ipswich. After all, the Town had spent the 60 years after their formation in minor competitions, and then a further decade and a half in Division 3 (S). Even when they eventually clambered into the higher grade, it was for just one term.

Relegation in 1955 was the cue for Ramsey's entrance, and a startling transformation. Within two campaigns they were back in the Second Division, but more momentous triumphs were in store: the Division 2 title and the League Championship were lifted in successive seasons.

Ramsey's 'miracle' was based on a sound defence, a midfield engineered by frail-looking Jimmy Leadbetter, and a lethal double spearhead of Ray Crawford and Ted Phillips. Of course, success on a shoestring could not be maintained and, Ramsey having departed, the Town soon went down. They rose again in 1968, the year before Robson took over to lead them into their longest period of First

Division membership. During his 13 campaigns they won two major cups, narrowly missed several titles and became established as a side to be respected, with many high-quality players such as defender Mick Mills and striker Paul Mariner. In 1986 Ipswich were relegated, but they are a well-run club with a proven record of doing well in an area which is hardly a soccer hotbed. It was hardly surprising, therefore, when they topped Division 2 in 1992 to earn a place in the new FA Premier League. However, competition with mega-rich opponents became ever more arduous and, in 1995, Town sank dismally once more to the second flight.

In 1960/61 Ipswich Town won the Second Division Championship. In the following year, the side photographed here won the First Division Championship. Many reasons have been suggested for their remarkable success. One factor is the loyalty of the players and the consistency of team selection by the manager Alf Ramsey. The numbers in brackets after each player's name represent the League appearances made for Ipswich Town FC: (left to right, back row) Baxter (409), Carberry (257), Bailey (315), Compton (111), Elsworthy (396); Stephenson (144), Moran (104), Crawford (320), Nelson (193), Phillips (269), Leadbetter (344). This constitutes a total of 2862 games and the holder of the Ipswich record for most appearances, Mick Mills with 591 League outings between 1965 and 1982, was still to join Town! The friendliness of the Suffolk club is one reason frequently put forward for the number of long-stayers although, of course, movement between clubs was less common when Ipswich won their Championship.

JAMES, Alex

1901 Born in Mossend, Lanarkshire, Scotland

1922 Debut for Raith Rovers

1925 Signs for Preston North End at a fee of £3250

1926 Wins first Scottish cap in 3-0 win over Wales at Cardiff

1928 James is brilliant in the 'Wee Blue Devils' 5-1 slaughter of England at Wembley

1929 Moves to Arsenal for £8750

1930 Helps 'Gunners' win FA Cup with Wembley goal against Huddersfield Town

1931 Picks up the first of four Championship medals

1936 Skippers 'Gunners' to FA Cup victory against Sheffield United

1937 Retires to become journalist

1947 Returns to Highbury as a coach

1953 Dies of cancer

James, the inspiration of Arsenal's all-conquering side of the 1930s, is one of the few figures in soccer history who may reasonably be described as legendary. The little Scot, whose trademark of baggy shorts was a cartoonist's dream, was the most influential player of his era, a master tactician blessed with sublime ball skills.

A natural showman, he took time to settle after manager Herbert Chapman brought him south from Preston. But after subjugating some of his characteristic individuality to the team cause, he became the darling of the Highbury faithful. Though a captivating dribbler when the mood took him, James usually opted to let the ball do the work, and his immaculate distribution to the likes of Cliff Bastin, Joe

Wearing his trademark – extra long shorts – Alex James is pictured (left) with his Arsenal team-mate from the 1930s, Cliff Bastin. The shirt badge reads '1935/36', a season in which Alex James skippered the Gunners to FA Cup victory against Sheffield United. There were also four League championships and another FA Cup triumph during his eight-year tenure at Highbury. James's inspirational scheming brought the best out of a multi-talented forward line, in which Bastin was also outstanding. 'Boy', as he was called for his youthful looks, was a dashing goal-scorer who usually operated from the left flank. Sadly his career was cut off in its prime by the Second world War.

Hulme and David Jack was the source of most Gunners goals.

Amazingly he played only eight games for his country, an absurd circumstance which was widely believed to be due to his 'Anglo' status. But James, who clashed publicly with Chapman on several occasions, was a supremely self-confident individual, a personality trait which may not have endeared him to the Scottish selectors.

JENNINGS, Pat

1945 Born in Newry, Northern Ireland

1963 Leaves Newry Town for Watford in £6000 deal

1964 Full international debut v Wales; June – joins Tottenham Hotspur for £27,000

1967 Jennings' first club honour as Spurs beat Chelsea to lift FA Cup

1971 Helps Spurs win first of two League Cups in three years

1972 UEFA Cup Final triumph over Wolves

1973 Footballer of the Year

1976 Players' Player of the Year and MBE

1977 Moves to Arsenal for £45,000

1979 Another FA Cup winner's medal as 'Gunners' beat Manchester United

1985 Returns to White Hart Lane as a first-team cover

1986 During Mexico World Cup he establishes then world record of 119 caps, then retires

Jennings, a softly spoken, modest man, is widely rated as one of the most outstanding goalkeepers of all time. His was a larger-than-life presence between the posts, and he exuded an impression of impregnability that calmed the most hesitant of defences. Tall, strong and athletic, and with a courageous style cultivated as a youthful Gaelic footballer, he also possessed well-nigh flawless technique.

The Ulsterman was blessed with a pair of huge hands which enabled him to field crosses with apparent ease, and sharp reflexes which made him a superb shot-stopper. Yet Jennings was perhaps at his best when faced with a solitary forward bearing down on his goal, never committing himself until the last moment and often beguiling his opponent into a rash move. He was also adept at unorthodox saves with almost any part of his anatomy.

His career with Spurs, during which he played nearly 600 matches, was enough to ensure him a place in soccer folklore. But when the club, wrongly supposing him to be nearing retirement, committed the howler of allowing him to join Arsenal, he underlined his greatness with a further 326 appearances. Few players will be remembered with more admiration and affection.

Pat Jennings scores for Spurs during the 1967 FA Charity Shield match played at Old Trafford. This remarkable feat is being acknowledged by surprised Spurs players as they turn to congratulate their goalkeeper. Jennings' upfield punt sailed first bounce over Alex Stepney in the United goal. The match ended 3-3 and the trophy was shared. Pat Jennings, of whom there is a clearer photograph on page 134, won his 119th Northern Ireland cap during the 1986 World Cup finals.

JONES, Cliff

1935 Born in Swansea, Wales

1950 Welsh schoolboy international

1952 Welsh youth international; signs as professional for Swansea Town

1955 Heads winning goal against England in his second international for Wales

1958 Signs for Tottenham

Hotspur for a record fee for a winger (£35,000); stars in Welsh World Cup success (quarter-finals); breaks leg in a pre-season training accident

1961 Plays in Spurs' double-winning team

1962 Helps Spurs to second successive Cup Final victory

1963 Plays in victorious European Cup Winners' Cup Final team

1967 A third Cup winner's medal for Spurs (as

substitute)

1968 Joins Fulham on a free transfer

1969 Wins the last of his 59 Welsh caps

1970 Retires from League football, later playing for King's Lynn and Wealdstone

Cliff Jones came from a Merthyr Tydfil family with the unique record of having at least one of its members registered as a professional with the Football League for

more than 50 years from 1918 when his father, Ivor, later a Welsh international, joined Swansea. A nephew of the great Bryn Jones, an outstanding inside-forward who became the most expensive player in the game when Arsenal signed him from Wolverhampton Wanderers in 1938, Cliff first came to prominence when Swansea defeated Manchester to win the Schools Shield.

By the time Cliff was sold to Tottenham Hotspur for £35,000 in February 1958, the Jones family thus setting another transfer record, he was established as an outstanding winger, skilful, brave and breathtakingly quick. But Cliff, in common with his uncle Bryn 20 years earlier, took a while to settle in London and it was not until after the lay-off enforced by a broken leg that Spurs saw the best of him.

Cliff, at his peak unquestionably world class, became one of the most popular figures in Tottenham's history, thrilling their supporters with his courage, pace and goalscoring feats. For a relatively small man, standing barely more than 5ft 6in, he scored an extraordinary number of goals with his head, coming in fearlessly at the far post like a centre-forward, requiring only a few steps to take off and climb above much taller men.

Cliff Jones, Dave Mackay, Danny Blanchflower and John White are the four players most obviously associated with the triumphs of 1961 when Spurs became the first team in modern times to achieve the 'double' of League Championship and FA Cup. Subsequent success in Europe further established Cliff Jones as one of the game's most thrilling attackers, as Atletico Madrid discovered in the European Cup Winners' Cup Final of 1963. No British club had won a European trophy until Spurs defeated the Spaniards 5-1 in Rotterdam,

A brave and classy winger for Swansea, Spurs and Wales, Cliff Jones's hard, low crosses were delivered from the left wing towards the frame of centre-forward Bobby Smith. Cliff was a member of the successful Spurs team of the early 1960s. After completing the League and FA Cup double in 1960/61, they repeated the Cup success the following season.

with their wingers, Jones and Dyson, outstanding.

Jones later moved on to Fulham and a spell in non-League football before retiring from the game to become a sports master in London.

KEEGAN, Kevin

1951 Born in Doncaster

1968 Turns professional with Scunthorpe United

1971 Moves to Anfield for £35,000

1972 England debut v Wales

1973 Keegan is key to Reds' League title and UEFA Cup success

1974 Stars, and scores twice, in Liverpool's 3-0 FA Cup Final victory over Newcastle United

1976 Footballer of the Year; another Championship/UEFA Cup double

1977 Bids farewell to the Kop by inspiring Liverpool to their first European Cup triumph, against Borussia Mönchengladbach in Rome; June – joins SV Hamburg for £500,000, a record fee for a Briton

1978 First of two consecutive European Footballer of the Year awards

1980 Re-enters English football with Southampton

1982 Players' Player of the Year; July – wins 63rd and final cap in World Cup clash with Spain; August – moves to Newcastle United

1984 Retires after helping to secure promotion to Division 1

1992 Returns to struggling Newcastle as manager

1993 In first full season in charge, takes United into the Premier League

1994 Magpies challenge for top domestic honours and enter Europe

Kevin Keegan was arguably the most influential player of his era. Never blessed with the extravagant natural talent of George Best, whom he

It is tempting to say that this photograph shows Keegan at his peak, playing for Liverpool against Queens Park Rangers at Loftus Road in 1973. Liverpool were moving towards their most powerful era and Keegan was in partnership with John Toshack. However, his spells at Southampton and Newcastle also saw him inspire the teams around him to considerable success. Apart from being a complete player, Keegan was a winner... as his recent record as manager of Newcastle has proved.

succeeded as the darling of the media, he possessed instead an overwhelming desire to succeed, and matchless application to his work. After being plucked from the obscurity of Scunthorpe – the deal was later described by Bill Shankly as 'robbery with violence' – Keegan could hardly have made a greater impact at Anfield. The irrepressible, dark-haired front-man became the vital additive the Liverpool boss needed to inspire and lift his rebuilt side.

Keegan was a darting imp, quick, brave and apparently inexhaustible. He had good ball control, a nimble brain and amazing power in the air for a small man. With the 'Reds' he formed a lethal duo with John Toshack, and became an integral part of the England side, which he captained for a spell. Indeed, many would contend that he was prematurely dropped by Bobby Robson.

After enduring unwarranted criticism for taking his skills to Europe, he returned home with spirited stints at Southampton and Newcastle, playing a dominant role in restoring the Magpies' First Division status. He then retired to Spain, having never given less than value for money. Seven years later, much to the surprise of the football world, he put his reputation on the line by rejoining Newcastle as manager. Within three months he had staved off a seemingly inevitable demotion, and a

year later had led the Magpies into the Premier League. In the top flight, Keegan's team played scintillating, attractive football and it seemed only a matter of time before the honours began to accumulate. Home was the hero, indeed.

KILMARNOCK

Founded 1869

Joined League 1895 (Division 2)

Honours Scottish League Division 1 Champions 1965; Division 2 Champions 1898, 1899; Scottish Cup Winners 1920, 1929

Ground Rugby Park

Scotland's second oldest club (after Queen's Park) took part in the first ever Scottish Cup tie on 18 October 1873 but waited until the 1960s for their greatest success. In 1965 they beat Hearts 2-0 at Tynecastle on the final day to win the Championship, edging the Edinburgh side out by 0.04 on goal average.

The 1960s side, often drawing on the guile of the

precocious Tommy McLean, enjoyed remarkable results in Europe. In 1964 they defeated Eintracht Frankfurt in a Fairs Cup tie after being 4-0 down on aggregate early in the second leg. Sterling deeds had also seen Kilmarnock win the Scottish Cup in 1920 and 1929.

KLINSMANN, Jurgen

1964 Born 30 July, near Stuttgart

1981 Represents West Germany at Youth level

1984 Signs for VfB Stuttgart from city neighbours Stuttgarter Kickers

1986 Scores five times for VfB in a Bundesliga fixture

1987 Makes full international debut in 1-1 draw with Brazil

1988 Top scorer in Bundesliga with 19 goals, Klinsmann earns his place in the national side for the European Championship finals

1989 Runners-up medal in UEFA Cup as Stuttgart lose out to Napoli; signs for Internazionale for £2.5m and joins fellow Germans Lothar Matthaus and Andreas Brehme in Milan

1990 Germany win World Cup, Klinsmann scores three times in the tournament and wins 25th cap in final

1991 Wins UEFA Cup with Inter in all-Italian final against Roma

1992 Reclaims place in national team for European Championship finals; leaves Inter for AS Monaco

1994 Monaco reach semi-finals of European Cup but lose out to AC Milan; Klinsmann on target five times for Germany in World Cup; moves to Tottenham for £2m

1995 Top scorer for Spurs with 20 Premiership goals; wins FWA Player of the Year award; leaves for Bayern Munich

When he signed for Tottenham Hotspur in the summer of 1994 – a sensational transfer which caught even the most accomplished 'sniffers' of the English press unawares – Jurgen Klinsmann was taking on a challenge to compare with any he had faced in his career. He was leaving the sleepy comforts of the South of France to step into the hothouse of English club football with its unique passions, prejudices and unrelenting physical demands.

The relish with which the German World Cup star set about this task was a revelation. He disarmed a suspicious public with his unassuming manner and modest lifestyle – the sight of his battered old Volkswagen Beetle alongside the Porsches and BMWs in the club car park always provoked a wry smile – and joked engagingly about the reputation for 'diving' he had acquired.

If the charm offensive was an unqualified success, it was mirrored on the pitch by a willingness to work for the team which meant that, with his powerful running and never-say-die attitude, Klinsmann often looked more English than his team-mates.

Then of course there were the goals, the blond striker's stock-in-trade: a powerful header on his debut at Sheffield Wednesday and a spectacular overhead strike in his first match at White Hart Lane were just the start, as Spurs were treated to the full Klinsmann repertoire in a season which saw him score 29 goals in all competitions. The highlight was a last-minute winner at Anfield in the quarter-finals of the FA Cup, and it looked then as if there might be a dream end to the season at Wembley. However, Spurs crashed to defeat in the semi-final at Elland Road, and the wanderer determined that his English adventure had run its course. Bayern Munich moved in to take 'Klinsi' home to Germany.

For Klinsmann it meant linking up once again with Franz Beckenbauer, who had given him his German debut back in December 1987 and launched an international career which reached its peak in the 1990 World Cup finals. Linking up with Rudi Voller, Klinsmann was on target in group matches against Yugoslavia and the UAE before playing the game of his life in the second round showdown with Holland, scoring in a 2-1 win after Voller was sent off. The partnership was reformed in 1994 in the USA and produced some spectacular goals, but Germany were eliminated in the quarter-finals by Bulgaria. Klinsmann went on to captain his country in 1995 and looked set to return to England for the 1996 European Championship finals.

Jurgen Klinsmann peeling away having scored his first goal in English soccer, against Sheffield Wednesday at Hillsborough during a 4-3 win for Spurs. Moments after this photograph Klinsmann dived to the ground, mocking those who had accused him of 'diving' to win penalties. His year in England was characterised by good humour; Klinsmann's charm certainly won over many doubters.

LAW, Denis

1940 Born in Aberdeen

1957 Turns professional with Huddersfield Town

1958 Scores on full Scottish debut, v Wales at Cardiff

1960 Moves to Manchester City for a British record fee of £55,000

1961 Scores six in abandoned FA Cup tie against Luton Town, all expunged from records; gets City's only goal in 3-1 replay defeat; Torino take Law to Italy for £110,000

1962 Joins Manchester United for £115,000, another record

1963 May – scores United's first goal in FA Cup Final victory over Leicester City; October – scores for Rest of the World against England in FA Centenary match at Wembley.

1964 European Footballer of the Year

1965 Wins first of two League Championship medals in three seasons

1968 Helps United reach European Cup Final, then misses match with injured knee

1973 Returns to Maine Road on free transfer

1974 April – backheels goal for City at Old Trafford which helps seal United's relegation; June – wins last of 55 caps against Zaire in World Cup finals, and retires, having scored 300 goals in 585 club games

Law was one of the most blindingly brilliant performers of the modern era, an inside-forward whose array of talents was virtually complete. His goals were many and spectacular, his all-round skills exemplary and his bravery a byword. On top of all that, he exuded a cocky panache which endeared him to the fans, who dubbed him 'The King' during his Manchester United heyday. The upraised fist, the spiky blond hair, the impudent grin, they were trademarks of the man who perhaps outdid even fellow heroes George Best and Bobby Charlton in earning the sheer affection of the Stretford End.

When he began his career at Huddersfield, he appeared so frail that it was difficult to believe he could survive in the professional game. But opponents soon discovered that the apparent weakling was rawhide tough and possessed of a fiery temperament which was often to land him in trouble with referees.

The acquisition of Law, on his return from an ill-fated sojourn in Italy, was unquestionably one of Matt Busby's master strokes. His later move to neighbours City was notable for the goal which helped to relegate United and which Law acknowledged with a mixture of pride (in the goal) and sadness (at its impact). After quitting football, Law became a radio commentator.

Characteristically saluting another goal (one hand raised, shirt cuffs pulled down) – this one for Manchester United against Crystal Palace in 1970 – Denis Law was one of the 'triumvirate' that electrified United's attack in the late 1960s and early 1970s. Playing alongside George Best and Bobby Charlton for United, the slim and quicksilver player excited strong emotions. His skills delighted his own supporters; his apparent cockiness infuriated those of his opponents, whether Law was playing for United or Scotland.

LAWS

A set of rules closely resembling today's Laws was drawn up at Cambridge University around 1848. Compared with the FA rules published in December 1863, they permitted more handling and contained a more severe offside ruling.

The 1863 FA rules helped to standardise some of the various approaches to the game, but there were still significant differences between the London Association and the Sheffield Association, most notably over the throw-in and offside. Sheffield Association clubs kicked the ball in from touch in any direction and needed only one player goal-side in their offside rule. London Association clubs threw the ball in straight from touch and needed three players goal-side in their offside rule. These differences were resolved in 1877 – a free throw in any direction and the three-person offside law. The 1925 change in this law – two opponents nearer to the goal-line rather than three – was probably the most dramatic change this century.

Many early laws proved well thought-out, but several familiar features of modern football came in only after the 1877 agreement between the London and Sheffield associations. These include the two-handed throw-in (1882), the penalty kick (1890), linesmen replacing umpires (1891), full control to the referee (1894), the goalkeeper restricted to handling inside his penalty area rather than anywhere on the field (1912), the 10-yard distance (rather than 6 yards) between defenders and ball at free kicks (1913) and also at corner-kicks (1914), no offside from a throw-in (1920), a goal scored direct from a corner kick (1924), the current offside law (1925), a goalkeeper to remain stationary on the goal-line for a penalty kick (1929), defenders no longer allowed to tap the ball into a goalkeeper's hands at a goal kick (1936), an increase of an ounce in the weight of the ball (1937), and obstruction included in indirect free-kick offences (1951).

The Referees' Chart and Players' Guide to the Laws of Association Football is the best source for understanding the laws of the game and international board decisions. It is updated annually. Experiments are sometimes operated in semi-professional leagues, such as replacing the throw-in with a kick-in.

One recent change to be adopted, provoking lively controversy in 1992, was the ban on goalkeepers handling back-passes. The rule was introduced to keep the game flowing and to stop deliberate time-wasting, but its opponents maintained it lowered the standard of play by encouraging defenders to kick the ball anywhere. Either way, it produced countless bizarre and entertaining incidents during its first season in force.

LAWTON, Tommy

1919 Born in Bolton

1936 Makes League debut for Burnley; December – moves to Everton for £6500

1938 Scores on England debut, v Wales in Cardiff

1939 Plays major part in winning League title

1945 Switches to Chelsea for £11,500

1947 Joins Notts County in first ever £20,000 deal

1948 Wins final England cap, against Denmark in Copenhagen

1952 Makes a £12,000 move to Brentford and soon becomes player-manager

1953 Signs for Arsenal

1955 Links up with non-League Kettering Town as player-boss

1957 Returns to Notts County as a manager

1958 Lawton is sacked and takes over a pub

No serious student of the game would deny Tommy Lawton his place among the all-time greats. The tall, muscular centre-forward, of the sleek centre-parting and jutting nose, has often been described as the finest header of a ball that ever lived, but there was much more to his game than mere aerial power. Lawton was blessed with the skill and pace to run at defenders, a searing and accurate shot, and deft distribution which brought many goals for his forward partners. He also had charisma. When he was in his pomp, the name of Lawton on the teamsheet was guaranteed to boost the gate, no matter how mundane the fixture. Sadly, his career was blighted by the war. In 1939, aged 19, he had already won a place in the England side and had just helped his new club, Everton, lift the League title. The soccer world was at his feet, and although his final goal tally – 231 in 390 League games and 22 in 23 internationals – was impressive by any standards, it would surely have

A smiling, dapper Tommy Lawton at the end of his career. Lawton played only 35 League matches for Arsenal following spells with Chelsea, Notts County and Brentford. He may be best remembered as an England player, his name fitting alongside those of Finney and Matthews among others, and for scoring 22 goals in 23 internationals.

reached awesome proportions if the conflict had not robbed him of seven seasons.

One of football's wanderers, Lawton was always very much his own man and was involved in several well-publicised disputes with clubs. After promising work at Kettering, his managerial career foundered and he made an unsatisfactory exit from the game he had graced so magnificently for 20 years.

LEEDS UNITED

Founded 1919

Joined League 1920 (Division 2)

Honours Division 1 Champions 1969, 1974, 1992; Division 2 Champions 1924, 1964, 1990; FA Cup Winners 1972; Football League Cup Winners 1968; European Fairs Cup Winners 1968, 1971

Ground Elland Road

Leeds United were formed to succeed Leeds City, who were expelled from the League and disbanded after a scandal over illegal payments. United's history was one of modest achievement – they had never fallen below Division 2 or finished higher than fifth in Division 1 – before Don Revie's appointment as player-manager in 1961.

The former England forward transformed Leeds into a club challenging consistently for major honours, at home and abroad. Using players who had graduated from the youth team, he built initially around Jack Charlton, a gangling centre-half who was to begin an England career at 28, and two small Scots, Bobby Collins and Billy Bremner, whose volatile temperaments accompanied great ability.

After several near misses, Leeds beat Arsenal in a dour League Cup Final in 1968. A year later, with ex-Manchester United player Johnny Giles by now partnering Bremner in midfield, they took their first Championship by drawing at Liverpool, and went on to finish with what was then a First Division record of 67 points after losing only two of their 42 fixtures. Further honours followed as the side began to win over those who had labelled them dirty and defensive. In 1972 Leeds won the FA Cup, again defeating Arsenal, but failed to clinch the Championship and the double 48 hours later at Wolverhampton.

Revie's departure for the England manager's job, following Leeds' second League title, caused player unrest. Brian Clough took over but departed barely seven weeks later. Leeds recovered to reach the 1975 European Cup Final against Bayern Munich in Paris, but lost against a backdrop of violence initiated by some of their followers.

The dual problem of diminishing success on the pitch and growing hooliganism off it dogged Leeds through the next decade and beyond. A succession of managers, among them three players from their heyday, were unable to arrest the decline. Financial difficulties, exacerbated by relegation in 1982, forced the sale three years later of Elland Road to the city council, who granted the club a 125-year lease.

In 1988 Leeds secured Howard Wilkinson from Sheffield Wednesday as manager. He dealt extensively in the transfer market, having spent £6

million and banked £3 million by the time Division 1 status was regained in 1990. Gordon Strachan, whose leadership and skill drew comparisons with Bremner, also finished top scorer in 1989/90, 16 goals leaving him the small matter of 26 behind John Charles's club-record tally in 1953/54.

With support running at levels not enjoyed since the Revie era, Leeds finished fourth on their return to the top flight despite playing under threat of expulsion from the FA, the result of incidents involving their fans at Bournemouth on the weekend promotion was achieved.

The renaissance was complete in 1992 when they pipped Manchester United for the Championship, with the evergreen Strachan, fellow midfielders David Batty and Gary McAllister, and marksman Lee Chapman among their most influential players. However, the following term brought dire anti-climax, with early elimination from the

Manager Don Revie attempts to console skipper Billy Bremner at the end of Leeds United's 1-0 shock defeat by Sunderland in the 1973 FA Cup Final. This disappointment followed the 'high' of beating Arsenal 1-0 to win the Centenary Fin al in 1972. The Leeds team of the early 1970s was an exceptional one, with players like Bremner, Johnny Giles, Allan Clarke (between Bremner and Revie in the photograph), Jack Charlton and Peter Lorimer.

European Cup at the hands of Glasgow Rangers and the controversial departure of star Frenchman Eric Cantona to Old Trafford. The mid-1990s were proving a trying period for Wilkinson, though the £3.4 million arrival of Ghanaian striker Tony Yeboah in the spring of 1995 offered fresh grounds for optimism.

LEICESTER CITY

Founded 1884

Joined League 1894
(Division 2)

Honours Division 2
Champions 1925, 1937,
1954, 1957, 1971, 1980;
League Cup Winners 1964

Ground Filbert Street

Leicester City are a frustrating club. They employ enterprising managers to build entertaining sides, only to see them fail, with agonising predictability, on the verge of major achievement.

The 'Foxes' have spent much of their history proving they are too good for the Second Division, only to fall out of the First with equal regularity. When they were relegated in 1995 it was their 18th journey between the top two flights, and not since 1908 have they spent more than a dozen successive campaigns at one level.

City first threatened to make a major impact in the late 1920s, when they twice came close to the League Championship and their stars included marksman Arthur Chandler and long-serving full-back Adam Black. But, typically, the impetus died and despite remarkable goalscoring feats by Arthur Rowley in the 1950s it was not until Matt Gillies became manager at the decade's end that some stability was achieved. The thoughtful Scot

constructed a fluent side in which 'keeper Gordon Banks and wing-half Frank McLintock were outstanding, but Leicester's near-miss syndrome was to continue. In 1961 they lost the FA Cup Final; two years later they squandered a promising First Division position and were beaten FA Cup finalists again. A solitary triumph in the infant League Cup was scant consolation.

The 1960s ended with City's fourth FA Cup Final defeat in 21 years, and another relegation. There followed splendid work by managers Frank O'Farrell and Jimmy Bloomfield, whose 1970s teams included the likes of Peter Shilton,

Banks's brilliant replacement, and forwards Keith Weller and Frank Worthington.

Nothing was won however, and the ups and downs continued unabated during the 1980s, despite prolific contributions from strikers Gary Lineker and Alan Smith, both sold for big fees. At least 1994 saw the end of the club's Wembley jinx; in addition to their FA Cup reverses, they had lost play-offs at the national stadium in 1992 and 1993, but this time they beat Derby County to earn a one-term sojourn in the top flight. Leicester are one of many Midlands sides battling each other for support. If they are to succeed, consistency must be their primary aim.

LEYTON ORIENT

Founded 1881

Joined League 1905
(Division 2)

Honours Division 3 (S)
Champions 1956; Division 3
Champions 1970

Ground Brisbane Road

Thrice rescued from the brink of financial disaster, Leyton Orient offer an inspiring example of what spirit and hard work can achieve for the least fashionable of clubs.

After election to the League, the east Londoners – at different times known as Clapton Orient and just plain Orient – were a very ordinary outfit and it was no surprise

Frank Worthington scored 72 goals in 209 appearances for Leicester. A much travelled footballer, Frank signed to 11 clubs in a career spanning 22 seasons and was still playing League football at the age of 39. Leicester City fans have enjoyed many special moments during their club's history, but few of major importance. There seems to be something preventing the club from reaching the very top. For instance, they have been the losing team in four FA Cup Finals.

when they slumped into Division 3 (S) in 1929. Not long afterwards they faced economic oblivion but were saved by Arsenal, who temporarily made the O's their nursery club.

More than two decades of mediocrity ensued until Alec Stock became manager, transformed their fortunes and led them back to the higher grade. Johnny Carey carried on the good work and amazed the football world by gaining promotion to Division 1 in 1962. But Orient were not ready for such a quantum leap, and near calamity followed: they finished 10 points adrift at the bottom of the table and then plummeted back to the Third Division, a descent which culminated in a second cash crisis in 1967. After salvation had been achieved, assisted by a collection organised by fans, a succession of enterprising managers, including Dave Sexton and Jimmy Bloomfield, brought better times at Brisbane Road, including an FA Cup quarter-final in 1971 and the semi-final seven years later.

By 1995, however, Leyton Orient were back in financial trouble. Closure was averted with the help of cash from sports promoter Barry Hearn, but he must have been disappointed by the relegation that ensued, putting the club back into the League basement.

LIDDELL, Billy

1922 Born in Dunfermline, Scotland

1939 Signs for Liverpool

1946 August – League debut v Sheffield United at Bramall Lane; October – wins first of 28 Scottish caps, v Wales at Wrexham; helps the Reds clinch the first post-war League Championship

1947 Plays for Great Britain against the Rest of Europe

1950 Takes home loser's medal as Arsenal beat Liverpool in FA Cup Final

1954 Despite the prodigious efforts of Liddell, the Reds are relegated to the Second

Division

1955 Liddell and Stanley Matthews are the only two players retained for Great Britain's second clash with the Europeans

1961 Retires after scoring 229 goals in 537 games for Liverpool

Any contemporary observer would confirm that Billy Liddell was Liverpool's finest player in the post-war years before Bill Shankly led the club towards lasting glory. Yet there is no shortage of shrewd pundits who would go even further; they would say the Scottish winger-cum-centre-forward was the Reds' greatest talent of all time, and that is with due deference to Messrs Dalglish, Keegan, Barnes and company.

Liddell's hallmarks were exhilarating pace and power, allied to the most delicate skill. Sadly, he lost his early prime

to the war, and then played in a poor side for much of his time at Anfield. Indeed, throughout the late 1950s he laboured nobly, though unavailingly, to lift them out of the Second Division.

Such application was typical of the man, who was beloved of the fans, not only as a fabulous entertainer but also as a chivalrous, down-to-earth personality. After retirement he became a youth worker, lay preacher and justice of the peace.

A Liverpool and Scotland star of the 1950s, Billy Liddell played more than 500 games for the Reds. Although he missed out on the glory days at Liverpool, he will always be remembered for his devotion to football and to his adopted home town.

LINCOLN CITY

Founded 1883

Joined League 1892 (Division 2, founder member)

Honours Division 3 (N) Champions 1932, 1948, 1952; Division 4 Champions 1976

Ground Sincil Bank

When Lincoln City dropped out of the League in 1987, it was no new experience for them. After being founder members of Division 2, the 'Imps' failed to gain re-election on three occasions before joining the newly formed Division 3 (N) in 1921.

There followed a roller-coaster existence between Second and Third Divisions which ended unhappily with a slump to the basement in the 1960s. Having narrowly survived a financial crisis during that decade, Lincoln toiled in the League's lower reaches until they were demoted to the Vauxhall Conference. They bounced back into the Fourth Division at the first attempt and now face the task of rebuilding in an area not renowned for its soccer tradition.

Notable managers have included long-serving Bill Anderson, whose side in the 1950s was one of Lincoln's most impressive combinations, and former England boss Graham Taylor, an ex-Imp who occupied the Sincil Bank hot seat in the mid 1970s.

LINEKER, Gary

1960 Born in Leicester

1978 Turns professional with Leicester City

1980 Wins Second Division title medal

1981 Struggles for his place as Leicester are relegated

1983 Boosts promotion campaign with 26 goals

1984 Makes England debut as substitute for Tony Woodcock, v Scotland at Hampden

1985 Joins Everton for £800,000 plus a third of

future profit

1986 Scoops two awards – Football Writers' and Players' Player of Year – after scoring 30 League goals; nets in FA Cup Final defeat by Liverpool; June – six strikes, including a hat-trick against Poland, make Lineker top scorer in Mexico World Cup; July – moves to Barcelona for £2.75 million

1989 Returns to Football League as Tottenham Hotspur pay £1.1 million

1990 Finishes first season at White Hart Lane with 26 goals; scores for England in World Cup semi-final against West Germany, his fourth goal of the tournament; September – becomes Graham Taylor's first England captain

1991 Passes the 150-goal mark in just over 300

League games; helps Spurs win FA Cup at end of season of financial turmoil

1992 January – OBE in New Year honours list; May – leaves Spurs for Japanese club Grampus 8; June – England career ends in anti-climax, though most people would be content with 48 goals in 80 games!

1994 Retires through injury to work in media

When Gary Lineker was substituted by England boss Graham Taylor during the second half of the 1992 European Championship clash with Sweden, it was a sad and frustrating moment. He was bidding farewell to the international scene just one goal behind Bobby Charlton's record of 49, and as captain of a discredited side. Such a prolific marksman and magnificent

ambassador for the game deserved a better fate and yet, in the context of his career as a whole, it was a minor blemish. Certainly, his place on his country's roll of honour was already secure.

Lineker made a startling impact at every level after building his reputation in a Leicester side of rather indifferent quality. With Everton he assumed world-class stature; in Spain he overcame illness and adapted his game to earn generous praise; at Tottenham he provided a much-needed cutting edge; and for England he was an inspiration.

Few defences were proof against his phenomenal acceleration, to which he allied enviable composure and a lethal instinct for arriving in front of goal at precisely the right moment. He was not a forager, however, and relied almost exclusively on intelligent

service from midfield. Blessed with an equable temperament and clean-cut image, Lineker excelled at public relations, and was an exemplary England captain.

Gary Lineker returns to England at the end of his playing career with Japanese side Grampus 8 to play in a friendly match against Leeds United. Lineker's achievements on the pitch have been matched by an ability to make the most of his life off it. He chose his clubs well, made the most of his spells playing abroad, learning the Spanish language and only narrowly failing to master Japanese. He has subsequently embarked upon a career in the media that looks like being every bit as successful.

LIVERPOOL

Founded 1892

Joined League 1893 (Division 2)

Honours Division 1 Champions 1901, 1906, 1922, 1923, 1947, 1964, 1966, 1973, 1976, 1977, 1979, 1980, 1982, 1983, 1984, 1986, 1988, 1990; Division 2 Champions 1894, 1896, 1905, 1962; FA Cup Winners 1965, 1974, 1986, 1989, 1992; League Cup Winners 1981, 1982, 1983, 1984, 1995; European Cup Winners 1977, 1978, 1981, 1984; UEFA Cup Winners 1973, 1976

Ground Anfield

In a journal of record such as this, the obvious has to be stated: Liverpool, quite simply, are the most successful club in English soccer history. Their exalted status comes courtesy of a phenomenal record in the modern era, which began with the arrival of Bill Shankly as manager in 1959. Yet, believe it or not, there was life at Anfield before Shankly.

In fact, the first stirrings were as an offshoot of local rivals Everton in 1890. After early vacillations between First and Second Divisions, the 'Reds' made their initial significant mark on the football world, winning two League Championships in the first decade of the new century, aided on the second occasion by England goalkeeper Sam Hardy. There followed a relatively uneventful spell before another brace of titles, with new custodian Elisha Scott and long-serving full-back Ephraim Longworth making prominent contributions.

The 1930s brought something of a decline, but Championship triumph in the first season after the war and the emergence of brilliant Scottish forward Billy Liddell boded well for the future. The 1950s, however, failed to live up to this promise and the unthinkable happened: Liverpool were relegated. Cue Shankly, and the revolution. The indomitable Scot swiftly revamped a nondescript side.

To promising youngsters such as goal merchant Roger Hunt and winger Ian Callaghan he added the likes of colossal centre-half Ron Yeats and Ian St John, a pugnacious, skilful centre-forward, and it wasn't long before the Reds were back in the top flight. But promotion was only the beginning. Having strengthened the team further with England flankman Peter Thompson and granite-tough local boy Tommy Smith, Shankly was ready to take on the elite. His new Liverpool served notice of the dominance in store by lifting two titles, and for good measure putting the club's name on the FA Cup for the first time – all in the space of three years.

By the early 1970s he had remoulded his side and with such men as inspirational forward Kevin Keegan, 'keeper Ray Clemence, midfielder-cum-defender Emlyn Hughes and goal-getter John Toshack now holding sway, the trophies continued to accumulate.

When Shankly surprised everyone by resigning in 1974, erstwhile back-room boy Bob Paisley moved into his seat and, astonishingly, the rate of success increased. New talents to savour included those of the superbly gifted Kenny Dalglish, Graeme Souness, an imperious play-maker, and Alan Hansen, the coolest central defender since Bobby Moore. Europe was conquered and fresh standards of achievement were set. After Paisley retired in 1983, first Joe Fagan and then Dalglish – who led Liverpool to the League/FA Cup double in his first term in charge – took up the challenge, establishing a supremacy which weighed heavily on their rivals and scotching former disparaging claims that the Reds were dull and machine-like. The sheer style of goal king Ian Rush, England striker Peter Beardsley, the magnificent John Barnes et al produced flowing one-touch football which was often a joy to behold. The 1980s were marred by the Heysel and Hillsborough tragedies but, in

With so many victories to celebrate and so many great players to feature, it is difficult to select one photo for Liverpool FC. This one shows Graeme Souness, Kenny Dalglish and Alan Hansen with the big prize, the European Cup, in 1981. Souness and Dalglish have moved into management and Hansen has become a media pundit. Although the 1990s have so far been less successful by Liverpool standards, the rebuilding of the side continues.

LOFTHOUSE, Nat

1925 Born in Bolton

1939 Signs for Bolton Wanderers

1950 Scores twice on England debut, v Yugoslavia at Highbury

1952 Press dub Lofthouse the 'Lion of Vienna'

1953 Footballer of the Year; scores in every round of the FA Cup, including the 'Matthews Final' against Blackpool, which Bolton lose 4-3; September – scores six for Football League against Irish League

1956 Tops First Division goal chart

1958 Skippers Bolton to FA Cup triumph over Manchester United, scoring both goals, the second through a controversial barge on 'keeper Harry Gregg; England swansong, v Wales at Villa Park, having scored 30 times in 33 internationals.

1960 Career ended by injury; joins Burnden Park coaching staff

1968 Takes over as Bolton boss

1971 Steps down to become chief scout

1985 Short spell as caretaker manager

1986 Becomes Bolton president

Lofthouse was an archetypal battering-ram centre-forward who, during his prime in the 1950s, terrorised defences all

Nat Lofthouse, left of photograph being hugged by manager Bill Ridding, captained the team and scored both goals for Bolton Wanderers against Manchester United in the 1958 FA Cup Final. However, the match will probably be remembered for his barge on United's goalkeeper Harry Gregg that sent man and ball over the line and gave Bolton the second goal of the game.

playing terms, the Liverpool story was one of unconfined delight.

The sudden departure of Dalglish as manager in 1991 opened a window of hope for the opposition and though new boss Souness lifted the FA Cup in 1992, he failed to build a successful side and was dismissed in 1994. His sucessor, long-serving Anfield boot-room graduate Roy Evans, made a promising start to the difficult job of restoring the Reds to something like their former eminence by winning the Coca-Cola Cup in 1995. His quiet style seemed in keeping with the Liverpool way, and European qualification might be a sign of success to come.

over the world. He followed another native of Bolton, Tommy Lawton, into the England side, and although he never had the craft of his illustrious predecessor, the tank-like Lofthouse could not be faulted for aggression, commitment and courage.

It was after a typically brave performance in his country's shirt that he was nicknamed the 'Lion of Vienna', his two-goal show setting up a memorable victory over Austria, then one of Europe's leading sides. Dynamic in the air, blessed with a vicious shot in either foot, and dedicated to chasing causes that were apparently lost, Lofthouse was a difficult man to play against, and there were times when he was accused of being over-physical in his approach.

A one-club man, he served Bolton royally as a player, netting 285 times in 503 games, and later as an administrator.

LOST CLUBS

Clubs have usually left the Football League after failing to gain re-election, but occasionally they have resigned from the League, recent examples being Aldershot in March 1992 and Maidstone United the following summer, both for financial reasons.

Since 1987 a club finishing

last in the lowest division has been automatically relegated to the GM Vauxhall Conference, except when other factors have intervened.

The most stable period in Football League history was between 1938 and 1960, when only New Brighton were lost. The elimination of Gateshead in 1960 came as a shock, especially as the north-eastern club had been relatively successful in the post-war period, had not faced re-election for 23 years and had not even finished bottom when Peterborough United replaced them. This demonstrates the unpopularity of geographically isolated clubs, many of which are under the most threat.

Clubs lost to the Football League are as follows (with League career in brackets): Aberdare Athletic (1921-27), Accrington Stanley (1888-93 and 1921-62), Aldershot (1932-92), Ashington (1921-29), Barrow (1921-72), Bootle (1892-93), Bradford Park Avenue (1908-70), Burton United (1901-07), Darwen (1891-99), Durham City (1921-28), Gainsborough Trinity (1896-1912), Gateshead (1919-60), Glossop North End (1898-1915), Halifax Town (1921-

93), Loughborough Town (1895-1900), Maidstone United (1989-92), Merthyr Tydfil (1920-30), Middlesbrough Ironopolis (1893-94), Nelson (1921-31), New Brighton (1898-1901 and 1923-51), Newport County (1921-31 and 1932-88), Northwich Victoria (1892-94), Southport (1921-78), Stalybridge Celtic (1921-23), Thames (1930-32) and Workington Town (1951-77). In addition, Burton Wanderers (1894-97) amalgamated with Burton Swifts (1892-1901) to form Burton United, and there are current League clubs with a discontinuous record: Blackpool, Chesterfield, Crewe Alexandra, Colchester United, Darlington, Doncaster Rovers, Gillingham, Grimsby Town, Lincoln City (now in their fifth spell), Luton Town, Port Vale, Rotherham United, Stockport County, Stoke City, Walsall and Wigan Athletic.

The list of lost Scottish League clubs is affected considerably by altercations involving rival Central and Western Leagues in the early 1920s. A deal was struck to incorporate the rival Leagues into the Scottish League, which was extended to three divisions. However, many of the new clubs were soon

threatened by an exodus of players and poor attendances. Division 3 collapsed in its third season.

The list of lost clubs from the Scottish League is as follows:

Abercorn (1890-1915), Armadale (1921-32), Arthurlie (1901-15 and 1923-29), Bathgate (1921-29), Beith (1923-26), Bo'ness (1921-32), Broxburn United (1921-26), Cambuslang (1890-92), Clackmannan (1920-22 and 1923-26), the original Clydebank (1914-30), Cowlairs (1890-91 and 1893-95), Dumbarton Harp (1923-25), Dundee Wanderers (1894-95), Dykehead (1923-26), Edinburgh City (1928-49), Galston (1923-26), Helensburgh (1893), Johnstone (1912-15 and 1921-26), Kings Park (1921-39), Leith Athletic (1891-1915, 1924-26 and 1927-53), Linthouse (1895-1900), Lochgelly United (1914-15 and 1921-26), Mid-Annandale (1923-26), Nithsdale Wanderers (1923-26), Northern club of Glasgow (1894-95), Peebles Rovers (1923-26), Port Glasgow Athletic (1893-1911), Renton (1890-98), Royal Albert (1923-26), St Bernards (1893-1915 and

Many clubs have been 'lost' to the Football League over the years. Aldershot FC was founded in 1926 and joined the Football League six years later. No honours came their way, and financial reasons forced the club to quit in 1992. Their small band of fans remained faithful to the end. The name of Accrington Stanley remains synonymous with football failure. They joined the list of 'lost clubs' in 1962 when they were forced to quite the Football League due to financial difficulties.

1921-39), Solway Star (1923-26), Third Lanark (1890-1967), Thistle (1893-94) and Vale of Leven (1890-92, 1905-15 and 1921-26). In addition, Ayr and Ayr Parkhouse merged in 1910 to form Ayr United.

LUTON TOWN

Founded 1885

Joined League 1897 (Division 2)

Honours Division 2 Champions 1982; Division 3 (S) Champions 1937; Division 4 Champions 1968; League Cup Winners 1988

Ground Kenilworth Road

Luton Town are a plucky club whose three spells in the top flight were achieved despite lack of consistently heavy support, a plight due largely to their position on London's doorstep.

The 'Hatters' early experience of Football League life was traumatic. After only three seasons they failed to gain re-election to the Second Division, and it was two decades before they were readmitted as founder members of the Third.

There they remained until 1937, when – boosted by 55 goals from Joe Payne, who had netted 10 times in one match during the previous campaign – they were promoted. They then consolidated before manager Dally Duncan led them into the top flight in 1955. Players such as centre-half Syd Owen, wing-half Bob Morton, 'keeper Ron Baynham and goal-scorer Gordon Turner impressed on the grander stage, but despite the purchase of talented forwards such as Billy Bingham and Allan Brown, Luton were relegated after five years. The highlight of this period was reaching the FA Cup Final in 1959, when they were beaten by Nottingham Forest.

Then came utter depression, followed by some solid rebuilding work. An alarming slide, all the way to the Fourth Division, was arrested when Brown returned to Kenilworth Road as manager. He took Luton back to the Third Division, Alec Stock led them to the Second, and Harry Haslam restored them to the First, though only for 1974/75. Seven more years in Division 2 were followed by promotion under David Pleat in 1982. Luton's first major trophy, the League Cup, arrived in the form of a dramatic late victory over Arsenal in 1988.

During these switchback years, star performers included forward Bruce Rioch (1960s), marksman Malcolm Macdonald (1969-71) and midfielder Ricky Hill (1970s and 1980s).

In recent years Luton have hit the headlines more through their controversial synthetic pitch and ban on away supporters, than for any great success on the field of play – although they are

Two-goal hero Brian Stein scores the winner in the League (then called Littlewoods) Cup Final in 1988 against Arsenal. This was the greatest season in Luton Town's history, as they also reached the semi-finals of the FA Cup. After gaining promotion to the first Division in 1982, Luton Town stayed there for the next nine seasons, finishing a respectable seventh in 1986/87.

always a team that are capable of turning in surprise performances. Having been relegated to the new First Division in 1992, the Hatters were looking to returned boss Pleat to restore their fortunes, but on a tight budget. Ever enterprising, he led them to an FA Cup semi-final in 1994, then showed his loyalty to the Kenilworth Road cause by spurning the chance of rejoining Spurs later in the year.

McCOIST, Ally

1962 Born in Belshill, Lanarkshire

1978 Signs for St Johnstone

1981 Swaps his midfield berth for striker's role and nets 22 times in season for Saints who narrowly miss out on promotion; McCoist is transferred to Sunderland for £400,000

1983 Moves back to Scotland and joins Rangers

1984 Hat-trick v Celtic in League Cup final

1986 Debut for Scotland in 0-0 draw v Holland

1987 Rangers are champions as McCoist hits 33 League goals

1988 October – scores twice v Aberdeen to earn Light Blues a third consecutive League Cup triumph

1990 Breaks post-war club record for League goals in 3-0 win v Celtic; plays in World Cup finals for Scotland

1992 Wins European Golden Boot with 34 goals; Scottish Player of the Year; collects first Scottish Cup medal as 'Gers do the Double

1993 Europe's leading scorer again, but suffers broken leg playing for Scotland in Portugal and misses out on final leg of Rangers' domestic treble; October – makes dramatic return with winning goal in League Cup final v Hibs

1994 Awarded MBE in Birthday Honours list

1995 Picks up eighth Championship medal as 'Gers make it seven in a row

The impish grin, good looks and 'cheeky chappie' personality may account for much of his popularity throughout Scotland but there can be no doubting that 'Super Ally' has proved himself a striker of the highest quality. As partners up front at Ibrox have come and gone, he has simply carried on scoring – 299 goals in all competitions for Rangers by the end of 1994/95, a total which would have been considerably larger but for several spells out of the side, most recently through injury.

Indeed what makes McCoist's achievements all the more admirable is that throughout his career he has consistently had to bounce back from adversity which at times has tested his cheerful nature to the limit. As a teenager he flopped at Sunderland and after two unhappy seasons had to be rescued by a call from Glasgow Rangers, the team he supported as a boy; then an inconsistent start at Ibrox saw the fans lose patience with him as he was famously barracked during a Cup tie

Ally McCoist in Scotland jersey tussles with Antonio Veloso of Portugal during a World Cup qualifier in 1992. The game finished 0-0, part of the reason for Scotland's non-qualification for the 1994 finals in the USA. McCoist never recaptured his club goalscoring touch at international level, but was (and is) still a national hero in a country possessing few such stars at the present time.

against Dundee, a devastating experience for a player who identified so much with the 'Teddy Bears'; and in 1990/91 he was forced to cool his heels on the substitutes' bench for much of the season after a personality clash with manager Graeme Souness.

McCoist enjoyed his most successful seasons playing alongside Mark Hateley, something of an irony in that the big Englishman had actually been bought by Souness to replace him. But when first Souness and then striker Maurice Johnston left the club in 1991, the way was clear for the Ally and Mark show to hit the road. As well as contributing over 50 League goals between them in consecutive seasons, they also linked up memorably in the 'Battle of Britain' European Cup tie against Leeds, scoring the goals that took Rangers through. Playing off a big man, McCoist, a natural 'snaffler' of chances, was in his element. He earned a regular place in the Scottish national side too, and although he was never quite so prolific a goalscorer in the dark blue jersey, his 15 goals in 46 appearances still made him the fifth highest goalscorer of all time for Scotland.

Since breaking his leg in a World Cup qualifier against Portugal in 1993, McCoist has been impaired by a succession of injuries in his struggle to return to form and fitness, but he remains a high-profile character north of the border.

McGRAIN, Danny

1950 Born in Glasgow

1967 Signs for Celtic

1970 Makes debut for Celtic at right-back

1972 Suffers fractured skull in clash of heads with Doug Somner (Falkirk)

1973 Wins first Scotland cap

1974 Is diagnosed diabetic after playing in 1974 World Cup Finals

1977 Voted Scottish Player of the Year; suffers

mysterious ankle injury, which sidelines him for over a year.

1978 Jock Stein appoints him Celtic club captain

1980 Captains Scotland for the first time

1987 Receives free transfer from Celtic

In his 20-year career at Celtic, Danny McGrain played in seven Scottish League Championship teams, the last four as an inspirational captain. He won 62 caps for Scotland, 10 as captain, and it could have been far more. When at his peak, he suffered an ankle injury which kept him out of internationals for three years. He was sadly missed at the 1978 World Cup Finals, when Ally MacLeod's team fared so capriciously without him.

Danny McGrain was one of Celtic's 'Quality Street Kids' of the late 1960s – Dalglish, Macari, Hay and Connelly were other examples – and a true example of courage. He overcame injury and illness to play more than 600 games

for Celtic. They included seven Scottish Cup Finals (five won) and seven Scottish League Cup Finals (two won).

On the field he had virtually everything except perhaps the clinical finish of a striker. Tall and lean, he had speed, beautiful ball control, strength in the tackle and the ability to trick players in the Scottish tradition. He read the play superbly and was so competitive that he could take over a game if it was going badly, overlapping as a full-back or moving into a midfield creative role. He was perfect for the era of 'total football'.

MACKAY, Dave

1934 Born in Edinburgh

1952 Turns professional with Heart of Midlothian

1955 Pockets first senior medal as Hearts win League Cup

1956 Helps the 'Jammies' lift the Scottish Cup

Danny McGrain is Celtic's most-capped player, appearing 62 times for Scotland. During his 20-year career with Celtic the club won the Scottish League Championship seven times and reached the Scottish Cup Final seven times. Danny's inspirational play and all-round ability was not widely recognised south of the border, perhaps because he never played English League football.

1957 Wins first of 22 Scotland caps, v Spain in Madrid

1958 Hearts' title triumph completes his set of medals

1959 Celebrates a second League Cup victory, then heads south to join Tottenham Hotspur

1961 Plays mammoth part in Spurs' League and FA Cup double

1962 Brilliant again as Bill Nicholson's side retain FA Cup

1963 Suffers first of two broken legs within a year

1967 Captains Tottenham to Wembley victory over Chelsea to claim his third FA Cup winner's medal

1968 Moves to Derby County

1969 Leads the 'Rams' to Second Division title and is voted joint Footballer of the Year with Manchester City's Tony Book

1971 Becomes player-manager of Swindon Town

1972 Takes over as Nottingham Forest boss

1973 Succeeds Brian Clough as Derby manager

1975 Mackay emulates his predecessor as Rams lift League Championship

1977 Takes over at Walsall

1978 Starts successful coaching stint in Kuwait

1987 Returns to Britain and slips into hot seat at Doncaster

In his Tottenham Hotspur shirt and using that trusty but twice-broken left leg, Dave Mackay contributed tenacity to the skilful Spurs side of the early 1960s. After 268 League appearances for Tottenham, he moved to Derby County where he was a favourite with their fans, both as a player and later as manager. According to Jimmy Greaves, if Dave Mackay was missing from the Spurs side 'the rest of us had to work twice as hard'.

1988 Rovers are relegated to the Fourth Division

1989 Switches to St Andrews to guide fortunes of ailing Birmingham City

1991 Resigns from 'Blues' job, finds new success in Middle East

With only a few hours left before the 1959 transfer deadline, Bill Nicholson, the manager of Tottenham Hotspur, persuaded Hearts to part with Dave Mackay. It turned out to be his best ever signing and, incidentally, not the fluke some people imagined. The story goes that Nicholson went for Mackay after Arsenal won the race to sign Mel Charles from Swansea, but in truth he had long since made the combative and marvellously gifted Scot his prime target.

For a fee of £30,000 that then equalled the British record for a half-back, Tottenham had a player who proved to be the most inspirational in their history. Possessing more skill than he was given credit for, a master of all the kicking skills and a shrewd tactician, Mackay did more than anyone to forge a great Spurs team.

Daring and dynamic, he recovered from a twice-broken leg and was admired throughout the game. 'He was the best I ever played with,' said Jimmy Greaves. 'If he was ever missing, the rest of us had to work twice as hard to make up for it.'

In December 1963 Mackay's left leg was broken

in two places during a European Cup Winners' Cup tie against Manchester United. A year later when attempting a comeback in the reserves against Shrewsbury Town, the leg went again. Now he became a legend, recovering to captain Tottenham and take a third FA Cup winner's medal in 1967.

Next came a move to Derby County. 'Signing Dave Mackay was the best day's work of my life,' said Brian Clough, the Derby manager. Playing alongside Roy McFarland, then a promising young centre-half, Mackay

found a new lease of life. He captained Derby to the Second Division title and shared the Footballer of the Year award.

Later he emulated Clough's managerial success at Derby before continuing his career in the Middle East and back in Britain.

MANCHESTER CITY

Founded 1887

Joined League 1892 (Division 2)

Honours Division 1 Champions 1937, 1968;

Division 2 Champions 1899, 1903, 1910, 1928, 1947, 1966; FA Cup Winners 1904, 1934, 1956, 1969; League Cup Winners 1970, 1976; European Cup Winners' Cup Winners 1970

Ground Maine Road

Manchester City have a special place in football's affections. Few clubs can match their range of performances, from brilliant to banal, always able to surprise and always likely to disappoint.

They began as West

Gorton, had five early homes, mostly in east Manchester, and entered the Second Division in 1892 as Ardwick, playing on Hyde Road. They fielded their first indisputably great player, Billy Meredith, in 1894, four years later had reached the First Division, and by 1904 had won the FA Cup and finished second in the League. That success brought allegations of illegal payments and the FA was severe: a former chairman, the secretary, two directors and 17 players were suspended, the club and each individual being fined. This setback enabled old rivals Newton Heath, under their new name of Manchester United, to emerge as the city's premier club for the first time.

In 1923 City moved into their present ground at Maine Road, went down again in 1926 despite scoring 89 goals and reaching the Cup Final, and saved an even bigger disappointment for the last day of the 1926/27 season. They were joint leaders with Portsmouth, goal average almost identical. City walloped Bradford at home, and Portsmouth were losing 1-0 to Preston, but promptly went on to score five second-half goals, pipping City for promotion by 0.002 of a goal.

Ironically, that near miss heralded a golden era: another 100-goal season brought City their fourth Second Division Championship which was followed by a Cup semi-final in 1932, a Cup Final victory in 1934 (that team, led by Matt Busby, is still regarded by some as the club's best) and their first League title in 1936/37. City were relegated, on goal average, before the war but returned in 1946/47, went down again in 1950, and rose again a year later to enter a period of stability and success under an innovative manager, Les McDowall, who turned Don Revie into a 'deep-lying centre-forward', Hungarian style, and paid a record fee for Denis Law.

City reached successive Cup Finals in 1955 and 1956 and played their first Cup tie

under lights in 1961, but after selling Law to Torino they were relegated again in 1962/63. This setback again proved to be a prelude to an astonishing spell that made the club's modern image. Joe Mercer was appointed manager in July 1965, bringing with him Malcolm Allison. Five magnificent seasons followed, featuring brilliant play from the attacking trio of Francis Lee, Colin Bell and Mike Summerbee and culminating in the European Cup Winners' Cup triumph in 1970.

After Mercer and Allison the team was still powerful, especially with enterprising new chairman Peter Swales leading the way. Allison's return as coach, then manager, initiated some big spending, but with little success. Season 1980/81 was extraordinary even by Maine Road standards. Twelve League matches without a win brought Allison's sacking, John Bond taking over in October; the team reached the League

Cup semi-final and the Centenary FA Cup Final, losing to Spurs in a memorable replay.

Trevor Francis became City's third £1 million player in 1981, but by 1983 the familiar spectre of relegation could be seen in Moss Side. City needed to draw with Luton in their last home game but lost by a late goal, and that drop set another 'yo-yo' pattern for the decade as Billy McNeill, Jimmy Frizzell and Mel Machin tried to give the club, still struggling with the debts of the Allison era, some stability. The early 1990s saw City back among the elite, with first Howard Kendall, then Peter Reid and Brian Horton bidding to uphold the honour of the blue and white legions. But there was constant criticism of chairman Swales, and he made way for former hero Francis Lee. The fans loved 'Franny', a self-made millionaire, and lived in the hope that they would soon be supporting the cream of Manchester.

The managerial team that led Manchester City to their greatest triumphs: Joe Mercer (left) and Malcolm Allison. In 1965 Joe was appointed manager and Malcolm became coach and master tactician. During the next five seasons, Manchester City won the Second Division Championship, the League Championship, the FA Cup, the League Cup and finally the European Cup Winner's Cup in 1970. Apart from this successful spell, City have rarely stolen the national headlines away from neighbours United. The happy and unflappable approach of Joe Mercer has not been emulated by his successors – perhaps not surprising given the pressure placed upon them. By the end of the 1994/95 season the tense, but likeable, Brian Horton was another Maine Road managerial casualty.

MANCHESTER UNITED

Founded 1878

Joined League 1892
(Division 1)

Honours Division 1
Champions 1908, 1911,
1952, 1956, 1957, 1965,
1967; Division 2 Champions
1936, 1975; FA Cup
Winners 1909, 1948, 1963,
1977, 1983, 1985, 1990,
1994; European Cup
Winners 1968; European
Cup Winners' Cup Winners
1991; Premier League
Champions 1993, 1994

Ground Old Trafford

Arsenal might have more tradition, and Liverpool have certainly won more trophies, but there is about Manchester United an indefinable aura of magic which still marks them out – even in times of travail both on and off the pitch – as the most glamorous club in English football.

Such a mantle was not always theirs. Early financial struggles saw them on the verge of extinction and it was not until the first decade of the twentieth century that success was achieved in major competitions, with their first star, winger Billy Meredith, playing a prominent part. There followed, between the wars, a distinctly mundane period during which United suffered three relegations to the Second Division, and although they made a swift return to the top rank after each demotion, there was little hint of the glories to come.

Then, into the ruins of an Old Trafford which had been gutted by Hitler's bombs, strode Matt Busby. The new manager revitalised the club, assembling a brilliant attacking side under the inspirational captaincy of Irishman Johnny Carey.

United won the FA Cup in 1948, with scintillating contributions from forwards Stan Pearson and Jack Rowley, and for five consecutive campaigns they narrowly missed the League Championship before finally lifting it – a triumph which, ironically, heralded the break-up of Busby's first great side.

In the early 1950s he introduced a crop of precocious hopefuls to the big time; the 'Busby Babes' were born. Among them were left-back and skipper Roger Byrne; centre-forward Tommy Taylor, one of the few who cost a fee; jaunty wing-half Eddie Colman; inside-forwards Dennis Viollet, Liam Whelan and Bobby Charlton; and, most colossal talent of them all, Duncan Edwards. They won two Championships and threatened to dominate English soccer for the foreseeable future. Then came the Munich air disaster of 1958, which claimed the lives of eight players and shocked the soccer world.

Busby himself was at death's door but, incredibly, he recovered and built a third magnificent team. This was

The Manchester United team, winners of the FA Cup in 1947/48, when they beat Blackpool 4-2 in the Final. Manchester United have a special place in British football, based largely on the exploits of the man in the middle of the front row, Sir Matt Busby, and the teams he built. This is the first of the great teams he assembled. They were a brilliant attacking side under the inspirational captaincy of Johnny Carey (seated to the left of his manager).

Ryan Giggs, Young Footballer of the Year in 1992 and 1993, typifies United's style. Although no longer the new kid, and not an automatic choice, he remains one of the crowd's favourites. His slight frame and close control encourage comparisons with George Best. Although Manchester United represent the top of the tree in terms of playing, there is also a downside. Having played for United it is hard for players to move elsewhere. It will be interesting to see, if Giggs should fail to achieve his full potential at United, whether he will move on successfully to another club. The best move, as with some of his predecessors, might be overseas.

an attractive team around England captain Bryan Robson and won two FA Cups but, having failed to win the League, he too was shown the door.

The expensive team created by the next manager, Alex Ferguson, was less easy on the eye at first, and with a background of boardroom unrest, United ended the 1980s in poor fettle. However, three cup triumphs at the dawn of the new decade gave birth to fresh hope and their vast legion of fans were granted, before too long, what they most dearly desired – an entertaining side capable of winning the Championship. When that longed-for success arrived, it did so with a vengeance. With a team of vibrant performers – the likes of Andrei Kanchelskis, Mark Hughes, Ryan Giggs and the incomparable Eric Cantona – they won back-to-back titles in 1993 and 1994. Their stature was underlined in the second of these two golden campaigns when they became the fourth club this century to win the League and FA Cup double. However, European Cup glory continued to elude them, a matter which was receiving Alex Ferguson's earnest attention.

the prime of Bobby Charlton, Denis Law and George Best, the glorious trinity whose combined talents simply took the breath away. More titles were won and in 1968 Busby experienced his crowning moment when United became the first English club to take the European Cup.

Thereafter, United experienced mixed fortunes.

Sir Matt, as he became, was not adequately replaced for nearly two decades and despite vast expenditure, none of his successors came close to emulating his achievements, although Tommy Docherty in the mid 1970s and Ron Atkinson in the early 1980s made stirring attempts.

Docherty took over a

poor side, reconstructed it during a one-term sojourn in Division 2, and returned to the top flight with a refreshingly positive line-up in which defender Martin Buchan and winger Steve Coppell were outstanding. But after winning the FA Cup the Doc was sacked following personal controversy. Atkinson built

MANNION, Wilf

1918 Born at South Bank, Teesside

1936 Turns professional with Middlesbrough

1938 Earns regular place in 'Boro side which challenges for the Championship

1941 Called up for first wartime international

1946 Scores hat-trick against Northern Ireland on full England debut

1947 Stars and nets twice for Great Britain against the Rest of Europe

1948 Spends six months out of game over wage dispute with 'Boro

1950 Shares in England's lowest hour, World Cup defeat by the USA

1951 Wins last of 26 England caps

1954 May – Middlesbrough relegated to Second Division, Mannion hangs up boots; December – emerges from retirement to play for Hull City

1955 Retires again amid controversy after making allegations concerning illegal payments to players

After one scintillating display for Great Britain in the 6-1 slamming of The Rest of Europe at Hampden Park in 1947, Wilf Mannion spoke of himself as 'a useful cog in a well-oiled machine.' What the diminutive inside-forward omitted to mention, with becoming modesty, was that he was the component which made a vital contribution to the smooth running of such big wheels as Stanley Matthews and Tommy Lawton.

Invariably Mannion was the creative fulcrum of any team for which he played. Weaving intricate patterns with his tiny, dancing feet, the stocky Teessider possessed captivating dexterity on the ball, exceptional balance and a knack of scoring goals as well as laying them on for others.

For all but his final season, Mannion served his local club, Middlesbrough, but he was no archetypal 'faithful retainer'. He stood up for his rights in an era when players were downtrodden and was involved in various controversies. However, it is for his frequently dazzling performances on the pitch, for both club and country, that Mannion deserves to be remembered.

MANSFIELD TOWN

Founded 1910

Joined League 1931 (Division 3 S)

Honours Division 3 Champions 1977; Division 4 Champions 1975

Ground Field Mill

Although Mansfield Town have led a largely tranquil League existence, there have been times when they have stirred themselves mightily in sudden-death competitions. In 1929, as a non-League outfit, they beat Wolves at Molineux to reach the FA Cup fourth round, and 40 years later made it to the quarter-finals at the expense of a West Ham United side boasting World Cup heroes Moore, Hurst and Peters.

Since then the 'Stags' have even experienced Wembley glory, winning the 1987 Freight Rover Trophy under the management of Ian Greaves, a wondrous achievement for a small club usually overshadowed by their Nottingham neighbours. Other leading figures have included pre-war goalscorer Ted Harston, 1960s forwards Mike Stringfellow and Ken Wagstaff, and bosses Raich Carter and Billy Bingham, though none of them was able to inspire even bread-and-butter success.

Mansfield did, however, establish a tradition for consistency: for four decades after joining the League they were solid members of the Third Division. Since 1960 there have been four spells in the basement and, in 1977/78, a single campaign in the Second, but their spiritual home has remained in between.

MARADONA, Diego

1960 Born in Argentina

1976 Makes League debut for Argentinos Juniors, short of his 16th birthday

1977 Wins first full international cap as substitute in crushing victory over Hungary

1978 National coach Cesar Menotti shatters Maradona by dropping him from the World Cup squad on the eve of the finals in his own country

1979 Captains Argentina to triumph in World Youth Cup

1981 Moves to the more fashionable Boca Juniors club

1982 June – disappoints in World Cup finals in Spain, and is sent off against Brazil for retaliation; July – joins Barcelona for £4.2 million

1984 Breaks world transfer record with £6.9 million switch to Napoli

1986 Leads Argentina to World Cup victory in Mexico

1987 Attains god-like status in Naples as he inspires his club to their first League Championship; they lift the Italian Cup for good measure

1990 Neapolitans take their second title; June – struggles with injury in World Cup finals in Italy, yet still skippers his team to the Final

Wilf Mannion was Middlesbrough's best known and most capped (26 times for England) player. He played for the club in the golden years of English soccer immediately after the Second World War when Middlesbrough were attracting huge gates and exciting their supporters with an attacking style of play that was to promise much but deliver nothing, in terms of major honours.

1991 Quits Napoli and is arrested in Argentina on drugs charge

1992 After serving a ban, joins Spanish club Seville

1994 Axed by his new club, Newell's Old Boys of Argentina, after series of rows; June – performs promisingly in early stages of his fourth World Cup Finals, then expelled from tournament for taking banned substances.

Maradona was the first man since Pele to be universally acclaimed as the premier footballer on the planet. On song and fully fit, he was practically unstoppable, equally devastating as a maker and taker of goals.

No one else in his era could control a ball so instantly, nor dribble past opponents with such utter certainty as the diminutive yet muscular Argentinian, and his shooting had the venom and accuracy of a striking snake. At turns awesomely powerful and delicately precise, he was the complete player.

Sadly, where Pele was loved and respected, Diego was often reviled, and it is undeniable that an apparently arrogant attitude did little to endear him to opponents or crowds. In England, any unpopularity is due largely to the infamous 'Hand of God' goal he scored against Bobby Robson's

team in the 1986 World Cup. However, it was Maradona's second strike in the same game – when he waltzed through the defence to beat Peter Shilton for the goal of the tournament – which bore most eloquent witness to his prodigious ability.

It should be remembered, too, that he lived with constant pressure to perform miracles while soaking up savage physical punishment, and it would be sad indeed if the memory of Maradona were unduly marred by bitterness or by criminal associations.

MATTHEWS, Sir Stanley

1915 Born at Hanley, in the heart of the Potteries

1932 Debut for Stoke City

1933 Helps win promotion from Division 2

1934 Celebrates England debut with goal against Wales at Cardiff

1947 Plays for Great Britain v the Rest of Europe, an honour repeated eight years later; joins Blackpool for £11,500

1948 Footballer of the Year

1953 The 'Matthews Final' in which he inspires Blackpool, 3-1 behind against Bolton with 20 minutes left, to a 4-3 victory

1957 Wins last of 54 caps, against Denmark in Copenhagen

1961 Returns to Stoke for nominal £2500 fee

1963 Matthews is voted Footballer of the Year after playing vital role in the 'Potters' climb to Division 1

Diego Maradona during Argentina's 2-1 victory over Nigeria in the World Cup of 1994. Although slightly stocky, Maradona's performances in the World Cup suggested he was still a major influence in the Argentine side... that was until his expulsion from the tournament for drug taking. This disgrace capped an unhappy few years in which he seemed to catch the headlines for all the wrong reasons, and during which time his football had been only intermittently effective.

For 30 years the name of Stanley Matthews was a byword for soccer excellence. He was a supremely gifted yet self-effacing individualist, a symbol of all that was good about the British game, and although he won comparatively few club honours, his fame eclipsed that of all his contemporaries.

A lean outside-right, whose obsession with physical fitness contributed hugely to his staggering professional longevity,

Matthews was a sublime dribbler and perhaps the most accurate crosser of a ball in living memory. His perfect balance and mesmeric skills would take him past the ablest of full-backs, and his astonishing speed from a standing start would render recovery impossible.

His critics said his trickery slowed the game down, yet in doing so it invariably pulled defenders out of position, thus creating space for team-mates. Others pointed to a modest goal tally of 71 in around 700 League games, a fatuous argument in view of his exploits as a provider. Amazingly, Matthews' international career was chequered, the selectors omitting him as often as they picked him. Had it been left to most fans, to whom he was an almost god-like figure, no England side would have taken the field without him.

This picture shows Stanley Matthews with his Stoke City team-mates on his 50th birthday. Yes, he was still playing in the First Division in 1965. Known as the 'wizard of dribble', Stanley Matthews was a superb winger and excellent crosser of the ball. The name of Sir Stanley Matthews would be on many people's team sheet for a side of all-time greats.

MEADOWBANK THISTLE

Founded 1974

Joined League 1974 (Division 2)

Honours Scottish League Second Division Champions 1987

Ground Meadowbank Stadium

Formerly Ferranti Thistle, Meadowbank gained their senior place when League reconstruction created a vacancy. Lacking their own ground and playing matches at Edinburgh's principal athletics venue made it difficult for them to settle, and they were initially regarded by their opponents as a source of easy victories.

That changed in the 1980s, and they are now established in the League. Talent-spotting is a necessity, and Premier Division men such as Darren Jackson (Hibernian), Peter Godfrey (St Mirren) and John Inglis (Aberdeen) came to notice with them.

MERCER, Joe

1914 Born at Ellesmere Port

1931 Signs for Everton

1938 England debut in 7-0 thrashing of Northern Ireland in Manchester

1939 Plays stirring part in winning League title

1940 Moves to Arsenal for £7000

1948 Captains 'Gunners' to Championship, a feat repeated five years later

1950 Leads Arsenal to FA Cup victory over Liverpool and is voted Footballer of the Year

1954 Broken leg ends playing career

1955 Becomes boss of Sheffield United

1958 Takes over at Aston Villa but can't avoid relegation

1960 Leads Villa to promotion, followed by League Cup triumph the following year

1964 Ill health forces temporary retirement

1965 Returns as manager of Manchester City, winning promotion two years later

1968 City win League Championship

1969 Mercer's men lift FA

Cup defeating Leicester 1-0

1970 Double triumph – League Cup and European Cup Winners' Cup

1972 Becomes general manager of Coventry City

1974 Stint as England's caretaker boss after Alf Ramsey departs

1990 Dies on Merseyside

Joe Mercer was a magnificent player, an inspiring manager, and a lovely man. As an attacking wing-half with Everton, he was one of the brightest pre-war talents in English football. It was fitting that he should have gone on to captain his country, though not that his tally of caps was limited to a mere five because of the war. In 1946, with his prime apparently behind him, Mercer switched to Highbury and underwent an amazing renaissance in a more defensive role. A spindly figure on bandy legs, he was a master of interception and distribution, a shrewd, cultured tactician with the ability to lift the spirits of the men around him.

This quality proved invaluable throughout his days as a manager, the most distinguished of which were spent in tandem with Malcolm Allison at Manchester City. He became one of the most popular personalities in the game; that famous lop-sided grin and self-deprecating wit is sorely missed on a British soccer scene increasingly devoid of good humour.

An attacking wing-half in his playing days and an inspirational manager, Joe Mercer is seen here leading out the Arsenal team during the 1952/53 season – his penultimate term as a player. So many stories are told about the man, nearly all of them relating to his humour and his refusal to get too wound up about soccer. He was also fond of telling jokes – most of which are unrepeatable on the printed page.

MIDDLESBROUGH

Founded 1876

Joined League 1899 (Division 2)

Honours Division 2 Champions 1927, 1929, 1974; Division 1 Champions 1995; Amateur Cup Winners 1895, 1898

Ground Ayresome Park (until 1995)

Middlesbrough have contributed richly to the English soccer scene throughout the twentieth century without having one major honour to show for their efforts. In local boy Wilf Mannion, who won 26 caps, they boasted one of the most extravagantly gifted inside-forwards League football has seen, although their traditional speciality has been prolific centre-forwards. There was England international Alf Common, subject of the first four-figure transfer fee when he arrived from Sunderland for £1000 in 1905; George Camsell, who notched 59 goals – still a Second Division record – in 1926/27; and Brian Clough, who struck 197 times in 213 outings in the late 1950s before embarking on an ill-fated sojourn at Roker Park.

Yet somehow all that talent has never translated itself into trophies, with eight FA Cup quarter-finals and two League Cup semi-finals ending in defeat. Such a lengthy period of poverty had hardly seemed likely when 'Boro won promotion to the First Division at the end of their third League campaign in 1902. They remained solidly in the top flight, finishing fourth in 1914, until the mid 1920s, when they made two brief visits to the Second Division. On either side of the war, inspired by Mannion, they were renowned for a flowing approach, but as Wilf waned, so did the team, and they were relegated in 1954.

Despite Clough's exploits,

John Hendrie and Paul Wilkinson celebrating a goal in the 2-0 win at Southend early in the 1994/95 campaign. With Bryan Robson as player-manager Middlesbrough were strongly tipped for honours. However, with only one automatic promotion place, and with strong competition from Wolves, Derby, Bolton and others, they did well to maintain the pace they established in the early days of the season.

they failed to bounce back and in 1966 slid into Division 3. Stan Anderson led them straight up, but it was not until Jack Charlton brought his long-ball game to Ayresome in the 1970s that the club returned to the First Division, this time for eight years. There followed interludes in every flight except the Fourth, and manager Lennie Lawrence's achievement in winning promotion to the new Premier League in 1992 augured well for the future. Demotion ensued, but soon 'Boro were buoyant again, as new boss Bryan Robson led them to the First Division Crown in 1994/95. With a move to a new stadium planned for 1995, and lowly Darlington and Hartlepool the only local competition for support, there seemed no reason why the Teessiders should not go on to greater things.

MILBURN, Jackie

1924 Born in Ashington, Northumberland

1946 Makes debut for Newcastle United

1949 Wins the first of 13 England caps v Scotland

1951 Scores in every round of the FA Cup including both goals in the Final, won 2-0 v Blackpool

1952 Second FA Cup winner's medal, 1-0 v Arsenal

1955 Scores after 45 seconds, fastest goal in Wembley FA Cup Final, for third winner's medal, 3-1 v Manchester City

1963 Retires after 354 League games for Newcastle (179 goals); appointed manager of Ipswich Town

1964 Leaves Ipswich and becomes a journalist with the News of the World

1988 Dies in Ashington

Jackie Milburn was the most revered of Newcastle heroes. A modest, unassuming man who suffered from an acute lack of confidence and was embarrassed by the adulation he received from his neighbours, he entered Geordie folklore as the player who led United to three FA Cup Final victories

Many Newcastle fans will say there has never been a player to match Jackie Milburn – although Kevin Keegan, Malcolm Macdonald and Chris Waddle have their supporters. Jackie Milburn is seen here in full flight playing for Newcastle United in 1955/56. He scored 179 goals in 354 games for Newcastle and played for England 13 times. Newcastle enjoyed a number of successful seasons while Milburn was playing and attracted large crowds both at home and away.

in the 1950s. To the end he was 'Wor Jackie'.

Blessed with extraordinary speed and pace of shot, he began his career as an inside-forward before moving to the right-wing and then to centre-forward. Wherever he played he had a tearaway style, verve and dramatic power. Len Shackleton, an illustrious contemporary, said, 'Jackie was one of the quickest players I have seen. Once he got going he was unstoppable. Whenever I think of Jackie I think of a greyhound going out of a trap.' His initials – J.E.T. – were wholly appropriate.

Milburn, member of a famous footballing family that also included Bobby and Jackie Charlton, succeeded Tommy Lawton as England's centre-

forward, scoring 10 goals in 13 internationals. But statistics alone cannot do justice to the man and the effect he had on those around him. He was a player who changed the course of games, a symbol of success.

At his funeral tens of thousands lined the streets of Newcastle to pay their respects. The grief was as genuine as the man.

MILLWALL

Founded 1885

Joined League 1920 (Division 3)

Honours Division 2 Champions 1988; Division 3 (S) Champions 1928, 1938; Division 4 Champions 1962

Ground The New Den

Until the late 1980s, when they reached the top flight for the first time in their history, Millwall had shown little likelihood of developing into a major soccer power. Their playing achievements had been moderate, and a distressingly high percentage of their headlines had been concerned with misdemeanours by unruly supporters.

There has, however, always been a warmth about Millwall that grander clubs have failed to emulate. They have produced unlikely folk heroes – such as Harry Cripps, the wildly enthusiastic full-back who epitomised the spirit of the 'Lions' throughout the 1960s and early 1970s – and their tough dockland environment has helped to breed a solidarity which, at times, is fearsome. No matter what the standard of the side at any given time, it was a rare opponent who relished a visit to The Den.

By the time Millwall settled at Cold Blow Lane in 1910 they had already made a considerable impact by reaching two FA Cup semi-finals – those of 1900 and 1903 – as a Southern League outfit, and when they became founder members of the Third Division, hopes of rapid progress were high.

They won the Division 3 (S) title twice before the Second World War, and beat three First Division sides before losing to Sunderland in the 1937 FA Cup semi-final.

But faced with fierce competition for support from the capital's more glamorous clubs, Millwall were forced to accept relative mediocrity, albeit enlivened occasionally by promotion campaigns and relegation battles. Bosses such as Benny Fenton (1966-74) and George Graham (1982-86), in his first managerial job, did sterling work but it was not until 1988, with John Docherty at the helm, that the Lions finally reached the premier grade. Alas, after leading the table during their first term, they fell away and were relegated after just two seasons.

The Lions' most recent claim to fame has been the New Den, a striking new ground appropriate to the modern image that enthusiastic chairman Reg Burr has tried to promote.

MONTROSE

Founded 1879

Joined League 1923 (Division 3)

Honours Scottish League Second Division Champions 1985

Ground Links Park

Montrose had been a club with an unobtrusive history until the Cup exploits of the 1970s and the mid 1980s. In 1975/76 they defeated Hibs en route to the semi-final of the League Cup and that same season they appeared in the quarter-finals of the Scottish Cup, a stage they had also reached in 1973. Season 1986/87 brought a League Cup defeat of Hearts.

In 1991 they achieved promotion to the First Division for the second time in their history, only to return immediately to the basement, before rising again in 1995.

MOORE, Bobby

1941 Born in Barking

1958 Signs for West Ham United

1962 Makes England debut in Peru

1963 Becomes England's youngest captain

1964 Helps 'Hammers' beat Preston North End to win the FA Cup, and is voted Footballer of the Year

Seen here playing in the 1964 FA Cup Final, Footballer of the Year Bobby Moore captained West Ham to a 3-2 victory over Preston North End. He amassed 108 England caps and lifted the World Cup in 1966 after the victory over West Germany. His apparent languid style of play belied his quick reactions and aggressive streak ...when they were needed. In the main, however, Bobby relied on timing and anticipation to perform his duties.

1965 Leads West Ham to glory against Munich 1860 in the European Cup Winners' Cup

1966 Lifts the World Cup after England beat West Germany

1970 Endures infamous Bogota incident in which he is accused of stealing a bracelet; then plays brilliantly in Mexico World Cup

1973 Wins 108th and final cap, against Italy at Wembley

1974 Joins Fulham for £20,000

1975 Plays for 'Cottagers' in FA Cup defeat – against West Ham

1977 Retires from League football

1984 Following managerial spell at non-League Oxford City, Moore takes over as boss of Southend United

1986 Leaves Southend; goes on to work in soccer media and promotions

1993 Dies of cancer just days after making last public appearance at Wembley; receives impressive tributes from players in Britain and around the world

Bobby Moore was the outstanding central defender in Britain – some would say the world – throughout the 1960s and early 1970s. Tall, calm and immensely skilful on the ball, he radiated an imperious authority at the heart of England's rearguard, and it surprised many that such an illustrious career should be spent with relatively unfashionable clubs. His greatest assets were an almost uncanny sense of anticipation and utter composure in the most hectic of circumstances, but they represented only part of his rich catalogue of gifts. Moore's immaculate distribution made him the springboard of countless attacks – his partnership with Geoff Hurst for both club and country was particularly productive – and his timing in the tackle was impeccable.

It's true that his aerial power did not always match up to his all-round performance, and certainly he lacked pace. But his superb reading of the game meant that such weaknesses were rarely exposed, and the way in which he rose above them is a further tribute to his greatness.

Though Moore often faced hostility – presumably born out of jealousy – from non-London crowds, it was invariably underpinned by respect. How fitting that a player of such consistent excellence should lead England to their finest footballing hour.

MORTON

Founded 1874

Joined League 1893
(Division 2)

Honours Scottish League First Division Champions 1978, 1984, 1987; Division 2 Champions 1950, 1964, 1967, 1995; Scottish Cup Winners 1922

Ground Cappielow Park

Scotland's first limited company football club (1896), Morton have had to be content with only one major trophy. They won the 1922 Scottish Cup, beating Rangers in the final with an irresistible free-kick goal by Jimmy Gourlay.

Celebrities have not been lacking. Jimmy Cowan was one of the few Scottish 'keepers to excel at Wembley (in Scotland's 3-1 victory of 1949). Current manager Allan McGraw created a club record back in 1963/64 with 58 goals. In the 1960s a series of ingenious signings from Denmark, in which Morton participated, brought freshness to the Scottish scene. And as recently as 1979, Morton had in Andy Ritchie Scotland's Player of Year.

MORTON, Alan

1893 Born in Partick, Glasgow

1913 Playing for Queen's Park

1920 Capped for Scotland, v Wales and Northern Ireland; turns professional, signing for Rangers

1921 Helps to win Scottish League Championship (eight were to follow up to 1930/31)

1928 Helps Rangers to Scottish Cup victory...

1930 ...and again

1932 Last international appearance v France in Paris

1933 Retires and becomes Rangers director

1971 Dies 15 December

Alan Lauder Morton of Rangers, the 'Wee Blue Devil', was the first of Scottish football's superstars. In a career spanning more than 20 years, first as an amateur with Queen's Park then as a professional with Rangers, he played for Scotland 31 times. It was a record set when international football meant little more than matches against England, Ireland and Wales, and it stood until George Young passed it after the Second World War.

Morton was an outside-left of dazzling skills. At 5ft 4in and seldom weighing more than 9 stone, he was small and slight but remarkably strong and resilient, and his dribbling talents, founded on exceptional balance, made him a master of all the defenders and defensive systems – and there were many – set to check him. One of the most potent weapons in his armoury was his ability to float hanging crosses just under the crossbar so that, quite literally, goalkeepers would often find themselves tumbling into the net with the ball.

He played 11 times against England, notably in the famous 'Wembley Wizards' team of 1928 which beat England 5-1. Only Alex Jackson, the outside-right, was taller than 5ft 6in in a forward line that read Jackson, Jimmy Dunn, Hughie Gallacher, Alex James and Morton. Jackson's three goals were all scored from Morton crosses.

Alan Morton was a professional man, a qualified mining engineer who was always a part-time professional; more than once he was at work on the Saturday morning of an international match. What is certain is that in the long and rich panoply of British football, Morton must stand in the first rank beside the likes of Stanley Matthews and Bobby Charlton. He is still considered Rangers' greatest player and his portrait in oils hangs in the entrance hall of the club's Ibrox Stadium. When he retired in 1933 he was made a director, surely the first player to go directly from dressing room to board room. He had played a total of 742 competitive games, 247 for Queen's Park and 495 for Rangers, scoring 166 goals.

MOTHERWELL

Founded 1886

Joined League 1893 (Division 2)

Honours Scottish League Championship, Division 1 1932; First Division 1982, 1985; Division 2 1954, 1969; Scottish Cup 1952, 1991; League Cup 1950/51

Ground Fir Park

Lanarkshire, with its history of heavy industry, is a hotbed of football in Scotland and its largest club, Motherwell, have reflected that vitality. Their glorious side at the beginning of the 1930s had an irresistible left-wing partnership in George Stevenson and Bobby Ferrier. The pair almost overshadowed centre-forward Willie McFadyen despite his 52 League goals in 1931/32.

They won the League Championship that year but lost Scottish Cup Finals in 1931 and 1933. There were further defeats before they collected the trophy in 1952. Despite a welter of young talent towards the end of the fifties, including Ian St John, success proved elusive. After financial crises in the early 1980s they prospered under Tommy McLean's management and won the 1991 Scottish Cup in glorious style. A Premier Division runner-up spot in 1994/95 augured well for the future.

Glasgow Rangers' Alan Morton (right) in a Scottish League line-up for a fixture against the English Football League at Ibrox. Alongside him is J. B. McAlpine of Queen's Park. Morton scored in the game, no doubt delighting the 63,000 Scots attending, but failing to give his side a win; the game ended 1-1.

NEWCASTLE UNITED

Founded 1881

Joined League 1893 (Division 2)

Honours Division 1 Champions 1905, 1907, 1909, 1927; Division 2 Champions 1965; FA Cup Winners 1910, 1924, 1932, 1951, 1952, 1955; European Fairs Cup Winners 1969; Division 1 Champions 1993

Ground St James's Park

Newcastle United are a club of proud traditions whose persistent under-achievement in modern times had sorely tried the devotion of what is possibly the most fanatical following in England.

The Tynesiders needed a Clough-like messiah to lead them out of the doldrums, and in 1992 he emerged in the enthusiastic form of Kevin Keegan. A St James's Park hero as a player, he was ideally suited to capitalise on the club's enormous bedrock of fervent support, and did so, first by steering Newcastle clear of relegation from the old Division 2, then by leading them into the Premier League in 1993, and on into European competition a year later.

The 'Magpies' built their reputation on two richly productive eras, the first of which dawned soon after the turn of the century when they won three titles in five campaigns and reached five FA Cup Finals in a seven-year span.

Unfortunately, careers of leading players were blighted by the First World War and subsequent triumphs were intermittent. Scottish marksman Hughie Gallacher skippered United to the 1927 League title, and five years later there was FA Cup glory thanks to a hotly disputed goal against Arsenal. The Magpies, however, were on the slide and were relegated in 1934.

They remained in the lower flight until 1948, when their return to the elite signalled the start of their second spell as a major power. With goal-merchant Jackie Milburn in the van, United won the FA Cup three times in the first half of the 1950s. 'Wor Jackie' was the undisputed idol of Tyneside, but he received splendid support from the likes of wing-half Joe Harvey and winger Bobby Mitchell. When that side – managed for most of the decade by Stan Seymour – broke up, the club was to embark on a perennial struggle for consistency. Defender Jimmy Scoular and schemer George Eastham were outstanding in the later 1950s, but Newcastle were down again by 1961. Harvey returned as manager, secured promotion and – with notable help from wing-half Bobby Moncur and goalscorers 'Pop' Robson and Wyn Davies – United went on to win a European competition, after qualifying by finishing tenth in Division 1.

The 1970s brought a new folk hero in centre-forward Malcolm Macdonald. 'Supermac' prospered for five seasons before heading for Highbury, but the nearest the Magpies came to an honour was a pitiful FA Cup Final display against Liverpool in 1974. Another demotion followed in 1978 and it was left to Kevin Keegan, approaching the end of his playing career but with ability and charisma to spare, to inspire a return to the top flight in the early 1980s.

New stars such as Chris Waddle, Peter Beardsley and Paul Gascoigne promised much but they were all sold on for big fees and United were relegated yet again in 1989. It seemed so long since 'Blaydon Races' had been sung with anything approaching conviction. Cue Kevin Keegan and the renaissance: the likes of Andy Cole, (sold controversially to Manchester United for £7 million in 1995), Robert Lee and the returned Beardsley played with sensational flair and inspiration, and the rafters of St James's Park were rattled once more by the strains of that famous anthem.

Sir John Hall, the chairman of Newcastle United whose cash and enterprise have helped restore the club's fortunes. In some ways he represents the new breed of club chairmen who are businessmen first and fans second. Counterparts can be found at Tottenham, Wolves, Blackburn, Everton, Carlisle, Birmingham City and elsewhere. With the fluctuating fortunes of the game, it is a brave man indeed who sinks money into the sport. In Sir John's case, the gamble seems to have paid off; but is there room at the top for all the ambitious chairmen?

NICHOLSON, Bill

1919 Born in Scarborough

1938 Signs for Tottenham Hotspur

1950 Helps Spurs win Division 2 title…

1951 … and then the League Championship; May – scores with first kick in sole appearance for England v Portugal at Goodison Park

1955 Retires as player to become coach at White Hart Lane

1958 Coaches England during World Cup in Sweden; October – succeeds Jimmy Anderson as Spurs manager

1961 Leads them to League and FA Cup double

1962 Back to Wembley to beat Burnley in FA Cup Final

1963 Spurs become first team from Great Britain to win European trophy as they slam Atletico Madrid 5-1 in European Cup

Nicholson was the architect of one of the finest club sides the world has ever seen. In the early 1960s his Spurs played exhilarating, flowing football, a devastating cocktail of subtlety and power, and were justly rewarded with an avalanche of honours.

That he should create such an entertaining team amazed many who had watched him as a sturdy, industrious yet unspectacular right-half in Arthur Rowe's push-and-rush combination of the early 1950s. Yet Nicholson's management approach was markedly more adventurous. He was always willing to back his judgement in the transfer market – as the likes of Dave Mackay, John White and Cliff Jones in the 1950s, and Jimmy Greaves, Alan Gilzean, Pat Jennings and company in the 1960s bore ample witness – but also had the priceless knack of blending them with more ordinary individuals. He was also the first man to bring the best out of Danny Blanchflower.

Not surprisingly, Nicholson's later sides could not match the standard of his first, yet were good enough to maintain his reputation as one of British soccer's most successful and positive post-war bosses. Hailing from the 'old school' of managership, he conducted his departure from Spurs, his later job with West Ham and his return to White Hart Lane with both honesty and dignity.

Bill Nicholson's managerial success of League and FA Cup double with Spurs in 1960/61 put him in a select band of managers who had previously won a Championship medal as a player with the same club. His Championship medal as a player was in 1950/51. Other notable members of this exclusive 'club' include Bob Paisley and Kenny Dalglish (Liverpool), George Graham (Arsenal) and Howard Kendall (Everton).

NICKNAMES

The 1990 World Cup finals were a reminder that nicknames help familiarise players and clubs, and make things easier for newspaper headliners. The top goalscorer in the tournament was Italy's Salvatore 'Toto' Schillaci, while England star Paul Gascoigne had such a popular nickname ('Gazza') that his agent took the precaution of registering it as a trademark.

Most players' nicknames are surname adaptations, but some are more inventive. Sometimes they are coined from a player's style of play. Ernest 'Nudger' Needham was a wing-half who excelled in nudging opponents in the tackle for Sheffield United and England at the turn of the century; Charlie 'Cannonball' Fleming of East Fife, Sunderland and Scotland had one of the most powerful shots of the 1950s; Ron 'Chopper' Harris was Chelsea's hard man of the 1960s and 1970s; Allan 'Sniffer' Clarke was renowned for sniffing out goal chances with Walsall, Fulham, Leicester City, Leeds United, Barnsley and England; and Clarke's Leeds United team-mate Norman Hunter became Norman 'Bites Yer Leg' – a self-explanatory sobriquet.

Perhaps the most famous inter-war nickname was that of Ralph William Dean, the Tranmere Rovers, Everton and England centre-forward. He was known as 'Dixie' Dean from an early age, either because he had a dark, southern-type complexion, or, much more likely, as an adaptation of 'Digsie' (because he dug his fingers in other children's backs when tagging them in street games). Football tradition caught up with John Deans, a 1970s striker with Motherwell, Celtic and Scotland; he was also nicknamed 'Dixie'.

Other sources of nicknames are family names (Ray 'Butch' Wilkins in the 1970s and 1980s), physical appearance (Billy 'Fatty' Foulke in the 1890s and 1900s), television names (Ron 'Rowdy' Yeats in the 1960s and 1970s) and the player's origins (1930s Welsh international Eugene 'Taffy' O'Callaghan). A Murphy often became 'Spud' as an association with Irish potato-growing, and Anglo-Scots have often become 'Jock' regardless of Christian name.

Manchester City had two players called William Smith in the 1890s, so they nicknamed them after their birthplaces – 'Stockport' Smith and 'Buxton' Smith. Gateshead remedied a similar problem more prosaically in the 1950s with Ken Smith No. 1 and Ken Smith No. 2.

Club nicknames also have various origins. Club colours are an obvious source, as with Coventry City (the 'Sky Blues'), Swindon Town (the 'Robins') and many clubs called the 'Reds' and the 'Blues'. Sometimes an old industry lives on in a nickname, such as with Sheffield United (the 'Blades') and Luton Town (the 'Hatters'). Other clubs rely on their specific location for a nickname, for example Brighton (the 'Seagulls') and Blackpool (the 'Seasiders').

However, many traditional nicknames are in decline and clubs are more likely to be known by other derivatives. West Brom, for instance, are as often known as the 'Albion' as the 'Throstles' or 'Baggies'. At other times, teams have been tagged with a topical nickname. Manchester United's young 1950s team were named the 'Busby Babes' after legendary United manager Matt Busby, while Tottenham Hotspur in the 1960s were 'Super Spurs'. Whatever the nickname, it seems to provide supporters with an extra sense of belonging to their club.

The second half of the 1990s were likely to be crucial for the future of association football in North America. The 1994 World Cup Finals in the United States proved a refreshing success, but next would come the acid test for a nation which to date had made only limited impact on the world of football. Would the impetus be maintained? Much will depend on the ultimate impact of Major League Soccer, which was planned for introduction in April 1995 as part of the deal which had facilitated USA '94; however, various problems – not least a disappointing public response to the prospect – resulted in the start date being put back to 1996.

That is for the future; what of the past? The first surge of public interest in soccer in the USA came after the 1966 World Cup Final was shown live on television, but there was already a solid base for the sport in America. The USFA had been recognised by FIFA for 53 years; the national team had been semi-finalists in the first World Cup (incidentally, the USA has entered for every tournament and on that basis alone surely merited the chance to host one of them); the new wave of immigrants and the return of Europe-based troops after the Second World War had given the game a minor boost; and, for the five summers preceding England's 1966 victory, New York had hosted a tournament featuring top clubs from around the globe which attracted crowds of up to 15,000.

Two rival bodies began operating in 1967: the National Professional Soccer League, which drafted European players into new teams set up in major cities, and the United Soccer Association, which imported whole teams such as Shamrock Rovers, Cagliari, Wolves and Dundee United to represent cities. (The game, then as now, was a summer one.) Some cities were therefore expected to support two teams in a minority sport. Moreover, the frequent commercial breaks in television coverage did not help the native audience to understand the dynamics of the game. The North American Soccer League was formed as a compromise in 1968 but it was almost too late; attendance figures plummeted and CBS declined to televise the 1969 season. However, financial backing and the dedication of men such as ex-Wales forward Phil Woosnam just saved the League from foundering.

In 1975 the status of American soccer was enhanced at a stroke by the signing of 34-year-old Pele by the New York Cosmos. The following season saw the arrival of, among others, George Best (Los Angeles Aztecs), Rodney Marsh (Tampa Bay Rowdies), Giorgio Chinaglia (Cosmos) and Eusebio (Toronto Metros-Croatia).

Others followed; many were second-rate or were top players past their peak, but the trick had worked. In 1977, when Franz Beckenbauer joined the Cosmos as Pele retired, the total NASL attendance figure was 3.5 million with an average of 13,000, and in 1980 there were 24 teams. Two years later, however, only 14 clubs contested the Championship and the NASL disbanded in 1985.

In addition to introducing

Diana Ross singing at the opening of the 1994 World Cup finals in the USA. Her performance preceded the opening match in which Germany beat Bolivia 1-0. Diana herself was asked to open the games by 'scoring' in an empty goal from a penalty spot some ten yards away from the goal. Sadly she missed, perhaps reflecting America's relationship with the game, particularly that of black Americans for whom she is an icon but who show little interest in football.

The World Cup was a stage on which the USA could parade its talents. As a team they were moderately successful and some individuals particularly caught the eye. Alexi Lalas, seen here scrapping for the ball with Romario from Brazil, was one such success who, following the tournament, went to play in Italy. Sadly the finals, although well attended, failed to ignite great enthusiasm for football in the US, even though other sports were going through difficult times. It's very possible that, despite many hopes over the years, soccer will never really succeed in the United States.

US-style razzamatazz and peripheral entertainments, the NASL had made many significant changes to the laws, including a 35-yard offside line (since abolished at FIFA's insistence) to compensate for the narrower pitches, sudden-death extra time followed by shoot-outs (5 seconds to dribble and score from 35 yards out) if necessary to ensure a result, and points for goals. This, plus the preponderance of artificial pitches, has done little to prepare Americans for international competition. The enterprising and skilful attacking play and creditable goalkeeping of the 1990 and 1994 US teams were

undermined by defensive naivety. The names of the players – Meola, Caligiuri, Ramos, Balboa, Lalas, Vermes – suggest that interest is still greatest among the immigrant populations. In 1978, 50 per cent of NASL players were British.

It was Scottish and French immigrants who, towards the end of the nineteenth century, introduced soccer to Canada, a country whose modern top teams, still drawn largely from immigrant groups, found themselves homeless with the demise of the NASL. Soccer's origins in the USA were more or less confined, predictably, to

New England and paralleled developments in the home country. In the mid nineteenth century there was a popular form of Shrove Tuesday football (with sightings in the Appalachians this century) and various college versions, 11-a-side, 20-a-side and so on with both handling and non-handling codes. In 1875 Harvard and Yale based their game on rugby, and gridiron was born; it could as easily have been soccer.

Canada qualified for the 1986 World Cup but today the Canadian Soccer League (formed in 1987) shares the same problems as US soccer in that top gates rarely exceed 5000.

Ironically, at grass-roots level the game is healthy – equipment is cheap and, unlike American football, children can play without fear of injury. It is as a spectator sport that soccer must grow in North America, and it could hardly have wished for a more propitious boost than the 1994 World Cup Finals. If the stateside game doesn't take off this time, then surely it never will.

NORTHAMPTON TOWN

Founded 1897

Joined League 1920 (Division 3)

Honours Division 3 Champions 1963; Division 4 Champions 1987

Ground Sixfields Stadium

Northampton Town are an unassuming club with a largely tranquil history – apart from one pulsating decade which pitched their supporters from one extreme of emotion to the other. The 'Cobblers' – so dubbed in honour of their town's shoe-making industry – began the 1960s in Division 4. In 1961 they rose to the Third, made the Second two years later, and in 1965 reached the lofty pinnacle of Division 1.

The fans pinched themselves in disbelief as their team, expertly managed by former Arsenal and Wales wing-half Dave Bowen and underpinned by an efficient defence in which Theo Foley, Joe Kiernan and Terry Branston stood out, met the giants of the day on equal terms, but sadly, it was not to last. After one season among the elite Northampton were relegated, somewhat unfortunately, and then failed to arrest a slide which took them back to the basement by 1969.

Before and since that uncharacteristic interlude, the club formed by a group of teachers just before the century's turn have made few waves, spending all their time in the Third and Fourth. However, there have

been occasional diversions, with progress to the FA Cup fifth round (three times) and to the same stage of the League Cup (twice).

Apart from Bowen, who served the Cobblers as general manager until 1985, major personalities have included Herbert Chapman (boss from 1907 to 1912, before going on to glory elsewhere), and goalscoring wingers of the 1940s and 1950s, Jack English and Tommy Fowler.

A not unfamiliar sight for Northern Ireland fans, as international opponents grab another goal. In this case it was Spain's Emilio Butragueño (right) who ran the ball past Pat Jennings. The game was won by Spain 2-1, ending Irish hopes of progress to the next round of the 1986 World Cup finals in Mexico. That they reached Mexico, however, was a great achievement.

How the Town needed men of comparable stature as they sank to the foot of the new Third Division in 1994. Unfortunately, there were none on the horizon and despite their move to a new ground, the Sixfields Stadium, immediate prospects seemed discouraging.

NORTHERN IRELAND

The first organised game played in Ireland was probably that in Belfast between Caledonian FC and Queen's Park (Scotland) on 24 October 1878. The Irish Football Association, formed on 18 November 1880, was plagued by disputes in its earlier years. In 1912 senior clubs were at loggerheads with the Irish FA and threatened to break off into a rival association. There was more acrimony in 1923 with the formation of the Republic's Football Association of Ireland after the political partition of the

island.

The Irish Cup, held since 1880, has one of the most interesting histories of national cup competitions. The Irish FA withheld medals in 1886, although Distillery successfully took the case to court, and on two other occasions the Final wasn't played. During the problems of 1912, Linfield were simply awarded the trophy by default. And Shelbourne were similarly awarded the title in 1919/20, when the Irish FA postponed the Final. They had been influenced in their decision by a riotous semi-final replay during which a player was sent off, stones were thrown, a gunman opened fire and over 80 people were injured.

The Irish League was formed in 1890 with eight clubs, including current Irish League members Cliftonville, Distillery, Glentoran and Linfield. In its early years it was an all-Ireland League, but the two Dublin clubs

(Shelbourne and Bohemians) left for good in 1920. Professionalism was accepted in 1894. The most successful team has been Linfield. One of their main rivals, Belfast Celtic, won the Irish League 14 times but resigned in 1949 following a crowd riot after a game against Linfield.

The Belfast Celtic directors vowed that their team would not perform in front of an Irish crowd again.

Clubs from Northern Ireland have achieved slightly more European success than those from the Republic. Linfield reached the last eight of the 1966/67 European Cup competition but lost 3-2 on aggregate to CSKA Sofia after comfortable wins against Aris Bonnevoie and Valerengen. Seven years later, Glentoran reached the European Cup Winners' Cup quarter-finals after wins against Chimia Ramnicu and Brann Bergen. Glentoran also came close to glory in 1967/68 when they drew 1-

1 and 0-0 against Benfica. They went out on the away-goals rule and Benfica went on to meet Manchester United in that season's European Cup Final. On the other hand, Crusaders lost a 1973 European Cup game 11-0 to Dinamo Bucharest, going out 12-0 on aggregate.

From 1969 civil unrest often led to careful choice of grounds. Sometimes Northern Irish teams played outside the country, and in 1972/73 there were no European club entries. Two days after the murder of Lord Mountbatten and three others, there were ugly scenes at the Dundalk v Linfield European Cup tie in the Republic. The second leg, Linfield's 'home' match, was played in Holland.

The 1980s were particularly dominated by Linfield. During manager Roy Coyle's spell of over 14 years he helped the club to more than 30 senior trophies, including 10 Irish League Championships (making 40 for the club overall). But while Linfield were dominating the League during the 1980s, Glentoran were achieving remarkable success in the Irish Cup – seven out of nine, including five in succession. In 1989/90 Portadown were surprise winners of the Irish League, for the first time, retaining the trophy in 1991 and lifting the Irish Cup for good measure. Linfield, however, continued to be the team to beat, following their League Championship of 1992/93 with the League/Cup double in 1993/94. The Irish League will be restructured for the 1995/96 season with a Premier Division and First Division each composed of eight clubs.

NORTHERN IRELAND NATIONAL TEAM

Northern Ireland's appearances in the World Cup finals have been very successful for such a small nation. In 1958 they drew with West Germany and twice beat Czechoslovakia (once in a play-off). A tired team lost 4-0 to France in the quarter-final. In 1982, under Billy Bingham's managership, two draws and a 1-0 victory over Spain enabled the Irish to win Group 5. Hopes of reaching a semi-final, however, were dashed by France, 4-1. Northern Ireland qualified for the finals again in 1986 but enjoyed little success in Mexico.

The 1958 team – famous for stars such as Danny Blanchflower, Billy Bingham, Jimmy McIlroy and Harry Gregg – shared the home international championship with England. They ended England's 18-match unbeaten run with a 3-2 win at Wembley, a result rivalled by Terry Neill's team in 1972 when Neill himself scored the only goal.

Shared home-championship success also came in 1955/56, 1958/59 and 1963/64, but the only outright wins came in 1979/80 and 1983/84 during the era of Gerry Armstrong, Sammy McIlroy, Billy Hamilton and Pat Jennings, veteran of 119 internationals. Northern Ireland have never qualified for the European Championship quarter-finals. In 1994, the retirement of the long-serving Bingham and his replacement by Bryan Hamilton ushered in a new era.

NORWICH CITY

Founded 1902

Joined League 1920 (Division 3, founder member)

Honours Division 2 Champions 1972, 1986; Division 3 (S) Champions 1934; League Cup Winners 1962, 1985

Ground Carrow Road

By the mid-1990s, Norwich City, for so long renowned merely as plucky Cup fighters, had seemed to be established in the top flight as regular purveyors of sweetly attractive football. Yet such are the economic realities in the soccer outpost of Norfolk that maintaining their position of eminence was likely to prove a daunting challenge, as the sale of several top players had already demonstrated. Accordingly, season 1994/95 proved bitterly disappointing and they were relegated. Not that the 'Canaries' have been used to an easy life. On becoming founder members of Division 3, they struggled for a decade before earning promotion in the 1930s and enjoying a five-year stint in the higher grade.

In the 1950s Norwich emerged as one of the more enterprising teams in the Third Division, but despite pocketing much-needed cash when future England defender Maurice Norman was sold, they ran into financial difficulties in 1957. A public appeal brought salvation, and two years later the Canaries reached the FA Cup semi-final disposing of Manchester United and Spurs on the way, with major contributions from forwards Terry Bly and Terry Allcock, and long-serving defender Ron Ashman.

Thus revitalised, Norwich went up in 1960 and consolidated their position. Highlights of the next decade included winning the League Cup, the buying and selling of star striker Ron Davies and, in 1967, a famous FA Cup victory at Old Trafford.

But it was in 1972, with Ron Saunders in charge, that the club really took off, reaching Division 1 for the first time. After this they were relegated four times, but on three occasions it was for one season only, and under the enlightened management of John Bond, Ken Brown – who presided over a second League Cup triumph – Dave Stringer, Mike Walker and John Deehan, they continued to gain in stature. Arguably the highlight of this period was the stirring UEFA Cup campaign of 1993/94, in which they saw off mighty Bayern Munich before bowing out heroically to Internazionale of Milan.

Influential players of the modern era have included 'keepers Kevin Keelan and England's Chris Woods and, more recently centre-forward Chris Sutton, who was sold to Blackburn Rovers for £5 million.

For many recent seasons Norwich City have been seen as a friendly, family club, frequently challenging for major honours and providing good entertainment. They won many friends, but few trophies. One success, however, was the 1985 League Cup victory against Sunderland and celebrating that victory is Norwich hero Mick Channon, seen here with his son and manager Ken Brown. The happiness that was attached to the club was soured slightly towards the end of the 1994/95 season when bad results were blamed on the club's policy of selling good players for big cash rewards.

NOTTINGHAM FOREST

Founded 1865

Joined League 1892 (Division 1)

Honours Division 1 Champions 1978; Division 2 Champions 1907, 1922;
Division 3(S) Champions 1951; FA Cup Winners 1898, 1959; League Cup Winners 1978, 1979, 1989, 1990; European Cup Winners 1979, 1980

Ground City Ground

Over more than 100 years Nottingham Forest had established a reputation as a club which invariably served up good football but usually lacked the ruthlessness needed to lift top prizes – and then along came Brian Clough. He transformed a team of also-rans into a combination which twice conquered Europe and became a lasting force on the domestic scene. Not that Forest were complete strangers to success. As stable members of Division 1, they won their first trophy, the FA Cup, towards the end of Queen Victoria's reign and continued to spend most of their time in the top flight until the mid 1920s.

Then came their dullest period. Forest remained in the Second Division for more than two decades, a period of

vegetation which ended not with the longed-for promotion but with an unprecedented slump into Division 3 (S).

It was then that the club showed both restraint and wisdom in standing by their manager, Billy Walker. He rebuilt the side, leading them back to the First Division in 1957 and winning the FA Cup two years later. His most outstanding player was centre-half Bobby McKinlay, who was to play more than 600 League games for Forest.

In 1967, with Johnny Carey at the helm, the club came close to the League and FA Cup double, finishing as runners-up and semi-finalists respectively. With fine players such as wing-half Terry Hennessey and forward Ian Moore, Forest were an attractive team, but a distressing decline was imminent. The ill-judged purchase of Jim Baxter, a once-great Scottish play-maker who was past his best, and a fire which destroyed the City Ground's main stand were followed by the

unpopular sale of several stars, and Forest were relegated in 1972.

Enter Clough, three years later, and the transformation was under way. Working closely with assistant Peter Taylor, he dumbfounded the soccer world by securing promotion, winning the League Championship and twice taking the European Cup, all in successive seasons. Key players during this heady interlude included winger John Robertson, 'keeper Peter Shilton, defenders Viv Anderson and Kenny Burns and forward Tony Woodcock. In the late 1980s he built another excellent side in which his son Nigel, a skilful forward, and England international defenders Des Walker and Stuart Pearce featured prominently.

Despite their success, Forest are not accustomed to huge support. But crowds were healthy even when their opening campaign in the Premier League ended in relegation, the retirement of Clough, and an exodus of star players. New boss Frank Clark supervised an immediate revival, securing promotion at the first attempt and turning out an attractive side illuminated by the attacking talents of Stan Collymore and Dutchman Brian Roy.

NOTTS COUNTY

Founded 1862

Joined League 1888 (founder member)

Honours Division 2 Champions 1897, 1914, 1923; Division 3(S) Champions 1931, 1950; Division 4 Champions 1971; FA Cup Winners 1894

Ground Meadow Lane

As the world's oldest surviving club, Notts County might be expected to boast an illustrious history. In fact, their achievements have been modest and their one major honour, the FA Cup, was won more than a century ago.

After helping to launch the League, County never enjoyed the success of most co-founders, dropping out of the top flight twice before the

John McGovern holds aloft the large European Cup after Forest's 1-0 final victory over Malmo in 1979. This was Forest's first European success – a feat which they repeated the following season. Manager Brian Clough assembled a team of stylish players, including goalkeeper Peter Shilton, Archie Gemmill and Trevor Francis. Although this European Cup success was largely unexpected, Forest had beaten holders Liverpool on the way to the final.

First World War. They returned in 1914, thanks enormously to the form of goalkeeper Albert Iremonger, an eccentric giant who won another Division 2 title medal in 1923 and still holds the club record of 564 League appearances.

Stability continued to prove beyond County's reach, and the late 1940s found them enduring their second sojourn in the Third Division. But in 1947 interest boomed with the unexpected purchase of England centre-forward Tommy Lawton, and promotion followed three years later. When the great man left, however, the good times went with him, and the end of the decade found the club in Division 4.

It was to be another 11 years before manager Jimmy Sirrel, who had three stints at Meadow Lane, began lifting them up the League, a renaissance capped by reaching the First Division in 1981. For a club with limited support and resources, survival at the top was always going to be hard, especially as influential schemer Don Masson was nearing the end of his career. But they clung on for three terms before sinking back into the shadow cast by neighbouring Forest.

There followed a five-year spell in the Third Division before Neil Warnock led them up to the top flight in 1991. But they never looked like retaining that status and were relegated back to the new First Division. Further demotion followed after a chronic start to 1994/95.

OLDHAM ATHLETIC

Founded 1895

Joined League 1907 (Division 2)

Honours Division 2 Champions 1991; Division 3 (N) Champions 1953; Division 3 Champions 1974

Ground Boundary Park

The Coronation Street comedian who said, 'Oldham Athletic – that's a contradiction in terms!' was forced to eat his words as Joe Royle, one of the most talented and loyal managers in the land, transformed the 'Latics' into a vibrant and entertaining side in the early 1990s.

In fact, although Oldham had experienced many a slough of despond down the years, they were not total strangers to success. After making an instant impact on Division 2, they were promoted and reached the FA Cup semi-final in 1913. Then, two years later, led by former Manchester United star centre-half Charlie Roberts, the Boundary Park club were runners-up in Division 1, missing the title by two points.

After the war Oldham fell away badly, however, spending most of their time in the Third Division, until they were allocated to the newly created Fourth in 1958. Five years later, inspired by Scottish schemer Bobby Johnstone, they were promoted but could not consolidate and soon returned to the basement.

Relief was at hand in the form of Jimmy Frizzell, who became manager in 1970 and within four seasons took them to Division 2. Royle assumed control in 1982 and gradually constructed a team which, by the end of the decade, was making its mark. In 1989/90 the Latics

Oldham Athletic, by 1995 back in the First Division, have enjoyed a recent spell in the top flight when their confident attacking play unsettled many bigger clubs. The nearest they came to a major success was in the 1994 FA Cup semi final when they were held to a 1-1 draw, in the last minute only, by Manchester United. Oldham's Richard Jobson (left) and Craig Fleming try to disposses United's Mark Hughes, the man who scored the heartbreaking goal.

narrowly missed elevation to the top flight, and reached the Final of the League Cup and semi-final of the FA Cup. In the process of Cup wins over Arsenal, Everton, Aston Villa and Southampton, men like defender Earl Barrett, midfielder Mike Milligan and striker Andy Ritchie caught the imagination of the footballing public, their exhilarating skills doing more than enough to deflect jibes about Boundary Park's then plastic surface.

Promotion – and a return to grass – followed in 1991 and Oldham, who have plenty of potential support despite their proximity to Manchester, were looking to the future with confidence. That was dented in 1994, first by relegation and then by Royle's departure to Everton, but having tasted a measure of success, the 'Latics' remained ambitious for more.

OLYMPIC GAMES

In the 1932 Los Angeles Olympics there was no football; the Depression and the prospect of a long sea journey kept many athletes away. Fifty-two years later, in the same city, 1,421,627 spectators paid to watch Olympic soccer, making it the best attended sport in the competition.

No such future for Olympic football could have been foreseen in 1896 when the ancient Greek games

were revived; and in fact, soccer did not feature in the programme of that first modern Olympics.

This is something of a surprise, since among the Olympic principles outlined in 1894 is one stating that the sports should be international and modern – two qualities possessed by the increasingly popular team game. Moreover, the founder of the Games, the visionary Baron Pierre de Coubertin, while insisting on the modern-day relevance of the events, intended the competition to recreate the ethos of the original festivals, and it was to the English public-school

sporting tradition – in particular their team games – that he looked for inspiration; he had also been encouraged by the public response to exhibition matches he had organised. By 1921, however, he was opposing team sports because he believed they brought out the worst aspects of nationalism. But the revenue they raised formed a convincing counter-argument.

At times in Olympic history, it cannot be denied, football has rivalled boxing for demonstrations of all that is worst in sport. In the 1906 Athens Interim Games there came a hint of future disputes

OLYMPIC GAMES				
Year	Venue	Gold	Silver	Bronze
1896*	Athens	Denmark	Greece	
1990*	Paris	Great Britain	France	
1904*	St Louis	Canada	USA	
1908	London	Great Britain	Denmark	Holland
1912	Stockholm	Great Britain	Denmark	Holland
1920	Antwerp	Belgium	Spain	Holland
1924	Paris	Uruguay	Switzerland	Sweden
1928	Amsterdam	Uruguay	Argentina	Italy
1932	Los Angeles	*no tournament*		
1936	Berlin	Italy	Austria	Norway
1948	London	Sweden	Yugoslavia	Denmark
1952	Helsinki	Hungary	Yugoslavia	Sweden
1956	Melbourne	USSR	Yugoslavia	Bulgaria
1960	Rome	Yugoslavia	Denmark	Hungary
1964	Tokyo	Hungary	Czechoslovakia	East Germany
1968	Mexico City	Hungary	Bulgaria	Japan
1972	Munich	Poland	Hungary	E Germany /USSR
1976	Montreal	East Germany	Poland	USSR
1980	Moscow	Czechoslovakia	East Germany	USSR
1984	Los Angeles	France	Brazil	Yugoslavia
1988	Seoul	USSR	Brazil	West Germany
1992	Barcelona	Spain	Poland	Ghana

*unofficial tournament

when Athens refused to play Thessaloniki because they had already defeated them earlier in the competition. In the 1920 final Czechoslovakia walked off in protest at certain refereeing decisions. Four years later in Paris, in the final, Uruguay insisted the Dutch referee be replaced because they anticipated bias. And the infamy of the 1936

The Great Britain team which won the 1908 Olympic football tournament at Shepherd's Bush in London were, in fact, all English: (back row, left to right) Barlow, Styles (FA official), Corbett, Bailey, Hawkes, David (FA official), Schumaker, Lewis (referee); Smith, Stapley, Woodward, Parnell, Hardman, Hunt; Berry, Chapman. Note the basketball-style panelling on the ball, held by Woodward. Only six teams participated, all of them European, and the sport enjoyed Olympic status for the first time. Convincing wins against Sweden, Holland and Denmark ensured triumph for the home team. Four years later in Stockholm there were 11 entrants, still all European, and Great Britain beat Denmark in the final. It was to be their last ever gold in the event, as the FA withdrew from FIFA over the issue of payments to players.

Olympics was not limited to the political sphere: the German referee was manhandled in the violent Italy-USA encounter (a dismissed Italian, Piccini, incredibly, refused to leave the field and his team won 1-0); Peru's entire contingent withdrew when a re-match was ordered after a pitch invasion during their defeat of Austria; Colombia withdrew in sympathy. And it was Peru's disallowed goal against Argentina in the 1964 preliminary round which sparked off riots resulting in 328 deaths. In 1968 there were brawls and four players were sent off in the final as the crowd threw cushions onto the pitch.

Nevertheless, not least thanks to some excellent football, the event has gained in strength. Before 1912 not all the teams were truly national, some countries entering more than one team to make up the numbers, and in the second and third Olympiads the sport had only exhibition status – a reflection of the uncertain start experienced by the Games themselves. In 1952, however, pre-Olympic knockout rounds became necessary because so many countries had entered.

Boycotts, bans and withdrawals have not caused as much damage as the amateur/professional dispute threatened to. When the Uruguayan footballers of 1924 and 1928 won the 1930

World Cup for their country, it was not regarded as significant. After the Second World War, however, Western amateurs had to compete against full-time Eastern-bloc 'amateurs' with World Cup experience. The 1964 Italian team had to withdraw for fielding players from European champions Internazionale, yet in 1952 Puskas had helped Hungary win the gold. Eventually the eligibility rules were changed to prevent anyone who had played in the World Cup finals from taking part, and thereafter to restrict the tournament to under-23 sides, professional or otherwise, which at least ensured a level playing field. It does not help the United Kingdom, however, which still feels unable to enter a side without jeopardising the separate status of the four home nations.

OXFORD UNITED

Founded 1893

Joined League 1962 (Division 4)

Honours Division 2 Champions 1985; Division 3 Champions 1968, 1984; League Cup Winners 1986

Ground Manor Ground

Oxford United have proved splendidly worthwhile members of the League since the withdrawal of Accrington Stanley gave them their big

chance in the early 1960s. Despite never attracting a huge following from the University town, United fought their way through the divisions to enjoy a short sojourn in the top flight; campaigned doughtily, and at times with inspiration, in the FA Cup; and actually won the League Cup.

Much of the early credit must go to two men, manager Arthur Turner and wing-half and captain Ron Atkinson. Turner took over Headington United in 1959, demanded the change of name, and led them to the Second Division, being sacked for his pains in 1972. Atkinson played more than 600 games for the club, in and out of the League, departing just a year before his boss to start his own successful managerial career. Other stalwarts of that era included defenders John Shuker and Maurice Kyle, and striker Graham Atkinson, Ron's brother.

The mid 1970s and early 1980s saw Oxford slip back to the Third Division, but Jim Smith started a revival that took them to the First and Maurice Evans – getting the best from such men as midfielder Ray Houghton and striker John Aldridge – kept them there for three years. It was during United's stint in the top division that they tasted Wembley triumph, crushing Queen's Park Rangers 3-0.

Prior to that, Oxford's most stirring exploit in a knock-out competition had been in 1964, when they had beaten Division 1 pacesetters Blackburn Rovers to become Division Four's first FA Cup quarter-finalists.

In the 1980s chairman Robert Maxwell proposed a merger with Reading, but that plan was discarded, and after dropping into the Second Division and selling talented forward Dean Saunders, United experienced boardroom changes. The future seemed likely to be a challenging one, but it was met with considerable zeal, and despite relegation to the Second Division in 1994, the club remained both enterprising and ambitious.

PAISLEY, Bob

1919 Born in Hetton-le-Hole, County Durham

1939 Helps Bishop Auckland win FA Amateur Cup; signs for Liverpool

1947 Wins Championship medal with 'Reds'

1954 Retires as player to join Anfield coaching staff

1959 Becomes Bill Shankly's first lieutenant as the Scot moves into manager's chair

1974 Succeeds Shankly as Liverpool boss

1976 Reds lift first trophies of Paisley era – League title and UEFA Cup

1977 Liverpool retain Championship and Paisley leads them to their first European Cup triumph; their second follows a year later

1979 Reds take first of four League titles in five seasons

1981 Liverpool win another European Cup and first of a hat-trick of League Cups for Paisley

1983 Steps down as manager

1985 Becomes adviser to new manager Kenny Dalglish, eventually taking a place on the Anfield board

1992 Leaves board through ill health

Paisley is, quite simply, the most successful manager in the history of English soccer. Never charismatic like Shankly, controversial like Clough or revered like Busby, he outshone them all in the quest for honours.

Some have denigrated the achievements of the modest north-easterner, contending that Shankly had already done the hard work, but such claims do not tally with the facts. Admittedly Paisley, who

Bob Paisley acknowledges the acclaim of the Liverpool crowd. Paisley's 1974 takeover from the legendary Bill Shankly was achieved with the minimum of fuss. He simply carried on from where Shankly left off. His nine-year reign at the helm brought an unprecedented six Football League Championships, three League Cup successes, the UEFA Cup once and the European Cup three times. Perhaps part of the success of Liverpool has been the saving of breath for where it's most needed – on the pitch.

played a more crucial role in his predecessor's triumphs than he is often credited with, inherited some top-class players, but many of his most glorious victories were won with a new side assembled by his own perspicacity in the transfer market. He it was who signed such magnificent

performers as Kenny Dalglish, Graeme Souness and Alan Hansen, and blended them into the Liverpool pattern.

Bob Paisley, an effective wing-half in his playing days, was a meticulous planner, shrewd tactician and canny judge of a footballer's strengths and weaknesses. Never one to shout the odds, he always preferred to let the men on the pitch do his talking for him. They did so, for nine fabulous years, with the utmost eloquence.

PARTICK THISTLE

Founded 1876

Joined League 1893 (Division 2)

Honours Scottish League First Division Champions 1976; Division 2 Champions 1897, 1900, 1971; Scottish Cup Winners 1921; Scottish League Cup Winners 1971/72

Ground Firhill Park

Despite being based in Glasgow, Partick Thistle have survived the Old Firm and sometimes confounded them. In 1971 they gave Celtic a comprehensive 4-1 beating in the League Cup Final. Between the posts that day was a young Alan Rough, who was to go on to win 51 caps while with the club.

In 1921, guided by Jimmy McMenemy (then in the veteran stage after a career with Celtic), they defeated Rangers to win the Scottish Cup.

Recently, Thistle persevered with costly attempts to restore the club to the Premier Division status it lost in 1982, succeeding eventually at the tenth attempt. In the 1980s they had the satisfaction of discovering striker Maurice Johnston, although he was soon sold to Watford.

As the 90s dawned they were experiencing a growth of support in Glasgow, with something of a cult following as a reaction to the 'big' clubs in the city.

PELE

1940 Edson Arantes do Nascimento (Pele), born in Tres Coracoes, Brazil; his father, 'Dondinho', is a lowly-paid professional footballer

1954 Starts to play for Bauru Athletic Club juniors in Sao Paulo; the coach, 1934 World Cup player Waldema de Brito, persuades him not to join senior team but to wait for Santos offer

1956 September – scores on his debut for Santos v Corinthians; finishes the season as club top scorer with 32 goals

1957 July – scores in first international v Argentina

1958 Still only 17 years old, scores twice in World Cup Final victory v Sweden, bringing his tournament total to six goals, despite missing first two games through injury

1959 Scores 126 first-class goals, many of them for the army (since he was doing national service at the time), the rest for Santos

1969 November – converts penalty v Vasco da Gama to score 1000th first-class goal

The most famous number 10 shirt in the world. When Pele left Santos, the shirt bearing that number was hung up, never to be used again. Who could fill it? The great man is seen here in October 1990 in an exhibition game to celebrate his 50th birthday. Pele's life epitomises the dreams of every Rio child who ever kicked a bundle of rags in a back street. His mother was dead set against him becoming a professional footballer. She had good reason: Pele's father barely scraped a living from the sport and economic pressure frequently forced him to play when he should have been resting an injury.

1970 Mature display helps Brazil secure possession of Jules Rimet Trophy in perpetuity

1971 July – 111th and final game for Brazil v Yugoslavia in Rio de Janeiro

1974 October – final game for Santos v Ponte Preta

1975 June – comes out of retirement to sign $4.5 million contract for New York Cosmos

1976 Voted NASL Most Valuable Player

1977 Helps Cosmos to victory v Seattle in Soccer Bowl Final; retires, having scored 1283 first-class goals; October – plays one half for each of his old teams, Santos and Cosmos, in emotional testimonial

1994 Becomes Brazil's sports minister

At times it seems as if half of the world's best players were nearly overlooked in their youth on account of being 'too slight'. The fact that this judgement was also made of Edson Arantes do Nascimento makes it incredible that coaches should ever again apply such a criterion.

Widely regarded as the greatest player in the world of his or any other era, Pele, as he was nicknamed, was also the most fêted footballer ever. Initially somewhat shy, resentful even, of the attention his talent brought him, he quickly learned to deal with it and was soon to be hailed as football's first ambassador. A similar pragmatism was evident in his tolerance of a different, less welcome sort of attention on the pitch; for much of his career he struggled with a knee injury sustained in a needle match when 16 years old, and he soon developed an instinct for self-preservation which became sharpened after the 1966 World Cup; even so, there was little to betray the fact that, as a youth, he had to work hard to curb a natural temper.

Pele has acted in films, is a keen amateur musician, and studied part-time for a degree in physical education while playing for Santos in the 1970s; he has served as a conscript, and has known poverty and wealth (the first footballer truly to appreciate the commercial potential of fame, his name is a worldwide registered trademark and he is said to have been a millionaire by the age of 22). His experience-crammed life has created a rounded personality so that his current ambition, to be President of Brazil, seems anything but ridiculous. Meeting Popes and heads of state is something he takes in his stride. Indeed, his power has, at times, proved to be greater than theirs; a two-day truce was called in the Biafra-Nigeria War so that both sides could see him play.

All great players seem to have that bit more time on the ball but Pele, despite his devastating speed, could appear positively languorous. His control was unsurpassed, the first touch absorbing all the impact of the ball; he could turn it with his chest. He would use his powerful physique to shield the ball, his balance and deft skills enabling him to take it right up to a defender, committing him to a futile tackle. Naturally right-footed, he developed his left foot to equal deadliness and scored 97 international goals. He was the most feared inside-forward of his day; of only average height, he had tungsten springs in his thighs and powerful neck muscles which, combined with the immaculate timing that allowed him to 'hang' in the air, made him as dangerous with his head as with his feet. Whether passing or shooting, dribbling or running off the ball, time and again he did the unexpected. He was imaginative, quick-witted and courageous. Pele was effectively kicked into submission in the 1962 and 1966 World Cups, but in 1970, aged 29, at the peak of his powers and vastly experienced, he returned to play in every qualifying and final round, producing exquisite performances in a highly talented and expressive Brazilian team.

The only aspect of Pele's game which went largely unexamined was his defensive ability – a fact for which football fans are surely grateful. Most of his European counterparts enjoyed no such exemption, tackling-back being an integral part of defence-based strategies.

Pele's participation in a game was always a celebration of the sport, his joy and delight in his own skills being communicated to the spectator. This enthusiasm has since been translated into the commitment he makes to football clinics (often for children as poor as he once was) all over the world. His dedication to football (in addition to financial considerations) brought him out of retirement to put a spark into United States soccer – he is often credited with single-handedly creating the football boom in that country.

PETERBOROUGH UNITED

Founded 1934

Joined League 1960 (Division 4)

Honours Division 4 Champions 1961, 1974

Ground London Road

When Peterborough United finally achieved League membership, it was long overdue. They had made 20 previous applications, often impressed in the FA Cup, attracted large crowds and won the Midland League with monotonous regularity. Having gained admittance, to the exclusion of Gateshead, they showed their quality immediately, romping away with the Fourth Division title and scoring a record 134 goals (52 of them from Terry Bly) in the process.

Then, securely ensconced in the Third Division and with striker Derek Dougan as their leading light, they beat Arsenal on the way to the 1965 FA Cup quarter-finals. The following year they disposed of Newcastle and Burnley to reach the League Cup semi-finals, and their future seemed bright.

But disaster was to follow. In 1968 they were relegated as punishment for financial irregularities, and then faced a severe cash crisis. They have since recovered, manager Noel Cantwell leading them back to the Third Division in the 1970s, only to return to the basement for the ensuing decade before rising again in 1991, then reaching the new First Division a year later. But 1993/94 proved a bittersweet campaign, with the disappointment of demotion being mitigated slightly by a run to the fourth round of the League Cup. Still, with better support than most of their opponents, there always seems to be potential for the 'Posh' to better their lot.

PLATINI, Michel

1955 Born in Joeuf, France

1972 Joins Nancy – scored 98 League goals for them in 175 appearances

1976 March – international debut v Czechoslovakia; scores in 2-2 draw

1978 Scores v Nice in Cup Final victory

1979 Bought by St Etienne

1981 Scores 21 goals on way to picking up League Championship medal

1982 Having scored 58 goals for St Etienne in 107 League appearances, moves to Italian club Juventus for £1.2 million

1983 Top scorer (16 goals) for new club; European Footballer of the Year

1984 Cup Winners' Cup medal, Italian Championship medal (18 goals); captains France to victory in European Championships, scoring a

record nine goals – not surprisingly, is again voted Europe's top player…

1985 …and again (three successive awards – a record); scores penalty v Liverpool to win European Cup for Juventus in notorious Heysel Final

1987 Retires and takes over as manager of French national team

1992 Resigns after disappointing European Championship finals, later works for French FA and on 1998 World Cup organising committee

Platini senior was coach at Nancy, Michel's first club, and the midfield player's dead-ball expertise was testimony to his father's belief in the value of practice. Michel's natural gifts alone, however, would have guaranteed him recognition as a world-class player. Perhaps his greatest asset was his vision; time and again his laser-guided passes opened up Europe's best defences. Elegant in movement, industrious when need be, he was comfortable in possession and a sweet striker of the ball. His scoring record is impressive for a midfield player and he was a cool penalty-taker for both national and club sides. No country is harder to score in than Italy, and his 68 goals in 147 League appearances for Juventus represents a remarkable ratio.

Platini won 72 caps for France, many of them as captain, and scored 41 goals. He played for his country in three consecutive World Cups and was the linch-pin of the sophisticated midfield quartet which so nearly steered France to the Final in 1982.

As a player he was occasionally wont to show impatience with less-gifted colleagues who were unable to anticipate his through-passes or were slow to deliver the ball as he made one of his finely timed runs. His footballing intelligence has never been in doubt, and there are high hopes

The French captain celebrates after scoring against Brazil in the 1986 World Cup Finals in Mexico. Michel Platini scored 41 goals in 72 games for his country. He was voted European Footballer of the Year three seasons running. On his retirement as a player in 1987 he was appointed manager of the French national team.

still for his managerial career. A true cosmopolitan, he once had his own slot on Italian television in which he discoursed, in Italian, on the subject of current soccer tactics.

PLAY-OFFS

Play-offs in the Football League were used in the 1986/87 season as a way to readjust the make-up of the divisions and, expressly, to produce a First Division of 20 clubs. Some automatic promotion and relegation still took place, but play-off matches were played to finalise the construction of the League for the following season. At the end of a round of home and away games, Swindon (third in Division 3) went to the Second Division (replacing Sunderland) and Aldershot (sixth in Division 4) went into the Third Division (replacing Bolton Wanderers).

Although the strain of these matches and the apparent unfairness of some of the promotions and relegations were pointed out by players, managers and fans, the general feeling was favourable. In particular the play-off system, coupled with three points for a win, meant that few League matches were played which did not affect either promotion or relegation, thus maintaining interest throughout the whole season. Although initially a short-term measure, play-offs have remained, in various formats, since, and clearly they are here to stay. The 1989/90 season culminated in successfully staged play-off finals at Wembley which further cemented support for the concept.

Play-offs are not new to the Football League. Called 'test matches' they were used in the early days of the League to determine promotion and relegation between the divisions. In the first season of Division Two (1892/93) Accrington (no relation to Accrington Stanley), Notts County and Newton Heath from the First played off against Small Heath, Sheffield United and Darwen from the Second for three Division 1 places. Newton Heath stayed up, to be joined by Sheffield United and Darwen.

Mike Newell scores from the penalty spot for Blackburn Rovers in the Second Division play-off final at the end of the 1991/92 season. Blackburn beat Leicester City by this solitary goal to gain promotion to the new Premier League. With new manager Kenny Dalglish at the helm, Blackburn had finished sixth in the Second Division. By beating Derby County 5-4 over two legs, home and away, they reached the play-off finals at Wembley.

PLYMOUTH ARGYLE

Founded 1886

Joined League 1920 (Division 3)

Honours Division 3(S) Champions 1930, 1952; Division 3 Champions 1959

Ground Home Park

Plymouth Argyle could hardly have a more apt nickname than the 'Pilgrims'. Isolated in deepest Devon, they are faced with regular marathon treks to the far corners of the country, which places significant drain on both resources and energy. In such circumstances, and in view of the West Country's traditionally lukewarm feeling for football, Argyle have done well to spend the majority of their campaigns in the old Second Division, and to avoid the basement until their relegation in 1995.

Their earliest League

efforts were encouraging, if extremely frustrating. For six consecutive seasons between 1922 and 1927 they were runners-up in Division 3 (S), with Sammy Black's goals and Welsh international Moses Russell's captaincy contributing largely to such astonishing consistency. They finally went up in 1930, and there followed 20 years in the Second Division before the 1950s brought two relegations and two promotions.

Wing-half Johnny Williams and marksman Wilf Carter were particularly influential in their Third Division title triumph of 1959, the last time an honour has landed at Home Park. Since then Plymouth have see-sawed between the Second and Third Divisions, with their most prominent character being flamboyant boss Malcolm Allison, who was in charge for a brief period in the mid 1960s. Other well-known Argyle figures have included Allison's protege, full-back Tony Book; striker Paul Mariner in the mid 1970s; and his successor in the number nine shirt, Tommy Tynan, in the 1980s; and former England goalkeeper Peter Shilton, who

lost his job as Argyle player-boss following personal financial problems in 1995. Plymouth's best knock-out sequences have taken them to the FA Cup semi-finals in 1984, and the same stage of the League Cup in 1965 and 1974.

PORTSMOUTH

Founded 1898

Joined League 1920 (Division 3 founder member)

Honours Division 1 Champions 1949, 1950; Division 3 (S) Champions 1924; Division 3 Champions 1962, 1983; FA Cup Winners 1939

Ground Fratton Park

Since the war only four teams have won consecutive League Championships: Manchester United (twice), Wolves, Liverpool (three times) and Portsmouth, a once powerful club who have languished out of the limelight – apart from one disastrous top-flight term in the late 1980s – for more than three decades.

After entering the League as original members of the Third Division, 'Pompey'

ascended quickly and – no small thanks to free-scoring Billy Haines – reached the First in 1927.

After surviving early struggles to avoid relegation, and recovering from the disappointment of FA Cup Final defeats in 1929 and 1934, they sold star centre-half Jimmy Allen and emerged as a major force.

Under the guidance of extrovert boss Jack Tinn, Portsmouth caused one of the biggest FA Cup upsets of the century by thrashing Wolves at Wembley in the last pre-war Final. After the conflict, with Bob Jackson now in charge, they entered their purple patch, chalking up their title double and remaining an accomplished team until well into the 1950s. The success was based on a splendid half-back line of Jimmy Scoular, Reg Flewin and long-serving English international Jimmy Dickinson, with wingers Peter Harris and Jack Froggatt also highly influential. The side broke up, however, and Pompey went down in 1959 to begin a lengthy mundane period spent mostly in Division 2, with low points including a financial crisis in the 1960s and a slide to the

Fourth Division in the late 1970s.

The 1980s saw a gradual recovery under managers Frank Burrows and Bobby Campbell, and in 1987 Alan Ball took them into the top flight. Sadly they were not good enough, Ball was sacked, and Portsmouth entered the 1990s as solid, if rather uninspiring members of the old Second Division. However, in 1992 they were desperately unlucky not to reach Wembley, losing an FA Cup semi-final replay to Liverpool only after a penalty shoot-out.

The season is 1946/47 and Portsmouth improve their position in Division 1 from 18th to 12th. The following season they finished 8th and then in 1948/49, and again the following season, they won the Football League Championship. Proudly displaying the famous badge on their club shirts are: (back row, left to right) Wharton, Scoular, Brooks, Walker, Ferrier, Dickinson, Stewart (trainer); Barlow, Reid, Froggat, McAlinden, Parker, Flewin.

PORT VALE

Founded 1876

Joined League 1892

Honours Division 3 (N) Champions 1930, 1954; Division 4 Champions 1959

Ground Vale Park

Port Vale took their unusual name from the house in the northern end of the Potteries where a dozen men gathered to launch the club. Only occasionally have they emerged from the lower divisions and out of Stoke City's shadow. Indeed, Vale have played in a higher division than their neighbours in just three seasons.

The club added the prefix 'Burslem' in 1886, and were elected to the new Division 2 six years later. Financial problems forced them out in 1907, but the suspension of Leeds City for making illegal payments allowed the club (by now plain Port Vale again) to return in 1919. In 1931 a best ever position of fifth in Division 2 was achieved.

In 1943 they sold the Old Recreation Ground in Hanley – known locally as 'th'owd wreck' – and laid ambitious plans for their sixth home. Vale Park, in Burslem, was to be the 'Wembley of the North'. It opened in 1950, but the original 50,000 capacity was tested only twice by FA Cup ties.

In 1953/54 Vale won the Division 3 (N) title, conceding a mere 7 goals at home and 21 overall in 46 games. They also reached the FA Cup semi-final in the same season, only for their former player Ronnie Allen to score West Bromwich's penalty winner.

Division 2 status was surrendered in 1957 and not regained until 1989. In between Vale became Division 4's first champions and rose from the bottom section a further three times. Sir Stanley Matthews briefly managed the club he had supported as a boy, but in 1968 Vale were expelled from the League – ironically for making illegal payments.

They were re-elected soon afterwards, but only stalwart defender Roy Sproson remained from the heady days of the 1950s. He later managed Vale, though it was not until John Rudge took the post in 1983 that they began to threaten Stoke's ascendancy in the Potteries.

The 1991/92 campaign began with Vale in Division 2, one division above their local rivals, but it was to end in relegation. In the previous season they had decided against moving to an all-purpose stadium proposed by Stoke-on-Trent council, and announced a multi-million-pound scheme to modernise the crumbling Vale Park.

With the extremely able Rudge still at the helm, Port Vale achieved promotion to the new First Division in 1994.

PRESTON NORTH END

Founded 1881

Joined League 1888 (founder member)

Honours Division 1 Champions 1889, 1890; Division 2 Champions 1904, 1913, 1951; Division 3 Champions 1971; FA Cup Winners 1889, 1938

Ground Deepdale

Young fans may find it hard to believe, but Preston North End, now a familiar sight in the lower reaches of the League, gave the world its first great football team. The 'Old Invincibles', as they were then known, lifted the inaugural Championship without losing a game, and in the same season took the FA Cup without conceding a goal.

Spearheaded by England marksman John Goodall, Preston – the first club to pay players openly – retained the title the following year and were runners-up in the next three terms before see-sawing between Divisions 1 and 2 for the first third of the twentieth century. Outstanding performers in this anti-climactic period were centre-half Joe McCall before the First World War, and schemer Alex James in the 1920s. By the mid 1930s greater consistency was found and, with Bill Shankly at right-half, Preston won promotion in 1934 and the FA Cup four years later.

After the war they slipped into the Second Division but soon returned to the top flight to embark on an era which, although yielding no trophies, offered rich entertainment. Architect of the improvement was winger Tom Finney, one of the finest footballers ever known, with wing-half Tommy Docherty also making a telling contribution. In 1953 the Championship was missed only on goal average, and the following campaign ended with a Wembley defeat by West Bromwich Albion, but nothing daunted, North End remained a major force until 1961. Then, with Finney retired and the disappearance of the maximum wage striking a body blow to Deepdale finances, relegation signalled the start of an inexorable decline.

Talented players such as winger Peter Thompson and wing-half Howard Kendall emerged but were sold through economic necessity, and the slide continued.

Preston did manage a further FA Cup Final appearance, their seventh –

Preston North End must look back to the end of the last century to find their most successful period in the game. The side photographed here were FA Cup winners in 1889, beating Wolverhampton Wanderers 3-0 at Kennington Oval: (back row, left to right) Drummond, Howarth, Mr Hanbury MP, Mr Tomlinson MP, Russell, Holmes, Mr Sudell (Chairman), Graham, Mills-Roberts; Gordon, Ross,. Goodhall, Dewhurst, Thomson. Importantly, the 1888/89 season was when Preston North End also won the first ever Football League Championship to complete the double. Their record over the first five years of the League's history was first twice and runners-up three times.

they unluckily lost to West Ham in 1964 – but little else went their way. In 1970 the club tasted Third Division fare for the first time. Subsequently there have been two spells in the old Second, but also two in the basement, and with the Lancashire giants tightening their grip on floating support, supreme efforts will be needed to restore even a vestige of former glories. Indeed, during the 1990/91 campaign they had to accept that promotion from the Third Division would actually be a financial disaster as, under new League rules, they would have had to take up their synthetic pitch – an asset to the club for the extra revenue it attracted. However, they were back on grass by mid-decade and making strenuous efforts to rise from the bottom division.

PUSKAS, Ferenc

1926 Born in Budapest, Hungary

1943 Makes debut for Kispest (Budapest) at 16

1945 Makes international debut for Hungary

1948 Heads Hungarian League goalscorers with 50 for Kispest

1949 Kispest become known as Honved, a Hungarian Army team

1952 Wins gold medal in Hungary's Olympic team

1953 Captains Hungary to 6-3 victory v England at Wembley

1954 Although injured, captains Hungary in World Cup Final

1956 Leaves Hungary during the People's Revolution

1957 Spends year in Austria but fails to get playing permit

1958 Joins Real Madrid

1960 Scores four goals in Real Madrid's fifth successive European Cup Final victory, 7-3 v Eintracht Frankfurt

1962 Scores another European Cup Final hat-trick

1964 Wins a second European Cup runners-up medal

1966 Retires as a player

1971 Coaches Panathinaikos of Greece to the European Cup Final

Ferenc Puskas scored 83 goals in 84 internationals for his home country before his Hungarian career was cut short by the popular uprising in October 1956. Two years later his career was revived in Madrid. He made four international appearances for Spain, and scored 35 goals in 39 European matches for Real. Puskas won one European Cup winner's medal and played in two other Finals. He won four Hungarian League Championships with Honved and five Spanish League Championships with Real. He was top scorer in the Hungarian League in four seasons, and in the Spanish League in four seasons.

Puskas made his impact on the British game at Wembley in 1953, in particular with the manner of the third Hungarian goal in a 6-3 victory. He changed direction by rolling back the ball with the sole of his foot before swivelling to hit a typical left-foot shot past Merrick. His left-foot power was legendary, but he also had deceptive acceleration combined with cunning anticipation. Unlike many stars, Puskas was stockily built and had obvious weaknesses – he was poor at heading, one-footed and not always at peak fitness – but

his left foot more than compensated. His record ranks with the world's best, and only Pele has scored more international goals.

THE PYRAMID

The Pyramid gives shape and structure to non-League football. It is a system which links the various leagues outside the Football League, ensuring that clubs can progress through a hierarchy. Since 1986/87 the GM Vauxhall Conference (Alliance Premier League) champions have been granted automatic promotion to the

Lining up at Wembley with the 'Magnificent Magyars' of 1953, is Hungary's captain, Ferenc Puskas (left). The rest of the side lines up: (left to right) Grosics, Lorant, Hidegkuti, Buzansky, Lantos, Zakarias, Czibor, Baszik, Budai and Kocsis.
Puskas is acknowledged as having inspired the 6-3 victory; he also amazed spectators and commentators with his ball artistry. How he moved his feet at all with such huge shinpads is a mystery.

Football League, providing they can satisfy League standards for ground capacity and facilities.

Three leagues feed into the GM Vauxhall Conference – the Diadora Football League (Isthmian League), the UniBond League (Northern Premier League) and the Beazer Homes League (Southern League). Clubs in the premier divisions of these three leagues compete for promotion to the GM Vauxhall Conference. Below these premier divisions, the league network escalates. There are more divisions to the main feeder leagues, which in turn have leagues which officially feed into them. The result is an integrated structure which is bottom-heavy with grass-roots leagues. This is the Pyramid.

The Alliance Premier League, formed in 1979, paved the way as the first national league outside the Football League. It later became known as the Gola League, later still the GM Vauxhall Conference. It is still the only national league in men's non-League football, but the opportunity for automatic promotion to the Football League means that in theory anyone can form a new club and reach the new Third Division within a decade.

Colne Dynamoes were formed in 1963 by eleven schoolfriends, and 25 years later they won the FA Vase at Wembley. In 1989/90 their team of full-time professionals won the HFS Loans League by 26 points, but promotion to the GM Vauxhall Conference was hampered by negotiations over grounds. Chairman Graham White put the club into voluntary liquidation, saying that his family had been under pressure – thus nipping in the bud a remarkable story of progress (nearly) to Football League status.

Each league outside the Football League has its own standards for football grounds and facilities, so clubs can prepare for the upward journey through the hierarchy. However, as both Kidderminster Harriers and Macclesfield found to their cost, the need to meet ground conditions imposed by higher grades of football can be frustrating. Both clubs topped the Vauxhall Conference, Kidderminster in 1994 and Macclesfield in 1995, but were denied entrance to the Football League because their facilities were inadequate. Yet it is often argued that many non-League clubs are better run than those in the League. In addition, there is growing support for non-League football.

Aside from the FA Cup there are three major knock-out competitions for non-League clubs: the Bob Lord Challenge Trophy (named after the late Burnley chairman), the FA Challenge Vase (1975) and the FA Challenge Trophy (1970). The Bob Lord Challenge Trophy is for GM Vauxhall Conference teams. Top non-League teams are excluded from the Vase, but all non-League teams can compete in the FA Trophy.

Manager Barry Fry (now in charge at Birmingham City), flanked by Barnet players as they celebrate winning the GM Vauxhall Conference after beating Fisher Athletic 4-2 in the final game of the 1990/91 season. The winners of the Conference now gain automatic promotion to the Football League, replacing whichever team finishes bottom of the lowest division.

QUEEN OF THE SOUTH

Founded 1919

Joined League 1923 (Division 3)

Honours Scottish League Division 2 Champions 1951

Ground Palmerston Park

Geographically remote (in Dumfries) from other clubs, Queen of the South have nonetheless made their presence felt. Their own rampaging Billy Houliston was centre-forward for Scotland in the 1949 Wembley victory against England, and 1920s attacker Hughie Gallacher was briefly with them before joining Airdrie.

They reached Division 1 in 1933 and were relegated from it only in 1950. Since those days life has grown considerably more difficult.

QUEEN'S PARK

Founded 1867

Joined League 1900

Honours Scottish League Division 2 Champions 1923, 1956; Second Division Champions 1981; Scottish Cup Winners 1874, 1875, 1876, 1880, 1881, 1882, 1884, 1886, 1890, 1893

Ground Hampden Park

Scotland's oldest club, Queen's Park take much of the credit for popularising the sport in that country. The game's development then left them stranded all the same. Professionalism was legalised in 1893 but they retained, as they still do, their amateur status.

Grandeur still attaches to the club whose early achievements included no less than ten Scottish Cups as well as appearances in the

FA Cup Finals of 1884 and 1885 in England. Charles Campbell won a record eight winner's medals in the Scottish Cup and other stars of the period included winger J.B.Weir.

Completion of Hampden Park (their third ground of that name) in 1903 gave Scotland a national stadium and Queen's Park a curious role – Scottish football's unofficial curators.

QUEEN'S PARK RANGERS

Founded 1885

Joined League 1920 (Division 3)

Honours Division 2 Champions 1983; Division 3 (S) Champions 1948; Division 3 Champions 1967; League Cup Winners 1967

Ground Loftus Road

As a football force to be reckoned with, Queen's Park Rangers are a thoroughly modern phenomenon. Throughout most of their first four and a half decades of League life they created few ripples, often struggling financially and languishing in the Third Division apart from four post-war campaigns in the Second. In the mid 1950s they were particularly mundane, but the early 1960s, with enterprising manager Alec Stock at the helm and Brian Bedford banging in more than 170 goals in six seasons, brought new optimism.

The long-awaited impact on the national scene came, with a vengeance, in 1967 when Rangers not only won the Third Division title by 12 points, but also came from two goals down to beat West Bromwich Albion in the first League Cup Final played at Wembley. Star of the show and symbol of the West London club's rise to prominence was flamboyant goalscorer Rodney Marsh, who netted 44 times during that glorious season. In the following term Rangers capitalised by earning top-

flight status for the first time, but they were not ready for such dizzy heights and immediately returned to the Second Division.

But genuine progress was being made, and after Gordon Jago led them to promotion in 1973, Dave Sexton polished them into an accomplished side which finished only a point behind champions Liverpool in 1976. The new hero was midfielder Gerry Francis, who became England captain, and there were also crucial contributions from 'keeper Phil Parkes, veteran defender Frank McLintock, schemer Don Masson and mercurial forward Stan Bowles.

When Sexton left, however, the momentum died and Rangers spent four more years in the Second Division during which they made a plucky attempt to upset Spurs in the replayed 1982 Cup Final – before rising again, under Terry Venables, in 1983. Since then they have been solid members of the top flight, with outstanding players including 'keeper David Seaman, sold to Arsenal in 1990, Paul Parker, who moved on to Manchester United in 1992, and England striker Les Ferdinand, sold to Newcastle United in 1995. Veteran schemer Ray Wilkins succeeded Gerry Francis as Loftus Road boss in 1994.

The mercurial Stan Bowles, seen here tormenting a Luton defender in April 1973. Stan was capable of flashes of brilliance. From 1969 to 1974 Queen's Park Rangers rose from the middle of the Second Division to 8th in the First. Indeed, by 1975/76 they were Championship runners-up. The QPR squad during this period also included Terry Venables, goalkeeper Phil Parkes, defender Frank McLintock and midfielder Gerry Francis who became England captain and later club manager.

RAITH ROVERS

Founded 1883

Joined League 1902
(Division 2)

Honours Scottish League
Division 2 Champions 1908,
1910 (shared with Leith),
1938, 1949; Division 1
Champions 1993, 1995;
Scottish League Cup
Winners 1994/95

Ground Stark's Park

Raith Rovers' greatest
episodes had always seemed
to end in disappointment. In
1913 they lost the Scottish
Cup Final to Falkirk, and the
League Cup Final of 1948/49
brought defeat by Rangers.
But their 1994/95 Scottish
League Cup win over Celtic
was sensational, bringing
them for the first time a place
in Europe. The renaissance
was confirmed when they
lifted the First Division title in
the same season.

Yet watching the Kirkcaldy
club has always had
substantial compensations.
Alex James, a brilliant play-
maker for Arsenal, learned his
trade with them in the 1920s.
A Scotland great of the 1960s,
Jim Baxter, also first caught
the eye at Stark's Park. Of the
stars who stayed, the half-
back line of the 1950s, Andy
Young, Willie McNaught and
Andy Leigh, is particularly
revered.

RAMSEY, Sir Alf

1920 Born in Dagenham

1944 Turns professional with
Southampton

1948 England debut, v
Switzerland at Highbury

1949 Moves to Tottenham
Hotspur, with Welsh winger
Ernie Jones going the other
way

1950 Helps Spurs take
Division 2 title…

1951 … followed by the
League Championship

1953 Wins last of 32 caps in
Hungary's famous 6-3
Wembley annihilation of
England

1955 Takes over as Ipswich
boss

1961 Ipswich win Division 2
title

1962 Surprise success as
Town lift the Division 1
crown

1963 Ramsey succeeds
Walter Winterbottom as
England manager

1966 Leads England to
World Cup victory

1967 Becomes Sir Alf

1970 Mexico World Cup
campaign ends at quarter-
final stage as England lose to
West Germany after leading
2-0

1974 Ramsey is sacked after
England fail to qualify for
World Cup

1977 Brief spell as
Birmingham City boss

England *will* win the World
Cup, Alf Ramsey announced
repeatedly in the months
leading up to the 1966
tournament. Few believed
him, some even ridiculed
him, but he it was who had
the last laugh – and a
knighthood to boot.

Ramsey, who enjoyed a
productive playing career as a
skilful right-back in Arthur
Rowe's innovative 'push-and-
run' Spurs team, made an
inspired start in management.
At Ipswich he achieved much
with little, moulding a group
of discards and previously
underrated performers into a
Championship side.

Next, faced with the
ultimate challenge at
international level, he
adopted a 4-3-3 system in
which wingers were
redundant, suffered constant
jibes for his so-called
negativity, and proceeded to
show the pundits that he was
right and they were wrong.

Ever cautious and
seemingly aloof, Ramsey
never truly captured popular
affection even after winning
the World Cup – although he

Alf Ramsey was the England manager at the time of their finest hour, namely winning the World Cup Final in 1966. Unfortunately, like all England managers, Ramsey later received criticism from fans and from the press. He was accused of being haughty and aloof and was eventually blamed for inflicting a 'dull' approach on the whole of English football. Sir Alf was dismissed after England failed to qualify for the World Cup in 1974.

rejoiced in the esteem and loyalty of his players – and was blamed often for inflicting a 'dull' approach on the whole of English football.

When England were eliminated in Mexico, Ramsey was again vilified for his tactics and few publicly mourned his dismissal. His achievements, if not his demeanour, had merited a more sympathetic send-off.

RANGERS

Founded 1873

Joined League 1890 (Division 1, founder member)

Honours Scottish League Division 1 Champions 1891 (joint with Dumbarton), 1899, 1900, 1901, 1902, 1911, 1912, 1913, 1918, 1920, 1921, 1923, 1924, 1925, 1927, 1928, 1929, 1930, 1931, 1933, 1934, 1935, 1937, 1939, 1947, 1949, 1950, 1953, 1956, 1957, 1959, 1961, 1963, 1964, 1975; Scottish League Premier Division Champions 1976, 1978, 1987, 1989, 1990, 1991, 1992, 1993, 1994, 1995; Scottish Cup Winners 1894, 1897, 1898, 1903, 1928, 1930, 1932, 1934, 1935, 1936, 1948, 1949, 1950, 1953, 1960, 1962, 1963, 1964, 1966, 1973, 1976, 1978, 1979, 1981, 1992, 1993; Scottish League Cup Winners 1947, 1949, 1961, 1962, 1964, 1965, 1971, 1976, 1978, 1979, 1982, 1984, 1985, 1987, 1988, 1989, 1991, 1993; European

Cup Winners' Cup Winners 1972

Ground Ibrox Stadium

Rangers Football Club is unique. It is unique because in the fabric of Scottish culture it is more, much more, than just a football club. It has dominated the Scottish game for a century, but more than that, the march of Scottish history has made it an institution which embodies the conservative, unionist, loyalist, Presbyterian ethic, in direct contrast to the other great Glasgow club, Celtic, which is identified with the Catholic religion and the Republic of Ireland. Other cities around the world – Milan, Turin, Madrid, Rio, Buenos Aires – have intense inter-club rivalries, but nowhere else are these based on religion.

The Rangers club was formed in Glasgow in 1872/73 by a group of youths from the Grairloch area of the west of Scotland. They first played on Fleshers' Haugh on Glasgow Green, the city's great open space, then moved west to Burnbank and Kinning Park before settling on the present location at Ibrox in 1899. In those early days the game in Scotland was amateur, centred on Glasgow and the west. The fixtures were friendly with the exception of the Scottish Cup, which began in season 1873/74. Queen's Park, the

George Young, one of the post-war greats of Scottish football, playing for his country in 1951/52. He was a strong tackling centre-half who starred in the treble-winning Rangers side of 1948/49. George won 53 caps for Scotland, making him the most capped Glasgow Rangers player.

dominant club of the time, won the first three competitions. Rangers were finalists in 1877 and 1879 but not until 1894 did they win, and their Scottish Cup record since has been uneven. From 1903 to 1928 they went 25 years without a win, and to date they have recorded 26 victories.

The Scottish League Championship was altogether another matter. Joint champions with Dumbarton in the very first year of the competition, 1890/91, Rangers, to the end of season 1994/95, have been outright champions a record 44 times.

Great names sprinkle the Rangers story. There was an outstanding team at the turn of the century, famous for the full-back partnership of Nick Smith and Jock Drummond, and Alec Smith, the outside-left with the club for 21 years from 1894 to 1915. In 1898/99 Rangers won all of their 18 League matches, considered to be a world record. Before the First World War, Neilly Gibson, Jacky Robertson, Alec Bennett and R.C.Hamilton were famous Rangers names.

The 1920s and 1930s were decades which saw brilliant Rangers teams and players such as the great Alan Morton, considered by many to have been the greatest Rangers player of all, Andy Cunningham, Davie Meiklejohn, an inspiring captain, Bob McPhail, George Brown, Dougie Gray and Jerry Dawson. After the Second World War there came the famous 'Iron Curtain' defence of Brown; Young and Shaw; McColl, Woodburn and Cox, backing exceptional forwards in Willie Waddell and Willie Thornton.

Since the passing of that team in the 1950s, outstanding Rangers players have included Eric Caldow, Ian McMillan, Jim Baxter, Willie Henderson, John Greig and Derek Johnstone, but perhaps the greatest of all Rangers names has been that of Bill Struth, manager from 1920 to 1957. In his reign, Rangers won 18 Championships and 10 Scottish Cups. In European competition, Rangers were finalists in the Cup Winners' Cup in 1961 and 1967, and winners in 1972.

The club has known tragedy. At a Scotland v England match in 1902, 25 fans died when part of Ibrox's wooden terracing collapsed. From then on, earthen embankments became the norm. Then on 2 January 1971, 66 lives were lost on embankment exit steps at the New Year game against Celtic. The same Willie Waddell, now the club manager, realised that the huge and old-fashioned Ibrox, which held 80,000 that day, was becoming obsolete. The rebuilding of a modern Ibrox eventually began in 1978 and was finished in 1981. On completion of additional work in 1993 it had a capacity of 50,000, all seated, all under cover.

There were critical dates for Rangers in the decade of the 1980s. In 1986 Graeme Souness was appointed manager of the club. Following a distinguished career with Scotland, Liverpool and Sampdoria, Souness brought an international flavour to

Rangers need to win the European Cup. This isn't official club policy but the trophy would be seen as the reward for the investment that has gone into the club; it would also equal Celtic's achievement, perhaps a more pressing requirement! In recent years there have been some stirring campaigns, but no real suggestion that success is just around the corner. A good Rangers side in 1992/93 played well, with Ally McCoist (seen here celebrating Nisbet's goal in a 2-1 defeat of Bruges at Ibrox) leading the line. They failed to progress beyond the group stages, however, as have successive sides. Some critics suggest that the overall quality of Scottish league football needs to improve before Rangers can match Europe's best.

Rangers by importing such exceptional English players as Terry Butcher, Chris Woods, Trevor Steven and Gary Stevens, paying huge transfer fees, and no doubt wages, to do it. Ray Wilkins from Paris St Germain, and Richard Gough, the Tottenham Hotspur captain, and the first Scottish 'Million Pound' player, were others. Souness left the club abruptly in April 1991 after five years to manage Liverpool and was succeeded by the assistant manager Walter Smith. In his first full season, Smith won the double of championship and League Cup, in his second, the treble, adding the Scottish Cup to the others. He continued the Souness policy of signing outstanding international players such as Alexei Mikhailichenko from Sampdoria, Brian Laudrup from A.C. Milan and Basile Boli from Olympique Marseille. Rangers have retained the championship each year that Walter Smith has been in charge and with seven consecutive wins after the 1994/95 season, they were in hot pursuit of Celtic's record nine successive wins.

RE-ELECTION

The original 1888 rule was that the bottom four Football League clubs would have to seek re-election at the end of each season. The number was reduced to three (in 1896) and two (in 1909). When the Division 3 (N) was formed in 1921, the number was again extended to four – two from Division 3 (N) and two from Division 3 (S). From 1958 it was the bottom four in the newly formed Fourth Division, until 1986/87, when the system of automatically relegating one club to non-League status was introduced.

Since the formation of the Third Division, the clubs facing re-election the most times were as follows: Hartlepool (14), Halifax Town (12), Barrow (12), Southport (11), Crewe Alexandra (10), Newport County (10) and Rochdale (10).

Re-election was determined by votes cast by League clubs and associate members. A variety of voting systems were used over the years, but the collective weight of higher division clubs was always greater than that of other interested parties. On occasions, the re-election voting resulted in a tie between two clubs. In second ballots, Stockport County defeated Doncaster Rovers in 1901, Torquay United defeated Aberdare in 1927, Chester defeated Nelson in 1931, Hereford United defeated Barrow in 1972 and Wigan Athletic defeated Southport in 1978. In 1950 Scunthorpe and Lindsey United defeated Wigan Athletic on a third ballot. But the closest voting came in 1908, when Tottenham Hotspur and Lincoln City tied on the first three ballots. The matter went to the League management committee, who voted five to three in favour of Tottenham.

New Brighton (1951), Bradford Park Avenue (1970), Barrow (1972), Workington (1977) and Southport (1978) have all lost Football League status on a post-war re-election vote. Three clubs have narrowly missed achieving League status: Mitchell St George's (by two votes in 1889), Yeovil Town (by three in 1976) and Altrincham (by one vote in 1980).

READING

Founded 1871

Joined League 1920 (Division 3, founder member)

Honours Division 2 Champions 1994; Division 3 (S) Champions 1926; Division 3 Champions 1986; Division 4 Champions 1979

Ground Elm Park

After half a century of League membership during which Reading experienced just one promotion from Division 3 and subsequent relegation, the 1970s and 1980s saw the 'Royals' transformed into soccer yo-yos. In two decades of frantic

activity they made eight trips between divisions, with three spells in the Fourth and one, from 1984 to 1986 under the guidance of Ian Branfoot, in the old Second.

Yet the Third, of which Reading were founder members, seemed to be their natural habitat.

After returning to it in 1931 following a five-year sojourn at the higher level, they remained there for 40 years despite many valiant attempts at betterment, notably under Ted Drake in the early 1950s.

Reading, whose greatest FA Cup achievement was defeating Manchester United and Portsmouth on the way to the 1927 semi-final, are disadvantaged in the quest for lasting progress by their proximity to London, whose major venues offer all-too-attractive alternatives to Elm Park. One avenue for possible advancement was closed when talks in the mid 1980s about a merger with Oxford United came to nothing. However, the picture changed with the arrival of Mark McGhee as manager in 1991. He constructed an entertaining side from a sound base, and in 1994 they lifted the new Second Division title. Then the ambitious Scot departed for Leicester, leaving Jimmy Quinn and Mick Gooding to become joint player-managers, a pairing that nearly brought premiership soccer to Elm Park.

REFEREES

In the early 1990s English football referees were under the microscope as at no other time. In an attempt to eradicate the 'professional foul', FIFA had directed 1990 World Cup referees to send off players committing such an offence, and the ruling was extended to national associations. Problems of interpretation soon arose, however, particularly with regard to such matters as intent, fouls in the penalty area, and handball. The result was inconsistency and confusion, with some baffling decisions.

This controversy highlights three crucial elements in modern refereeing which have broader implications: the role of television, the assimilation of law changes and new directives, and the referee's right to use his discretion.

The first is of increasing significance. The luxury of slow-motion replays allows studio pundits to analyse and criticise the instantaneous decisions of officials. In December 1990 the FA declared that, in exceptional circumstances, video evidence might be used in a player's prosecution or appeal. The lower reaches of football not having access to such resources, this runs counter to the unspoken principle of the uniformity of the laws and their implementation, regardless of the level. Similar objections are voiced against the idea of replays on giant screens in the major stadiums, which would permit a referee to change a decision but might also undermine his authority. However, another possible American import – microphone-linked referees explaining their decisions to the crowd – seems a logical extension of the red and yellow card system which was first introduced in the 1970 World Cup. Such striking additions to the referee's traditional equipment of stopwatch, wristwatch, coin, pencil, notebook whistle and cards may well become a reality one day.

Short-term problems of interpretation occur, typically, when new or modified laws are introduced. More lasting, and more irritating, are the varying interpretations throughout the world. British referees, for example, are generally considered too lenient in permitting challenges from behind – the subject of an international crackdown from the 1994 World Cup onwards – whereas continental referees are seen as naive in matters of time-wasting and play-acting.

English Premiership referees receive £300 per match, linesmen half that, with extra payment for Cup Finals and internationals;

How times change. Neatly bow-tied and jacketed, referee J.T. Howcroft supervises the toss-up at the start of the match with Billy Flint (Notts County) and Frank Barson (Aston Villa, right), respective captains in this 1925 First Division encounter.

their Football League equivalents receive £165 and £82.50p. In 1888 referees got 10s 6d (52$\frac{1}{2}$p) and in 1896 linesmen got 5s (25p).

Expenses were first allowed in 1946. There are frequent calls for full-time professional referees. In 1993/94 Italian referees joined their Brazilian counterparts with salaries starting from £48,000.

A good referee is unobtrusive, demonstrates a sense of humour and explains decisions if necessary. Using his discretion, he is guided by the spirit and feel of the game as much as by the letter of the law.

The referee's authority goes beyond the confines of the pitch and the time-span of the game. Players have been booked for comments made in the car park after a game, and in the changing room before a game. The referee can caution managers and trainers. He judges the suitability of the pitch, the equipment and the players' apparel.

Surveys show managers, teachers and lecturers to be the main professional groups among League referees.

It can be a hazardous occupation, with such ignominies as assault, kidnapping, and death at the hands of enraged spectators not unknown. All this is a far cry from the nineteenth century when players appealed, in the manner of cricketers, to the umpire (each team supplied one) officiating in the relevant half of the pitch.

In the 1871 FA Cup a neutral referee was used to make decisions when the umpires could not agree. Gradually the referee's powers increased until in 1891, disputes having become wearyingly common, he controlled the game from the pitch and the umpires helped from the

touchlines, thus establishing the system used today. Three years later the referee made decisions without waiting for players' appeals. Today's linesman is a fully qualified referee, but usually specialises; problems arise, as in the 1990 World Cup, when officials not used to running the line take on that duty.

The diagonal system of refereeing was introduced after the Second World War to halve the distance covered by linesmen.

In addition to earning their FA badge, League officials have to pass a fitness test. (It is estimated that referees cover, on average, 7 miles in a match.) They also, despite the belief of partisan spectators, undergo an eyesight test. The age limit is 47, but that is currently under review and expected to drop. Referees may be subject to assessment at any time as they carry out their duties. There are regular seminars and meetings as governing bodies seek to improve the officiating of matches.

In 1974 Englishman Jack Taylor became the first referee to award a penalty in a World Cup Final – almost as soon as the game started. In the same half he awarded one to the other side, West Germany, who beat Holland 2-1. His contemporary Clive Thomas, George Courtney

and Gordon Hill were other British referees with great FA Cup and international experience. A prominent name from the past is Major Francis Marindin who played in two FA Cup Finals, refereed eight and retired as FA President in 1890.

Compared with other sports, football administrators have generally left the rules of the game alone. Some well considered changes have led to considerable improvement, and others have caused some controversy. One recent alteration required referees to send off players who deliberately prevented a goalscoring opportunity by a so-called 'professional' foul. Goalkeepers were frequently early victims of this rule, pulling down players who tried to round them, both conceding a penalty and getting themselves sent off. Oldham Athletic 'keeper Paul Gerrard is shown the red card by referee Mike Bailey from Cambridge. Gerrard had just downed Southend United's Ricky Otto. Southend won the match 1-0, and Oldham were left to rue the rule changes and the referees' interpretation of them.

REPUBLIC OF IRELAND

Organised football in the southern part of Ireland began in 1883 when the Dublin Association club was formed. From the earliest days, however, Irish soccer clubs have had to compete for spectator interest with rugby, hurling and gaelic football.

Ireland's achievement of independence from British rule led to the formation of the Republic of Ireland (Eire) in December 1921. The six northern counties remained part of the United Kingdom (Northern Ireland). One consequence of this split was the formation of the Football Association of Ireland (FAI). This was recognised by FIFA in August 1923 but opposed by the British FAs, especially the Irish Football Association (Northern Ireland). A temporary change of name, to the 'Football Association of the Irish Free State', helped appease the Northern Irish for a while, but it remained an issue until after the Second World War.

The Football League of Ireland began in 1921/22, and that season St James's Gate won the League and Cup double. This has since been achieved by Shamrock Rovers (six times), Bohemians, Cork United, Cork Athletic, Dundalk and Derry City. Shamrock Rovers' record number of Cup wins (23) includes six in succession in the 1960s. Cork United won five League titles out of six in the 1940s – the League of Ireland continued throughout the war – and Shamrock Rovers won four on the trot from 1983/84 to 1986/87, taking their record of League wins to 14, extended to 15 in 1994. The League has usually contained a dozen teams, a separate shield competition extending the season.

In 1985 the League was extended to two divisions – the Premier Division and the First Division. This led to the fascinating rise of Derry City, a team from Northern Ireland with a Catholic, nationalist following. Derry had played in the (Northern) Irish League until 1972, but now re-formed to join the Republic's First Division across the border. This meant that Derry played all their away games in another country. They won promotion at the second attempt and two years later won a remarkable treble: the League of Ireland Championship, the FA of Ireland Cup and the League Cup.

Since 1957/58 Irish teams have competed in the three major European club competitions but have never got beyond the second round. Finn Harps have the unenviable record of losing one game 12-0, to Derby County in 1976.

One of the features of Irish soccer is that promising young players are quickly whisked away to mainland Britain. Some of the most famous post-war players in the Football and Scottish Leagues grew up in the Republic, men such as John Carey, Charlie Hurley, Johnny Giles, Tony Dunne, Noel Cantwell, Gerry Daly, Don Givens, Pat Bonner, Liam Brady, David O'Leary, Frank Stapleton and Ronnie Whelan, but between them they played very few League of Ireland games. Others, such as Alan Kelly, Paddy Mulligan and Mick Martin, won their first caps for Irish clubs before being quickly

Ray Houghton's goal, the fans' delight, Jack Charlton's disbelief... all of these remind us of 13 June 1994, when the Republic beat Italy 1-0 in New York. The game also provided other memories, not least the performance of 'unknowns' such as Jason McAteer, the young Bolton midfielder/forward. It was the determination, and confidence, of youngsters like McAteer which helped unsettle the bigger names in the Italian side.

signed by English clubs, in their cases Preston North End, Chelsea and Manchester United. Over the years, Manchester United have signed more players from the Republic than any other British club.

Irish soccer received a boost in 1971, when a rule change allowed countries to field non-native players in internationals, providing that such players had an Irish (in this case) parent and their native country had not claimed them first. The rule was later extended to include other close relatives, and more than 40 non-nationals have been adopted into the Irish team, including stalwarts like Tony Grealish, Mark Lawrenson, Mick McCarthy, John Aldridge, Andy Townsend and Ray Houghton.

REPUBLIC OF IRELAND TEAM

An international team representing the Republic of Ireland played its first games at the 1924 Olympic Games and reached the quarter-finals. On 21 September 1949 the Republic became the first country outside the United Kingdom to defeat England on English soil, winning 2-0 at Goodison Park, Everton. The team included nine players from English clubs and two from Shamrock Rovers.

The Republic of Ireland entered the World Cup qualifying competition as early as 1934, failing to qualify for the finals on goal average. In 1966 they lost 1-0 to Spain in a qualifying play-off, and in 1982 failed on goal difference after taking three points from World Cup runners-up Holland and beating France (who finished fourth in the competition).

Success finally came in 1990, when Englishman Jack Charlton successfully managed the team through the qualifying group to the Italia '90 tournament. In Italy they drew four games – beating Romania in an exciting penalty shoot-out – before losing 1-0 to the hosts in the quarter-finals. Four

years later Charlton led them to the second phase of the final tournament, beating Italy thanks to a sensational strike by Ray Houghton, but then falling away in intensely humid conditions, losing to Mexico and drawing with Norway before bowing out to Holland. The Republic reached the quarter-finals of the European Championship as early as 1964 (when the tournament was known as the European Nations' Cup), losing heavily to Spain over two legs. Although always capable of producing a good result such as the 2-1 win in Czechoslovakia in 1967 and a 3-0 home win against USSR in 1974, the Republic did not qualify for the last eight until Charlton's team did so in 1988. They began the European finals with a 1-0 win over England, drew with the USSR and then lost narrowly to Holland. The late Dutch winner stopped the Republic from reaching the semi-finals.

RIVELINO, Roberto

1946 Born in Sao Paulo, Brazil

1964 First appearance for Corinthians

1968 International debut for Brazil, v Mexico

1970 Scores three goals in World Cup finals, helping Brazil to win the trophy for third time

1975 Signs for Fluminense

1978 Signs £4 million contract with Saudi Arabian team Al-Ahly

Even among that most colourful collection of Brazilian footballers, the 1970 team that won the Jules Rimet Trophy for ever, Rivelino stood out. A small, mustachioed figure, his buccaneering style and flamboyant gestures seemed to be the essence of Latin American football and he was popular with the spectators, who loved to watch his long-range pots at goal, readily forgiving his wilder efforts. The Brazil team of that era was one of the most fluid, their intricate

passing and switching runs around the penalty area resembling, at times, nothing so much as the exhibition teamwork of the basketball entertainers the Harlem Globetrotters. Such a framework suited the Corinthian, as he alternated between left-wing and left of midfield. He was a superb passer of the ball, but will be best remembered for his shooting. Even by Brazilian standards he was an exceptional striker of the ball, whether in open play or from a free kick. He could swerve, bend or dip the ball like no one else, negating the opposition's defensive wall, and such was the ferocity of his shots it is hard to believe that, on starting his career, he had to go on a special diet to build up his strength. Referees and opponents might be more inclined to recall the extravagant rolling he would indulge in when fouled in order to cross the 18-yard line and persuade the official to award a penalty instead of a free-kick!

Rivelino came to wide notice in the 1970 World Cup tournament with three goals – a feat he was to repeat four years later. The 1978 tournament, however, was a

Roberto Rivelino scored three goals in the 1970 World Cup finals, helping Brazil to win the trophy for the third time. The club for which Rivelino played during the greater part of his career, Corinthians, took their name from the famous club of the same name, whose all-conquering tour of Brazil in 1910 fired the imagination of the public. In 1926 Corinthians Paulisto (to give them their full name) had their own tour of Europe.

disappointment both personally and nationally, and precipitated his move to the Middle East. He won 120 caps – more even than Pele – but whether all of those matches truly merited full international status is often the subject of debate.

ROBSON, Bobby

1933 Born in Sacriston, County Durham

1950 Gives up job as apprentice electrician to sign for Fulham

1951 Makes senior debut as inside-forward

1956 Joins West Bromwich Albion for £25,000

1957 Wins first of 20 England caps, scoring twice in 4-0 Wembley defeat of France

1958 Plays in World Cup finals in Sweden, losing place to Peter Broadbent after two games

1960 England comeback, at wing-half, against Spain in Madrid

1962 August – returns to Craven Cottage for £20,000

1967 Gives up playing to become manager of Vancouver Royals

1968 Back to Fulham as manager; gets sacked after nine months

1969 Becomes boss of Ipswich Town

1978 East Anglians beat Arsenal to win FA Cup

1981 Leads his club to UEFA Cup triumph and second place in League

1982 Another runners-up spot for Ipswich, then Robson succeeds Ron

Greenwood as England manager

1984 England fail to qualify for European Championship finals

1986 Robson's men reach World Cup quarter-finals, then fall victim to Maradona and the 'Hand of God'

1988 The team flop in the European Championships, losing all three matches

1990 England ride their luck into the last four of the World Cup; Robson resigns to take over the Dutch club PSV Eindhoven

1992 Moves to Portugal as coach of Sporting Lisbon

1993 Though Sporting are riding high in League, they sack Robson following surprise UEFA Cup exit

1994 Robson guides new club, Porto, to European Cup semi-finals

Bobby Robson's eight-year reign as England manager ended on a higher note than had seemed remotely likely to anyone who had followed the team's fortunes in the run-up to the 1990 World Cup. An exit at the semi-final stage – and then only by means of a penalty shoot-out – represented riches indeed for a man who had been hounded mercilessly by the press for several years.

He was accused of inept selection, an excess of tactical caution and a general failure to knit a collection of talented individuals – the likes of John Barnes, Gary Lineker and Glenn Hoddle – into a winning team. The vilification, much of which was cruel, hysterical or both, caused deep hurt to a sensitive, decent man who probably should have stepped down after his side's disastrous showing in the 1988 European Championships. Their subsequent improvement in the latter stages of Italia '90 came only after the pressure was lifted by close wins over Belgium and Cameroon.

As a player Robson had been at his best as his country's midfield foil for Johnny Haynes in the early 1960s, while his managerial peak was at Ipswich where,

The England manager from 1982 to 1990, Bobby Robson, discusses strategy with his captain and namesake Bryan. This photograph was obviously taken early in Bobby Robson's England managerial career as his hair is not yet grey, the weight of the world does not appear to be on his shoulders and Bryan Robson looks fit. Bryan was his manager's ideal player: wholehearted, fearless and tireless. It is Bryan Robson's level of skill, however, that sets him aside from other lesser players who, nonetheless, show the same commitment to their game. Although some international teams may be ahead in technique, they know that British players will not be outplayed through a purely physical approach.

had he had the resources to assemble a bigger squad, he might have lifted several League Championships.

ROBSON, Bryan

1957 Born in Chester-le-Street, County Durham

1974 Turns professional with West Bromwich Albion

1976 Suffers first of three broken legs in one season

1980 Wins first England cap, v Republic of Ireland at Wembley

1981 Joins Manchester United for £1.5 million, becoming Britain's most expensive player

1982 June – scores against France just 27 seconds into England's World Cup campaign in Spain; succeeds Ray Wilkins as captain of club and country

1983 Lifts the FA Cup after netting twice in replayed Final against Brighton

1985 May – another FA Cup triumph, this time against Everton; Aug-Oct – skippers United to 10 straight League wins at start of season; then sustains injury and 10-point lead disappears

1986 Dislocates collar-bone and is forced out of Mexico World Cup

1990 May – first captain to collect third FA Cup; pulls out of second successive World Cup due to injury

1991 Captains United to triumph in European Cup Winners Cup

1993 Finally pockets League title medal...

1994 ... then makes it two in a row, before leaving to manage Middlesbrough; also joins England set-up as one of Terry Venables' right-hand men

1995 Leads 'Boro' to First Division title.

When Manchester United manager Ron Atkinson wondered how much he should offer for the signature of Bryan Robson, no less a soccer sage than Bill Shankly had no doubt: 'Pay whatever you have to, just make sure you get him.' As usual, the shrewd Scot was offering gilt-edged advice. Atkinson took it, and Robson went on to become, in the reckoning of most observers, the dominant British midfielder of the 1980s. A dynamo in defence, attack and all points between, he became a motivator supreme for the 'Red Devils' and England. At its peak the Robson game had no discernible weakness; his tackling, passing, shooting and heading were exemplary, he was quick and strong, and he read the game immaculately.

His sole bane was injury, which disrupted some of United's most promising campaigns as well as depriving England of their most inspirational figure. Some claimed he was too brave, but to ask him to hold back would have been to deny his nature and nullify his special talent. After winning two Championship medals, Robson kicked off his managerial career at Middlesbrough, where he began by lifting the First Division Championship. Many within the game foresee the day when he will return to Old Trafford as successor to Alex Ferguson – a tall order, even for Captain Marvel.

ROCHDALE

Founded 1907

Joined League 1921 (Division 3 N)

Honours None

Ground Spotland

Despite their tradition of travail as one of Lancashire's football minnows, Rochdale can claim one distinction which is unlikely to be equalled: they are the only club from the Football League basement to reach the final of a major competition. That was in 1962, when they contested the two-leg climax of the League Cup with Norwich City, losing 4-0 on aggregate. Admittedly, many top sides had not entered a competition which was still in its infancy, but it was nevertheless a remarkable achievement.

The Spotland club's League record, in contrast, has been wholly humble. After 38 years in Division 3 they were relegated in 1959, since when they have been promoted once, only to drop again. Their most promising period was in the mid 1920s, when three attempts to reach the Second Division ended in narrow failure.

In view of the local competition, Rochdale – managed for a spell in the 1950s by Harry Catterick – have done well to survive for so long. Their finances were boosted in 1990 when they reached the last 16 of the FA Cup.

ROMARIO

1966 Born into poor family in Jacarezinho, a shanty suburb of Rio

1983 Signs for first professional club, Olaria

1985 Joins Vasco da Gama, scoring 73 times in 123 outings

1987 Helps Vasco win Rio State Championship for first of two successive years

1988 Debut for Brazil, scoring winner against Australia in Melbourne; top scorer and silver medallist in Olympic Games

1989 Moves to Dutch club PSV Eindhoven, with whom he pockets three championship medals and two cup winner's gongs; helps Brazil win Copa America, grabbing only goal of final against Uruguay

1993 Top scorer in Dutch league for fourth time in five years, netting a total of 125 times; joins Barcelona and helps them to Spanish title

1994 By common consent, Romario is the brightest star as Brazil win the World Cup in the United States

1995 Clashes with Barcelona boss Johan Cruyff, joins Rio club Flamengo for £4 million

It was the most widely quoted football prophesy since Alf Ramsey had pledged England's victory in 1966. It came 28 years later and ran along these lines: 'This is *my* World Cup; nobody is closer to the yearning of Brazil's people; nobody is more likely to fulfil their dreams.' The words came

Unlike some of his South American contemporaries, Romario had a very successful career in Europe, playing for very different clubs in PSV Eindhoven and Barcelona. He is seen here playing for the Spanish side in their 2-2 draw with Manchester United in the 1994/95 European Cup. Close skills and sudden acceleration helped him record many of his goals – as did his abundant confidence.

at the outset of USA '94 from Romario de Souza Faria. It was an immodest little speech, entirely in character with the man, but in the end it was substantially accurate. When the dust had settled on Brazil's triumph in Pasadena, who would argue with the stocky striker's assessment of himself as the planet's foremost footballer?

Romario has the priceless knack of scoring goals, no matter how tightly he is marked. One moment strutting with apparent indolence, the next he can be searing the grass, tearing into space to receive a pass and drill a ferocious shot into the net, usually giving the goalkeeper no vestige of a chance to save it.

The effectiveness of the Brazilian's staccato bursts are underpinned by exquisite control, immense strength and the intelligence to time his runs to perfection.

True, he can be selfish, sulky and prone to unbecoming tantrums, as many a coach will testify. But Romario's moments of quicksilver intuition, his incisive distribution and, above all, his golden goals, pay for everything.

ROSS COUNTY

Founded 1929

Joined League 1994

Ground Victoria Park Dingwall

The story of senior football in Dingwall goes back to 1888, when Ross County were founder members of the North of Scotland FA. Their first stay in the Highland League was brief, but in 1929 football in Dingwall was revived, and since then County have been Highland League champions three times, and winners of all the trophies in Northern football. Twice winners of the Scottish Qualifying Cup, in 1973/74 and 1993/94, the nineties saw County with the most successful team in the club's history, winning and retaining the Highland League championship (1990/91 and

91/92) and the Highland, North of Scotland and Inverness Cups. Indeed in 1991/92 they won all three cups in addition to their league championship.

In the Scottish Cup proper, they had done their share of giant-killing against League clubs. In 1965/66, they beat Forfar and Alloa before Rangers were more than happy to leave Dingwall with a 2-0 win. Ross County were invited to join the new Third Division when the Scottish League was extended from 38 to 40 clubs in the summer of 1994. On the eve of the vote, as it were, Ross County made their point in another memorable cup run, beating St Cuthbert's 11-0 and Forfar Athletic 4-0. In the league they missed promotion by only one place in 1995.

ROTHERHAM UNITED

Founded 1884

Joined League 1893 (Division 2)

Honours Division 3 (N) Champions 1951; Division 3 Champions 1981; Division 4 Champions 1989

Ground Millmoor

United, who took their current title when Rotherham Town and Rotherham County merged in 1925, have made a fair fist of surviving and, at times, prospering in the shadow of Sheffield.

Town spent three seasons in Division 2 but were not re-elected in 1896 and

Sir Stanley Rous, seen here on Wembley duty, had his active career cut short by the Second World War. However he had refereed many important games before becoming an administrator. Sir Stanley loved the game of football passionately. He saw football on a global scale and as president of FIFA did much to encourage the growth of European club competitions, and to aid the development of the sport in emerging nations.

Rotherham's name did not appear in the League again until 1919, when County entered the same flight. After relegation in 1923, the club was to spend nearly 30 years in the Third Division, despite spirited and narrowly unsuccessful efforts to gain promotion in the immediate post-war years. They finally made it in 1951, a triumph which signalled the start of their finest era.

Under the management of former Millmoor stalwart Andy Smailes and driven on by long-serving wing-half Danny Williams, United missed a Division 1 place on goal average in 1955. Though never coming so close again, they remained a solid member of the Second Division until 1968, and in 1961 reached the first Final of the League Cup, losing on aggregate to Aston Villa.

Much commuting between divisions followed, with the old Third being their usual berth. Notable former players include Dave Watson, who went on to become

England's centre-half in the 1970s, and among big-name bosses have been Tommy Docherty, Norman Hunter and Emlyn Hughes.

Like most small clubs the recent past is peppered with financial crises – the club was in receivership at one stage. Current Chairman, Ken Booth, who owns the huge scrap yard adjoining Milmoor, has brought stability but has indicated that he wants to sell out. A recently appointed management duo of ex-Clough prodigies Archie Gemmill and John McGovern have placed the accent on youth with Bermudan international Shaun Goater looking set for a higher division.

ROUS, Sir Stanley

1896 Born in Norfolk

1934 Referees FA Cup Final between Manchester City and Portsmouth; succeeds Sir Frederick Wall as Football Association Secretary

1946 Plays prime role in promoting England's first national coaching scheme

1949 Receives knighthood in recognition of services to soccer

1962 Leaves FA post, becomes President of the International Federation of Football Associations

1974 Retires from FIFA

1986 Dies at the age of 91

Sir Stanley Rous stands unrivalled as the premier administrator – perhaps statesman would be a more apt description – in the history of world football. A tall, distinguished individual of immense personal presence, he was that rare being, an original thinker. Sir Stanley never progressed beyond village football as a player but he loved the game passionately, and his refereeing, which dovetailed neatly with his duties as a sports master, allowed him to keep in close touch with football at all levels.

One of his earliest innovations was the diagonal system of refereeing, a more efficient and logical way of doing the job than the traditional haphazard method, but it was later, in his roles of FA Secretary and FIFA President, that he exerted his greatest influence. Sir Stanley – along with his protege Walter Winterbottom, the first England team manager – was responsible for the introduction of organised coaching, which did much to change the face of the British game. He saw football on a global scale, encouraging the growth of European club competitions, urging the home countries to overcome their prejudices and enter the World Cup for the first time, and aiding the growth of the game in developing countries. How delighted he would have been to have witnessed the progress of Cameroon in 1990.

Sir Stanley Rous was a true visionary; international soccer needs a figure of similar stature to guide the game into the new century.

The side that Arthur Rowe built at Tottenham Hotspur in the early 1950s outplayed opponents by virtue of skill and good passing. It was Rowe who introduced the 'push and run' style which involved quickfire passes by all ten outfield players. His 1950/51 Spurs side won the League Championship for the first time in the club's history.

ROWE, Arthur

1906 Born in Tottenham, London

1929 Turns professional with Spurs

1933 Plays major part in gaining promotion to First Division; December – wins sole England cap, v France at White Hart Lane

1935 Rowe's captaincy cannot avert relegation

1939 Cartilage operations end playing career; coaches in Hungary until outbreak of Second World War, then assumes control of British Army team

1945 Takes over at Chelmsford City, transforming them into one of the country's top non-League clubs

1949 Returns to White Hart Lane as manager

1950 Leads Spurs to Division 2 title…

1951 …and then lifts the Championship for the first time in Tottenham's history

1955 Retires from the game due to ill health

1960 Makes comeback, as boss of Crystal Palace

1963 Steps down at Selhurst Park as Dick Graham moves in

1971 Takes control of Soccer Hall of Fame in London

1993 Dies in London

Rowe was one of the major influences on British soccer in the post-war years. The clue to his success as an innovative manager with Tottenham Hotspur came in his playing days with the club; although a centre-half, he was never a mere stopper, employing a more constructive, thoughtful approach than most of his contemporaries.

When injury forced him to quit, Rowe took his expertise to Hungary, a nation which appreciated his reliance on skill. He was offered the job of managing the Magyars, but his ambitions in that direction were frustrated by the war.

Back at White Hart Lane, after a sojourn in the Southern League, he introduced his famous 'push and run' method, which involved quickfire 'wall passes' by all 10 outfield players. Using the nucleus of the squad assembled by his predecessor Joe Hulme – his

only expedition into the transfer market was to acquire the services of full-back Alf Ramsey – he brought unprecedented honours to the club. Some said he subsequently allowed his splendid side to grow old together, which is a matter for debate, but there is no doubting that Rowe – a man of intelligence and integrity, who worked himself into the ground – deserves his exalted place in the folklore of his beloved Spurs.

RUSH, Ian

1961 Born in St Asaph, Wales

1979 Turns professional with Chester

1980 April – signs for Liverpool in £300,000 deal; May – makes debut for

Wales, v Scotland at Hampden

1981 Picks up first of four consecutive League Cup winner's medals

1982 Helps the 'Reds' win first of four League titles in five years

1984 Takes part in European Cup Final victory over Roma

1986 Scores twice against Everton at Wembley as Liverpool secure the League and FA Cup double

1987 Joins Juventus for £3.2 million

1988 Returns to Anfield at a slightly reduced fee

1989 Comes on as substitute to net twice as Liverpool beat Everton to win the FA Cup

1990 Returns to peak form

as the Championship goes back to Anfield

1992 Pockets third FA Cup winner's medal and scores as Reds defeat Sunderland

1995 As new team captain, Rush leads Liverpool to Wembley triumph in the Coca Cola Cup

Rush is a predator supreme. No one since the heyday of Jimmy Greaves and Denis Law has shown a more ruthless aptitude for finding the net. Throughout the 1980s – with the exception of one unhappy season in the Italian sun – he contributed an avalanche of goals to the Liverpool cause.

After taking a season to settle at Anfield, the lean, angular Welshman played a huge part in keeping his new club's trophy cabinet well stocked, at first forging a

scintillating partnership with Kenny Dalglish, and later combining destructively with Peter Beardsley and John Barnes.

Rush's most obvious asset is speed, but he is also a delightfully crisp striker of the ball, boasts a finely-honed positional sense, and possesses more ball skills than he has been given credit for, although for a tall man he is not strong in the air.

On his return from Juventus, where he had suffered from a debilitating illness, he struggled for a time to find his form. When he succeeded, however, the Kop saw a more complete performer than ever before, a leader of the line who could shield the ball and create chances for colleagues, as well as adding to his own phenomenal tally for the Reds, which by 1995 stood at well in excess of 300.

Ian Rush, master goalscorer, tucks away Liverpool's second goal against Sunderland in the 1992 FA Cup Final. It is perhaps appropriate that Ian Rush's picture should appear alongside that of Arthur Rowe because it serves to remind us that good passing has always been an important part of soccer. Rush scores most of his goals as a result of being on the end of intricate passing movements by his Liverpool team-mates. Many of Rush's goals – over 300 for Liverpool — have been scored from close in, without great power but perfectly timed and angled.
Like some other great goalscorers, Rush also has the ability to remain cool when closely marked and heavily tackled.

ST JOHNSTONE

Founded 1884

Joined League 1911
(Division 2)

Honours Scottish League
Championship, First
Division, 1983, 1990;
Second Division, 1988;
Division 2, 1924, 1960,
1963

Ground McDiarmid Park

St Johnstone have a new
stadium (opened 1989) and a
lively side.

Perth's population is only
50,000 but its club has often
belied those limited
resources. Under future
Scotland manager Willie
Ormond they were
particularly unwelcome
opposition, narrowly losing
the League Cup Final of
1969/70 and, in 1971,
thrashing Hamburg 5-1 on
aggregate in a UEFA Cup tie.
At one point in 1986 they
were 38th and last in
Scotland but manager Alex
Totten engineered a
remarkable upsurge and
Premier League status was
regained in 1990. Under the
management of Paul
Sturrock, they were relegated
from the Premier Division
following league
reconstruction in 1994/95.

ST MIRREN

Founded 1877

Joined League 1890
(Division 1 founder club)

Honours Scottish League
Championship, First
Division, 1977; Division 2,
1968; Scottish Cup, 1926,
1959, 1987

Ground Love Street

St Mirren's attainment of
three Scottish Cups is a
remarkable achievement. In
1926 they beat Celtic
decisively in front of 100,000

at Hampden and the
supporters hastened back to
Paisley to watch footage of it
all that same evening at the
local cinema.

There was further work
for the cameras in 1959
when Aberdeen were
beaten 3-1 in the Scottish
Cup Final. The Saints'
dynamic young manager
Alex Ferguson succeeded in
rousing the citizenry (often a
problem for the club) in the
late seventies with a
precocious team. The
impetus hasn't totally died
away. One of Ferguson's
proteges, Tony Fitzpatrick,
later to manage the club,
played in the 1987 Final
when St Mirren beat
Dundee United to take their
third Scottish Cup. But
relegation from the Premier
League in 1992 was an
ominous setback.

SALARIES

Professionalism was not
recognised by the Football
Association until 1885, but
for almost ten years before
this players had various
financial arrangements with
clubs.

From 1901 to 1961 clubs
were bound to the Football
League's maximum-wage
rule. The weekly wage limit
varied – £4 (1901),
£5 (1910), £9 (1920),
£8 (1922), £10 (1946),
£12 (1947), £14 (1951),
£15 (1953), £17 (1957) and
£20 (1958) – but not all
players could be paid the
maximum, and the close-
season maximum was a
lower figure. In 1909 only
one Barnsley player was
paid the £4 maximum, two
earned 70 shillings (£3.50)
but the other first-teamers
were paid between 50
shillings (£2.50) and £3 a
week. The total wage bill for
23 players came to £57 10s
(£57.50).

Richard Holt summarises
the history of players' wages
in Sport and the British
(1989): 'Until very recently
professional sportsmen have
been regarded by directors as
skilled workmen; footballers'
incomes were not calculated
in the same way as transfer
fees according to market

value but in relation to what
other working-class men
could expect to earn… they
were paid about double
what a skilled man could
expect for a fifty-hour week
in return for working part-
time at something they
enjoyed.'

Clubs had the discretion
to pay loyal players benefit
money: a maximum of £750
for five years' service in the
post-war period. Top
footballers always had the
chance to supplement their
earnings but the post-war
advertising boom provided
more opportunities, probably
beginning with Denis
Compton and the hair lotion
called Brylcreem.

The late 1950s brought
opportunities to earn higher
salaries abroad, particularly
in Italy. In England, pressure
was put on the Football
League to find ways of
improving salaries. When
the players threatened to
strike – the proposed date
was 21 January 1961 – the
League agreed to a number
of alterations, the most
important of which was the
removal of the maximum
wage. This paved the way
for salary rises and playing
staff reductions. The
Eastham case (1963) showed
that clubs were in restraint of
trade unless they permitted
players a transfer, and even
greater bargaining power for
players came in April 1978,
when the old retain-and-
transfer system was replaced
by freedom of contract.

In the year ending 31
May 1976, Manchester City
had 13 employees earning
'emoluments' over £10,000.
This was a top First Division
club with eight internationals
and 31 professionals. Seven
years later the same club had
14 employees who earned
over £20,000, including one
in the £70,000 range. Stars'
wages have continued to rise
– in 1990 Derby County had
12 employees who earned
over £50,000, including
three £100,000 plus men –
and today it is not unknown
for a player to negotiate with
the help of an accountant, a
solicitor and an agent.
Figures of up to £20,000 per
week have been mentioned.
The sky, it seems, is the limit.

SANTOS, Nilton dos

1925 Born in Ilha do
Governador, Brazil

1942 Joins Botafogo

1950 International debut v
Uruguay

1958 Member of first
Brazilian team to win
World Cup

1962 Another World Cup
medal – at the age of 37

When, in 1956, Santos was
given the run-around by
Stanley Matthews at
Wembley in England's 4-2
victory, many felt that the
left-back was getting too old
for international soccer. Yet
he kept his place in the
victorious World Cup team
two years later,
demonstrating his attacking
ability in the Final against
Sweden, having scored
against Austria in one of the
earlier rounds. Such
versatility was a hallmark of
his style; strong on the ball,
he and the other Santos,
Djalma, his partner full-back,
would augment the attack
with their overlapping runs.
The pair teamed up again in
1962 to help Brazil retain
the trophy for another four
years.

Santos was captain of
Botafogo, the Rio de Janeiro
club, and his disciplinary
record was a good one; his
dismissal in an ill-tempered
match against Hungary in
the 1954 World Cup must
be counted as something of
an aberration. The lengthy
span of his service to the
national team means that at
various times he played
alongside Ademir, Pinto and
Julinho and the new
generation of stars such as
Amarildo and Pele.

SCARBOROUGH

Founded 1879

Joined League 1987
(Division 4)

Honours None

Ground McCain Stadium

Scarborough are a sparky
little outfit determined to
carve a lasting niche for
themselves in League

football, not the easiest of tasks in a Yorkshire seaside resort far removed in atmosphere from the traditional hotbeds of soccer passion.

Then bossed by Neil Warnock, they entered the League as the first club to earn automatic promotion as Vauxhall Conference champions, and made a solid start with 12th place in their first season. Better was to come in 1988/89 when a fifth-place finish put them in the play-offs, where they lost narrowly to Leyton Orient at the semi-final stage.

Thereafter, for several seasons, the 'Boro' consolidated their status and under manager Ray McHale turned their sights towards gradual betterment, though inevitably they must operate on a tight budget – travelling by car to away games within an 80-mile radius, and having to sell promising young players, such as defenders Chris and Craig Short, to survive.

A memorable highlight of 1992/93 was their League Cup triumph over Premier League Coventry City, coming back from a two-goal deficit to win late in the game, then going on to perish gloriously against Arsenal in the fourth round. However, come 1994/95 they were struggling to keep away from the foot of the Third Division and the spectre of a return to non-League football loomed menacingly.

SCHOEN, Helmut

1915 Born in Dresden

1932 Debut for Dresdner FC

1937 November – international debut v Sweden in which he scores twice

1940 Wins Cup medal for Dresdner FC

1941 Sweden are the opponents again, this time in his last international appearance; Dresdner win the Cup again

1943 League

Championship medal with Dresdner...

1944 ...and again

1955 His playing days over, Schoen is appointed assistant national team

The mild-mannered West German team manager raises the new World Cup trophy in 1974. This was the highlight of his managerial career and a just reward for years spent keeping the

West German team in competition for top honours. The only other national team manager with as long and successful a career as Schoen's is Argentina's Cesar Menotti.

1964 Becomes team manager on Herberger's retirement

1966 Takes West Germany to World Cup Final

1972 West Germany win European Championship

1974 World Cup victory

1976 West Germany lose European Championship to Czechoslovakia on penalty shoot-out

1978 Without Beckenbauer and Muller, Schoen's inspiration dries up and West Germany do not get beyond second round of World Cup finals; Schoen retires

Schoen scored 17 goals in 16 appearances for Germany but, inevitably, his international career was interrupted by the war, and a knee injury brought his playing days as an inside-forward to a premature end. His background was, in fact, an academic one, and he became a foreign correspondent after the war, learning French and English. He first took up coaching at a regional level, in the Saar, before getting involved with the national squad.

Germany, and then West Germany, had been a significant force in international football since the 1930s, but their claim to supremacy in Europe began with Schoen's managership. Some of soccer's finest ever players came under the diffident manager's command; there was no lack of skill or application on the pitch and Schoen was able to develop a fluid system, trusting his players' maturity and footballing intelligence to steer them through games.

Franz Beckenbauer was to Schoen what Fritz Walter had been to Sepp Herberger, and it is unfortunate that they should have fallen out after the national team's debacle in the 1978 World Cup, in which the manager's inconsistency in team selection and tactics exposed

his confusion. It is equally unfortunate that Schoen's retirement should be associated with defeat. He had brought together a splendid side to conquer Europe in 1972, and his 1974 World Cup-winning team, drawn largely from Bayern Munich, showed great character and resilience. Schoen had made changes throughout that 1974 tournament, like a mechanic tinkering with a Formula 1 engine; he unveiled a finely tuned machine when it mattered – in the Final.

SCHOOLBOY FOOTBALL

There are more children playing football regularly in Britain than there are adults. The growth and development of schools' football in England is linked largely with the English Schools' Football Association, acknowledged as the largest movement of its kind in the world. Similar programmes are provided by the Schools' Football Associations of Scotland, Wales and Northern Ireland.

Founded in 1904, the English Schools' FA has 468 member organisations, the 44 County Schools' Football Associations being subdivided into Area Associations. Some associations organise football for pupils of all ages (9-19), while others cater for either secondary-school pupils or pupils at primary and middle schools. All associations field representative teams, organise coaching and arrange league and cup competitions for schoolboys at different age levels. Nearly 14,000 schools are affiliated.

The English Schools' FA organises six national competitions. The oldest is the inter-association trophy for under-15s, which began in 1905. The most successful associations are Liverpool (12 wins), Sheffield (8), Manchester (7), Swansea (5), West Ham (4), Barnsley (3), Middlesbrough (3) and Sunderland (3). There are also national county

championships and individual schools' competitions at under-19 and under-16 levels, and, finally, the ESFA-Smith's Crisps 6-a-side Cup. This is the largest competition of its kind in the world. Almost 9000 primary schools enter, and the semi-finals and final are played at Wembley Stadium.

Internationals are played at under-15 and under-18 levels, and the four home countries compete for the Victory Shield. The two annual under-15 games played at Wembley attract crowds of up to 60,000. In 1959 Martin Peters (England) and Wolfgang Overath (West Germany) were Wembley opponents in a schoolboy international. Seven years later they met again in the same stadium in the World Cup Final.

Football authorities combine to promote festivals, coaching courses and award schemes, and every year fifteen or sixteen 14-year-olds are selected to attend the Football Association School of Excellence at Lilleshall. Promising players can link with professional clubs as 'associate schoolboys' when they reach the age of 14. Many schoolboys also represent county FAs in youth competitions, in particular the FA County Youth Challenge Cup.

SCOTLAND

In the mid-1800s, chasing and kicking a football took over from caber-tossing as the major leisure interest of the men in the Highlands. The 1860s Glasgow building boom spread this football interest to the Lowlands, and on 9 July 1867 Queen's Park Football Club was formed. For the first two years it was almost impossible to find

opponents, and the score of an 1869 game against Hamilton – Queen's Park won by four goals and nine touchdowns – shows that soccer was still evolving.

The first professional footballers were Scots. John Lang and Peter Andrews moved south from Glasgow to Sheffield in 1876 for the

Jimmy McGrory (left) and Jimmy McStay, both Celtic players, before a match between a Scottish League XI and an English League XI in 1928. They are wearing different socks, presumably because the players had to provide their own. The style of shirt is reminiscent of those worn by rugby players.

specific purpose of earning money. The Scottish FA, however, held out against legalising professionalism until 1893. As in England, though, players were paid for some years before professionalism was officially recognised.

Queen's Park dominated the early years of Scottish football, with 10 Scottish Cup wins in the first 20 seasons of the trophy (1873-93), but slipped away as a twentieth-century competitive force by remaining loyal to the amateur ethic. Their touch of class has been maintained by their presence at Hampden Park, Scotland's major stadium, opened by Queen's Park in 1903.

The history of professional soccer in

Scotland became dominated by the two big Glasgow clubs, Celtic and Rangers, nicknamed the 'Old Firm'. Rangers made their first appearance in a Scottish Cup Final in 1879 but failed to turn up for the replay with Vale of Leven after being incensed at a decision in the first game. Celtic were formed later (1887) and, more importantly, from a Catholic background. Religion became an omnipresent conflict between the Old Firm. In recent years, however, the fervently Protestant Rangers have departed from their policy of not signing Catholics, the most controversial acquisition being the ex-Celtic player Maurice Johnston for £1.5 million in July 1989.

The health of Scottish football does sometimes appear to go in tandem with the success of the national team. Scotland have achieved against the odds in reaching the final stages of recent World Cups, but have never done very well once at the tournament. In 1990 (they failed to qualify in 1994) their final group match was against Brazil. Scotland lost 1-0 when a draw might have seen them qualify beyond the initial stage. In the last minute of the game the ball fell to Maurice Johnston. He appeared to do everything right, hitting the ball cleanly and fiercely. It was only a remarkable reflex save by Brazilian 'keeper Taffarel that kept the ball, and Scotland, out.

Celtic had the edge in the period before the First World War, but Rangers won the Scottish League in 15 out of the 20 inter-war seasons. This was during the heyday of players such as Alan Morton, Davie Meiklejohn and Bob McPhail. In 1931 Celtic goalkeeper John Thomson was accidentally fatally injured when diving at the feet of a Rangers player during a game at Ibrox.

The dominance of Rangers continued after the Second World War when Jock Shaw captained a team known for 'iron curtain' defenders like George Young and Willie Woodburn. Rangers won the greater share of silverware in the first 20 post-war years. Then came Jock Stein's great Celtic team which took nine successive Scottish League Championships. In 1967 Celtic became the first British team to win the European Cup, beating Internazionale 2-1. The team that day was Simpson, Craig, Gemmell, Murdoch, McNeill, Clark, Johnstone, Wallace, Chalmers, Auld and Lennox. In the midst of Celtic's greatest consistent League success, Rangers also had to endure the tragedy of the 1971 Ibrox disaster, which took 66 lives.

There were occasional interruptions to the stranglehold of Rangers and Celtic. Hibernian produced a great team in the immediate post-war period, winning the League three times with their 'Famous Five' forward line of Gordon Smith, Bobby Johnstone, Lawrie Reilly, Eddie Turnbull and Willie Ormond. East Fife won both the Scottish Cup (1938) and the League Cup (1947/48) as a Second Division team; Aberdeen, Hearts and Kilmarnock all came through to win the League in the late 1950s or early 1960s; and Partick Thistle surprisingly smacked four early goals past Celtic in the 1972 League Cup Final.

But the removal of the maximum wage in England encouraged more Scottish players to move south in the 1960s. Only Rangers and Celtic were able to hold on to star players, and then only some of them. Indeed, the history of the English Football League is also the history of Scottish footballers.

The 1980s brought another eastern challenge to the Old Firm. In that decade, Aberdeen won the League Championship three times, the Scottish Cup four times and the League Cup twice. Central defenders Alex McLeish and Willie Miller were particularly important to that success. In 1982/83 they emulated Rangers in 1971/72 by winning the European Cup Winners' Cup, beating Real Madrid 2-1 after extra time. Dundee United were champions in 1982/83 and four years later became the first Scottish club to reach the UEFA Cup Final, losing 2-1 on aggregate to Gothenburg. But after Hearts had failed on goal difference to win the League in 1985/86, the next run of League champions had a familiar ring: Celtic, Rangers, Celtic and Rangers. The traditional Scotland-England exodus was now reversed. Star Englishmen such as Terry Butcher, Trevor Steven and Chris Woods moved north of the border to Rangers.

Football is one of the few remaining ways that Scotland can show it is not consumed by its British political identity. Scottish football retains its legacy of passion, pride and skill, and yet, during the 1980s, Scottish supporters behaved far better than their English counterparts.

There is much more to Scottish football than Scottish League clubs and internationals. The Highland League has existed since 1893, and 'Junior' football has always been a rich source of talent for the English game. And if you ever wish to rediscover the roots of soccer, walk across Glasgow Green on a fine spring evening. You will see all kinds of football games, a reminder of where the world's first professional soccer players learned their trade.

Don Masson scoring for Scotland past Welsh goalkeeper Dai Davies in the World Cup qualifier played at Anfield in 1977. This helped Scotland to a 2-0 victory and a place in the 1978 finals. This was the fourth time in succession that Scotland had beaten Wales in a World Cup match and the resultant qualification led to some hopes that the team might get near to lifting the trophy in Argentina. Disappointments against less fancied sides Peru and Iran sent the Scots home after the first round.

SCOTLAND NATIONAL TEAM

After the world's first international match – Scotland v England in 1872 – the early years belonged to Scotland, who lost only one of 31 internationals between 8 March 1873 and 17 March 1888. The decline in the early 1890s was largely self-inflicted since professional 'Anglo-Scots' were outlawed by the Scottish FA.

The Scots dominated British internationals again in the 1920s, culminating in a superb exhibition by the 'Wembley Wizards' in 1928 when England were beaten 5-1. Captained by Jimmy McMullan, the team became a legend, in particular the forward-line of Jackson, Dunn, Gallacher, James and Morton. But Scottish stars were again lured to England, there were difficulties obtaining releases for internationals, and Scotland slumped in the 1930s.

In the immediate post-war period, Scotland, like England, were faced with improving sides from mainland Europe. Slow to react to World Cup opportunities – Scotland qualified in 1950 but did not attend the finals – no impact was made until the 1974 World Cup, when Scotland started an incredible run of playing through five successive World Cup

qualifying tournaments. Managed by Willie Ormond, the 1974 team was one of Scotland's finest, boasting players of the calibre of Bremner, Law, McGrain, Hay, Dalglish and Lorimer. Although unbeaten, they failed to qualify for the second stage of the finals in West Germany.

There were also near misses in the World Cup finals in 1978 (when Ally McLeod's team came unstuck

against Peru and Iran), in 1982 (when Jock Stein's men went out on goal difference), in 1986 (when a team under the temporary charge of Alex Ferguson failed to beat 10-man Uruguay) and in 1990 (when Andy Roxburgh's team were eliminated by a late Brazilian goal).

Some memorable performances include post-war wins against England at Wembley in 1963 (2-1) and 1967 (3-2), and against Italy (1-0 in 1965), Holland (3-2 in 1978), Spain (3-1 in 1984) and Sweden (2-1 in 1990). Kenny Dalglish is the only player to have appeared in over 100 internationals, and Dalglish and Denis Law have scored most goals for their country (30 apiece). Scotland qualified for the European Championship Finals for the first time in 1992. They lost to Germany and Holland, and beat C.I.S.

SCOTTISH CUP

In 1873, 15 clubs subscribed towards the purchase of the Scottish Cup. The trophy and a set of medals cost £56 12s 11d. Since then Celtic (29) and Rangers (26) have won the trophy the most times, but Aberdeen won four in five seasons in the 1980s. Bob McPhail (Airdrie and Rangers), Jimmy McMenemy (Celtic and Partick Thistle) and Billy McNeill (Celtic) all won seven Scottish Cup winner's medals. Bobby Lennox (Celtic) won eight, but two were as a non-playing substitute. A history of the Scottish Cup, *100 Cups*, was written by Hugh Keevins and Kevin McCarra.

Perhaps the most famous match in Scottish Cup history is the 1885 game that ended Arbroath 36 Bon Accord 0.

SCOTTISH CUP

Year	Winners	Runners-up	Score	Year	Winners	Runners-up	Score
1874	Queen's Park	Clydesdale	2-0	1934	Rangers	St Mirren	5-0
1875	Queen's Park	Renton	3-0	1935	Rangers	Hamilton Academical	2-1
1876	Queen's Park	Third Lanark	2-0 after 1-1 draw	1936	Rangers	Third Lanark	1-0
1877	Vale of Leven	Rangers	3-2 after 0-0 and 1-1 draws	1937	Celtic	Aberdeen	2-1
1878	Vale of Leven	Third Lanark	1-0	1938	East Fife	Kilmarnock	4-2 after 1-1 draw
1879	Vale of Leven	Rangers	1-1***	1939	Clyde	Motherwell	4-0
1880	Queen's Park	Thornlibank	3-0	1947	Aberdeen	Hibernian	2-1
1881	Queen's Park	Dumbarton	3-1	1948	Rangers	Morton	1-0 after 1-1 draw
1882	Queen's Park	Dumbarton	4-1 after 2-2 draw	1949	Rangers	Clyde	4-1
1883	Dumbarton	Vale of Leven	2-1 after 2-2 draw	1950	Rangers	East Fife	3-0
1884	Queen's Park	Vale of Leven	****	1951	Celtic	Motherwell	1-0
1885	Renton	Vale of Leven	3-1 after 0-0 draw	1952	Motherwell	Dundee	4-0
1886	Queen's Park	Renton	3-1	1953	Rangers	Aberdeen	1-0 after 1-1 draw
1887	Hibernian	Dumbarton	2-1	1954	Celtic	Aberdeen	2-1
1888	Renton	Cambuslang	6-1	1955	Clyde	Celtic	1-0 after 1-1 draw
1889	Third Lanark	Celtic	2-1	1956	Hearts	Celtic	3-1
1890	Queen's Park	Vale of Leven	2-1 after 1-1 draw	1957	Falkirk	Kimarnock	2-1 after 1-1 draw
1891	Hearts	Dumbarton	1-0	1958	Clyde	Hibernian	1-0
1892	Celtic	Queen's Park	5-1	1959	St Mirren	Aberdeen	3-1
1893	Queen's Park	Celtic	2-1	1960	Rangers	Kilmarnock	2-0
1894	Rangers	Celtic	3-1	1961	Dunfermline	Celtic	2-0 after 0-0 draw
1895	St Bernards	Renton	2-1	1962	Rangers	St Mirren	2-0
1896	Hearts	Hibernian	3-1	1963	Rangers	Celtic	3-0 after 1-1 draw
1897	Rangers	Dumbarton	5-1	1964	Rangers	Dundee	3-1
1898	Rangers	Kilmarnock	2-0	1965	Celtic	Dunfermline Athletic	3-2
1899	Celtic	Rangers	2-0	1966	Rangers	Celtic	1-0 after 0-0 draw
1900	Celtic	Queen's Park	4-3	1967	Celtic	Aberdeen	2-0
1901	Hearts	Celtic	4-3	1968	Dunfermline	Hearts	3-1
1902	Hibernian	Celtic	1-0	1969	Celtic	Rangers	4-0
1903	Rangers	Hearts	2-0 after 1-1 and 0-0 draws	1970	Aberdeen	Celtic	3-1
1904	Celtic	Rangers	3-2	1971	Celtic	Rangers	2-1 after 1-1 draw
1905	Third Lanark	Rangers	3-1 after 0-0 draw	1972	Celtic	Hibernian	6-1
1906	Hearts	Third Lanark	1-0	1973	Rangers	Celtic	3-2
1907	Celtic	Hearts	3-0	1974	Celtic	Airdrieonians	3-1
1908	Celtic	St Mirren	5-1	1976	Rangers	Hearts	3-1
1909	Cup witheld after riots; Rangers v Celtic Final			1977	Celtic	Rangers	1-0
1910	Dundee	Clyde	2-1 after 2-2 and 0-0 draws	1978	Rangers	Aberdeen	2-1
1911	Celtic	Hamilton Academical	2-0 after 0-0 draw	1979	Rangers	Hibernian	3-2 after 0-0 and 0-0 draws*
1912	Celtic	Clyde	2-0	1980	Celtic	Rangers	1-0*
1913	Falkirk	Raith Rovers	2-0	1981	Rangers	Dundee United	4-1 after 0-0 draw
1914	Celtic	Hibernian	4-1 after 0-0 draw	1982	Aberdeen	Rangers	4-1*
1920	Kilmarnock	Albion Rovers	3-2	1983	Aberdeen	Rangers	1-0*
1921	Partick Thistle	Rangers	1-0	1984	Aberdeen	Celtic	2-1*
1922	Morton	Rangers	1-0	1985	Celtic	Dundee United	2-1
1923	Celtic	Hibernian	1-0	1986	Aberdeen	Hearts	3-0
1924	Airdrieonians	Hibernian	2-0	1987	St Mirren	Dundee United	1-0*
1925	Celtic	Dundee	2-1	1988	Celtic	Dundee United	2-1
1926	St Mirren	Celtic	2-0	1989	Celtic	Rangers	1-0
1927	Celtic	East Fife	3-1	1990	Aberdeen	Celtic	0-0**
1928	Rangers	Celtic	4-0	1991	Motherwell	Dundee United	4-3*
1929	Kilmarnock	Rangers	2-0	1992	Rangers	Airdrieonians	2-1
1930	Rangers	Partick Thistle	2-1 after 0-0 draw	1993	Rangers	Aberdeen	2-1
1931	Celtic	Motherwell	4-2 after 2-2 draw	1994	Dundee United	Rangers	1-0
1932	Rangers	Kilmarnock	3-0 after 1-1 draw	1995	Celtic	Airdrie	1-0
1933	Celtic	Motherwell	1-0				

* after extra time ** won on penalties *** losers failed to attend replay ****losers failed to turn up

SCOTTISH FOOTBALL ASSOCIATION

The Scottish Football Association was formed at Dewar's Hotel, Glasgow, on 13 March 1873. Representatives of eight clubs were present at the meeting: Clydesdale, Dumbreck, Eastern, Granville, Queen's Park, Rovers, Third Lanark and Vale of Leven; Kilmarnock had also pledged support. The centenary was 'celebrated' in 1973 with a Hampden Park game against England which was lost 5-0! Scotland had no international team manager for much of the 1950s but the World Cup qualifying successes in the 1970s and 1980s owed much to good administration and commercial sense. The Scottish FA also launched a Travel Club in the early 1980s.

SCOTTISH LEAGUE

The Scottish League was formed in 1890 with 11 founder members: Abercorn, Celtic, Cowlairs, Cambuslang, Dumbarton, Hearts, Rangers, St Mirren, Renton, Third Lanark and Vale of Leven.

SCOTTISH LEAGUE CHAMPIONSHIP

Year	Winners	Runners-up	Year	Winners	Runners-up
1890/91	Dumbarton	Rangers	1946/47	Rangers	Hibernian
1891/92	Dumbarton	Celtic	1947/48	Hibernian	Rangers
1892/93	Celtic	Rangers	1948/49	Rangers	Dundee
1893/94	Celtic	Hearts	1949/50	Rangers	Hibernian
1894/95	Hearts	Celtic	1950/51	Hibernian	Rangers
1895/96	Celtic	Rangers	1951/52	Hibernian	Rangers
1896/97	Celtic	Rangers	1952/53	Rangers	Hibernian
1897/98	Hearts	Hibernian	1953/54	Celtic	Hearts
1898/99	Rangers	Hearts	1954/55	Aberdeen	Celtic
1899/1900	Rangers	Celtic	1955/56	Rangers	Aberdeen
1900/01	Rangers	Celtic	1956/57	Rangers	Hearts
1901/02	Rangers	Celtic	1957/58	Hearts	Rangers
1902/03	Hibernian	Dundee	1958/59	Rangers	Hearts
1903/04	Third Lanark	Hearts	1959/60	Hearts	Kilmarnock
1904/05	Celtic	Rangers	1960/61	Rangers	Kilmarnock
1905/06	Celtic	Hearts	1961/62	Dundee	Rangers
1906/07	Celtic	Dundee	1962/63	Rangers	Kilmarnock
1907/08	Celtic	Falkirk	1963/64	Rangers	Kilmarnock
1908/09	Celtic	Dundee	1964/65	Kilmarnock	Hearts
1909/10	Celtic	Falkirk	1965/66	Celtic	Rangers
1910/11	Rangers	Aberdeen	1966/67	Celtic	Rangers
1911/12	Rangers	Celtic	1967/68	Celtic	Rangers
1912/13	Rangers	Celtic	1968/69	Celtic	Rangers
1913/14	Celtic	Rangers	1969/70	Celtic	Rangers
1914/15	Celtic	Hearts	1970/71	Celtic	Aberdeen
1915/16	Celtic	Rangers	1971/72	Celtic	Aberdeen
1916/17	Celtic	Morton	1972/73	Celtic	Rangers
1917/18	Rangers	Celtic	1973/74	Celtic	Hibernian
1918/19	Celtic	Rangers	1974/75	Rangers	Hibernian
1919/20	Rangers	Celtic	1975/76	Rangers	Celtic
1920/21	Rangers	Celtic	1976/77	Celtic	Rangers
1921/22	Celtic	Rangers	1977/78	Rangers	Aberdeen
1922/23	Rangers	Airdrieonians	1978/79	Celtic	Rangers
1923/24	Rangers	Airdrieonians	1979/80	Aberdeen	Celtic
1924/25	Rangers	Airdrieonians	1980/81	Celtic	Aberdeen
1925/26	Celtic	Airdrieonians	1981/82	Celtic	Aberdeen
1926/27	Rangers	Motherwell	1982/83	Dundee United	Celtic
1927/28	Rangers	Celtic	1983/84	Aberdeen	Celtic
1928/29	Rangers	Celtic	1984/85	Aberdeen	Celtic
1929/30	Rangers	Motherwell	1985/86	Celtic	Hearts
1930/31	Rangers	Celtic	1986/87	Rangers	Celtic
1931/32	Motherwell	Rangers	1987/88	Celtic	Hearts
1932/33	Rangers	Motherwell	1988/89	Rangers	Aberdeen
1933/34	Rangers	Motherwell	1989/90	Rangers	Aberdeen
1934/35	Rangers	Celtic	1990/91	Rangers	Aberdeen
1935/36	Celtic	Rangers	1991/92	Rangers	Hearts
1936/37	Rangers	Aberdeen	1992/93	Rangers	Aberdeen
1937/38	Celtic	Hearts	1993/94	Rangers	Aberdeen
1938/39	Rangers	Celtic	1994/95	Rangers	Motherwell

Unlike the English League, the clubs were still bound to amateur status. Renton were banned by the Scottish FA after only five League matches; their crime was playing against a club convicted of professionalism.

Division 2 was formed in 1893 and re-formed in 1921 after a gap of seven years. Automatic promotion and relegation was also introduced in 1921.

Division 3 was formed in 1923 but did not complete its third season, although a Third Division reappeared between 1946 and 1955.

In 1975 the basic modern-day structure was introduced – a Premier Division, First Division and Second Division. A Third Division was started in 1994. Premier Division clubs now play each other four times. Only 11 clubs have won the Scottish League, and only six of these have done so more than once: Rangers (44), Celtic (35), Aberdeen (4), Hearts (4), Hibernian (4) and Dumbarton (2)

SCOTTISH LEAGUE CHAMPIONSHIP

The Championship of the Scottish League from 1890/91 until 1974/75 was for the top team in Division 1. Since 1975/76 the title has been bestowed on the champions of the new Premier Division.

Whatever the top division is called, the domination of Rangers and Celtic has been overwhelming, despite some periods of limited success from teams such as Aberdeen, Hearts and Dundee United in recent years.

SCOTTISH LEAGUE CUP

The Scottish League Cup, once the Skol Cup but now known as the Coca-Cola Cup after its sponsors, has had a chequered existence since its inception following the Second World War. It has been played with qualifying groups before a knock-out phase (in its early years) and

SCOTTISH LEAGUE CUP

Year	Winner	Runners-up	Score
1946/47	Rangers	Aberdeen	4-0
1947/48	East Fife	Falkirk	4-1 after 0-0 draw
1948/49	Rangers	Raith Rovers	2-0
1949/50	East Fife	Dunfermline Athletic	3-0
1950/51	Motherwell	Hibernian	3-0
1951/52	Dundee	Rangers	3-2
1952/53	Dundee	Kilmarnock	2-0
1953/54	East Fife	Partick Thistle	3-2
1954/55	Hearts	Motherwell	4-2
1955/56	Aberdeen	St Mirren	2-1
1956/57	Celtic	Partick Thistle	3-0 after 0-0 draw
1957/58	Celtic	Rangers	7-1
1958/59	Hearts	Partick Thistle	5-1
1959/60	Hearts	Third Lanark	2-1
1960/61	Rangers	Kilmarnock	2-0
1961/62	Rangers	Hearts	3-1 after 1-1 draw
1962/63	Hearts	Kilmarnock	1-0
1963/64	Rangers	Morton	5-0
1964/65	Rangers	Celtic	2-1
1965/66	Celtic	Rangers	2-1
1966/67	Celtic	Rangers	1-0
1967/68	Celtic	Dundee	5-3
1968/69	Celtic	Hibernian	6-2
1969/70	Celtic	St Johnstone	1-0
1970/71	Rangers	Celtic	1-0
1971/72	Partick Thistle	Celtic	4-1
1972/73	Hibernian	Celtic	2-1
1973/74	Dundee	Celtic	1-0
1974/75	Celtic	Hibernian	6-3
1975/76	Rangers	Celtic	1-0
1976/77	Aberdeen	Celtic	2-1*
1977/78	Rangers	Celtic	2-1*
1978/79	Rangers	Aberdeen	2-1
1979/80	Dundee United	Aberdeen	3-0 after 0-0 draw
1980/81	Dundee United	Dundee	3-0
1981/82	Rangers	Dundee United	2-1
1982/83	Celtic	Rangers	2-1
1983/84	Rangers	Celtic	3-2*
1984/85	Rangers	Dundee United	1-0
1985/86	Aberdeen	Hibernian	3-0
1986/87	Rangers	Celtic	2-1
1987/88	Rangers	Aberdeen	3-3**
1988/89	Rangers	Aberdeen	3-2
1989/90	Aberdeen	Rangers	2-1 *
1990/91	Rangers	Celtic	2-1*
1991/92	Hibernian	Dunfermine Athletic	2-0
1992/93	Rangers	Aberdeen	2-1*
1993/94	Rangers	Hibernian	2-1
1994/95	Raith Rovers	Celtic	2-2**

* after extra time ** won on penalties

as a knock-out only competition. The final has been played both before Christmas, as in 1994/95 with the Final in October, and at the end of the season. The Finals have been decided on corners (1942/43 and 1943/44) – then the "Southern League Cup" – and on penalties (1987/88 and 1994/95). Today the trophy is accepted as a valid part of the Scottish 'treble' and, like much else in Scottish football, it has a history dominated by Rangers and Celtic.

SCUNTHORPE UNITED

Founded 1899

Joined League 1950 (Division 3 N)

Honours Division 3 (N) Champions 1958

Ground Glanford Park

It was never going to be easy for a club based in a small Humberside steel town to make headway in the Football League, but Scunthorpe United have made plucky efforts, with occasional success.

The 'Iron', as their fans lovingly know them, consolidated their new-found status through the early and mid 1950s, with long-serving full-back and penalty-king Jackie Brownsword outstandingly consistent, before rising to the Second Division and then, in 1962, failing by two places to reach the First. Sadly for United, they were then forced by economic pressures to sell free-scoring centre-forward Barrie Thomas, and a decline set in which saw them in the basement by the end of the decade. Since then they have remained in the lower reaches, and have been best known for producing 'keeper Ray Clemence and forward Kevin Keegan, who were both to find fame with Liverpool.

Towards the end of the 1980s they left the Old Show Ground and entered a new era at Glanford Park, one of very few modern grounds in the Football League. Any quest for honours, however, was likely to be sublimated to the struggle for survival which faces most small clubs.

SEELER, Uwe

1936 Born in Germany

1952 Debut for Hamburg

1954 International debut v England at Wembley

1958 Plays in the first of his four World Cups

1966 Captains national team in the World Cup and makes his only appearance in a World Cup Final – West Germany lose to hosts England

1968 Captains Hamburg to Final of Cup Winners' Cup

1970 Captains West Germany in his last World Cup

Over four consecutive World Cup finals series Uwe Seeler played 21 games, scoring in each competition. He made 72 international appearances in all, captaining the national team for many of those games, and yet never won a

The 1974 World Cup in West Germany. Uwe Seeler (right) is holding the new trophy, as Pele holds the Jules Rimet Trophy, the original World Cup which had been won outright by Brazil four years earlier. Seeler was never to hold either Cup as a player. He must have watched the 1974 tournament with mixed emotions. His country were winners but his days as an international were over and he witnessed younger men achieve what he had been unable to in four attempts. He did, however, have the satisfaction of being able to contribute tactically to later German teams.

major honour with West Germany, thus proving that football is indeed a fickle master. There have been many footballers, less consistent, less reliable, and less dedicated, who can boast a fine collection of silverware. Seeler's rewards with Hamburg, a club he represented for 20 years, were – a few domestic triumphs apart – equally meagre; at times he might have wondered at his

decision not to join Internazionale when they offered £60,000 for him in 1961.

But there never was a more steadfast player than this stocky, hard-working striker. Early in 1965 an achilles tendon injury threatened to end his career; in September of that year, still not fully recovered or match-fit, he turned out to play against Sweden in a World Cup qualifying round. His loyalty and courage were never in question, and the second of these qualities, a vital ingredient for any close-range goalscorer, combined with his great acrobatic ability to produce an exciting footballer who could score from almost any position.

By the 1970 World Cup he had dropped to more of a midfield role, another instinctive and chunky striker by the name of Gerd Muller having earned a team place, and manager Helmut Schoen greatly valued his captain's contributions to tactical discussions. Two years later, victory in the European Championship initiated a period of German supremacy, but for Uwe Seeler it was too late.

SHACKLETON, Len

1922 Born in Bradford, Yorkshire

1936 Plays for England Schoolboys

1938 Joins the Arsenal ground staff but is rejected within a year

1939 Spends a year working with London Paper Mills

1940 Working for GEC, signs as a part-time professional for Bradford Park Avenue

1946 League debut for Bradford; moves to Newcastle United for £13,000 (the third biggest fee at the time) and scores six on Newcastle debut (13-0 v Newport County)

1948 Signs for Sunderland for a British record £20,000; wins first England cap

1954 Recalled to the England team

Len Shackleton did not win a major medal, and he played only five England games (plus one wartime international), but his non-conformist flair made him one of soccer's greatest entertainers. His type of individualism is now relegated to a bygone post-war era, surfacing only sporadically through the likes of Best, Marsh, Hoddle and Le Tissier.

An inside-forward, he could juggle the ball, deceive defenders and turn a game with an unorthodox move. In six wartime seasons he scored over 160 goals for Bradford Park Avenue. But he could also frustrate team-mates, and England selectors considered him too individualistic. Overlooked for five years, he was recalled for two England games in 1954, when he was 32 years old. Against West Germany – World Cup winners but under-strength – he graced Wembley with a typical 'Shack' goal, tricking two defenders and coolly chipping the ball over the goalkeeper's head.

Shackleton was contemptuous of authority. His nickname, the 'Clown Prince of Soccer', was also the title of his autobiography. Chapter 9, entitled 'The average director's knowledge of football', consisted of one blank page. Len later became a sports journalist in the North-East.

SHANKLY, Bill

1913 Born in mining village of Glenbuck, Ayrshire

1927 Leaves school for job in local pit

1929 Signs for Carlisle United

1933 Joins Preston North End

1938 Wins first of five caps as Scotland beat England at Wembley; helps Preston win the FA Cup

1949 Quits playing to become Carlisle United boss

1951 Takes managerial reins of Grimsby Town

1953 Workington are his new employers

1956 Accepts managership of Huddersfield Town

1959 The Shankly era dawns at Anfield

1962 Leads Liverpool to Second Division title

1964 Wins League Championship

1965 'Reds' lift FA Cup for first time in their history

1966 Another League Championship

1973 Wins double of Championship and UEFA Cup

1974 FA Cup triumph, and retirement

1981 Dies of heart attack

Shankly was the messiah-like figure who transformed Liverpool from a slumbering mass of unfulfilled potential into a soccer institution revered throughout the world. When he breezed into Anfield in 1959 his managerial credentials were not especially impressive, yet he exuded enthusiasm and a burning desire for success, and it was not long before the Reds were on the move.

He quickly assessed the merits of his inherited squad and found that many players were simply not up to the task of lifting the club out of Division 2, let alone winning the glittering prizes on which he had set his heart. Accordingly he discarded many, retained a few gems, and crossed the Scottish border to sign two men around whom he would build his first great side. Having secured centre-forward Ian St John and stopper Ron Yeats, Shankly embarked on the glory trail which brought a hat-trick of major trophies to Anfield in the mid 1960s.

Towards the end of the decade he began breaking up the side, going on to construct another in which Kevin Keegan was a vital constituent. Further triumphs followed, and it was a major surprise when he announced his retirement, a decision which, perhaps, he came to regret as he witnessed the subsequent runaway success of Bob Paisley.

But no one could take away from Shankly – as famous for his scything wit and utter devotion to the club as his actual achievements – the fact that it was he who had made it all

possible. He will go down as one of the truly great soccer managers.

SHEFFIELD UNITED

Founded 1889

Joined League 1892 (Division 2)

Honours Division 1 Champions 1898; Division 2 Champions 1953; Division 4 Champions 1982; FA Cup Winners 1899, 1902, 1915, 1925

Ground Bramall Lane

Apart from one spell stretching from the reign of Queen Victoria to the mid 1930s, Sheffield United have never quite managed to settle in the top division. There have been five other stints but none longer than seven years, and for much of their history the 'Blades' have languished in the shadow of the more glamorous Sheffield Wednesday.

United owe their existence to Yorkshire Cricket Club, who introduced soccer to

The Liverpool manager in 1974 holding the Charity Shield, after his team beat Leeds United on penalties following a 1-1 drawn match. Bill Shankly will be remembered as one of the game's great characters. There are numerous anecdotes about his wit and devotion to football. He once quipped, 'The two best teams in the land are Liverpool and Liverpool Reserves.' The main entrance at Anfield was named 'The Shankly Gates' after him.

Bramall Lane to keep their players fit during the winter. Their first season ended with promotion to the First Division, and then began their golden era. In six years around the turn of the century, the Blades appeared in three FA Cup Finals (winning two), lifted one League Championship and

The Sheffield United side of 1902 who beat Southampton 2-1 (after a 1-1 draw) to lift the 1902 FA Cup. The original photo caption lists the team (back row left to right) as Johnson, Thickett, Foulkes, Boyle, Wilkinson, Needham (capt.); Barnes, Common, Hedley, Priest and Lipsham. Foulkes is the 'keeper commonly known as 'Fatty' for fairly obvious reasons. Common is the man who became involved in the first £1000 transfer and Needham, pictured here towards the end of his career, won 16 caps for England between 1894 and 1902.

twice finished as runners-up in the title race. Stars of the day included 22-stone goalkeeper William 'Fatty' Foulke and wing-half Ernest 'Nudger' Needham, so nicknamed for his tackling expertise.

Even after the decline of that vintage combination, United continued in relative prosperity. Twice more they won the FA Cup and by the 1920s could field a useful team which included Irish international inside-forward Billy Gillespie and marksman Harry Johnson. But then the rot set in; United were relegated in 1934, and they proceeded to switch regularly between the top two divisions until they slumped to the Third in 1979 and the Fourth two years later. Since then they have recovered to remind themselves what life was like among the elite, but failed to create an impression of permanence at that exalted level and were relegated again in 1994.

Outstanding players down the years have been schemer Jimmy Hagan in the 1940s and 1950s, goalkeeper Alan

Hodgkinson and unrelated defenders Joe and Graham Shaw (1950s and 1960s), forwards Mick Jones and Alan Birchenall (both sold to raise much-needed cash in the 1960s), and England play-maker Tony Currie, winger Alan Woodward and defender Len Badger (1960s and 1970s). Among influential managers have been Joe Mercer, John Harris and Dave Bassett.

SHEFFIELD WEDNESDAY

Founded 1867

Joined League 1892 (Division 2)

Honours Division I Champions 1903, 1904, '

A rather disconsolate Trevor Francis giving vent to his feelings following Sheffield Wednesday's defeat by Blackburn Rovers in the early part of 1995. Wednesday were struggling badly in the league during a season in which they narrowly avoided relegation. Francis, like other Premiership managers, knew only too well that relegation would be a financial disaster in 1995, as the Premiership became both more profitable and harder to get into. Few managers seemed secure in their jobs either, as Francis discovered when he was edged out at season's end.

1929, 1930; Division 2 Champions 1900, 1926, 1952, 1956, 1959; FA Cup Winners 1896, 1907, 1935;

League Cup Winners 1991

Ground Hillsborough

Sheffield Wednesday are a big-city club with a sumptuous stadium, yet somehow they have failed to fulfil their potential as one of the superpowers of British soccer.

The 'Owls' early years betrayed few hints of future frustrations as they garnered a succession of honours around the turn of the century. But all too soon their successful combination, in which goalscorer Andy Wilson was prominent, lost momentum and Wednesday were demoted after the First World War. Recovery was swift, however, as manager Bob Brown assembled the greatest side in the Owls' history, which won four trophies and starred inside-forward Jimmy Seed, winger Ellis Rimmer and full-back Ernie Blenkinsop.

Sadly, a rapid decline set in and Wednesday were relegated in 1937, not rising again until 1950. That promotion set off a merry-go-round of despair and elation, encompassing three further demotions, each followed by an immediate return to the top flight, by the end of the decade. The idol of Hillsborough in the early 1950s was Derek Dooley, who scored 63 goals in as many senior games before his leg was amputated following an injury. But despite the efforts of Dooley, and those of inside-forwards Jackie Sewell, Redfern Froggatt and Albert Quixall, consistency eluded Wednesday until the early 1960s.

Then, with Harry Catterick taking over from Eric Taylor as team boss – the latter continued as general manager and was largely responsible for ambitious ground improvements – the Owls showed signs of new stature. In 1961, with major contributions from 'keeper

Ron Springett, centre-half Peter Swan and wing-half Tony Kay, they were title runners-up, and even after Catterick's departure they remained a solid force.

But then Hillsborough was rocked by a bribes scandal involving Swan, Kay and David Layne, and morale was damaged. Losing the 1966 FA Cup Final did nothing to help and Wednesday began to slide, plumbing the hitherto unknown depths of Division 3 by 1975. The managerial efforts of Jack Charlton and Howard Wilkinson eventually restored Wednesday to the First Division before yet another relegation interrupted their progress in 1990. Under the guidance of Ron Atkinson, however, they won the League Cup and promotion in 1991, only to lose their new messiah to Aston Villa. New manager Trevor Francis inherited a firm foundation for future success and

Wednesday's third place in the 1992 title race was highly encouraging. The following term was intensely frustrating as they lost both domestic cup finals to Arsenal; meanwhile the search for greater consistency in the League continued.

SHILTON, Peter

1949 Born in Leicester

1965 Wins English Schools Trophy (Under-15) with Leicester Boys and first of four England schoolboy caps

1966 Joins Leicester City on apprentice terms

1967 First team chance as Gordon Banks leaves Leicester

1969 FA Cup Final defeat, 1-0, by Manchester City

1971 Second Division Championship medal and first full England cap

As captain of England, Peter Shilton shakes the hand of Diego Maradona before the match against Argentina in the 1986 World Cup Finals. Shilton compiled a record 125 England caps, before his retirement from internationals in 1990. He made a virtue of hard training, something that kept him playing throughout his managership at Plymouth and for Bolton in a 1994/95 play-off semi-final.

1974 Transferred to Stoke City

1977 Transferred to Nottingham Forest under Brian Clough

1978 Wins League Championship and Players' Player of the Year award

1979 First of two successive European Cup Final victories

1982 Transferred to Southampton

1987 Joins Derby County

1990 Following mixed form in the World Cup finals he retires from international football with a record 125 England caps

1991 Derby County relegated to Second Division

1992 Takes over as player-boss of Second Division Plymouth Argyle but cannot avert relegation

1995 Resigns following personal financial difficulties

Everything written about the young Peter Shilton suggests that there was nothing else in his life except soccer.

His years at Leicester, marked by impressive displays and continual improvement, were contrasted with a few unhappy years at Stoke. It was under Brian Clough at Nottingham Forest that he came into his own, making the England position safe and finding himself regularly acclaimed 'the best goalkeeper in the world'.

Throughout his career he has been noted for his professional approach to the game, with a harsh training regime matched with great attention to both goalkeeping theory and practice. Never noted for spectacular saves, his reputation has been built on a good reading of the game, an excellent understanding of angles and exceptional reflexes. With both Southampton and Derby he frequently found himself starring in an average side. It was really when he pulled on the England jersey that the stage seemed appropriate for this remarkable player.

SHREWSBURY TOWN

Founded 1866

Joined League 1950 (Division 3 N)

Honours Division 3 Champions 1979, 1994

Ground Gay Meadow

For a provincial, small-town club, rather isolated in deepest Shropshire, Shrewsbury Town have given a good account of themselves since becoming members of the Football League. After struggling to adjust to life in the Third Division throughout most of the 1950s, they found themselves in the newly created Fourth at the end of the decade. Lifted by the lethal marksmanship of Arthur Rowley – who became the highest goal-scorer in League history during his six-year playing stint at Gay Meadow – Shrewsbury rose again to spend the next 15 years back in the Third Division.

There followed a second one-term spell at the bottom level before, in 1979, the Town ascended to the unheard-of eminence of the old Second Division, where they remained for 10 campaigns, eventually slipping back to the Third, and then down to the basement in 1992. Two seasons later they rose again, as divisional champions.

They have often excelled in knock-out competition, winning the Welsh Cup six times, reaching FA Cup quarter-finals in 1979 and 1982, and going one stage further in the 1961 League Cup.

SOUNESS, Graeme

1953 Born in Edinburgh

1968 Scotland schoolboy international

1968 Joins Tottenham Hotspur as an apprentice

1970 FA Youth Cup winner's medal for Spurs

1973 Signs for Middlesbrough for £30,000

1974 Second Division Championship medal with Boro

1975 Wins first Scotland international cap

As player-manager of Glasgow Rangers, Graeme Souness lifts the Scottish League Championship trophy in 1990. Souness had an incredible record in domestic competitions during his time as manager at Rangers: from 1986 to 1991 they won the League Championship and the Scottish League Cup four times out of five. On returning to Anfield, however, he struggled to reproduce the consistency and style that had been Liverpool's hallmarks for so many years and he was dismissed in 1994.

A hard, skilful Scot, Graeme Souness had one of the most successful playing careers of the 1970s and 1980s. He started with Spurs and in the four-game FA Youth Cup Final of 1970 he scored two goals and was sent off. Then he made his mark with Jack Charlton's Middlesbrough team before joining Liverpool. In a little over six years at Anfield he won five League Championship medals, three European Cup winner's medals and played in Liverpool's four successive League Cup Final victories (although he missed the 1981 replay which brought the trophy to Anfield for the first time). Altogether he played 352 first-class games for Liverpool, scoring 56 goals. He played 54 games for Scotland, half of them as captain. His internationals included Scotland's famous World Cup defeat of Holland in Argentina in 1978 and he scored against the Soviet Union in Spain four years later.

Souness had perfect poise when in possession of the ball, controlling games by accurate passing and fearsome tackling. He also had a strong shot which could bring vital goals, such as the Milk Cup winner against Everton in 1984. But his aggression brought occasional trouble. He caused outrage when, in his autobiography No Half Measures, he admitted throwing a short right-hook which broke Lica Movila's jaw during a European Cup game with Dinamo Bucharest.

When he returned to Scotland as Rangers' player-manager in 1986, it was in character that he was sent off in his first-ever Scottish League match. It was also typical that he brought success to his new club: three League Championships in his four full seasons in charge, and four League Cup wins.

Soon after succeeding his friend Kenny Dalglish as Liverpool boss, he survived major heart surgery, then received the perfect tonic as the Reds lifted the FA Cup a month later. Souness then set about rebuilding the side, with woefully disappointing results. Though riding high enough in the League to satisfy most clubs, the Reds slipped well below their own incredible standards, with several humiliating cup eliminations by 'giant killers' providing the low lights. Stories of internal strife and claims that the manager had departed from the tried–and–tested 'bootroom' training methods lost him much public sympathy, already eroded by his links with The Sun newspaper (reviled on Merseyside over its coverage of the Hillsborough disaster). His transfer record, too, attracted much criticism and in the circumstances there was only one outcome. Early in 1994, Souness was sacked. Though he was a wealthy man with a history of heart problems, it was difficult to believe he had finished with football for good – as evidenced when he became manager at Galatasary.

SOUTH AMERICA

Latin America followed hard on the heels of Europe in taking up football and establishing associations and competitions. The two continents have dominated the World Cup and the Olympic soccer competition, exhibiting playing styles which have served as models throughout the rest of the world. South America is passionate about and dedicated to the game; at times the boundaries between enthusiasm, fanaticism and over-reaction become blurred, as do those between competitiveness and gamesmanship. Volatile or violent behaviour always seems a possibility when South Americans and football get together; but the brands of soccer on display have enlivened and coloured the international scene and produced some of the world's greatest players.

The Brazilians, frequently described as the most natural footballing nation on earth, could easily have adopted basketball or baseball as their national sport. The first indigenous Brazilian club, the Mackenzie Athletic Association, found itself rebelling against faculty efforts to establish these North American sports as official games.

Although British sailors played matches among themselves in the coastal towns of Brazil, the introduction of soccer to the continent's largest country is credited to Charles Miller, born in Sao Paulo of English parentage. After a spell as an amateur with Southampton he returned to his native town in 1864 and began to organise matches. In 1902 the club Fluminense was founded in Rio de Janeiro; so it was that the two poles of Brazilian football were established, providing a rivalry which has not always been beneficial to the national team. The great World Cup teams of 1958-70 owed much to a fresh spirit of co-operation between the two geographical centres which, despite the inauguration of a national championship in 1967, have also maintained the regional competitions set up in the 1900s (an expedient system, given the size of Brazil).

Brazil's victory in the 1989 Copa America (South American Championship) was their first major trophy in

19 years. The decline of Brazilian football coincided with Pele's departure; the public yearned for new players to match his stature, and that of Falcao, Tostao, Didi, Rivelino and Carlos Alberto. Experiments in the 1970s and 1980s with defence-based European tactics stifled the innate expressiveness of the players and the 1990 World Cup revealed a disappointing national team suffering from a footballing identity crisis, with natural flair and a systematic approach vying for the upper hand. However, World Cup triumph in 1994, with dazzling contributions from the likes of Romario and Bebeto, restored Brazil to pre-eminence, even if the current side does not match the Pele vintage for sheer style.

Argentina has the most convincing football pedigree in the continent, the first club, Buenos Aires FC, having been formed in 1865 by the British influx which also introduced polo and the railways. (About that time there were some 30,000 British nationals in the capital.) Their Football Association was founded 30 years later and the game was given a boost by Italian immigrants after the First World War. The disgraceful exhibition by the national team in the 1966 World Cup and their continued physical approach since have reinforced a poor image of Argentinian football which began with violent public demonstrations against the Argentinian FA prompted by the World Cup failures in 1958 and 1962; the intimidating performances by their club sides in the World Club Championships of the 1960s and 1970s did little to dispel this reputation. It was not always thus; the elegance, artistry and sportsmanship of Argentinian football before the Second World War saw their players being sought by top European clubs. In the 1940s the centre-forward Adolfo Pedernera was as highly acclaimed as near-contemporary and Brazilian counterpart Artur Friedenreich.

The team of the late 1970s, inspired by Mario Kempes and Osvaldo Ardiles, stands out as worthy of future emulation. But the 1990 World Cup, with Maradona, arguably the preceding tournament's most exciting player, failing to find the net once, featured a lacklustre national side who many felt were fortunate to reach the Final. In 1994, they didn't get beyond the second phase of the finals, and their tournament was marred by the Maradona drugs scandal.

The South American competitions have been dominated by teams from Argentina, Brazil and Uruguay – hosts (on the basis of their 1924 and 1928 Olympic football successes) and winners of the first World Cup in 1930. Uruguay is a relatively small country but it possesses a great footballing heart, typified by the successes of Peñarol and Nacional in the South American Cup and the World Club Championship. After the late 1950s, however, the national team's game became imbued with cynicism and was characterised by temperamental outbursts and tackles whose legality no interpretation of the game's Laws could admit. The ultimate effect of this betrayal of the skill and spirit of early Uruguayan soccer was a dramatic slump in interest in the domestic game after the 1986 World Cup. Victory in the following year's South American Championship, however, unveiled a new team and a fresh approach, and hopes for Uruguayan football have been revived.

In contrast to the three most successful nations in South America there stand Ecuador and Venezuela, countries which have made little footballing impact within the continent and virtually none outside it. Both set up their professional leagues late (1957) and in the case of Venezuela the game is second in popularity to baseball. The Brazilian international Jairzinho is the biggest name associated with Venezuelan football, signing as he did for top club Portuguesa Acarigua in 1977. Ecuador's best-known player, on the other hand, forged his career in Uruguay: Alberto Spencer played centre-forward for Peñarol in the 1960s.

Chile's professional league dates from 1933 and its governing body from 1895, but its achievements are modest and the sport is rarely free from financial difficulties. It hosted the 1962 World Cup, widely regarded as the most disappointing post-war tournament, and took third place. Bolivia's record is equally undistinguished, its sole victory in the Copa America having been achieved at home, 3660 metres above sea-level in 1963, and its few World Cup appearances , including that of 1994, having been largely colourless.

Scratchy photos like this back up the stories of the delightful soccer played in South America in the first decades of this century. There is also film available of training sessions and top-class games. Two things stand out from the footage. The first is the skilful ball control – remarkable when you consider the bulky boots with inflexible toe-caps that were worn then, and the heavy laced ball. The player in possession would often stand still before deciding on his course of action, confident that he could dribble past any opponent who came near. The second thing which strikes the modern viewer is the bravery of the 'keepers who, at that time, could be shoulder-charged while catching the ball. This photo from the first ever World Cup Final in 1930 shows Argentina's 'keeper Botasso denying Hector 'Manno' Castro of Uruguay. Castro had the last laugh though, scoring in the home side's 4-2 win.

Peru and Paraguay, like Ecuador, have rarely been able to keep their best players, who have been easily tempted by the higher wages and bonuses offered by other South American clubs. This was particularly evident in the 1950s when football in both countries was going through a good phase. It was to be the same story 20 years later: Peru's goal-scoring forward Teofilo Cubillas was among those to leave for Europe after his country's creditable display in the 1970 World Cup, but he returned to his old club Lima Alianza before demonstrating his long-range shooting in the 1978 competition.

Paraguay's best player of recent times, Julio Cesar Romero, began the 1980s with New York Cosmos. In 1979 Paraguay had won the South American Championship and their top club Olimpia had won the South American Cup and the World Club Championship; but despite this high point in Paraguayan football, and his relative youth, the talented Romero chose to play in the NASL. Both countries have had intermittent success in the Copa America and have proved to be forces to reckon with in quite a few World Cups. It is tempting to believe that a sounder economic background in both cases would provide serious rivals to the 'big three'.

Watching South American teams parading their skills in neat, colourful kit, it is easy to forget that South America is still a continent beset with poverty and hampered by a tempestuous political tradition, and that it is in these difficult circumstances that soccer continues to thrive. Colombia's 1989/90 season neatly epitomises the paradox; the league competition was suspended because the game had become linked with the lucrative illegal cocaine trade and the laundering of drug money. In addition, there were allegations of rigged results, and a referee was shot. Meanwhile, Nacional Medellin became the first club from that country to win the South American Cup.

It was with a scandal that Colombian football first came to international attention: in 1950 a pirate league, operating without the approval of the Colombian FA or FIFA, poached top European players without paying transfer fees. Di Stefano was the most famous name attracted by the higher wages, but the league soon disintegrated. Colombia's national side has become stronger in recent years but their performances in the 1990 and 1994 World Cups didn't live up to expectations, their best player, Carlos Valderrama, failing to make his mark on the competition. However, at least he fared better than defender Andres Escobar, who was murdered on his return home to Colombia, apparently because of his own goal in the humiliating defeat by the USA.

Most football associations in the continent have had their scandals and disruptions to deal with; but football survives as an intrinsic part of Latin American life and culture – and not just as an escape from poverty and the consequences of political instability. There is a strong middle-class following but it is a game appreciated by all sections of society, by both sexes and by all generations. It is impossible to imagine a future South America without soccer – or vice versa.

SOUTH AMERICAN CHAMPIONSHIP

South America's most important international competition has enjoyed a long but unsettled life. Falling attendances in the 1960s seemed to herald its demise but, after an eight-year hiatus, the competition was reorganised in 1979 to accommodate all of the 10 principal footballing nations; the league system was replaced by group tables and knock-out semi-finals and a final.

The Championship is now contested every two years; originally it was intended to be annual but after 1927 no

regularity is discernible. There have always been gaps and – as if to compensate – extraordinary tournaments.

The infrequent appearance of Brazil's name in the roll of honour is striking; this is due in part to that country's absence from the tournament from 1923 to 1936 owing to disputes, but credit must also be given to the enduring strength of Argentinian and Uruguayan football.

SOUTH AMERICAN CHAMPIONSHIP	
Year	Winners
1910	Argentina
1916	Uruguay
1917	Uruguay
1919	Brazil
1920	Uruguay
1921	Argentina
1922	Brazil
1923	Uruguay
1924	Uruguay
1925	Argentina
1926	Uruguay
1927	Argentina
1929	Argentina
1935*	Uruguay
1937	Argentina
1939	Peru
1941*	Argentina
1942	Uruguay
1945*	Argentina
1946*	Argentina
1947	Argentina
1949	Brazil
1953	Paraguay
1955	Argentina
1956*	Uruguay
1957	Argentina
1958	Argentina
1959*	Uruguay
1963	Bolivia
1967	Uruguay
1975	Peru
1979	Paraguay
1983	Uruguay
1987	Uruguay
1989*	Brazil
1991	Argentina
1993	Argentina

*extraordinary tournament, cup not awarded

SOUTH AMERICAN CLUB CUP

The Copa Libertadores, first contested in 1960, was modelled on the European Cup. All rounds, including the Final, are decided over

two legs. As from 1966 two clubs from each of the 10 main soccer nations have been invited to compete. The quality of the football has often been eclipsed by corruption, and violence on and off the field. Argentinian teams, Independiente and Estudiantes in particular, have had the greatest success in the competition.

SOUTHAMPTON

Founded 1885

Joined League 1920 (Division 3 founder member)

Honours Division 3 (S) Champions 1922; Division 3 Champions 1960; FA Cup Winners 1976

Ground The Dell

After spending the bulk of their history as also-rans, Southampton have elbowed aside Portsmouth as the south coast's leading light and, against the odds for a provincial club, have emerged as a genuine force in British football.

Their early days, however, were not devoid of achievement. Formed as Southampton St Mary by a group of sporty churchgoers – hence their enduring nickname of the 'Saints' – they were never cowed by the giants of the day and, while competing in the Southern League, reached the FA Cup Finals of 1900 and 1902. After entering the senior competition as founder members of Division 3, Southampton lost little time in gaining promotion as the Southern section's first champions, and remained in the Second until 1953.

Most of that sojourn was uneventful, but the immediate post-war years brought spirited bids to reach the top echelon, with the efforts of full-back Alf Ramsey and goalscorer Charlie Wayman catching the eye. They never made it, instead dropping a level, and it was left to new manager Ted Bates – who was to remain at the helm until 1974 – to lead them back up in 1960, with the goals of Derek Reeves and

George O'Brien playing a crucial part.

Boosted by the consistent excellence of winger Terry Paine, and the marksmanship of Martin Chivers, Ron Davies and Mick Channon, Bates built an impressively firm edifice and reached the First Division in 1966. There they remained for eight years before, with Lawrie McMenemy now in charge, they were relegated.

The fall caused no lasting harm – indeed, it was while in the Second Division that the Saints earned their

Many teams have a big day. Southampton's 'big day' came in 1976 when they beat Manchester United in the FA Cup Final, 1-0. After that victory, achieved as a Second Division side, Southampton soon won promotion to the First and have been putting in consistently good performances ever since, although rarely threatening to win the title. Here Southampton's Peter Osgood (left) is challenged by Stewart Houston with Brian Greenhoff lending a helping hand.

greatest triumph, the famous FA Cup victory over Manchester United – and when they were promoted again in 1978 they exuded stability. The following year they reached the League Cup Final and improved steadily until, in 1984, they were runners-up in the title race.

McMenemy's policy was to bring top players to the Dell – the likes of Alan Ball, Kevin Keegan and Peter Shilton – and his boldness paid off. The Saints have since enjoyed the services of outstanding young players such as Matt Le Tissier, Rod Wallace, Neil Ruddock, Tim Flowers and Alan Shearer, who was sold for a record £3.6 million in 1992. Come mid-decade, with Ball at the helm, Southampton continued to hold their own in the Premiership, a huge achievement considering their comparative lack of resources.

SOUTHEND UNITED

Founded 1906

Joined League 1920 (Division 3)

Honours Division 4 Champions 1981

Ground Roots Hall

It's a fact of football life that smaller clubs sell their best players to keep bank balances in the black. Southend United purchased Stanley Collymore from Crystal Palace in late 1992 for little over £100,000... and some nine months later he left the club to join Nottingham Forest for more than £2m. Those nine months were important for both player and club. Collymore, with a regular first team place, scored some outstanding goals and attracted interest from many top teams. Southend, thanks to Collymore, avoided relegation and collected the cash that enabled them to buy a training ground and fund substantial improvements to their Roots Hall base. Collymore has now won an England cap (and moved to Liverpool) and Southend completed the 1994/95 season with a healthy league position and record season ticket sales.

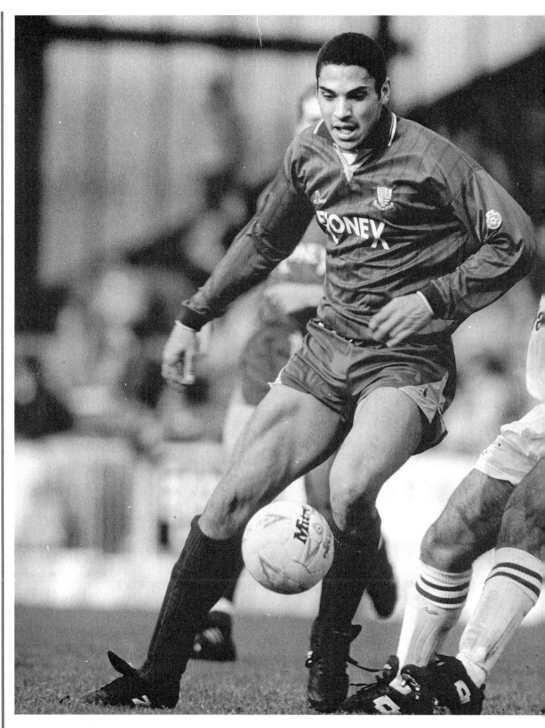

Southend United have never set the football world alight. They remained in Divisions 3 and 3 (South) for 46 seasons, rarely threatening promotion, until they were relegated to Division 4 in 1966. After a few near misses they were returned to Division 3 in 1972 to begin a period as a 'yo-yo' club, achieving their fifth promotion from the lowest level in 1990 and following that with a move to the old Division 2 in 1991.

This step-up at least meant exemption until the third round of the FA Cup – a tournament in which they always fared very badly until reaching the fifth round in 1993.

Although a large catchment area appears to exist for the club, much of the potential support is easily lured away to London sides, many of which can be reached in little over an hour's travel time. In recent years, with only a solid bedrock of support attending matches, a degree of dissatisfaction over managerial changes has cast a shadow over the team's modest successes. And while older fans fondly recall the likes of Scotsman 'Sandy' Anderson (a record 451 League appearances between 1950 and 1962) and Northern Ireland international Sammy McCory (1955-59), the younger supporters are a little short of heroes of real substance. However, they were treated to the talents of striker Stan Collymore during 1992/93 and when veteran Irish midfielder Ronnie Whelan arrived from Liverpool in 1994, at least they could crow, occasionally, about having a player away on international duty!

SPONSORSHIP

The era of sponsorship began in earnest in the 1970s. Pre-1970 sponsorship was often of the level shown in this quote from a 1969 Mansfield Town programme: 'The match ball for this game was kindly donated by Ind Coope (Northern Ltd).' Today everything is affected – even the FA Cup has fallen under the wing of Littlewoods Pools – and about 10 per cent of all sport's sponsorship money goes into football.

The longest-running major soccer sponsor was Bell's Whisky, who put their name to the 'Manager of the Month' awards between 1965 and 1988. The first match sponsor accepted by the Football League was Watney in 1970. The brewery financed a new knock-out tournament for the previous season's two top-scoring teams in each division; the competition lasted for four years. A similar competition, the Drybrough Cup, was organised in Scotland, where the four highest-scoring teams in the Scottish League's two divisions competed between 1971 and 1974.

A more complex competition was the Texaco Cup (1970/71 to 1973/74), sponsored by the oil company not long after its name change from Regent to Texaco. Sixteen teams represented four countries – England, Scotland, Northern Ireland and the Republic of Ireland – with a guaranteed Irish semi-finalist. Gillette and Ford sponsored early sportsmanship awards.

Tobacco companies, banned from television advertising, found a more inventive promotion method in sponsorship. Rothmans linked themselves with football's classic reference book, Rothmans Football Yearbook, first published in 1970, and then financed non-League football, beginning with the Isthmian League in 1973. (John Player and Benson & Hedges targeted cricket.) Later, however, the Football League excluded tobacco companies, breweries and South African companies from sponsoring its major competitions.

The first Football League sponsor was Canon in 1983. The electronics company was happy with its three-year deal. Company awareness grew considerably and the name was spread all over Europe by television. But the League's next deal, with Today newspaper in 1986/87, experienced problems, and the newspaper company gave way to Barclays Bank in 1987, then Endsleigh Insurance in 1993. The FA Premiership was sponsored by Carling from 1993.

The League Cup has a longer sponsorship history than the Football League. The Dairy Council sponsored the Milk Cup from 1982 to 1986, Littlewoods took over the competition from 1986 to 1990, then Rumbelows until 1991/92, after which the Coca-Cola Cup came into existence. In Scotland, first Bell's and then Skol (from 1985) sponsored the Scottish League Cup, while the 1986

Scotland-Luxembourg game was the first British international to be sponsored.

A double-glazing firm craftily overcame the Rangers-Celtic problem by sponsoring both clubs in 1984. A club's sponsor is not always a profit-making organisation, as evidenced by deals between Millwall and Lewisham Borough Council (1987) and West Brom and Sandwell Council (1989). By the early 1990s there was an incredible range of sponsorship opportunities. It cost Wagsport only £15 to sponsor the gloves of Stafford Rangers goalkeeper Ryan Price, whereas Glasgow Rangers signed a deal valued around £6 million with McEwan's lager.

STADIA

Few aspects of football have been more controversial or newsworthy in recent years than the stadia in which the professional game is staged. The devastating fire at Bradford City's Valley Parade in May 1985, in which 55 people died, followed in April 1989 by the deaths of 95 Liverpool fans at Hillsborough, awoke everyone to the need for wholesale changes in the design, construction and even location of Britain's ageing, outmoded football grounds.

When football first became a mass spectator sport in the late nineteenth century, most clubs rented fields or cricket grounds with rudimentary wooden stands and ropes around the pitch.

Everton and Celtic were among the first clubs to create purpose-built grounds, in 1892, and within a decade the three largest football grounds in the world were in Glasgow; Hampden Park, Ibrox Park and Celtic Park. A Scottish engineer, Archibald Leitch, carved a niche for himself in football history by designing the grounds and grandstands of several major clubs between 1900 and 1936, including those of Tottenham, Everton, Chelsea and Aston Villa. Many of his distinctive grandstands, such as those at Fulham, Sheffield Wednesday, Rangers and Dundee, are still in use today.

In Leitch's era the emphasis was on utilitarian structures providing seats on one side of the pitch with open terracing on the remaining three sides. Terrace covers were gradually added, as, in the 1950s, were floodlight pylons. The 1960s saw the introduction of executive boxes (first at Manchester United) and, sadly, anti-hooligan perimeter fences.

But football ground developments in Britain were always piecemeal – a stand here, a cover there – with few aesthetic considerations or hints of a master plan. By contrast, European and South American governments and civic authorities have, from the 1920s onwards, spent large sums building impressive stadia for their tenant clubs and local communities. Germany pioneered the concept of a stadium as part of a larger sports complex. Cantilevered roofing to facilitate a clear view of the pitch was developed in several countries during the 1930s but did not reach Britain until 1958 (at Scunthorpe United, surprisingly).

Change in Britain came about mainly as a result of disasters. The first Ibrox tragedy of 1902 signalled the end of high wooden terracing. Wembley Stadium's chaotic opening in 1923 forced the introduction of all-ticket matches and the division of terraces into manageable pens.

Vittorio Gregotti's distinctive corner towers at the Genoa stadium were completed for the 1990 World Cup Finals in Italy. Few English stadia can match those of the Italians for sheer architectural style.

In 1946 the death of 33 supporters at Bolton warned of the dangers of poor control and overcrowding, but it took the second Ibrox disaster in 1971, when 66 died on a steep stairway, finally to alert the government to the need for legislation. The resulting Safety of Sports Grounds Act of 1975 began a system of inspection by local authorities which was to cost clubs a great deal in improvement work and to see once massive grounds drastically reduced in capacity.

The Bradford fire in 1985 increased the Safety Act's jurisdiction to Third and Fourth Division clubs, but its implementation was found tragically wanting by the Hillsborough disaster in 1989. As a result of this debacle, the government set up an enquiry under Lord Justice Taylor, who recommended in January 1990 that all Football League grounds be converted to all-seating – in the top two Divisions by 1994 and the rest by 1999. The shattering impact of this ruling on terrace regulars was hardly softened by parallel directives on all-seating from both UEFA and FIFA.

The Football League estimated that it would cost its clubs between £300 and £700 million to implement the Taylor Report. The government responded by reallocating some £150 million of pools betting tax over a five-year period. But the shortfall still presents the clubs with a Herculean task. Fans, meanwhile, worry that seats will be badly installed, will destroy the traditional atmosphere at matches, and will price the ordinary spectator out of football. But the Taylor Report has at least had the desired effect of forcing British clubs to reassess completely their own grounds, many of which are hardly worth converting.

British stadia are not alone in facing huge repair bills. The largest venue in the world, the Maracana Stadium in Rio de Janeiro, had its capacity cut from 200,000 to 150,000 as a result of its crumbling infrastructure. The Heysel Stadium was cruelly exposed in 1985 when Liverpool fans rioted before the European Cup Final, resulting in 39 deaths.

Many of Germany's stadia were modernised in the 1970s but still have large expanses of uncovered terracing which must be converted. Britain now boasts some of the most modern and atmospheric grounds in the world, such as Old Trafford and the newly revamped Ibrox Park. The difference is that whereas in Britain most stadia are privately owned, in Europe central and local governments play an active role in funding sports facilities. The Italians spent £600 million on modernising just 12 stadia for the 1990 World Cup, not a penny of which came from the tenant clubs.

To help pay for the modernisation of British grounds, future developments will undoubtedly incorporate commercial and leisure facilities, such as shops, offices, social clubs and cinemas. In the absence of public grants, British clubs which can move will mainly follow the example of Scunthorpe, St Johnstone, Walsall, Yeovil Town, Wycombe Wanderers , Millwall and Huddersfield Town by selling their old inner-city grounds for commercial development and replacing them with smaller purpose-built stadia, often on green-field sites.

Although the use of synthetic pitches in Britain has proved unpopular in first-class football since its introduction at Queen's Park Rangers in 1981, future developments abroad are likely to include retractable roofs, sections of movable seating and even moving pitches – all of which are technically possible but, at present, unproven economically.

STEIN, Jock

1922 Born in Burnbank, Lanarkshire, Scotland

1942 Signs part-time for Albion Rovers while still a miner

1950 Joins Llanelli as full-time professional

1951 Signed by Celtic mainly to help with reserve and youth team coaching – and becomes first-team captain.

1954 Celtic complete League and Cup double

1955 Injury – and Stein becomes reserve team coach

1960 Appointed manager of Dunfermline Athletic

1964 Appointed manager of Hibernian

1965 Rejoins Celtic – as manager. They win Scottish Cup; also temporary Scotland manager for World Cup qualifying matches

1966 First of nine Scottish Championships in a row

1967 Celtic become first British club to win European Cup

1977 Last of 10 Championships and 8 Scottish Cup victories with Celtic

1978 Becomes manager of Leeds United – to leave later in the same year to become Scotland team manager

1979 Awarded the CBE

1985 Dies at the end of the match at Ninian Park, Cardiff, in which Scotland drew 1-1 with Wales to ensure qualification for the 1986 World Cup finals in Mexico

Never can the Scottish tag of the 'Big Man' have been more appropriately applied than in the case of John (Jock) Stein. He stood head and shoulders above many others in his profession due to his honesty, loyalty and modesty.

Stein's phenomenal success at Parkhead will probably always be remembered for the European Cup victory in Lisbon in 1967. That victory, achieved by attacking flair against the defensive Italian champions Internazionale, has a permanent place in Scottish soccer folklore.

Stein's eventual departure

Jock Stein, in his prime, with yet another trophy. This time it's the Scottish Cup for 1977 following Celtic's 1-0 win over rivals, Rangers. No wonder he's smiling. Although always determined in his approach to football, Jock Stein's modesty ensured he never glorified victory and never gloated over beaten opponents. His sudden death in 1985 meant the loss of another strong influence for good in the game.

from the Glasgow club was both unexpected and sad; the board wanted him to move on to promotional work to make room for Billy McNeill to return as manager. Although Stein, characteristically, treated the affair with dignity, he was known to be hurt by the 'dismissal' and reluctantly moved south to Leeds United. He was with the Yorkshire club for only a few months when he was enticed back to Scotland to look after the national side.

His fatal heart-attack, moments after a World Cup qualifier in 1985, occurred on just the kind of emotional and stirring night that Stein had provided for Scottish fans for so long.

STENHOUSEMUIR

Founded 1884

Joined League 1921 (Division 2)

Honours None

Ground Ochilview Park

Ochilview was the scene of the first senior match in Scotland under modern floodlighting (v Hibs, 7 November 1951), but Stenhousemuir have not always been seen as part of the future of the game. Proposed reconstruction in 1964 threatened to push them out of the League, but legal action followed and an out-of-court settlement secured their place.

The judiciary was also

involved after a bookmaker attempted unsuccessfully to bribe goalkeeper Joe Shortt in 1925. It was one of the few attempts at match-fixing ever uncovered in Scottish football.

Stenhousemuir's most distinguished discovery was Willie Ormond, a star winger of the 1950s with Hibs and later Scotland's manager.

More recently, a run of 17 matches without defeat astonished the Scottish football scene in 1994/95, and saw "The Muir" top of Division Two. They ended the season, however, in fourth place.

STIRLING ALBION

Founded 1945

Joined League 1946 (Division C)

Honours Scottish League Division 2 Champions 1953, 1958, 1961, 1965; Second Division Champions 1977, 1991

Ground Annfield Park

The club's early days reflected the makeshift nature of the post-war period. Their first stand, for example, rested on two lorries. By 1949, however, they had been promoted all the way to Division 1.

League success was difficult to sustain but Albion, in the 1970s and 1980s, consistently discovered good young players. They were also the first senior club in Scotland to play on artificial turf (laid in 1987) but were compelled to return to grass by 1992. In season 1984/85 they had a 20-0 victory over Selkirk in the Scottish Cup, a record margin for the competition in the twentieth century.

STOCKPORT COUNTY

Founded 1883

Joined League 1900 (Division 2)

Honours Division 3 (N) Champions 1922, 1937; Division 4 Champions 1967

Ground Edgeley Park

Just down the road from Manchester is hardly the most viable location for a club of modest means but, in those daunting circumstances, Stockport County have been making a plucky fist of League life throughout the twentieth century.

Formed by members of the Congregational church, they occupied numerous grounds before settling at Edgeley Park two years after joining Division 2. In 1904 they failed to win re-election but gained their status the following season, then embarked on an up-and-down existence which saw them sink to the Third Division on three occasions. In 1959 they dropped to the Fourth, where they remained for three decades apart from three seasons at the end of the 1960s. During that enterprising but gimmicky period, in which dancing girls provided pre-match entertainment and the slogan 'Go Go County' was employed, hopes ran high.

But public support was not forthcoming, results declined and Stockport resumed their familiar role in the soccer hierarchy until promotion in 1991 brought relief. Diversion through success in knock-out competitions came in 1935 and 1950, when they reached the last 16 of the FA Cup, and in 1972/73, when similar progress was made in the League Cup.

Understandably, star names have been few, although 'keeper Harry Hardy won an England cap in 1924 and former England defender Neil Franklin finished his playing days with County in the late 1950s. Former managers include Andy Beattie, Jimmy Meadows, Bert Trautmann and Mike Summerbee.

STOKE CITY

Founded 1863

Joined League 1888 (founder member)

Honours Division 2 Champions 1933, 1963; Division 3 (N) Champions 1927; League Cup Winners 1972; Division 2 Champions 1993

Ground Victoria Ground

Toil has featured more prominently than triumph in the story of Stoke City, yet the long years of striving have been enlightened by occasional high spots which have produced an intensity of emotion quite out of character with the normally down-to-earth 'Potters'.

Stoke's early League experiences were not auspicious. After propping up the table for two seasons they were not re-elected, and even after returning a year later they continued to struggle. Cash was short and in 1908, having been relegated, they went into liquidation.

The Potters regrouped after the First World War, spent the 1920s division-hopping, and finally, in the 1930s, built a side capable of making its mark. With a young winger named Stanley Matthews showing rich promise, Stoke ascended to the First Division, where they were to stay for 20 years. Managed by their former defender Bob McGrory, and with the future knight forming a potent combination with marksman Freddie Steele, they offered real hope for the future.

In the first season after the war – with accomplished centre-half Neil Franklin at his peak – Stoke missed the Championship by just two points. But then Matthews went to Blackpool, Franklin to Bogota, and in 1953 the Potters found themselves back in the Second Division.

Revival was heralded by the arrival of Tony Waddington as boss in 1960. He re-signed Matthews, recruited other veterans including forwards Jimmy McIlroy and Dennis Viollet, and achieved promotion in 1963. The town had never witnessed such scenes of celebration. Continuing to buy seasoned campaigners, Waddington consolidated Stoke's status, and 1972 brought the club's first major trophy, the League Cup, with telling contributions from the likes of schemer George Eastham, attacker Peter Dobing and 'keeper Gordon Banks. In the mid 1970s, inspired by front-man Jimmy Greenhoff and Peter Shilton in goal, they rode high in the table, but when that side broke up, the club's fortunes faded. Two spells in the Second Division followed, and in 1990 came a slump to the Third.

Support in the Potteries has been traditionally luke-warm, perhaps because the five towns lack a focal point and the increase of easy motorway travel has lured many fans to plusher venues. But success for City in the new Second Division, which they topped in 1993, followed by Port Vale's promotion a year later, seemed to galvanise the area.

STRANRAER

Founded 1870

Joined League 1949 (C Division)

Ground Stair Park

Although created by the banding together of local clubs, Stranraer have rarely been secure. League membership was slow to arrive and, tended to reside in the lowest possible division.

As with Queen of the South, a distant location has created difficulties. While Queen of the South's players train in Glasgow, Stranraer's travel to Kilmarnock. Despite that, however, attendances have been comparatively sound.

Stranraer's 1990 victory over Kilmarnock was the first Scottish Cup tie ever to be decided by penalty shoot-out. In the 1993/94, season they dominated the Second Division, and won promotion by eight points!

SUNDERLAND

Founded 1879

Joined League 1890 (Division 1)

Honours Division 1 Champions 1892, 1893, 1895, 1902, 1913, 1936; Division 2 Champions 1976; Division 3 Champions 1988; FA Cup Winners 1937, 1973

Ground Roker Park

Sunderland, one of the first titans of British soccer, have had to settle for a more humble position in the game's hierarchy during recent decades. It has not been easy for such a proud club, whose expensive transfer policy has often proved ill-advised, and whose fervent fans demand success no matter that the facts of modern football life decree otherwise.

The Wearsiders got off to a magnificent start to their League tenure. They were champions within two years of entry, and went on to take the trophy three times in four campaigns. As the century turned their dominance decreased, but with the brilliant Ted Doig between the posts and centre-forward Johnny Campbell scoring freely, they managed another title.

Even when the 'team of all the talents', as they were dubbed, broke up, it didn't herald an immediate decline. A new side was built, in which inside-forward Charlie Buchan was majestic, and in 1913 they narrowly missed the League-FA Cup double.

Another team has its 'big day': this time Sunderland taste success in May 1973. Here popular manager Bob Stokoe holds aloft the Cup above his victorious team on their return home to Roker Park. Sunderland, then in the Second Division, beat mighty Leeds 1-0. Ian Porterfield's goal and 'keeper Jim Montgomery's remarkable save from Peter Lorimer are part of football folklore and will grow in stature with the retelling.

The 1920s proved anti-climactic, but the 1930s saw the rise of what has proved, to date, to be Sunderland's last great team. The star was inside-forward Raich Carter, who was well supported by fellow attackers Patsy Gallacher and Bobby Gurney, a trio who contributed hugely towards bringing major prizes to Roker Park.

The war stopped their momentum, and when life returned to normal the club attempted to buy glory. Costly arrivals included inside-forward Len Shackleton, striker Trevor Ford and winger Billy Bingham, yet their most impressive performer was locally born wing-half Stan Anderson. The spending spree failed, and in 1958 Sunderland were relegated after a record 68 years in Division 1. Sterling efforts by centre-half Charlie Hurley and goal-machine Brian Clough helped to pave the way for promotion six years later, but further questionable judgement – witness the purchase of gifted but wayward play-maker Jim Baxter – precipitated another demotion in 1970.

This time, with shrewd guidance by Bob Stokoe, their stint in the Second Division was enlivened by a stirring FA Cup victory against Leeds United, featuring a heroic performance by 'keeper Jim Montgomery. But although Sunderland went up three years later, they could not consolidate, and were off on

a roller-coaster tour of divisions which reached its lowest point in 1987/88, which was spent in the Third.

Since then the Rokerites have returned to the top division – albeit in controversial circumstances involving the financial difficulties of Swindon Town – only to drop out after a single season. It was a sickening blow to the morale of an economically depressed area. In 1992 there was a little light relief as Sunderland reached the FA Cup Final, only to lose to Liverpool. More far-reaching, however, was a plan to leave Roker for a new custom-built stadium, a radical move that would launch a new era for the hard-pressed Wearsiders.

SUPPORTERS

Tony Mason, in *Association Football and English Soccer* (Harvester, 1980), concluded that throughout the late 1870s and 1880s football of a

good standard could be watched for anything between threepence and sixpence. He says: 'There is no doubt that by 1915 the majority of spectators who went to watch professional football matches were working-class in origin, occupation and life style. They paid 6d and stood on earth mounds or terracing, often made of cinders edged with wood. They might or might not be under cover.'

In the period after the First World War, more formal supporters' clubs first began, and the National Federation of Football Supporters' Clubs was formed in 1927. In the post-war period, when supporters first used cars to travel to

more successful clubs, supporters' clubs helped keep some lower-league clubs solvent. Money was raised through social events and, once the Betting and Lotteries Act permitted, small-scale gaming activities. Later, football clubs took over their own commercial activities.

Supporters have always dressed for the match. In the early post-war days fans took rattles, rosettes and scarves. Of these, only the scarf has lasted. The tossing of toilet rolls was a disruption that began in the 1960s, and in the 1970s there was much talk of the hooligan's tools: boots to kick with, sharpened pennies to throw from the terraces, and so on. York

A section of the Kop at Anfield, with Liverpool supporters in full voice. This photograph was taken in the days before crash barriers were added on terraces to prevent mass surges of fans towards the front. With the implementation of the Taylor Report there are no longer terraces such as this. The famous Kop, for example, became a seated stand in the 1994/95 season. All major stadia are now seating only, and most smaller grounds are following suit. Football fans everywhere appreciate the need to prevent another Hillsborough disaster, but many of them still prefer to stand.

police once held a press conference to parade a multitude of confiscated weapons. In the late 1980s, however, there was a new fad – inflatables. Manchester City fans brandished inflatable bananas, Grimsby Town supporters went for 'Harry the Haddock', and many others caught on.

Whereas some sports personalities, such as golfers and tennis players, require quiet spectators, footballers thrive on a noisy environment. There have always been ritualised chants, such as the Pompey chimes at Portsmouth, and supporters have always adopted popular songs in the way West Ham supporters did with 'I'm Forever Blowing Bubbles' for the 1923 Wembley FA Cup Final. In the 1960s the South American chanting of team names ('Bra-sil, Bra-sil') was taken up by English supporters ('Liv-er-pool, Liv-er-pool'), and messages are now sent to the players through chants: 'One nil, One nil', 'Here we go, here we go', 'Cham-pi-ons'.

One outcome of the Taylor Report into the Hillsborough disaster was the recognition that supporters deserved a stronger say in the management of football clubs. Attempts in the 1950s and 1960s to co-opt supporters' club officials as directors sometimes ran into difficulties, and one Midlands director once complained that board meetings clashed with his night-shift at the pit.

However, supporters had long-standing complaints about ticket allocations, ground facilities and the direction of the club. At Oxford United in April 1983 a game was delayed for 33 minutes when 1500 fans staged a sit-in on the pitch to protest at news of a possible merger with Reading. In 1990 Charlton Athletic fans, incensed at Greenwich Council's opposition to plans for a refurbished Valley Stadium, formed a political party to protest. The Valley Party scored a massive 14,838 votes in 60 council seats.

Supporters' complaints are usually about the team. 'I'm never going to watch them again,' says the true supporter before turning up at the next home game. For some supporters, winning is the only thing. Others perform best in adversity, sharpening their wit on a referee or manager. When Derby County had serious problems with results, creditors and hooliganism in 1984, supporters warned each other to be careful outside the ground: 'They'll try to push season tickets into your pockets.'

Not all supporters are partisan to one particular team. Some are more general in their support for football, travelling around the country to see grounds and games that interest them. The Ninety-Two Club was formed in 1978 for supporters who had attended a first-team competitive fixture at all current home grounds of the 92 Football League clubs. By the early 1990s there were some 700 members.

The Football Supporters' Association, formed after the 1985 Heysel disaster, also gained momentum very quickly. It now has a regional network, and details are available through its postal address: PO Box 11, Liverpool L2X 1XP. The rapid growth of 'fanzines' during the 1980s has provided evidence of supporters' energy, humour and insight. In the past, supporters have been sadly neglected in football literature. One exception is Fever Pitch by Nick Hornby which captures the essence of life as a supporter rather than those of players, managers, directors, referees or hooligans. Perhaps the late 1990s will see a move away from 'the match' and towards 'the experience of supporters'. After all, supporters are football's largest sponsors.

Twice in their history, Swansea have shown top-flight potential. The first time, in the 1950s, it disappeared when a succession of richly talented youngsters were sold through economic necessity; on the second occasion, in the early 1980s, John Toshack actually led the 'Swans' into Division 1, whence they disappeared after two campaigns to resume their struggles in the League's lower reaches. By the 1990s, with the eternal problems of poor attendances and the Welsh passion for rugby, there was little sign of a third opportunity.

Swansea were founder members of Division 3, from which they soon rose with a sprightly side which beat Arsenal to reach the 1926 FA Cup semi-finals. They could attain no more than Second Division mediocrity, however, and were relegated soon after the war despite the emergence of young centre-forward Trevor Ford. Manager Billy McCandlass took them up in 1949 and, though he sold wing-half Roy Paul, he introduced youthful entertainers such as schemer Ivor Allchurch, wingers Cliff Jones, Terry Medwin and Ivor's brother Len, and utility man Mel Charles. Each was transferred and, with a 1964 FA Cup semi-final appearance the only highlight, Swansea sank eventually to the Fourth Division, where Toshack joined them in 1978.

Leaning heavily on his Liverpool connections and boosted by stalwart forward Robbie James, Toshack assembled a team which climbed all the way to the First Division and finished a creditable sixth in 1981/82. But he left, reality returned, and by 1986 Swansea were back at the bottom level. Promotion followed two years later, but a return to Europe via the Welsh Cup seemed their most likely way of getting back into the big time – though even that avenue would soon be closed by UEFA.

Frank Swift, like some other famous goalkeepers, was known and respected as much for his personality as for the list of honours he achieved. Big 'Swifty' (six feet tall, with enormous hands) was everybody's favourite; loved within the game for both his humour and modesty, he was admired by fans around the world for his agility and skill.

As he came from a family that already possessed one professional footballer, scouts were aware of the potential of the young Swift. He wasn't old enough to sign professional forms on leaving school and so took a job at Blackpool Gas Works, playing for them and Fleetwood before joining City. He soon won a first-team place, and in the following five eventful seasons he missed only one match.

Although he was able to complete his playing career, Frank Swift – seen here in goal for Manchester City – died in the prime of his life in 1958. 'Big Swifty' was awarded 19 England caps. He was a much respected goalkeeper.

For a club who have spent more than 50 of their first 70 years of League life in Division 3, and who until 1993 had never entered the top flight, Swindon Town have had a considerable impact on English soccer. They first made their mark just before the First World War when, as a Southern League outfit inspired by schemer Harold Fleming, they reached two FA Cup semi-finals. There followed a long, grey period, which ended in the early 1960s with the emergence of a bright young team under the guidance of manager Bert Head.

Wingers Don Rogers and Mike Summerbee took the eye, but there was also a major contribution from full-back John Trollope – later to break the club's appearance record – as the 'Robins' won promotion. But leading players departed and Swindon were relegated two years later, before bouncing back to enjoy their most successful campaign in

The Second World War meant that his first (of 19) full England cap came as late as 1946, although he played in 17 wartime and 'Victory' internationals. Swift thought it was a great honour to represent his country and was delighted to become the first goalkeeper to captain England in 1948 – a 4-0 victory against Italy in Turin.

In his later playing years Swift was active in working for improved conditions and contracts for footballers, and also in coaching goalkeepers. Despite all this, he may go down in history as the player who fainted at the final whistle of an FA Cup Final – when reaching for his gloves after City's 1934 Wembley win. A photographer sitting behind the goal had 'counted down' the last moments, adding to the young Swift's excitement.

Frank Swift died in the Munich air disaster; he had attended Manchester United's match in Belgrade as a newspaper reporter.

SWINDON TOWN

Founded 1881

Joined League 1920 (Division 3)

Honours Division 4 Champions 1986; League Cup Winners 1969

Ground County Ground

Happy days for Swindon Town as manager Ossie Ardiles and ever-present midfielder Alan McLoughlin celebrate victory in the 1989/90 Division 2 play-off final against Sunderland. McLoughlin scored (or was it a Gary Bennett own goal?) the only goal of the match, watched by 72,873 at Wembley. Due to breaches of League rules, however, Swindon were not promoted and Sunderland found themselves in the First Division for the 1990/91 season.

1968/69. With Rogers in the van, they overturned Arsenal to win the League Cup and also reached Division 2, with average gates of nearly 20,000. Sadly they could not maintain progress and by 1982 were in the Fourth.

Lou Macari lifted them back to the old Second, and his successor, Osvaldo Ardiles, transformed a workmanlike side into an attractive unit which won a place in the 1990 Division 1 play-offs. A Wembley triumph over Sunderland apparently earned promotion, but celebrations were halted when the League ruled that Swindon must stay down as punishment for financial irregularities during the Macari years. Ardiles was replaced by Glenn Hoddle, and in a growing town with limited local competition for support, there seemed a fair chance that – despite the club's heavy debts – he might succeed. So he did, leading them into the top flight via the play-offs in 1993 before leaving for Chelsea. Sadly John Gorman could not keep the 'Robins' among the elite and it was left to his sucessor, Steve McMahon, to try and halt the slide in 1995. He failed, and Swindon suffered a second successive demotion.

SYSTEMS OF PLAY

'Of late dribbling has given way to a more effective, if less scientific, kind of play,' wrote FA Secretary Charles Alcock in 1876. He was mourning how the dribbling and 'backing-up' approach had been replaced by the 'passing-on' game, 'first introduced in any degree of perfection by the Northerners in the early matches between London and Sheffield'.

Whereas teams in the dribbling era consisted almost entirely of forwards, the passing game gradually brought a better balance. The classic 2-3-5 system – two full-backs, three half-backs, and five forwards – became commonplace in the mid 1880s. But the full-backs were positioned more centrally – to watch three forwards down the middle –

Billy Bremner of Leeds and Peter Storey of Arsenal clash during a match in the early 1970s. Both players were renowned for their tough tackling. The Leeds midfield in their glory days of the late '60s and early '70s had the stylish artistry of Johnny Giles alongside the tenacity of Billy Bremner. This partnership was often compared to the Spurs pairing of Mackay and Blanchflower of the early '60s (see page 195). The system of play in the 1970s was 4-4-2 or 4-3-3, but no longer 2-3-5; gone were the days of inside-forwards and wing-halves.

the centre-half went up and down the field in the manner of a central midfield player, and the two wing-halves played wider and marked wingers.

A major change was sparked by the 1925 offside law. Full-backs such as Morley and Montgomery (Notts County) and Hudspeth and McCracken (Newcastle United) had used the old law by putting players offside rather than waiting for them to stray into an offside position. But when only two defenders were required behind the ball to keep players onside, the centre-half was needed in a more defensive role – as a 'stopper' centre-half. Full-backs moved wider to watch wingers, and wing-halves took on a more vital role in midfield. This new system was the W-M formation, so called because defenders lined up on the points of a W, attackers on the points of an M.

After the 'stopper' centre-half came the deep-lying centre-forward. Hungary excelled against England at Wembley in 1953 with an elusive centre-forward called Nandor Hidegkuti. Don Revie helped Manchester City to Wembley in 1955 and 1956 with a similar plan, confusing centre-halves who relied on close-marking a centre-forward.

Former footballers argued that many such tactics had

been tried in other eras without being given fancy names like 'the Revie plan', 'overlapping full-backs' and 'near-post centres'. However, these and other moves became commonplace in the 1960s, complete with grand and scientific names. Similarly, the tactic of employing a defensive wing-half alongside the centre-half – as adopted by Joe Mercer at Arsenal in the late 1940s – became very popular in the 1960s. Based on the 1958 Brazilian system, a deep-lying forward and attacking wing-half worked as link men

between attack and defence in a formation known as 4-2-4. But the 4-2-4 system needed two attacking wingers. When Alf Ramsey found himself without wingers of the calibre of Matthews or Finney, he shifted to a 4-3-3 formation for England's 1966 World Cup win. Other managers resorted to 4-4-2, 5-3-2 – all kinds of shapes.

The zonal marking system was an alternative to man-to-man marking, and an additional option was the libero, a player given the freedom to hang behind other defenders and use his vision of the whole pitch to 'sweep' up dangerous situations. People became more system-conscious. Managers later talked of a team's 'shape'.

The variety of systems was made more confusing for spectators by tricks with players' numbers. Dick Graham was one manager who kept the public guessing, as summarised with inimitable humour by Eric Foster in a scouting report of a 1967/68 game between Oxford United and Orient: 'The Orientals were running true to form. Number 2 was at inside-left, number 8 was at left-back, number 4 at outside-left. For one exciting moment it looked as though the goalkeeper was going to stay between the posts, but, typically he was nowhere to be seen when Oxford's goals went in.'

Yet Graham was prescient. A system of interchangeable players, later known as 'total football', was perfected in the early 1970s by teams such as Ajax, Holland and West Germany. The Dutch were attackers and defenders, free from constraints, as long as they did not sacrifice the overall system. Men such as Johan Cruyff and Wim van Hanegem had no obvious position. A libero like Ruud Krol was often seen in midfield or attack.

British football became more European in the 1970s, clubs such as Liverpool and Nottingham Forest dominating the European Cup, but in the 1980s some teams returned to the direct strategy of long passes and old-fashioned wing play. Game analysis showed that most goals came from moves of fewer than four passes. The quicker the ball was played into the penalty area, the more defensive chaos, some coaches argued. This direct approach helped Watford's rise to the First Division, manager Graham Taylor blending two strong central attackers (Luther Blissett and Ross Jenkins) with two fast, penetrative wingers (Nigel Callaghan and John Barnes). The long-ball (Taylor prefers to call it the 'long-pass') game thrilled some pundits, while others moaned that they needed the roof taken off the stand to see their team's best passes. Wimbledon also reached the First Division with this system.

Other successful teams between 1966 and 1986 are analysed in The Winning Formula, a book and series of five video tapes produced by Charles Hughes, the FA Director of Coaching. Coaches, however, stress that individual skills – ball control, passing, defending, shooting – are more important than a system of play. Liverpool's team success had much to do with individual responsibilities: working hard at not losing the ball, not wasting a pass and supporting team-mates. And any system should suit the strengths of individual players. In the final analysis, systems of play may not be as important as a team's ability to turn set-plays into goals or, indeed, a goalkeeper's ability to save them.

As systems of play have changed, so has numbering. There was a time when the number of a player gave a good indication of his position. First came tactical changes, with numbers 7 and 11, for example, possibly playing in midfield. Then came the Premiership's demand that players use the same numbers throughout the season, creating scenes like this one of Arsenal players in a wall.

TAYLOR, Graham

1944 Born in Worksop

1962 Signs for Grimsby Town; plays 189 games

1965 Qualifies for full FA coaching badge

1968 Joins Lincoln City; 150 appearances

1972 Becomes manager of Lincoln City

1976 Lincoln are Champions of Division 4, losing only four league games and scoring 112 goals

1977 Appointed manager of Watford who win the Division 4 championship in Taylor's first full season

1979 Watford promoted again

1982 ...and again

1983 First season in the top flight and Watford finish as runners-up; The Hornets reach the FA Cup Final, which they lose to Everton.

1987 Taylor joins Aston Villa who win promotion from Division 2

1990 Appointed England manager in succession to Bobby Robson

1992 England flop in European Championships - failing to win a match and finishing bottom of their group

1993 Criticism of Taylor mounts as England struggle in World Cup qualifiers; November – he resigns as England boss after failing to reach America

1994 March – becomes manager of Wolves and in two successive seasons narrowly misses promotion

When Bobby Robson announced he would quit as England's manager after the 1990 World Cup finals in Italy, the FA acted swiftly. The then Aston Villa manager Graham Taylor was offered a four-year contract and so was completed the rise from being manager of 4th Division Lincoln City to supremo of the national side.

Taylor's playing career as a defender was largely undistinguished. However, on entering management, he soon made his mark. He became the youngest ever to be appointed an FA staff coach and transformed Watford from a sleepy 4th Division team to a respected 1st Division side challenging for honours and playing in Europe. During his successful period at Vicarage Road he became England Youth team manager.

In his brief but successful spell at Aston Villa he took the club back into the 1st Division and to runners-up position in the top-flight.

When Taylor was appointed England manager he had a tough act to follow. Bobby Robson had just led England to fourth place in the 1990 World Cup Finals. However, he began well. In his first dozen games he was as successful as any of his predecessors. Taylor stuck to his principles, favouring the more direct style and picking players to match that method of play.

His first target was achieved, albeit narrowly, when England qualified for the 1992 European Championships, but their performance in Sweden was hugely disappointing. Injuries to key players Paul Gascoigne, John Barnes and Mark Wright meant Taylor could not field a settled side and his decision to substitute Gary Lineker in the game against Sweden won him few friends. Like previous England managers, he found the tabloid press to be unforgiving.

A satisfactory start to the qualification stages of the 1994 World Cup meant Taylor began 1993 with the dream of leading England into the World Cup Finals very much alive. His composure in front of the press and the loyalty he won from players were key factors in helping him ride early criticism. But the 'knocking', especially in the tabloid press, reached an hysterical level – though it must be said that some of Taylor's team selections and tactics were bizarre – and when England failed to qualify for the finals, Taylor had little choice but to resign. Soon, though, he was back in football at club level, taking on the task of making Wolves great again.

Graham Taylor in his days as manager of Aston Villa. He is smiling broadly. This may have something to do with the fact that after gaining promotion in 1988, Aston Villa finished runners-up to Liverpool in Division 1 two years later. After the resignation of Bobby Robson in 1990, Taylor was appointed England manager. After an indifferent 1992 European Championships, Taylor's next target was England qualifying for the 1994 World Cup Finals... but he was struggling.

TAYLOR REPORT

Lord Justice Taylor chaired a two-month enquiry into the disaster which claimed the lives of 95 people at Hillsborough, Sheffield, on 15 April 1989. The enquiry, which heard evidence from over 170 witnesses, provided the most searching look at football in modern times. The judge produced a 71-page interim report on 4 August 1989, to permit some changes before the 1989/90 season, and the final report was released at the end of January the following year. The report ruled that the main cause of the disaster had been a failure of police control. However, Taylor was also critical of football club management for its failure to improve spectator conditions and safety.

The interim report contained 43 recommendations, and the final report a further 33. The most dramatic was that all clubs in England's top two divisions should have all-seater stadia by August 1994, and that Scottish Premier League and other Football League clubs should follow suit by August 1999. It was later deemed impractical for clubs in the bottom two divisions of the Football League to follow Taylor's edict to the letter, though stringent rules on terrace safety encouraged compliance. The judge recommended that certain activities should be made criminal offences, namely the throwing of missiles at sports grounds, ticket touting, the chanting of racist or obscene abuse and running on to the pitch without reasonable excuse. Taylor's recommendations included methods for better police communications, electronic 'tagging' to detect convicted hooligans at grounds, and ways of improving first-aid and medical facilities (although he stressed that there was no criticism of the response by ambulance and fire services at Hillsborough). One specific recommendation was for one trained first-aider per thousand spectators.

Many of Taylor's recommendations concerned very specific safety issues. He suggested reductions in terrace capacities and improved systems for filling grounds and monitoring the progress of crowds. One recommendation was that the spikes be removed from fences, which should be no higher than 2.2 metres. Emergency gates should be patrolled to allow swift opening. There were a number of specific points made about crush barriers, gangways, escape routes from terraces, stewarding, crowd partitioning and safety certificates, and the judge felt a need to spell out the duties of football clubs. Overall, the report highlighted the poor state of football grounds and management.

The Conservative government suffered a setback from the Taylor Report in that the judge recommended that the proposed computerised identity card scheme should be rejected. Taylor believed that the scheme would increase chances of congestion and disorder outside grounds. He also recommended that all sports grounds, including those for cricket and rugby, should be subject to a Football Licensing Authority, set up under the new Football Spectators Bill.

TELEVISION

Television coverage of football has gradually increased, but not without conflict between the television companies and football authorities. Careful negotiations have often been needed to resolve issues of finance, the distribution of money among clubs, shirt advertising, overseas rights, live television and compensation for loss of attendance.

Part of the 1937 FA Cup Final – Sunderland v Preston North End – was shown on television; then, after the war, it became common for the FA Cup Final to be broadcast live. Internationals and other Cup games were occasionally edited for BBC's Sports Special programme, which began in September 1955. ITV was the first channel to televise a Football League game – a Division 1 clash between Blackpool and Bolton Wanderers on 10 September 1960.

A major breakthrough came in August 1964 when BBC2 launched a 45-minute programme showing highlights of a top League game. The programme, Match of the Day, was so successful that it was moved to BBC1 to reach a bigger audience.

The late 1960s brought experiments with closed-circuit television. On Wednesday 7 October 1965 Coventry City erected four screens on their own ground so supporters could watch a Division 2 match taking place in Cardiff. The game was watched by 12,639 in Cardiff and 10,295 in Coventry. Far more watched the 1967 Everton v Liverpool fifth-round Cup tie: 64,851 live at Goodison Park and 40,149 in front of screens at Anfield.

The power of television was apparent by the end of the 1960s. Instant joy was brought into millions of British homes when big events were televised live, such as the 1966 World Cup Final, Celtic's 1967 European Cup Final victory and Manchester United's 1968 European Cup Final win. But television also brought controversy. The Celtic-Racing

A crowd of 35,534, mostly standing, at Tottenham's White Hart Lane for Spurs v Sheffield United in the Second Division, January 1936. The picture shows Taylor, the Spurs 'keeper saving from Dodds (who later scored in the 1-1 draw). Modern spectators are unlikely to see either standing crowds of this size or pitches in such bad condition. Neither will they see the large white letters along the side lines that were used to give spectators half-time scores of other matches.

brawl in Montevideo, in which six players were sent off, brought outraged reactions. And in 1971 referee Ray Tinkler was subjected to a nationwide trial when he allowed a Jeff Astle goal for West Bromwich Albion against Leeds United – Astle's team-mate Colin Suggett was in an offside position.

Negotiations for television deals were often difficult. As sponsorship came into football, so television contracts became even more important. There were fears that 'American' problems – one referee complained he had to blow for stoppages to allow advertisements to be shown – would be replicated in Britain, but the most common debate surrounded whether television was good for the game. Would the revenue compensate for lower attendances and controversial publicity? In the late 1970s the Football League struck a special exclusive deal with ITV, nicknamed 'Snatch of the Day', but it was later set aside by the Office of Fair Trading.

In 1983, for the first time, games were played on Sunday especially for the benefit of live television. The first was Tottenham Hotspur against Nottingham Forest on Sunday 2 October, and the audience was 5 million. (A month later a man murdered his girlfriend because she turned off the television when a football match was being shown.)

Predictably, there was one season when talks between the Football League and the television companies broke down completely. There was no television coverage during the first half of 1985/86. Agreement was finally reached in December.

With satellite and cable television, networks grew even bigger. It was estimated that over half the human race watched at least one game during the 1990 World Cup finals. In Britain, a major new deal with Sky satellite television in 1992 saw live coverage of League fixtures trebled under a four-year contract worth over £300 million.

TORQUAY UNITED

Founded 1898

Joined League 1927

Honours None

Ground Plainmoor

Torquay United's mark on soccer history has not, so far, been a notable one, as might be expected of a club based in a tourist resort on the south coast of Devon. Professional soccer has never figured highly among the local entertainment options, and with almost every away game bringing steep travel bills, it would appear that, for United, becoming a major soccer force presents a well-nigh insurmountable task.

Early omens were not good. For more than 30 years after applying for re-election at the end of their first League campaign, Torquay remained members of the lowest available flight. Then, during the 1960s, they twice won promotion before returning both times to the basement.

Their most exciting spell came in the middle of that decade when, with Frank O'Farrell in charge, they rose to the Third Division and twice came close to reaching the Second. In 1991 they won promotion again, only to go down once more after one term. United's best-known

players down the years have tended to be goalscorers, with Sam Collins in the 1950s and Robin Stubbs in the 1960s springing to mind.

TOTTENHAM HOTSPUR

Founded 1882

Joined League 1908 (Division 2)

Honours Division 1 Champions 1951, 1961; Division 2 Champions 1920, 1950; FA Cup Winners 1901, 1921, 1961, 1962, 1967, 1981, 1982, 1991; League Cup Winners 1971, 1973; European Cup Winners' Cup Winners 1963; UEFA Cup Winners 1972, 1984

Ground White Hart Lane

Even though their recent achievements have hardly matched their illustrious past, Spurs remain one of the glamour clubs of world soccer. Usually ready to compete for the most expensive players in the transfer market, and renowned for attractive football, they take the eye and dominate the back pages in a way that makes them the southern counterpart of Manchester United.

Yet Tottenham were comparatively late starters on the glory trail. In fact, when

The power of television... the Sky Strikers at the Arsenal v Manchester City match. Sky TV has brought a number of new ideas into football, and a lot of new money. Never before has television coverage been so complete. Apart from Sky's exhaustive recording and live screening of Premiership matches, all Endsleigh League (Divisions 1-3) matches are now watched by independent television cameras.

they won their first major trophy, the FA Cup, just after the turn of the century, they were in the Southern League, and a further seven campaigns passed before they were elected to the senior competition. Once in, they were promoted at the end of their opening campaign, but then struggled in the top grade and were relegated in 1915. After the war Spurs were a more buoyant force, with the likes of wing-half and skipper Arthur Grimsdell, inside-forward Jimmy Seed and left-winger Jimmy Dimmock in their prime, and success in both Division 2 and the FA Cup soon came. There followed a lengthy period of mediocrity during which they twice slid back to the Second

Division, and it was not until the late 1940s that Tottenham's star began to rise again.

The manager responsible was Arthur Rowe, a former White Hart Lane player, whose famous 'push-and-run' style not only achieved the longed-for promotion but also lifted the League Championship in the following term. Rowe's most influential players were goalkeeper Ted Ditchburn, full-backs Alf Ramsey and Ron Burgess, and inside-left Eddie Baily.

The mid 1950s saw the arrival of brilliantly constructive right-half Danny Blanchflower, bustling centre-forward Bobby Smith and wing speedster Cliff Jones, but it was not until Bill Nicholson, who played under Rowe, took over as manager in 1958 that the most famous side in Tottenham's history was assembled. In came ultra-combative left-half Dave Mackay, schemer John White and 'keeper Bill Brown, all from Scotland, and within two and a half years Spurs had become the first club this century to win the League and FA Cup double. They were a wonderful side, skilful and adventurous yet with a core of steel. With ace goalscorer Jimmy Greaves added, they went on to further achievements, notably becoming the first British team to win a European trophy.

The inevitable break-up came and Tottenham, while winning cups on a fairly regular basis, have never since been such a force in the League, although there has been no shortage of stars to thrill the fans. Among the most dazzling have been subtle striker Alan Gilzean and inspirational 'keeper Pat Jennings in the post-double era, England forwards Martin Chivers and Martin Peters in the early 1970s and Argentinians Ossie Ardiles and Ricky Villa who arrived in 1978. Ardiles was still captivating White Hart Lane towards the end of the following decade, his creative talents complementing those of his visionary midfield colleague Glenn Hoddle, often to spectacular effect.

By the dawn of the 1990s with former Spur Terry Venables in charge, it was England striker Gary Lineker and media plaything Paul Gascoigne who held the stage, before both departed overseas. Entertainment value was high, but financial problems following the club's flotation on the Stock Exchange cast uncertainty over the future. Then in 1991, with debts amounting to some £18 million, Tottenham were bought by a partnership that included businessman Alan Sugar and Venables himself. Thus the 'Lilywhites' prepared for a new era with fresh hope. Unfortunately, much dirty linen was to be washed in public before the club regained an even keel. Sugar and Venables fell out bitterly and the latter departed to be replaced as manager by Ardiles in June 1993. Under the Argentinian, Spurs played attractive but not always practical football, though many fans believed he was the correct long-term choice. However, his chances took a severe jolt during the summer of 1994 when Tottenham were found guilty of financial irregularities – dating from the 1980s – and

Few teams can have had such a well-known line-up as the Tottenham Hotspur 'double' side of the early 1960s: (back row, left to right) Henry, Norman, Brown, Smith, Baker; Jones, White, Blanchflower (captain), Allen, Dyson, Mackay. The balance of the team was often used as a model for other sides: the tall Maurice Norman dominated the air in defence, while gritty, ball-winning half-back Dave Mackay complemented the passing abilities of Danny Blanchflower. Up front, the bustling Bobby Smith often won the ball for the quicksilver John White, both being supplied by fast wingers Dyson and Jones.

were fined heavily, banned from the 1994/95 FA Cup and had 12 League points deducted from the forthcoming season. After lengthy and acrimonious legal wrangles, the penalty was reduced to a merely financial one, but by then Ardiles - who had acquired the services of World Cup stars Jurgen Klinsmann of Germany and Rumanians Ilie Dumitrescu and Gheorghe Popescu – had been dismissed. His team had been exhilaratingly entertaining but, too often, defensively inept and he paid the traditional price. Enter Gerry Francis, who brought a more pragmatic approach; fortunes revived at once and, suddenly, Tottenham's prospects, despite Klinsmann's departure after only one season, were the brightest they had been for a long time.

TRANMERE ROVERS

Founded 1885

Joined League 1921 (Division 3 N)

Honours Division 3 (N) Champions 1938

Ground Prenton Park

If the Mersey Tunnel had never been built, life would have been easier for Tranmere Rovers. Yet, despite the regular exodus of Wirral football fans to sample the more exalted delights on offer across the river at Anfield and Goodison Park, the Birkenhead club has striven valiantly to record more than seven decades of League existence.

Until the 1990s, all but one campaign – 1938/39, when Rovers proved incapable of meeting the standard demanded in Division 2 – had been spent in the lower reaches, and the club had been periodically troubled by cash crises. But there had been compensations. Tranmere it was who unearthed two of England's greatest pre-war centre-forwards – Bill 'Dixie' Dean and Tom 'Pongo' Waring – and in the 1960s they gave a start to centre-half Roy McFarland, who also became an international star.

In 1987 Tranmere came perilously close to dropping into the Vauxhall Conference but since then, improving rapidly during manager John King's second spell at Prenton Park, they have lifted the Leyland DAF Cup and risen to challenge for a place in the new Premier League. In 1994 they were unlucky to be defeated by Aston Villa in the Coca-Cola Cup semi-finals. Then 1995 saw their third successive failure to reach the top flight via the play-offs.

TRANSFERS

When a player changes clubs, his new club pays compensation to the old. Transfer fees have risen steadily through the century, although a dramatic rise in the late 1970s threatened to send them out of control. Since 1980 fees have been decided by a Football League tribunal if clubs cannot agree or a player thinks the fee being asked is prohibiting him getting another club.

A transfer deadline – the second Thursday in March each season – was introduced in 1911 to prevent clubs engaged in relegation and promotion issues from strengthening their teams after that date. Football League permission is needed for a player to play a League game if he is signed in the last few weeks of a season. This is usually granted only for games not affecting the top or bottom places.

As transfer fees are private and confidential matters, and as deals sometimes take in more than one player, transfer fees quoted in the press are not always reliable. However, certain symbolic transfer barriers are often associated with certain players. Alf Common (£1000 from Sunderland to Middlesbrough in 1905); Syd Puddefoot (£5000 from West Ham to Falkirk in 1922) and David Jack (£10,890 from Bolton Wanderers to Arsenal in 1928) all broke significant thresholds.

Tony Hateley's move from Aston Villa to Chelsea in 1966

Prolific goalscorer John Aldridge celebrates his second goal on his debut for Tranmere Rovers against Brighton in the Second Division at the opening of the 1991/92 season. John has scored consistently at all levels – from Newport County to Tranmere, via Oxford and Liverpool, and even at international level for the Republic of Ireland. Tranmere Rovers have benefited immensely from Aldridge's goals, but have just failed to get to the Premiership.

was the first £100,000 transfer between British clubs.

Dennis Tueart's transfer from Sunderland to Manchester City in 1974 broke the £250,000 barrier. And four years later Gordon McQueen was the subject of the first £500,000 fee, Manchester United paying Leeds United.

In 1979 Trevor Francis became the first £1,000,000 British player when he moved from Birmingham City to Nottingham Forest. This transfer sparked a rush of seven-figure deals, the most dramatic being those of Steve Daley (Wolverhampton Wanderers to Manchester City for £1,437,500), Andy Gray (Aston Villa to Wolverhampton Wanderers for £1,469,000) and Bryan Robson (West Bromwich Albion to Manchester United for £1,500,000). Tony Cottee's transfer from West Ham United to Everton in 1988 broke the £2 million barrier, and he was soon followed by Paul Gascoigne (Newcastle United to Tottenham Hotspur). In 1989 Manchester United paid £2.3 million to Middlesbrough for the transfer of Gary Pallister; then came Dean Saunders' £2.9 million switch from Derby County to Liverpool in July 1991, and Alan Shearer's £3.6 million transfer from Southampton to the nouveau riche Blackburn Rovers a year later. In the summer of 1994, it was Chris Sutton's turn to be record-breaker, leaving Norwich to link up with Shearer at Ewood Park for a little matter

of £5 million. Then in January 1995, Andy Cole's £7 million move from Newcastle to Manchester United made him the most expensive player in British football history. But for how long?

Allan Clarke and Alan Ball go down in transfer price history by twice figuring in British record deals. In the late 1960s Clarke moved from Fulham to Leicester City for £150,000 and then to Leeds United for £165,000. Ball went from Blackpool to Everton for £110,000 in 1966 and on to Arsenal for £220,000 five years later.

Two earlier transfers are important for their legal implications. In March 1912 the judge ruled in favour of Aston Villa in the test case of Lawrence J Kingaby v Aston Villa. Kingaby claimed that another club had offered him employment but the transfer fee fixed by Aston Villa was stopping him taking it up. The judge felt the club was justified. In 1963, however, George Eastham (Newcastle United) successfully brought a case against his club to show that the system of retaining a player after expiration of contract was not binding in law.

Denis Law's transfer from Huddersfield Town to Manchester City in 1960 – the first over £50,000 – was soon followed by two more big transfers involving the same player. Law went from Manchester City to Torino for £100,000 in 1961 and from Torino to Manchester United for £115,000 in 1962. Both

were records for transfers involving a British club.

In 1982 Diego Maradona was transferred from Argentinos Juniors to Barcelona (Spain) for £4.8 million. Two years later he moved to Napoli for £6.9 million. Both were world records.

Major deals involving British clubs included Chris Waddle (Tottenham Hotspur to Marseille for £4.25 million in July 1989), then three all priced at £5.5 million – David Platt (Aston Villa to Bari, August 1991), Trevor Steven (Rangers to Marseille, same month), Paul Gascoigne (Tottenham Hotspur to Lazio, May 1992). May 1990 saw a new world record when Robert Baggio moved from Fiorentina to Juventus for £7.7 million, but that was eclipsed in 1992 when AC Milan paid Torino approximately £13 million for Gianluigi Lentini.

Of course, when large sums of money change hands there is a good deal of interest. Recent years have

No doubt pushing up the final asking price, Andy Cole scores against Manchester United for Newcastle United in August 1993. The match finished 1-1 in a season which Cole was to dominate from a goalscoring point of view. United signed Cole for around £7m in 1995 and, although his early form was disappointing, he soon proved he could take chances close to goal. The football world waits to see who the first £10m signing in Britain will be. Certainly the day cannot be very far away, as powerful and ambitious chairmen compete with each other.

seen the rise of players' agents who, apart from securing good deals for their clients take a significant cut of money themselves. And others may benefit from transfers too. Arsenal manager George Graham, one of the most successful and respected bosses in the land, was accused of taking a £285,000 'bung' as part of one major deal. His alleged misdemeanour came to light while the soccer authorities were undertaking a wide-ranging investigation into more than 20 transfers involving Scandinavian players. Individuals and clubs may eventually be charged with financial irregularities – and some famous names have been mentioned in this connection.

Roberto Baggio (left) and Gianluca Vialli – two very expensive signings for Juventus. The Italian club are reputed to have paid £7.7 million to Fiorentina for Baggio and £12 million to Sampdoria for Vialli. Both players ultimately proved their worth in 1994/95 as they helped Juve to land the 'Scudetto'.

UEFA

UEFA (Union Européen de Football Association) is the controlling body of national associations in Europe and the organiser and authority for the European club and national competitions. Based on the South American model, it was formed under the auspices of FIFA, to which it remains responsible, in Basle, Switzerland on 15 June 1954. The headquarters were established in Berne. The first president was Ebbe Schwartz of Denmark, and the current one is another Scandinavian, Lennart Johansson of Sweden. The organisation's first coup was to secure a deal with Eurovision which made the new European Cup competition feasible.

Two recent UEFA decisions have had a great impact on British soccer. The first was the banning of English clubs from European competitions after the 1985 Heysel disaster; this resulted in many English players going to Scotland in order to qualify for football in Europe. In 1990 the ban was lifted from all clubs except Liverpool, who were readmitted in 1991/92 to play in the UEFA Cup. The second was the ruling that clubs may only field three 'foreign' players in European ties, with England, Wales, Scotland, Northern Ireland and the Republic of Ireland to be considered separate nations since they put out individual national teams. This has severely limited the prospects of most British clubs in Europe.

UEFA CUP

This competition started life as the International Inter-City Industrial Fairs Cup, a tournament set up by UEFA in its inaugural year and designed to coincide with trade fairs held in major European cities, which were

invited to enter teams. In practice the competition was as unwieldy as its name; in the first five years only two tournaments were completed – not a situation guaranteed to maintain public interest. Club sides as well as ad hoc city teams such as London and Frankfurt entered.

From 1960/61 the competition began to take on a more familiar shape; club sides competed in the course of one season, each round (Final included) being contested over two legs – still the case today. After a series of

The rather splendid UEFA Cup being held aloft by Graham Roberts, the Spurs captain, after the second leg of the 1983/84 Final. The score in both legs was 1-1, so the dreaded penalty shoot-out was necessary. Anderlecht lost 4-3 on penalties. Essentially, the UEFA competition is open to also-rans in domestic league competitions. Tottenham Hotspur had finished fourth in the English First Division in 1982/83.

bewildering modifications to its name, it was rechristened the UEFA Cup in 1971/72. Like all aspects of the competition, the admission criteria have fluctuated, but essentially it has been open to also-rans in domestic league competitions, thus giving less glamorous clubs a chance of glory. Further changes were planned during the mid-1990s. With only a limited number of clubs eligible for the new Champions League, it was decided that the champions from smaller countries should be placed in the UEFA Cup. Another new way to qualify was by reaching the last four of the InterToto Cup, a long-established summer competition created for the benefit of pools companies and featuring predominantly central European clubs.

The spread of winning nationalities is wide. Spanish clubs dominated the tournament's early years and English clubs won every year from 1967/68 to 1972/73.

Winter of Ajax thwarted by keeper Marchegiani during the 2nd leg of the 1992 UEFA Cup Final. How things have changed in football. Players from an earlier generation would not understand how two matches could be drawn and yet one side be awarded the trophy – on 'away goals'. And they might not have appreciated the dive that the Dutchman seems to be launching into!

UEFA CUP			
Year	Winners	Runners-up	Aggregate Score (two leg)
1972	Tottenham Hotspur	Wolverhampton W	3-2
1973	Liverpool	B. Mönchengladbach	3-2
1974	Feyenoord	Tottenham Hotspur	4-2
1975	B. Mönchengladbach	Twente Enschede	5-1
1976	Liverpool	FC Brugge	4-3
1977	Juventus	Athletic Bilbao	2-2*
1978	PSV Eindhoven	Bastia	3-0
1979	B. Mönchengladbach	Red Star Belgrade	2-1
1980	Eintracht Frankfurt	B. Mönchengladbach	3-3*
1981	Ipswich Town	AZ 67 Alkmaar	5-4
1982	IFK Gothenburg	Hamburg	4-0
1983	Anderlecht	Benfica	2-1
1984	Tottenham Hotspur	RSC Anderlecht	6-5*
1985	Real Madrid	Videoton SC	3-1
1986	Real Madrid	FC Köln	5-3
1987	IFK Gothenburg	Dundee United	2-1
1988	Bayer Leverkusen	Espanol	6-5**
1989	Napoli	VfB Stuttgart	5-4
1990	Juventus	Fiorentina	3-1
1991	Internazionale	Roma	2-1
1992	Ajax	Torino	2-2*
1993	Juventus	Borussia Dortmund	6-1
1994	Internazionale	Salzburg	2-0
1995	Parma	Juventus	2-1

* won on away goals ** after extra time and penalties

W

WALES

The foundations of Welsh soccer were in North Wales. The epicentre was an unlikely place – a tiny border mining village called Chirk. T. E. Thomas, a Chirk schoolmaster and Welsh FA administrator, is credited with introducing 49 future Welsh internationals to the game. Even so, early Welsh administrators did not find it easy to put together a team to travel long distances. In 1878 the Scottish FA Secretary had to journey south to help round up Welsh players for the 9-0 Scottish win in Glasgow.

One Chirk coal-miner was Billy Meredith, one of the most famous Welsh footballers. Meredith played for 30 years in England. He captained Manchester City in the FA Cup Final of 1904, helped Manchester United to their 1909 FA Cup win and played in the 1924 semi-final for City when aged nearly 50. He first played for Wales in March 1895, and his last international, 25 years later, brought a famous 2-1 win against England at Highbury, a victory which welcomed one of the greatest eras in Welsh football.

By 1921 there were six Welsh clubs playing in the Football League: Cardiff City, Swansea Town, Wrexham, Newport County, Merthyr Tydfil and Aberdare Athletic.

In 1921/22 Cardiff City finished fourth in Division 1 at the first attempt. Two seasons later they missed the Championship by one goal, finishing behind Huddersfield Town on goal average. (Had today's goal difference system been operating, Cardiff would have been champions.) In 1927 there was the compensation of the FA Cup.

Seven years after winning the FA Cup, Cardiff City were seeking re-election to Division 3 (S). They were successful, unlike Aberdare (1927) and Merthyr Tydfil (1930). The era had ended, although Swansea Town continued as a steady Second Division team.

Between 1939 and 1955 Swansea won four of eleven English Schools Trophy competitions. The supply of excellent young players promised well for the Welsh international team, but Welsh clubs failed to win honours. When First Division football finally came to Swansea it was part of one of the most incredible rise-and-fall stories of soccer. Swansea City went from 22nd in Division 4 in 1974/75 to 6th in Division 1 in 1981/82. Five seasons later they finished 12th in Division 4.

From 1961 until the proposed change in 1996 a Welsh club has qualified for the European Cup Winners' Cup by means of the Welsh Cup. In 1962/63 the Welsh representatives were Bangor City, who took Napoli to a play-off in the first round. The following year Borough United progressed to the second round by beating Sliema Wanderers (Malta). There were more memorable performances from Cardiff City. In 1967/68 Cardiff beat Shamrock Rovers, NAC Breda (Holland) and Torpedo Moscow to reach the semi-final. They drew 1-1 away to SV Hamburg but lost the return 3-2 at home. Cardiff also suffered two odd-goal defeats at the quarter-final stage – to Real Zaragoza in 1964/65 and Real Madrid in 1970/71. Wrexham (1975/76) and Newport County (1980/81) have also reached the quarter-final of the European Cup Winners' Cup, the latter being unfortunate to go out 3-2 on aggregate to Carl Zeiss Jena. In 1987/88 Merthyr Tydfil fared very well against Italian Cup winners Atalanta, winning 2-1 at home but losing 2-0 away.

WALES TEAM

In the inter-war years, Wales won the British international championship outright on six occasions. Fred Keenor, captain for much of the 1920s, provided the springboard for this success. Other inter-war stars were Bob John, Bryn Jones, Stanley Davies and Len Davies.

After sharing the British international championship in 1951/52, Wales qualified for the 1958 World Cup finals in Sweden with a team managed by Jimmy Murphy and including some of the most famous players in Welsh history: goalkeeper Jack Kelsey, the Charles brothers (Mel and John), Ivor Allchurch and Cliff Jones.

Wales have not qualified for the final stages of a World Cup since 1958. The nearest they came was before the 1994 finals when a penalty miss by Paul Bodin (he hit the crossbar) contributed to a 2-1 home defeat by Romania. A packed Cardiff Arms Park were left to rue the near miss. Welsh crowds had more to mourn when the early matches for qualification for the 1996 European Championships brought defeats and almost certain failure.

Three drawn group games led to a play-off against Hungary, which Wales won 2-1. In the quarter-final Wales, without the injured John Charles, lost 1-0 to Brazil, 18-year-old Pele scoring the goal. The Welsh have not qualified for the World Cup finals since, but have often come close. They were kept out of the 1978 and 1986 World Cup finals by late penalties in vital qualifying games against Scotland. In 1982 they failed, on goal difference, to pip Czechoslovakia.

Their best European Championship performance came in the 1976 tournament, when Wales won a qualifying group which contained Austria, Hungary and Luxembourg. In the two-leg quarter-final against Yugoslavia, Wales lost 2-0 in Zagreb and drew 1-1 in Cardiff. Frustrations continued with near qualification in 1984, a year in which Yugoslavia won a tight group that included an amazing 4-4 draw in Titograd. In 1988, when defeats in Denmark and Czechoslovakia ended hopes, and in 1992, when Wales were thrashed by West Germany in Nuremberg after defeating Matthäus and company at Cardiff, the team also came close to qualification. Some of the modern stars, such as Neville Southall, Ian Rush, Mark Hughes, Ryan Giggs and Dean Saunders, have deserved appearances on a grander stage. But in the mid-1990s, results under Mike Smith, who had replaced Terry Yorath as manager, were dismal.

WALSALL

Founded 1888

Joined League 1892 (Division 2)

Honours Division 4 Champions 1960

Ground Bescot Stadium

Situated on the doorstep of Birmingham, not far from Wolverhampton, and with the M6 – an avenue to numerous Premiership venues – nearby, little Walsall are hardly well placed to make an impact on the football world.

Yet, in their time, the club who twice failed to gain League re-election in their early years and made four successive applications in the 1950s have experienced their moments of heady triumph. Among them have been a sensational FA Cup defeat of Arsenal at their mightiest, in 1933, and progress to the League Cup semi-finals, again at the Gunners' expense, in 1984.

After re-entering the League's Third Division in 1920, they remained in the lower levels until the early 1960s, when they reached the Second, thanks largely to the goals of Colin Taylor and Tony Richards. They lasted

just two terms, however, then fell to the Fourth by 1979, before rising again to the Second a decade later and plummeting back to the basement through successive relegations.

Noteworthy talents whose transfer fees have helped the 'Saddlers' survive include 1930s 'keeper Bert Williams and, in the 1960s, Phil Parkes, another custodian, and England striker Allan Clarke.

As the 1980s closed, Walsall left their long-time home at Fellows Park for a purpose-built stadium, despite their disadvantages they are not short of ambition.

FOOTBALL DURING THE WARS

The Football League programme continued through the 1914/15 season, although there was much opposition. Thereafter it was suspended for the remainder of the First World War, although makeshift leagues were introduced. League fixtures were immediately suspended on the outbreak of the Second World War, three games into the 1939/40 season. The FA Cup was also abandoned, leading to Portsmouth's bizarre record of holding the trophy for seven years (1939-46).

The blanket ban on sport in September 1939 was lifted within a few days. Football resumed with regional friendlies, and soon these were converted into regional leagues. However, players' contracts were suspended for the duration of the war. They were paid a match fee – 30 shillings in England (£2 from 1943) and £2 in Scotland – but their availability was unpredictable. Clubs often relied on guest players from other sides. There are many tales of teams being cobbled together at the last minute.

Clubs maintained a good standard if they had war-workers (e.g. coal miners) or members of the armed forces stationed nearby. Aldershot were helped by an army base which housed international footballers. Portsmouth had the legacy of a good team and

were potentially well-served by the navy. As an example of an unpredictable game, consider Portsmouth against Clapton Orient in the London League in February 1942. Clapton arrived without a goalkeeper, Pompey were at their best, and the final score was 16-1. Andy Black scored eight.

League champions in the First World War were Manchester City, Liverpool, Stoke and Everton in the Lancashire section; Nottingham Forest and Leeds City (twice each) in the Midlands section; and Chelsea (twice), West Ham and Brentford in the London Combination.

After the fragmented system of the interrupted 1939/40 season, the League programme was divided into North and South. Beginning with 1940/41, the northern winners were Preston North End, Blackpool, Blackpool, Blackpool, Huddersfield Town and Sheffield United. The southern winners were Crystal Palace, Leicester City, Arsenal, Tottenham Hotspur, Tottenham Hotspur and Birmingham. In three seasons the north had a second Championship, won by Liverpool (1942/43), Bath (1943/44) and Derby County (1944/45).

League War Cup winners were West Ham United (1939/40), Preston North End (1940/41), Wolverhampton Wanderers (1941/42), Blackpool (North), Arsenal (South) and Swansea (West) in 1942/43, Aston Villa (North), Charlton Athletic (South) and Bath (West) in 1943/44, and Bolton Wanderers (North), Chelsea (South) and Bath (West) in 1944/45. Arsenal's 7-1 victory over Charlton Athletic in 1943 was a record score for a Wembley Cup final.

In addition to the club fixtures, wartime football saw regular representative matches. Towards the end of the Second World War, England dominated the domestic scene in a way rarely seen in peacetime internationals. They could call on players such as Frank Swift, George Hardwick, Joe Mercer, Stanley Matthews,

Raich Carter, Tommy Lawton and Jimmy Hagan. In a two-year period, Scotland were beaten 4-0, 8-0, 6-2, 3-2, 6-2, 3-2 and 6-1.

WATFORD

Founded 1891

Joined League 1920 (Division 3)

Honours Division 3 Champions 1969; Division 4 Champions 1978

Ground Vicarage Road

It all happened for Watford in the 1980s. League Championship runners-up in 1983 and FA Cup finalists the following year, they sold striker Luther Blissett to AC Milan for £1 million; nurtured the talents of two international stars-to-be, John Barnes and Mo Johnston; were managed by Graham Taylor, who was destined to become England boss; and, as if that were not enough, they were chaired by one of the world's most famous pop stars, Elton John.

Such personalities and events seemed far removed from the bulk of the 'Hornets' history, which was uneventful to put it mildly. After becoming founder members of the Third Division, Watford remained in that grade for 38 years, occasionally flirting with betterment but always falling short. When they finally departed in 1958, it was to join the newly created Fourth Division, from which they rose after two years, largely due to Cliff Holton.

The 1960s proved a more enterprising decade – thanks largely to managers Bill McGarry and Ken Furphy – with two splendid players, 'keeper Pat Jennings and schemer Tony Currie, being discovered and sold, and promotion twice being missed only on the season's final day. In 1970 Liverpool were defeated on the way to the FA Cup semi-finals, and with a solid following established despite the proximity of London, the future looked bright. But Furphy left and by 1975 the Hertfordshire club were in the Fourth Division.

WEST BROMWICH ALBION

Founded 1879

Joined League 1888 (founder member)

Honours Division 1 Champions 1920; Division 2 Champions 1902, 1911; FA Cup Winners 1888, 1892, 1931, 1954, 1968; League Cup Winners 1966

Ground The Hawthorns

A picture to treasure for West Bromwich Albion fans as Ronnie Allen scores from the penalty spot to help his side to a 3-2 victory over Preston North End in the 1954 FA Cup Final. The team finished as runners-up in the First Division that season, but have had only modest success since. Imagine a penalty kick today where players do not encroach as the kick is taken and the goalkeeper stays on his line, not moving until the ball is kicked.

Watford's years under the spotlight were masterminded by three men who, either before or since, have enjoyed fame beyond Vicarage Road. For Elton John (centre, wearing hat), being chairman of Watford meant a chance to indulge his passion for football. He spent some of the vast wealth he had accumulated as a top international pop star. For Bertie Mee (on his left), having had 10 successful years as manager of Arsenal, joining the Watford administration was probably a good way to stay involved in football without managerial hassle. And for Graham Taylor (on Elton John's right), the time as manager of a team on the rise stood him in good stead for future promotion to Aston Villa and then to the England manager's job.

Fortunately, the illustrious rescue party was at hand, and the Hornets rose rapidly to spend six seasons in the top flight. Since then, Taylor has departed, Elton John is no longer as closely involved, and Watford's fortunes have declined. In the absence of another football-crazy millionaire, manager Glenn Roeder faces a challenging task in saving Vicarage Road from a return to obscurity.

WELSH CUP

From its outset in 1877, the Welsh Cup has been open to all clubs in Wales and clubs in bordering English counties. Wrexham beat Druids 1-0 in the first Final. Unfortunately, neither Cup nor medals were ready when the game was played, but when it did arrive the 100-guinea Welsh Cup proved a spectacular trophy worth competing for.

Between 1886 and 1894 Chirk appeared in the final six times and won the Cup five times. Billy Meredith played in two of these Finals, and later became the first Welsh player to win Welsh Cup and FA Cup winner's medals. A team from South Wales did not reach a Final until 1903 (Aberaman lost 8-0 to Wrexham); the first southern success came from Cardiff City in 1911. South Wales dominated the inter-war Welsh Cup. In 1927 Cardiff City won a remarkable treble: FA Cup, Welsh Cup and Charity Shield. In 1929 there was a surprise winner – Connah's Quay – while in 1934 Bristol City beat Tranmere Rovers in an all-English final. The post-war period brought new names on the Cup: Lovells Athletic (1948), Merthyr Tydfil (1949), Rhyl (1952), Flint Town United (1954), Barry Town (1955), Bangor City (1962) and Borough United (1963).

The qualification for Europe gave the competition an added interest from 1961, but it also brought out the best from Football League clubs. Cardiff City won 10 out of 13 between 1964 and 1976. English clubs continued to compete for the Welsh Cup but were not eligible for the European Cup Winners' Cup as a result of winning it. When Hereford United won in 1990, for instance, runners-up Wrexham qualified for Europe. The picture is due to change in 1996/97, when victory in the Welsh Cup will no longer qualify *any* Football League teams for the Cup Winners' Cup. Any winners who play their football in a Welsh League, however, will still have the chance of European glory.

A history that takes in 13 major finals has built for West Bromwich Albion a Cup tradition that few can match. Yet there is frustration among supporters that the exhilarating football which has been the hallmark of many Hawthorns combinations has been marred by inconsistency, a serious handicap in their quest for League honours.

The pattern was established early on. After losing the FA Cup Finals of 1886 and 1887, Albion claimed their first trophy in the following campaign, with winger Billy Bassett – destined to be club chairman until 1937 – in irresistible form. But they struggled in the League, being twice relegated to Division 2 during the early 1900s.

However, under the leadership of Fred Everiss – a secretary-manager from 1902 to 1948 – they improved after the First World War and took what remains their only Championship, a fitting climax to the career of majestic defender Jesse Pennington. There followed a runners-up slot in 1925, then Albion slumped and spent four years in the Second Division before Billy Richardson's marksmanship helped to clinch promotion and the FA Cup in 1931.

Mediocrity reigned subsequently, and the 'Throstles' – or 'Baggies' to locals – started the post-war era back in the lower flight. They rose again and in 1953/54, with Vic Buckingham in charge, enjoyed a brilliant season, beating Preston at Wembley and narrowly missing the title. Stars included goal merchants Ronnie Allen and Johnny Nicholls, and wing-half Ray Barlow.

Bolstered by youngsters such as full-back Don Howe and wing-half Bobby Robson, Albion promised much and remained a solid First Division force until the early 1970s, but the only silverware they had to show for it was another FA Cup, courtesy of a Jeff Astle goal in 1968, and the League Cup two years earlier.

Come 1973 and, despite the efforts of long-serving forward Tony Brown, the Throstles were demoted. Johnny Giles led them back up, then Ron Atkinson created an entertaining team, with midfielder Bryan Robson and striker Cyrille Regis taking the eye. But stars departed, impetus faltered and Albion were relegated in 1986, after which performances declined so drastically that they slumped to the Third Division, for the first time in their history, in 1991. Two terms later they rose to the new First Division via the play-offs, but since then have stuggled to remain there. With a fine ground and plenty of traditional support, the Throstles should be flying higher.

WEST HAM UNITED

Founded 1895

Joined League 1919 (Division 2)

Honours Division 2 Champions 1958, 1981; FA Cup Winners 1964, 1975, 1980; European Cup Winners' Cup Winners 1965

Ground Upton Park

West Ham United have long been surrounded by a romantic aura. They are known as a friendly club who endeavour to serve up skilful, entertaining football even when a more down-to-earth approach might better serve their needs. In fact, such an image – exemplified by their whimsical anthem 'I'm Forever Blowing Bubbles' – is less appropriate in modern times, and a new pragmatism has become evident.

The 'Hammers' started life as Thames Ironworks – they are still known as the 'Irons' to many supporters – but were rejoicing under their current title when they made their League debut, getting off to a brisk start by winning promotion to Division 1 in 1923. In the same year they reached the first Wembley FA Cup Final, tasting defeat at a venue which was later to be the scene of their greatest triumphs. But despite the prolific plundering of centre-forward Vic Watson, they went down in 1932 to commence an uneventful quarter of a century in the Second Division, the first stage of which was adorned by the talents of England inside-forward Len Goulden. By the 1950s the side contained original thinkers such as Malcolm Allison, Dave Sexton, Frank O'Farrell, Noel Cantwell and John Bond, all destined for managerial success, and it was a stimulating combination that Ted Fenton led back to the First Division in 1958. Three years later Ron Greenwood took over as boss and the Hammers embarked on their most successful era.

With stars such as wing-half and captain Bobby Moore, midfielder Martin Peters and striker Geoff Hurst, all to become England World Cup heroes in 1966, supplemented by the subtle contribution of deep-lying forward Johnny Byrne, West Ham covered themselves in Cup glory, but failed to find consistency in the League. By the end of the decade Greenwood was spending

The West Ham United line-up that played in Division 2 in 1955/56: (back row, left to right) Sexton, Bond, Gregory, Allison, Cantwell, O'Farrell; Musgrove, Hooper, Dare, Dick, Tucker. An extraordinary number of this West Ham side went on to become managers: David Sexton, John Bond, Malcolm Allison, Noel Cantwell, Frank O'Farrell and Malcolm Musgrove.

heavily on the likes of defender Billy Bonds, though the most notable newcomer, schemer Trevor Brooking, emerged from the Upton Park youth set-up.

As John Lyall succeeded Greenwood in 1974, a similar pattern was maintained, with two further FA Cup victories and an appearance in the 1976 European Cup Winners' Cup Final being balanced against brief spells in the Second Division at the end of both the 1970s and the 1980s. In the wake of Lou Macari's short but tempestuous reign as manager, and with Bonds – who served long and nobly as

a player – in charge, the newly promoted Hammers seemed well prepared for the 1990s. Yet they went down to the new First Division in 1992 and though they bounced back at the first attempt, Bonds was replaced by Harry Redknapp in 1994. Nevertheless, West Ham are blessed with a loyal bedrock of support – a minority of which tends towards over-enthusiasm – and a tradition for stability which has seen only eight bosses in their history. Such clubs deserve to succeed.

WIGAN ATHLETIC

Founded 1932

Joined League 1978 (Division 4)

Honours None

Ground Springfield Park

When Wigan Borough folded and resigned from the League in 1931, it seemed there was little future for soccer in such a traditional stronghold of rugby. Yet within a few months Wigan Athletic were born. Although it took them 46 years to reach the league, the 'Latics' quickly began

making up for lost time after entering Division 4. Within four seasons they had risen to the Third, and came close to a Second Division place in both 1986 and 1987, when they also reached the quarter-finals of the FA Cup. Their crowning moment, though, was a Freight Rover Trophy triumph at Wembley in 1985.

They returned to the basement, but for a club sandwiched between the giants of Manchester and Merseyside, and faced with heavy competition for support from a clutch of other Lancashire sides, not to mention their famous Rugby League neighbours, Wigan have done well. They appear to have the resolve to continue achieving modest success.

WIMBLEDON

Founded 1889

Joined League 1977 (Division 4)

Honours Division 4 Champions 1983; FA Cup Winners 1988

Ground Selhurst Park

The phenomenal rise of Wimbledon since their election to the Football League represented an achievement of fairy-tale proportions, although the mantle of a simpering Cinderella sat ill on the feisty little outfit. In fact, since arriving in Division 1 in 1986, the Dons' uncomplicated long-ball style and combative outlook have earned them a reputation more in keeping with the ugly sisters, although as the 1990s dawned they hinted at entering a more attractive phase. Under successive managers Ray Harford and Joe Kinnear, Wimbledon were playing brighter football and the soccer world wondered what further miracles might emanate from the former non-League outfit.

Before joining Division 4 at the expense of Workington Town, the Dons were best known for their FA Cup exploits, the most famous of which came in 1975 when Dickie Guy saved a Peter Lorimer penalty and Leeds United were taken to a fourth-round replay. Within two years they were in the Third Division, but twice returned to the basement

before embarking on their amazing ascent. In 1986 they reached Division 1, finished sixth in their first top-flight term, and then stunned the establishment by winning the FA Cup – against Liverpool, of all clubs – in their second. Leading players have included forward Alan Cork, a constant factor throughout the fantastic journey, midfield hard-nut Vinnie Jones, 'keeper Dave Beasant and striker John Fashanu. But Wimbledon owe most to the managers who guided them to the heights on gates more appropriate to the Fourth Division, such men as Allen Batsford, Dario Gradi, Dave Bassett and Bobby Gould.

As dozens of clubs with infinitely more glorious traditions struggled to survive, the facts of soccer life proclaimed that the Wimbledon bubble must burst, especially when they were forced to leave their Plough Lane home and move in with Crystal Palace at Selhurst Park. However, come 1995 it had yet to happen.

WINTERBOTTOM, Walter

1913 Born in Lancashire

1934 Leaves amateur football to join Manchester United

1936 Makes senior debut as wing-half

1937 Spinal injury ends League career after 25 matches; recovers to guest for Chelsea and lead representative sides during the war

1946 Becomes England's first manager and FA Director of Coaching

1950 Presides over debacle in Brazil as England are dumped out of their first World Cup, losing to the unfancied United States

1954 Leads his men to World Cup quarter-finals in Switzerland, where they fall to Uruguay

1958 England flop in Sweden World Cup

1962 Another quarter-final of soccer's premier tournament; this time England are beaten, in Chile, by Brazil

1963 Winterbottom steps down to join Central Council of Physical Education; Alf Ramsey takes over England job

1978 Receives knighthood for services to sport

Walter Winterbottom is the one England manager who cannot be judged by his results. Though his record

over 27 years, which includes four World Cup failures, is modest in the extreme, he was handicapped by the presence of a selection committee which often saddled him with baffling and unnecessary team changes.

In fact the one-time teacher, who initiated

England's first national team manager, Walter Winterbottom, was also the longest serving, lasting from 1946 to 1963. Under Winterbottom's managership, the England side was often picked by a selection committee. So perhaps he should not be held too responsible for the infamous 1-0 defeat by the unfancied United States during the 1950 World Cup finals in Brazil.

England's under-23 and youth teams, arguably had his greatest influence in his role as FA Director of Coaching. As such he offered organised instruction to various levels of the game for the first time, and though he was occasionally vilified for introducing too much theory, he can take much credit for advocating the importance of ball skills.

It had been widely expected that when Winterbottom relinquished the managership of his country, he would replace his mentor, Sir Stanley Rous, as FA Secretary. But the job went to Denis Follows, and the RAF's wartime head of physical education was left to serve sport in other capacities. He later became a member of the Sports Council.

WOLVERHAMPTON WANDERERS

Founded 1877

Joined League 1888 (founder member)

Honours Division 1 Champions 1954, 1958, 1959; Division 2 Champions 1932, 1977; Division 3 (N) Champions 1924; Division 3 Champions 1989; Division 4 Champions 1988; FA Cup Winners 1893, 1908, 1949, 1960; League Cup Winners 1974, 1980

Ground Molineux

The mighty Wolves; the very name thunders from the pages of English football history, evoking memories of proud achievements and stirring deeds. Yet, in truth, the club's greatness relates largely to just one era, in which the inspired leadership of one man created a tradition that none of his successors has come close to equalling.

Yet Wolves did exist – enjoying some success – before Stan Cullis took over as manager in 1948. Indeed, they finished third in the Football League's inaugural season and won the FA Cup five years later, but as the twentieth century got under way, mediocrity beckoned. The Midlanders slumped into the Second Division and, although another Cup triumph soon followed, they were to plumb the depths of the Third before resuming their place among the elite in the early 1930s.

With Major Frank Buckley in charge, Wolves again challenged for honours, and were surprisingly slammed by Portsmouth in the 1939 FA Cup Final. The war destroyed the team's impetus and Buckley, having unearthed many youngsters who were to become top names, left the club. It was the cue for Cullis, himself a Buckley discovery, to lead Wolves to unprecedented glory.

The new boss believed firmly in the effectiveness of the long-ball game played with pace and power, and on these principles he built a formidable team. His stars included half-back Billy Wright, who was to play 105 times for England, 'keeper Bert Williams, goalscorers Roy Swinbourne and Dennis Westcott, wingers Johnny Hancocks and Jimmy Mullen, schemer Peter Broadbent, and defenders Ron Flowers and Bill Shorthouse. As well as stringing together an enviable sequence of domestic trophies, Wolves played a major part in blazing English soccer's trail to Europe. During the 1950s they took on top continental opposition in what were ostensibly friendlies but which were played with fiercely competitive spirit.

When new tactics overtook the Cullis method, Wolves' fortunes declined. In 1964 Cullis was sacked amid loud controversy. Over the next 20 years Wolves twice won the League Cup, and in 1972 they reached the Final of the UEFA Cup where they lost to Spurs, but they also experienced three demotions to the Second Division. Top players of this period included strikers Derek Dougan, John Richards and Andy Gray, wing-half Mike Bailey, and full-back Derek Parkin.

The Wolverhampton Wanderers side with the League Championship trophy won in the 1957/58 campaign. Wolves went on to win the title again in the following season, missing a hat-trick by one point from Burnley in 1959/60. The team: (back row, left to right) Clamp, Murray, Harris, Finlayson, Slater, Flowers, Stuart; Mason, Deeley, Wright, Cullis (manager), Broadbent, Booth, Mullen. Stan Cullis showed his true ability as a manager by replacing several of this side but still keeping the Wolves at the top.

The 1980s brought a disastrous slide to the Fourth Division which almost ended in financial oblivion, but inspired by England striker Steve Bull and ably led by manager Graham Turner, they climbed back to the old Second. Given a successful team, which former England boss Graham Taylor was striving to provide in the mid-1990s, the support can surely be found for a return to eminence. With multi-millionaire Sir Jack Hayward providing financial backing, the future looked bright for the old-gold-and-black brigade.

WOMEN'S FOOTBALL

In the 1890s Nettie Honeyball, Secretary of British Ladies, pioneered women's soccer in England. A typical example was the North-South game at Crouch End Athletic Ground in 1895. The Manchester Guardian reported 'The ladies of the 'North' team wore red blouses with white yolks, and full black knickerbockers fastened below the knee, black stockings, red beretta caps, brown leather boots and leg-pads.' The North won that game 7-0. A similar initiative took place in Scotland in the same decade – a travelling team under the management of Lady Florence Dixie.

On 25 August 1902 the FA Council issued instructions to its affiliated associations not to permit matches against 'lady teams'. It was not until the First World War that women's football boomed. Dick-Kerr's Ladies (Preston) was formed in 1917 to raise money for a military hospital. After the war Dick-Kerr's toured the country playing to large crowds, including one of 53,000 at Goodison Park, but in December 1921 the FA stopped women's football at Football League club grounds. Dick-Kerr's continued throughout the inter-war period, however, raising an estimated £70,000 for charities.

Local women's football continued after the Second World War, but other European countries offered more opportunities. In the 1960s a few British players went to Italy as professionals, a pattern which was repeated in the 1980s when Scottish international Margaret Wilson had two years with Bari and several England players joined other Italian clubs.

England's 1966 World Cup success attracted more women to the game. In December 1969 the FA recognised women's football, and the Women's Football Association was soon formed (officially recognised by the FA in November 1971). The Women's FA Cup was launched in 1971, and the first official international in Britain was played at Greenock on 18 November 1972. England beat Scotland 3-2.

In 1971 England had 44 women's clubs, but by the end of the decade there were

Mia Hamm from the USA dispossessed by Norway's Kristin Sandberg during an Algarve Cup match in Portugal 1991. The Algarve Cup reflected the growth of the women's game worldwide. England's relatively new National League has upped interest in the UK

five times that number. The WFA was affiliated to the FA in May 1984, the year which also saw the completion of the first ever UEFA international competition. England lost 4-3 on penalties to Sweden in the Final.

Interest in the game in Britain was raised by television coverage in the late 1980s, but women's football is still far behind other countries in terms of registered players. In the mid-90s Arsenal and Doncaster Belles were the two major contenders for honours in the British game.

WORLD CLUB CHAMPIONSHIP

The World Club Championship, started with the intention of finding the best club side in the world, is an annual competition between the winners of the European Cup and the winners of the South American Champions Cup (Copa Libertadores). Inaugurated in 1960 as a two-legged competition, at a time when jet travel began to make such events possible, the first winners were Real Madrid. Santos (1962 and 1963), Internazionale (1964 and 1965), AC Milan (1989 and 1990) and Sao Paulo (1992 and 1993) have won the trophy in successive seasons.

Culture clashes were frequent in the 1960s. Santos and AC Milan each had a player dismissed in the 1963 play-off, which was won by a penalty kick. Another play-off decider, between Racing (Argentina) and Celtic in 1967, saw six players sent off. The Manchester United-Estudiantes (Argentina) confrontation in 1968 brought another three dismissals, including United's Stiles and Best, before Estudiantes won 2-1 on aggregate. The 1969 and 1970 World Club Championships, also featuring Estudiantes, were again no place for faint hearts.

Consequently, European Cup winners often spurned

WORLD CLUB CHAMPIONSHIPS

(European team in italics)

Year	Winner	Runners-up	Scores
1960	*Real Madrid*	Penarol	0-0, 5-1
1961	Penarol	*Benfica*	0-1, 2-1, 5-0
1962	Santos	*Benfica*	3-2, 5-2
1963	Santos	*AC Milan*	2-4, 4-2, 1-0
1964	*Internazionale*	Independiente	0-1, 2-0, 1-0
1965	*Internazionale*	Independiente	3-0, 0-0
1966	Penarol	*Real Madrid*	2-0, 2-0
1967	Racing Club	*Celtic*	0-1, 2-1, 1-0
1968	Estudiantes	*Manchester United*	1-0, 1-1
1969	*AC Milan*	Estudiantes	3-0, 1-2
1970	Feyenoord	Estudiantes	2-2, 1-0
1971	Nacional (Uruguay)	*Panathinaikos*	1-1, 1-2
1972	*Ajax*	Independiente	1-1, 3-0
1973	Independiente	*Juventus*	1-0
1974	*Athletico Madrid*	Independiente	0-1, 2-0
1976	*Bayern Munich*	Cruzeiro	2-0, 0-0
1977	Boca Juniors	*Borussia Mönchengladbach*	2-2, 3-0
1979	Olimpia	*Malmo*	1-0, 2-1
1980	Nacional (Uruguay)	*Nottingham Forest*	1-0
1981	Flamengo	*Liverpool*	3-0
1982	Penarol	*Aston Villa*	2-0
1983	Gremio	*SV Hamburg*	2-1
1984	Independiente	*Liverpool*	1-0
1985	*Juventus*	Argentinos Juniors	2-2*
1986	River Plate	*Steaua Bucharest*	1-0
1987	Porto	Penarol	2-1
1988	Nacional (Paraguay)	*PSV Eindhoven*	2-2*
1989	*AC Milan*	Nacional (Colombia)	1-0
1990	*AC Milan*	Olimpia	3-0
1991	*Red Star Belgrade*	Colo Colo	3-0
1992	Sao Paulo	*Barcelona*	2-1
1993	Sao Paulo	*AC Milan*	3-2
1994	Velez Sarsfield	*AC Milan*	2-0

*match decided on penalties

opportunities to compete in the 1970s. Only Ajax (1972) and Bayern Munich (1976) took part. Among the absentees were Liverpool (twice) and Nottingham Forest. The European Cup runners-up usually deputised but there were no matches in 1975 and 1978. The World Club Championship received a boost in 1980, however, when the format was changed to a single match played in Tokyo.

Nottingham Forest did compete this time, losing 1-0 to Nacional (Uruguay), who with Peñarol (Uruguay) and AC Milan have the most World Club Championship wins (three). The Italians have twice missed the chance to claim the record outright, losing out in 1993 – when they were drafted in to replace Marseille after a bribes scandal involving the French

club – and 1994.

Overall, South American clubs have been more successful in a tournament that has been notable for poor matches, bad behaviour and unseemly squabbling. Perhaps it is the lack of success by European sides, having to play the match (or matches) in the middle of a domestic season, that has led to its less than enthusiastic reception in this part of the world; there's certainly no such reticence about the competition in South America.

THE WORLD CUP

The first World Cup competition was staged, amid some controversy, in 1930 in Uruguay, then the reigning Olympic champion nation. It was instigated by FIFA under

the auspices of its President, Jules Rimet, after whom the trophy was initially named. England, Scotland, Wales and Northern Ireland were not eligible, having withdrawn from FIFA in 1928, and indeed it was to be another twenty years before England, who had played such a large part in introducing football to the world, made their first appearance in the tournament. Thirteen countries, predominantly from the Americas, took part in the competition, and the host nation took the first title, beating Argentina 4-2 in the Final. Italy was the venue for the tournament in 1934, and once again the host nation triumphed. Mussolini attended the Final, against Czechoslovakia, and the Italian team gave the Fascist salute before the match, which they won 2-1.

Maintaining their supremacy in the following tournament, held in France in 1938, Italy beat Hungary 4-2 in the Final, and the subsequent intervention of the Second World War saw that they held on to the trophy for 12 years.

England made their World Cup debut in the next competition, staged in Brazil in 1950, where their hitherto acknowledged mastery of the game was brought to an ignominious end, as a side which included Alf Ramsey were beaten by rank outsiders the USA. It was not until sixteen years later that England established any sort of presence in the competition. The Final of 1950 was a fine match between Uruguay and Brazil, but this time the host nation couldn't quite make it, and the trophy returned to Montevideo.

In 1954 Hungary, the 'Marvellous Magyars', were the team to beat, and they started out as firm favourites with a side including the remarkable striking quartet of Toth, Kocsis, Puskas and Czibor, and the all-time great 'keeper Grosics. They stormed through to the Final, but, facing a strong West German line-up, they allowed over-confidence and German exploitation of their tactical weaknesses to get the better of them. After taking an early two-goal lead, they lost 3-2.

In the 1958 competition in Sweden, all four British nations qualified for the finals. Northern Ireland were the least rated of the four, but under the guidance of Danny Blanchflower they succumbed only in the quarter-finals to France. Wales also progressed to a quarter-final against Brazil, but the combination of Pele, Garrincha and Didi was too powerful for them, and they went down 1-0. The supposedly stronger teams of England and Scotland were both eliminated in the first round, England perhaps still suffering from the reverberations of the Munich air disaster earlier that year. The Final was contested by Sweden and the elegant Brazilians, and was the first competition in which the latter staked their claim to footballing supremacy by beating the host nation 5-2.

Czechoslovakia emerged as strong European contenders in Chile in 1962, and were beaten only in the Final by Brazil, who thus took their second successive title and confirmed their reputation as the best in the world. England, the only British nation to qualify, were also put out of the tournament by the Brazilians in the quarter-

finals, having narrowly scraped through the first round.

While the legality of England's third goal of the 1966 Final at Wembley, scored by Geoff Hurst in extra time, will always be debated, the West Germans' second goal just before full-time was also dubious because of an alleged handball by Schnellinger, so that the final scoreline of 4-2 to England might seem a fair reflection of the game. Alf Ramsey's commitment to building a team which would win the World Cup had finally come to fruition. However, his concentration on physical stamina, his use of ball-winners (such as Nobby Stiles, who successfully restricted the remarkable Eusebio of Portugal in the semi-final), and his scorn for public relations also left a negative imprint, perhaps leading to the more cynical and less stylish football of subsequent competitions.

The 1970 tournament in Mexico saw the rise of the strongest post-war Italian team, which reached the Final against the supreme Brazil, who took a third title. In recognition of this achievement, the Jules Rimet Trophy departed with the Brazilian team to a permanent home in Rio de Janeiro. This tournament also

witnessed perhaps England's most unfortunate exit from the competition, in their quarter-final against West Germany. Peter Bonetti, finding himself in goal at two hours' notice and unable to settle, made two errors which saw England's two-goal lead disappear. A goal from Gerd Muller wrapped it up for the Germans in extra time.

For the 1974 tournament in West Germany a new trophy was supplied by FIFA (despite Brazil's offering to provide the replacement), which has since been known as the 'FIFA World Cup Trophy'. Scotland were the only British side to qualify, but they found themselves in a tough group with Brazil and Yugoslavia and narrowly failed to progress beyond the first round. The Dutch were the most exciting side to watch in this competition, playing inventive and intelligent football. A world-class line-up, including the masterful Johan Cruyff, Neeskens, Rep and Krol, appeared set to beat West Germany in the Final, but over-confidence seemed to play its part, and while the Dutch players toyed with the ball, Helmut Schoen's Germans gritted their teeth and put themselves 2-1 ahead, a position from which Holland never recovered.

After managerial problems,

England failed to qualify for the 1978 finals in Argentina. Scotland, on the other hand, were on a wave of misplaced patriotic fervour under the managership of the inexperienced Ally MacLeod. They did qualify but came home after the first round, having suffered defeat by Peru (for which match Gemmill, Souness, Macari and Derek Johnstone were available but not selected) and an embarrassing draw with Iran. The Final in 1978, between Holland and Argentina, was strongly criticised for the standard of its refereeing and there were hints that Peru, Argentina's last opponents before the Final whom they needed to defeat heavily to qualify, were in fact bought off by an unpopular Argentinian regime desperate to improve its standing. However, Cesar Menotti's Argentinians included players of the calibre of Ardiles and Passarella, with Fillol in goal, and they took the title 3-1 with a less cynical display than they had shown for some time.

England, Scotland and Northern Ireland all qualified for the 1982 finals in Spain, and it was the Irish under Billy Bingham who provided the most inspired British contribution. Their brave challenge took them through to the second round, when the French, and in particular the relentless attacking of Michel Platini, showed their superiority and put out the Irish 4-1. Scotland, under Jock Stein, battled hard in what was again a tough group, but could not find

Sweden 1958: Brazil became the first and only team so far to win the World Cup outside their own continent. Pictured with the trophy are: (back row, left to right) Feola (coach), D. Santos, Zito, Bellini, N. Santos, Orlando, Gilmar; Garrincha, Didi, Pele, Vava, Zagalo, Brito. Eight of this squad played in the team which won the Final in Chile four years later.

enough to get past the first round, while England, unable to score against Spain, just missed getting through to the semis. Diego Maradona made his first appearance in these finals, but he could not single-handedly take his country to a credible defence of their title. The Final, between Italy (who had failed to win any of their group matches) and West Germany, again saw poor refereeing against a plethora of fouls. The first half was dull, but action improved in the second with goals from Rossi, Tardelli and Altobelli for Italy and a late one from Breitner for West Germany, Italy thereby equalling Brazil's tally of three titles.

The 1986 tournament took place in Mexico – the first time a nation had hosted the competition for a second time. Once again, England, Scotland and Northern Ireland all qualified, but only England progressed beyond the first round, after a sparkling match against Poland in which Gary Lineker scored a hat-trick. Argentina proved too much for them in the quarter-finals, however, putting them out of the competition 2-1. The most exciting match of the tournament was probably that between the USSR and Belgium, which the latter won 4-3 after extra time, with Ceulemans and Scifo outstanding. The Final, between Argentina and Franz Beckenbauer's West Germans, provided five goals for the watching millions,

two for Germany from Rummenigge and Völler, and three – the last in the 84th minute – for Argentina, thus securing the Argentinians' second title.

Of the 24 nations competing in Italy for the 1990 World Cup, Brazil began as many people's favourites. The draw was managed so that all early England matches would be played on the island of Sardinia, with the aim of containing any supporter violence. Happily this did not materialise. England progressed to the semi-finals, their best performance since 1966, thanks to some skilful contributions from players such as Lineker, Platt, Wright, Walker and emerging star Paul Gascoigne. Their semi against West Germany was probably the finest match of

the competition, lost only on a penalty shoot-out after extra time. There was some consolation for England in winning the Fair Play award of the tournament.

Brazil won the 1994 World Cup on penalties having fought out 120 minutes of the final without a goal. Although no one person wins or loses a penalty shoot out, many will remember Roberto Baggio's miss as critical in his side's 2-3 defeat. This was a special irony because Baggio had been instrumental in taking Italy to the final by virtue of some good performances and great goals.

Brazilian captain Dunga with the World Cup following the 3-2 penalty triumph in 1994.

Americans, who had eschewed their negativity of four years earlier to perform with splendid verve. All eight of the quarter-finalists had much to commend them, and many pundits were surprised by the departure at this stage of the ultra-professional Germany (to Bulgaria), Spain (to Italy) and Romania (to Sweden, on penalties), while Holland, faced by favourites Brazil, perished honourably by three goals to two.

In the semi-finals, the ever-improving Italy, who had come perilously close to elimination in the first stage, saw off Bulgaria 2-1, while a late goal by Romario ended the challenge of Sweden. Thus the stage was set for a mouth-watering finale, with both Brazil and Italy bidding to land the trophy for the fourth time. Alas, it never quite materialised. There was plenty of technical excellence, but it seemed the stakes were too high for either side to express themselves fully. The upshot was 120 minutes of goalless football, followed by a harrowing penalty shoot-out resulting in a 3-2 triumph for the South Americans. The result, if not the manner of achieving it, received widespread acclaim. Without touching the heights of previous magnificent Brazilian sides, this one had been just about the best team in the tournament, and the feel-good factor they delivered was sorely needed by the world of football.

The World Cup finals continue to be the showpiece of football for millions of fans worldwide. Unlike the Olympic Games, the tournaments have rarely been subject to political manipulation or boycottings – it would be a very brave or a very foolish leader indeed who would deny his country the chance to participate in this most celebrated

Scotland also qualified in 1990 but once again left their best performance until too late, and made an early trip home. The Republic of Ireland, under the managership of Jack Charlton, qualified for the first time and fared better, with some determined if sometimes over-defensive play, but were eventually ousted by Italy 1-0 in the quarter-finals. The hosts, who took third place in the tournament, saw the rise of a new goalscoring talent in the relatively unknown Salvatore Schillaci, who was top scorer of the finals. Holland, expected to do well, were disappointing, but Cameroon astonished the footballing world by reaching the quarter-finals – the first African nation to do so – thanks to some prolific goalscoring by 38-year-old substitute Roger Milla.

The Final, once again between Argentina and West Germany, was a shambles in which the football took a poor second place to the histrionics. Refereeing was confused and arbitrary and cynical fouling was rife, particularly from the defending champions. The scenes culminated in arguments with the referee and two Argentinians being sent off, Monzon becoming the first ever player to be shown the red card in a World Cup Final. After the match a tearful Maradona refused to shake hands with the President of FIFA. West Germany won the title 1-0 after Brehme scored from a penalty, but international football was the overall loser.

After the cynical, soulless impression left by Italia '90, the global game received a breath of fresh air from USA '94. The choice of the States as venue for the tournament had been greeted with howls of dismay by many traditionalists, who feared that American razzmatazz and commercialism would submerge the football itself. Far from it. What the world got was a carnival of adventurous entertainment which, unfortunately but inevitably, deteriorated in excitement value towards the end as the fear factor took over.

From a parochial British point of view, involvement was sadly lacking. With England, Scotland, Wales and Northern Ireland all having failed to qualify, it was left to Jack Charlton's Republic of Ireland – who had performed so creditably four years

earlier – to provide the local interest.

In the face of chronic heat and humidity – which players from all competing nations were required to endure, at times merely to fit in with European TV schedules – the Irish battled with characteristic determination, but in the end lacked the necessary elan. In fact, they began brilliantly, a wonderful goal from Ray Houghton earning an uplifting 1-0 victory over eventual finalists Italy, but in the end succumbed to the much classier Holland in the second phase.

Though there was no truly 'great' team on show, and no individuals to rank with Pele or Maradona (in his pomp), Cruyff or Beckenbauer, there was a refreshingly high overall standard of technique and, until the last stages, uninhibited ambition. This made for some scintillating matches, none better than the second-phase clash between Romania and Argentina. The East Europeans, inspired by the often-breathtaking skills of Gheorghe Hagi and Ilie Dumitrescu, gave a classical display of counter-attacking to overcome the South competition. The vastly improved performances of African and Asian nations in recent tournaments are an indication of the ever increasing popularity of the game throughout the world – Japan hopes to stage the first finals of the 21st Century – and there are no longer any 'minnows' who can be written off before a ball is kicked.

The depth of feeling aroused by the competition has in fact been the subject of psychiatric research, which indicates that in the weeks leading up to the finals there is a marked increase in reported cases of mental disorders, while during the tournament itself there is a sharp downturn in such cases.

For once FIFA could congratulate themselves on a job well done. The introduction of three-points for a win in the first-phase matches, the outlawing of the dangerous tackle from behind, the change in the offside law to favour attackers, the introduction of stretcher-wagons to curtail time-wasting – they all played their part in making USA '94 a success. Large, enthusiastic and well-behaved crowds also deserve a major share of the credit. What a swell party that was! France will host the tournament for a second time in 1998.

WORLD YOUTH CHAMPIONSHIPS

The World Youth Championship was launched by FIFA in 1977 as a competition for under-18s held every two years. Past winners have been the Soviet Union (1977 in Tunisia), Argentina (1979 in Japan), West Germany (1981 in Australia), Brazil (1983 in Mexico), Brazil (1985 in the Soviet Union), Yugoslavia (1987 in Chile), Portugal (1989 in Saudi Arabia and 1991 in Portugal) and Brazil (1993 in Australia). The last two competitions had an under-20 age limit.

In 1985 FIFA inaugurated an under-16 World Cup, and the first finals were held in China. The hosts and Australia were among the surprise quarter-finalists. West Germany's Mercel Witsczek scored hat-tricks in the quarter-final and semi-final, but his country lost the final 2-0 to Nigeria. The second under-16 World Cup, in 1987, took place in Canada. Again the 16 teams produced surprise quarter-finalists – Australia, South Korea and Ivory Coast among them – but the Cup went to the Soviet Union after a penalty shoot-out against Nigeria. The 1989 Finals, held in Scotland, saw the host nation progress to the Final. Opponents Saudi Arabia, 2-0 down in the first half, fought back to draw 2-2 after extra time; Saudi won the penalty shoot-out 5-4 to take the trophy. In 1991 the first FIFA under-17 World Championship, superseding the under-16 competition, was won by Ghana. In 1993/94, Ghana reached the final again, but lost to Nigeria.

These tournaments run alongside the longer-established UEFA Youth tournament, won initially by England in 1948 and most recently by Turkey in 1994 at under-16 level, and the UEFA under-18 trophy last won by Portugal in 1994.

WREXHAM

Founded 1873

Joined League 1921 (Division 3 N)

Honours Division 3 Champions 1978

Ground Racecourse Ground

Wrexham, the oldest surviving club in Wales, have broken out of their lower-division strait-jacket but once. That was in 1978 when young manager Arfon Griffiths, who as a skilful midfielder played more than 600 games for the 'Robins', led them into the Second Division. There they struggled for four campaigns before relegation restored them to more familiar surroundings. The only other League triumphs in Wrexham's history have been three promotions from the bottom division, the vast majority of their seasons having been spent at the lowest level, although knock-out exploits – in 1978 they reached the quarter-finals of both League and FA Cups – brought some relief. Indeed, this tradition was upheld memorably in 1992 when the 'Robins' dumped Arsenal out of the FA Cup in the third round.

Despite some enterprising cash-raising schemes, Wrexham have faced a continuing economic struggle, with many North Wales fans being attracted to Manchester and Liverpool. Occasional European forays, courtesy of victories in the Welsh Cup, a trophy they have won on 22 occasions, have helped keep interest alive, and there was another boost when Brian Flynn led them into the new Second Division in 1993.

WRIGHT, Billy

1924 Born in Ironbridge, Shropshire

1941 Turns professional with Wolverhampton Wanderers

1942 Recovers from serious ankle injury

1946 Makes full international debut, against Northern Ireland in Belfast

1947 Takes over club captaincy

1949 Collects the FA Cup as Wolves defeat Leicester

1950 Skippers England through the first of three World Cups

1952 Footballer of the Year

1954 Leads Wolves to League title

1958 Holds aloft the Championship trophy

1959 Caps his Molineux achievements with a third title medal; May – makes 105th and last appearance for England, against the United States in Los Angeles, and then retires

1960 Becomes manager of England youth and under-23 teams

1962 Takes job as Arsenal boss

1966 Sacked by the 'Gunners'; goes on to work in television, with huge success

1994 Dies in London

Wright, the leading English defender of the 1940s and 1950s, enjoyed a golden playing career which might have been scripted for a comic-strip hero. He won the game's top club honours, captained his country 90

Billy Wright in his Wolverhampton Wanderers strip. The club apprentice responsible for cleaning and polishing the skipper's boots had obviously not been doing his job properly. Wright played nearly 500 games for Wolves. He was a natural general, captaining Wolves for 12 seasons – three of which ended with Wright lifting the Championship trophy – and captained his country 90 times in 105 internationals.

times, and was the first player to win a century of international caps. Wright's image of perfection was heightened by his blond, clean-cut looks, a modest personality, and his marriage to pop singer Joy Beverley, an event greeted ecstatically by the nation.

Yet, despite the euphoria, he was not a footballer of great natural talent, his distribution being distinctly average and his ball skills unremarkable. He more than made up for it, however, with a fierce tackle, an instinctive ability to read the game, exceptional power in the air for a stocky man, and an inspiring knack of leading by example. The early part of his career was spent as a defensive right-half, but many believe he was more effective at centre-half, the role to which he was converted during the 1954 World Cup finals.

Sadly, Wright's management days were less than glorious. At Highbury – where he initiated a youth policy which bore fruit under his successor, Bertie Mee – he was judged 'too nice' for such a ruthless profession. His subsequent decision to forsake football for television proved to be eminently wise.

WYCOMBE WANDERERS

Founded 1884

Joined League 1993

Honours None

Ground Adams Park

Like Barnet before them, when Wycombe Wanderers rose to League status as champions of the GM Vauxhall Conference, they had well and truly paid their dues. In 1992 the Blues, also known as the Choirboys, had been denied on goal difference by Colchester United; but a year later they were in a class of their own, leading the table all season and finishing streets ahead of the nearest opposition. Having reached the Football League, they demonstrated their class by winning promotion, via the play-offs, at the first attempt.

Wycombe began the 1990s with an enterprising young manager in former Nottingham Forest and Northern Ireland winger Martin O'Neill, and a smart, custom-built stadium at Adams Park. Add an enlightened administration and, most important of all, a talented and versatile playing staff, and the reasons for their advance become clear.

But while the Wanderers appear to be very much a club of the future, they also have a proud past. Having begun life in the Southern, then moved on through the Great Western Suburban and Spartan Leagues, they began an illustrious 59-year sequence in the Isthmian in 1921. During this time they won seven championships and earned widespread renown as aristocrats of the amateur game, exuding charisma and tradition, and their sloping Loakes Park headquarters became one of the most famous non-League venues. The FA Cup has added spice to their history, most notably in 1974/5 when First Division high-fliers Middlesbrough overcame them only through a late penalty in a third round replay.

Based in High Wycombe, west of Watford and north of Reading, the Blues are well placed to add to their already fervent bedrock of support. For Wycombe Wanderers in 1995, the future beckoned brightly.

YASHIN, Lev

1929 Born in Moscow

1953 Makes debut for Moscow Dynamo

1954 Wins first of 78 caps, 3-2 v Sweden

1955 Wins Soviet League Championship medal

1956 Olympic gold medallist

1957 Second Soviet Championship

1958 World Cup quarter-finalist

1959 Soviet Championship

1960 Wins European Championship medal, 2-1 v Yugoslavia

1962 World Cup quarter-finalist

1963 Soviet Championship; European Footballer of the Year

1964 European Championship runner-up, 1-2 v Spain

1966 World Cup fourth place

1967 Retires

1991 Dies, and is mourned around the world

The Soviet Union's initial distaste for international competition meant that Yashin's arrival at the World Cup was delayed until Sweden in 1958, when he was 29. But what an impact he made. The black-clad figure guarding the Russian goal made it seem almost impregnable. Thirty years on, when sports journalists voted him into their all-time team, only Pele was a more indisputable choice.

Yashin played for only one club throughout his career but when, in 1953, he found it difficult to emerge from the reserves, he was tempted to turn his back even on his beloved Moscow Dynamo. He was proficient at basketball and volleyball, but it was ice hockey that was the rival attraction and it was fortunate for football that Yashin succeeded his country's other truly great goalkeeper, 'Tiger' Khomich, at club level in time. A year later, in September 1954, he embarked on an international career that extended to 78 caps and earned him international renown, not only for his saves, which bordered on the miraculous, but also for his sportsmanship.

After his World Cup performance in Sweden it came as a shock when Yashin proved vulnerable four years later in Chile. Against Colombia he let in a goal straight from a corner, while the host country beat him twice from long range in the quarter-finals. L'Equipe noted that the match 'marked the end of the greatest modern goalkeeper, if not of all time'. Completely wrong. A year later Yashin had a magnificent match for the Rest of the World against England at Wembley, and in 1966 he was still in the Soviet goal when they reached the semi-finals in the World Cup, their best performance in that competition.

At club level Yashin collected four Soviet Championship and two Cup winner's medals. One last honour was to come: his country's highest award, the Order of Lenin.

YORK CITY

Founded 1922

Joined League 1929 (Division 3 N)

Honours Division 4 Champions 1984

Ground Bootham Crescent

A tradition for stirring deeds in knock-out cups has brought much-needed consolation to York City fans, who have had little to shout about in more than 60 years of League life. A two-season sojourn in the Second Division during the mid 1970s has been the highlight of an otherwise disappointing history in the bread-and-butter competition, though the 1990s brought signs of improvement.

The 'Minstermen's' finest hour came in 1955 when they beat Blackpool (complete with Matthews, Mortensen et al) and Spurs on their way to an FA Cup semi-final against eventual winners Newcastle United, going out only in a replay. Stars of this heroic campaign included goalkeeper Tom Forgan and marksmen Arthur Bottom and Norman Wilkinson. Among other exhilarating exploits was a run to the quarter-finals of the 1962 League Cup.

Influential figures have included managers Tom Johnston, who led the club into the Second Division, and Wilf McGuinness, who couldn't keep them there. In fairness, with most Yorkshire supporters favouring the bigger clubs, the task of bringing regular top-level soccer to Bootham Crescent has always been little short of Herculean, which made their promotion to the new Second Division, courtesy of a penalty shoot-out in the 1993 play-offs, all the more commendable.

YOUNG, George

1922 Born in Grangemouth, Scotland

1941 Joins Rangers from Kirkintilloch Rob Roy

1943 Plays at right-back for Scotland against England in a wartime international

1948 First captains Scotland

1953 Completes run of 34 consecutive Scotland appearances (a record until Kenny Dalglish)

1957 Retires from Scottish League football

1959 Takes over as Third Lanark manager (until 1962)

A giant of a man, 6ft 2in tall and heavily built, George Young became a giant also in stature and personality during soccer's post-war golden age. He played 53 Scotland internationals (plus two unofficial wartime games) and 22 times for the Scottish League. He captained Rangers to six Scottish League Championships, four Scottish Cup triumphs and two League Cup wins. In 1948/49 Rangers won all three major Scottish competitions, their success founded on a strong defence in which Young was outstanding.

Young, who captained Scotland a record 48 times, developed a close working relationship with Scottish FA Secretary George Graham. In Young's era there was no Scotland manager – except for a brief period during the 1954 World Cup when Andy Beattie was in charge – so he became as much a player-manager as a captain. He captained Scotland eight times against England, and although never on the winning side at Hampden against the 'auld enemy', he led the Scots to famous Wembley victories in 1949 and 1951.

Carrying around a lucky champagne cork from a Rangers Cup win, George Young was nicknamed 'Corky'. Scottish Player of the Year in 1955, he was still an international when he retired from playing.

ZICO

1953 Born in Rio de Janeiro, Brazil

1968 Joins Flamengo

1969 First-team debut

1975 Scores on Brazil debut, v Uruguay

1977 South American Footballer of the Year

1978 Brazil take third place in World Cup

1979 Scores 89 goals in one season

1981 South American Footballer of the Year…

1982 …and again

1983 Transferred to Udinese, Italy, for £2.5 million

1985 Returns to Flamengo

1986 Plays in World Cup quarter-finals

It is one of the injustices of football that Brazil failed to win the World Cup in Zico's time. But by the same token, it was injuries to the midfielder/striker that almost certainly denied his country the prize.

Artur Antunes Coimbra, nicknamed 'Zico', scored 66 goals in 88 internationals but suffered varying degrees of disappointment in the World Cup. In 1978 and 1986 he carried wounds that restricted his appearances, while in 1982 a marvellous Brazilian team was undermined only by the eccentricities of its defence.

By 1983, when Zico went to Italy, he had won three Brazilian titles and South American and World Club Championships with Flamengo. In his first season with Udinese he was top scorer, with 19 goals. Zico always appeared to be an injury ready to happen, however, and after a second year largely on the sidelines he returned to his former club.

At the age of 33 he played in his third World Cup, but it summed up rather than crowned his career. In the opening group games he played only 22 faultless minutes against Northern Ireland; he then came on as a late substitute against Poland, and missed a crucial penalty against France. A great player whose reputation survived bad fortune, yet one whose memory will evoke frustration as well as delight.

ZOFF, Dino

1942 Born in Mariano del Friuli, Italy

1961 Concedes five goals on

Another Brazilian, another nickname. The fondness of that country for bestowing two-syllable handles on their favourite players is of great relief to commentators, fans and football book writers alike. Zico's career illustrates another tradition – the purchase of South American players by European clubs after an impressive World Cup showing. The few who come to Britain, however, don't seem to stay long. One exception is Ossie Ardiles, seen here playing for Argentina as Zico unleashes a powerful shot. The South Americans who play on the continent of Europe seem to fare a little better.

debut for Udinese against Fiorentina

1963 Transferred to Mantova

1965 Relegated to Italian Second Division

1966 Promoted

1967 Transferred to Napoli

1968 Wins first of 112 caps; European Championship win, 2-0 v Yugoslavia

1972 Transferred to Juventus

1973 Runner-up, European Footballer of the Year

1977 Wins UEFA Cup medal, on away goals v Athletic Bilbao

1978 Plays in World Cup – fourth place

1982 Captains Italy to win World Cup, 3-1 v West Germany

1988 Appointed coach of Italian Olympic team; becomes Juventus coach

1990 Sacked by Juventus; takes over as coach at Lazio, where eventually he graduates to an executive role, with Zdenek Zeman taking over as coach.

Zoff, in terms of honours, is one of the most successful footballers of all time. Capped 112 times by his country, he gained World Cup and European Championship winner's medals and, at club level, five Italian Championships, two Italian Cups and the UEFA Cup.

Yet until he reached the age of 30, Zoff appeared to be heading for a talented but largely unfulfilled goalkeeping career. Spells with Udinese, Mantova and Napoli were fruitless and included two relegations. When he was transferred to Juventus in 1972 for £400,000, however, he embarked on an orgy of conquest of Napoleonic dimensions.

At the same time, his move to Turin cemented a permanent place in the Italian team and, shortly afterwards, the record books. After conceding a goal to Yugoslavia in September that year he was unbeaten in 12 international matches. In the 13th, a 1974 World Cup game against Haiti, he finally conceded a goal a minute after half-time, setting a world record of 1143 minutes without letting the opposition score. His prowess at club level was such that he also established a national record of 903 unblemished minutes.

Zoff was an agile player whose courage, anticipation and reflexes were honed in the ultra-defensive Italian League where packed penalty areas often give goalkeepers little time to adjust. Supremely talented, it was strength of character and the confidence he inspired in the men in front of him that were his greatest assets. His position in the national team was in jeopardy after he let in two long, searing drives against the Netherlands in the 1978 World Cup, but it was Zoff who was chosen not only as goalkeeper but as captain in Spain four years later.

Italy's most capped player, Dino Zoff. At the end of the 1982 World Cup Final against West Germany, the 40-year-old Zoff, as captain, had the enviable duty of lifting the trophy. Goalkeepers' careers often last longer than those of outfield players, partly because stamina isn't such an important factor in their craft. Confidence and positional sense increase with experience to compensate for diminishing reflexes. Peter Shilton of England and Pat Jennings of Northern Ireland are two other goalkeepers who represented their countries way past the footballer's average retirement age. The number of clean sheets kept by Zoff as an international is testimony to the efficiency of Italian defences as much as to his goalkeeping ability.